MW01629159

ONE DAY IN WASHINGTON

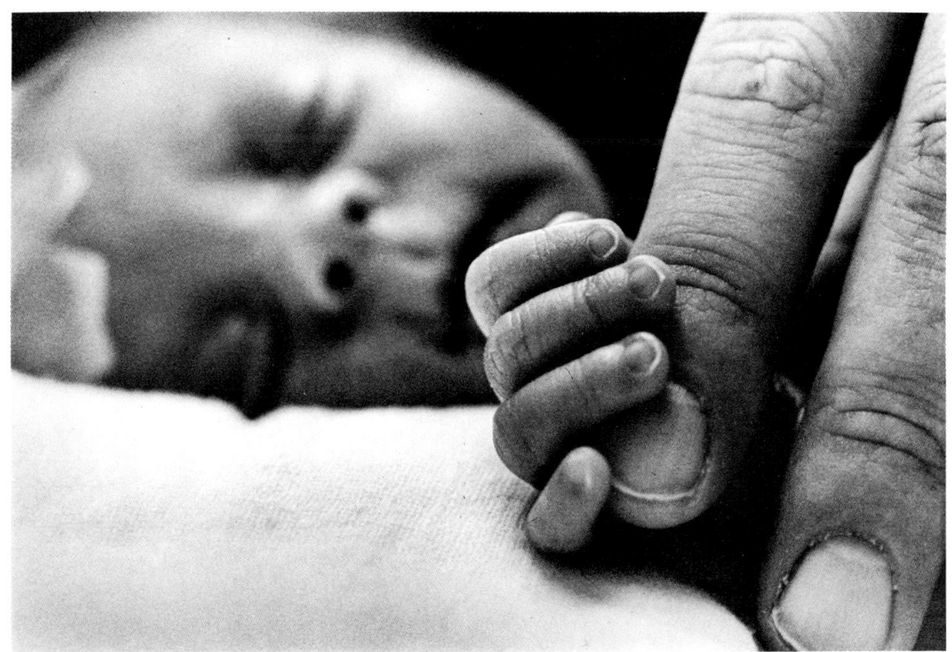

THERESA AUBIN

Christian Noble, 11 weeks premature, and her mother, Gail, at Tacoma General Hospital.

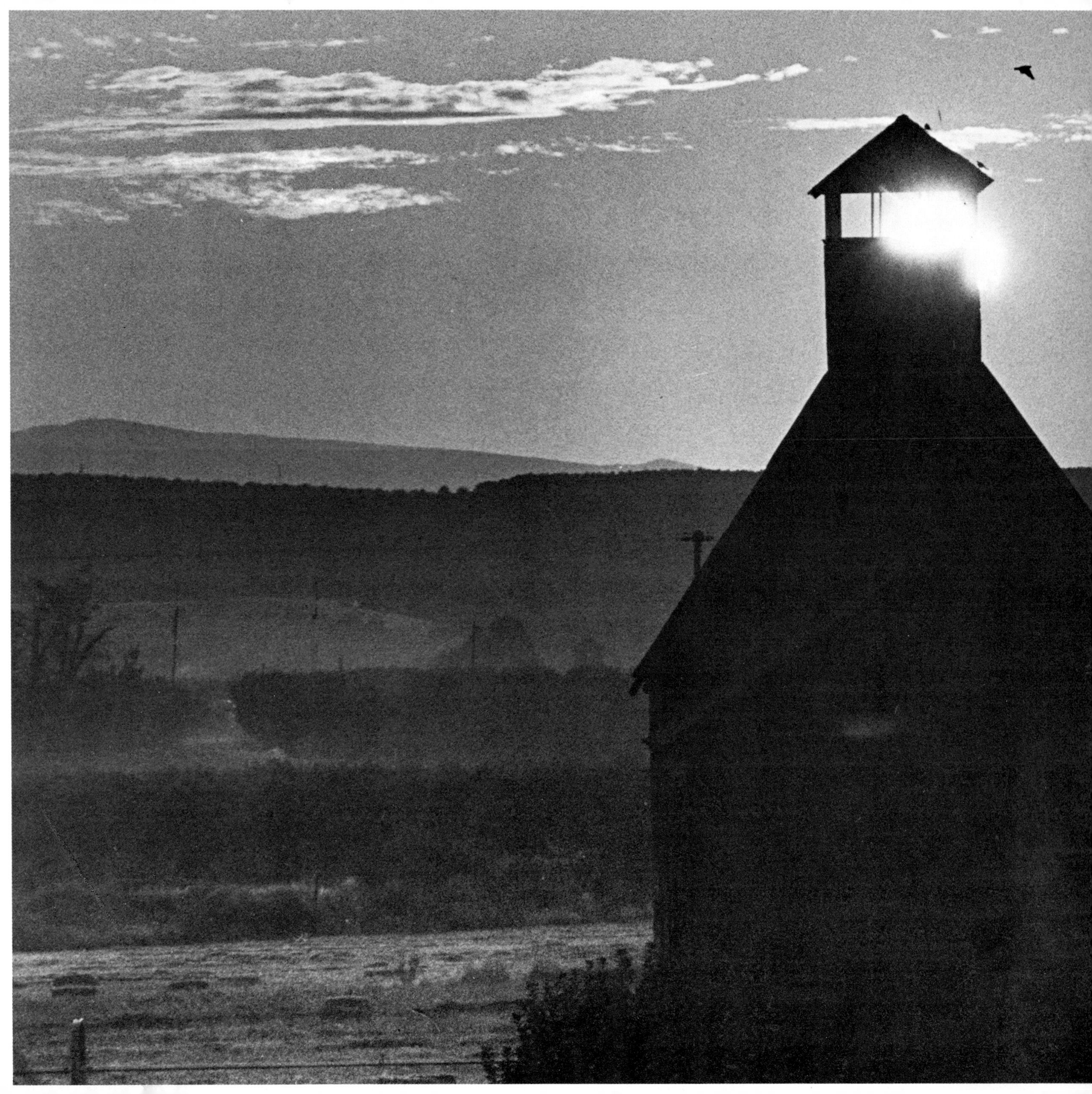

LARRY STEAGALL

One Day in Washington

National Press Photographers Association, Region II

MADRONA PUBLISHERS
SEATTLE

A hop kiln at sunrise at Wapato.

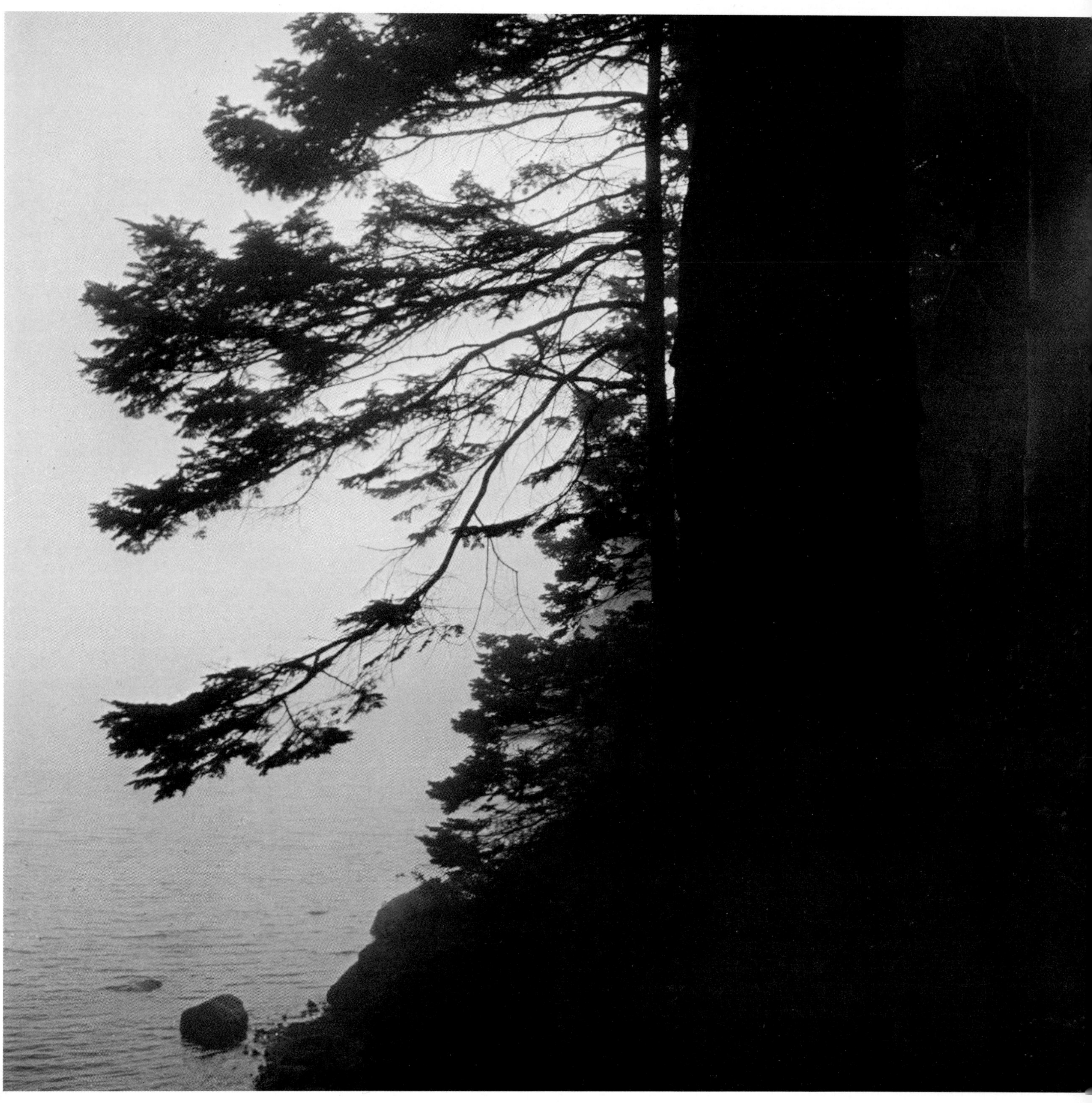

ART GRICE

Night begins to fall at Deception Pass.

First edition
10 9 8 7 6 5 4 3 2 1

Published by
Madrona Publishers
P. O. Box 22667
Seattle, WA 98122

Library of Congress Cataloging in Publication Data
Main entry under title:

One day in Washington.

1. Washington (State)—Description and travel—1981- —Views. I. National Press Photographers Association (U.S.). Region 11.
F892.054 1985 979.7'043 84-21818
ISBN 0-88089-005-3

Printed and bound in Hong Kong

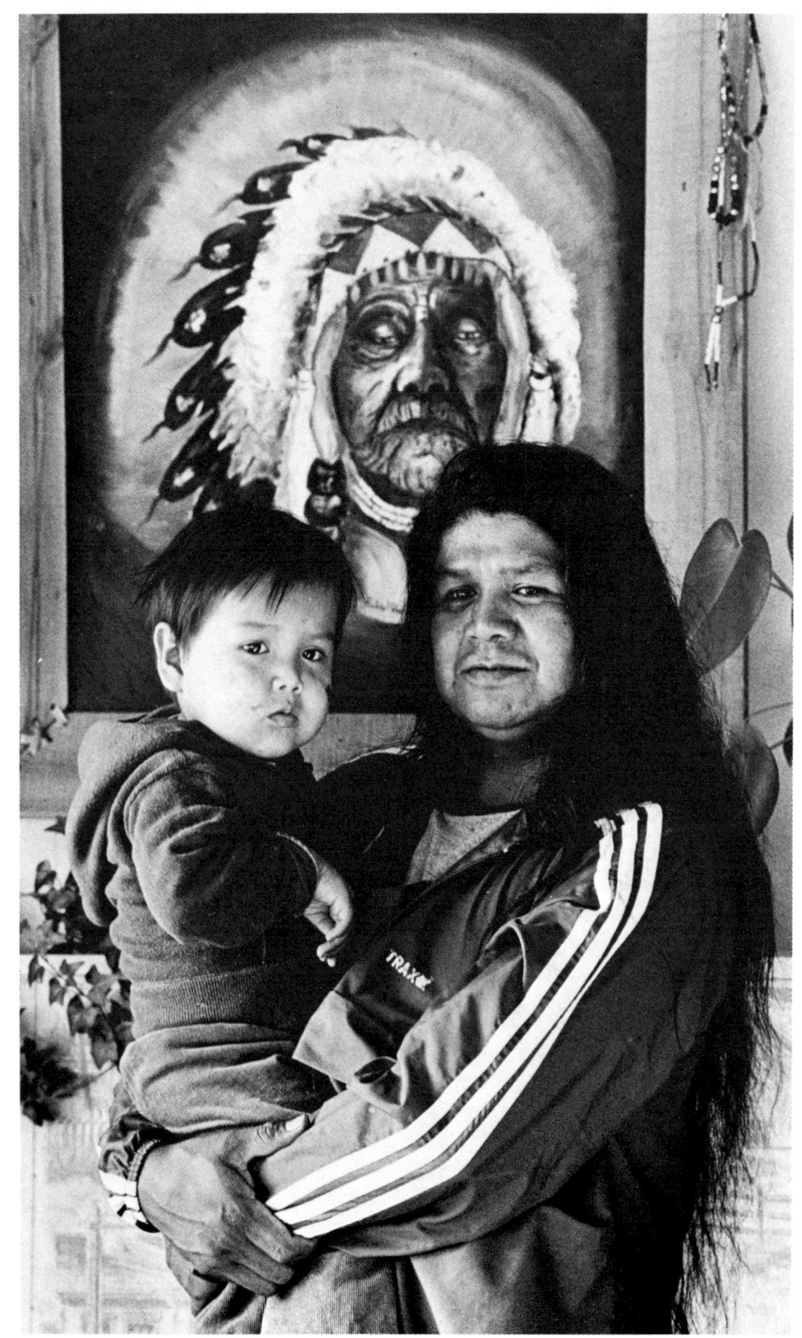

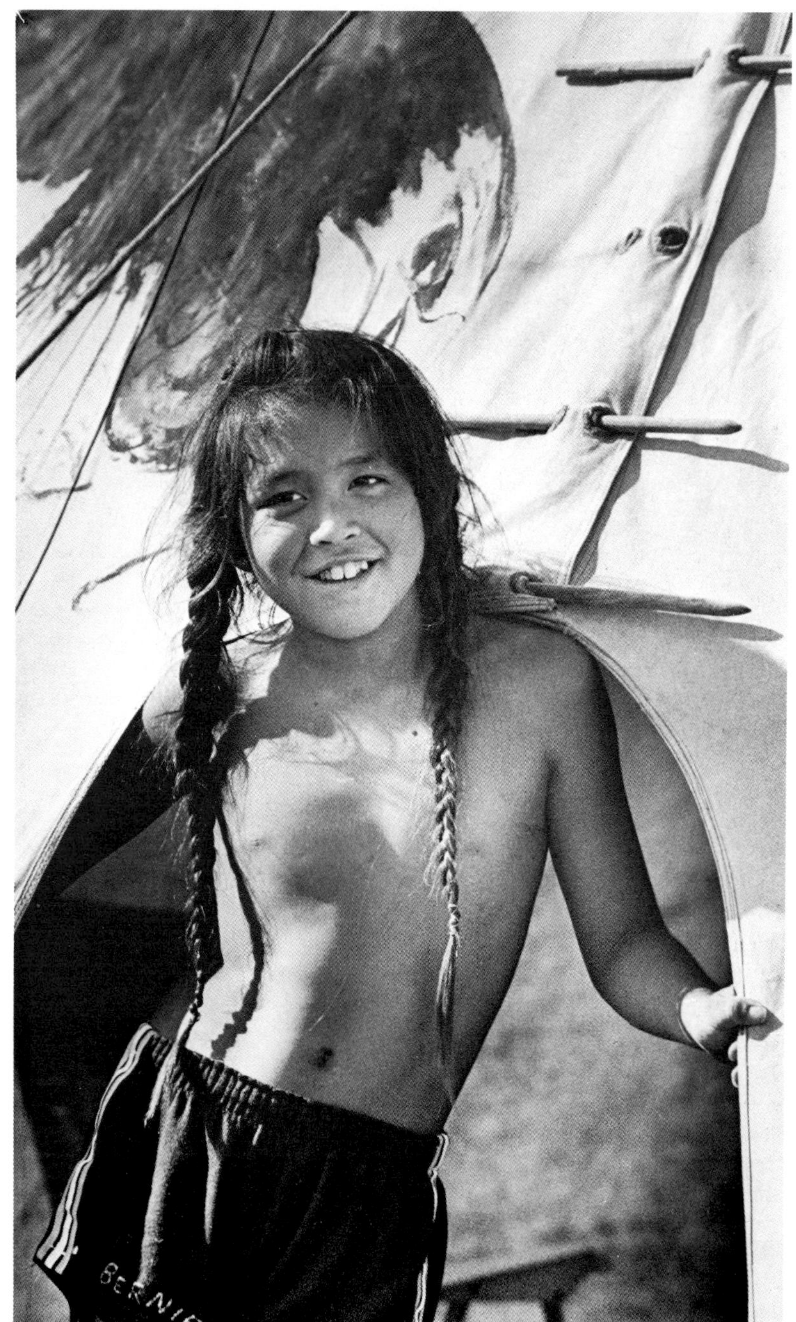

PHOTOS BY LARRY STEAGALL

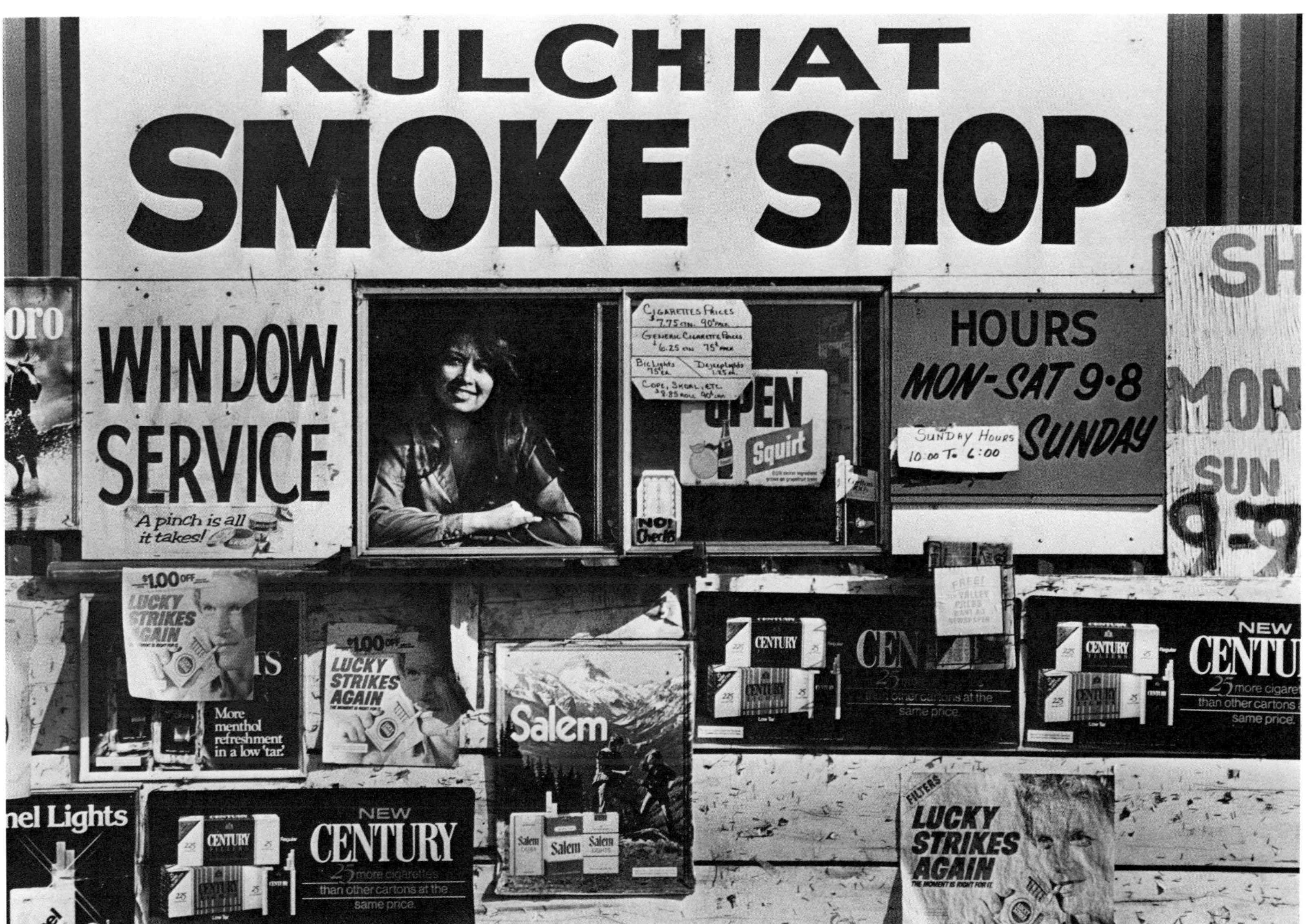

Left: *Francis Williams, 10-year-old Yakima Indian.*

Far left: *Glen Lucei and his son, J.D., 2, at the Hartline Cafe in Wapato in front of a portrait of Chief Tommy Thompson.*

Above: *Debbie McLavey sells tax-free cigarettes on Yakima Indian land.*

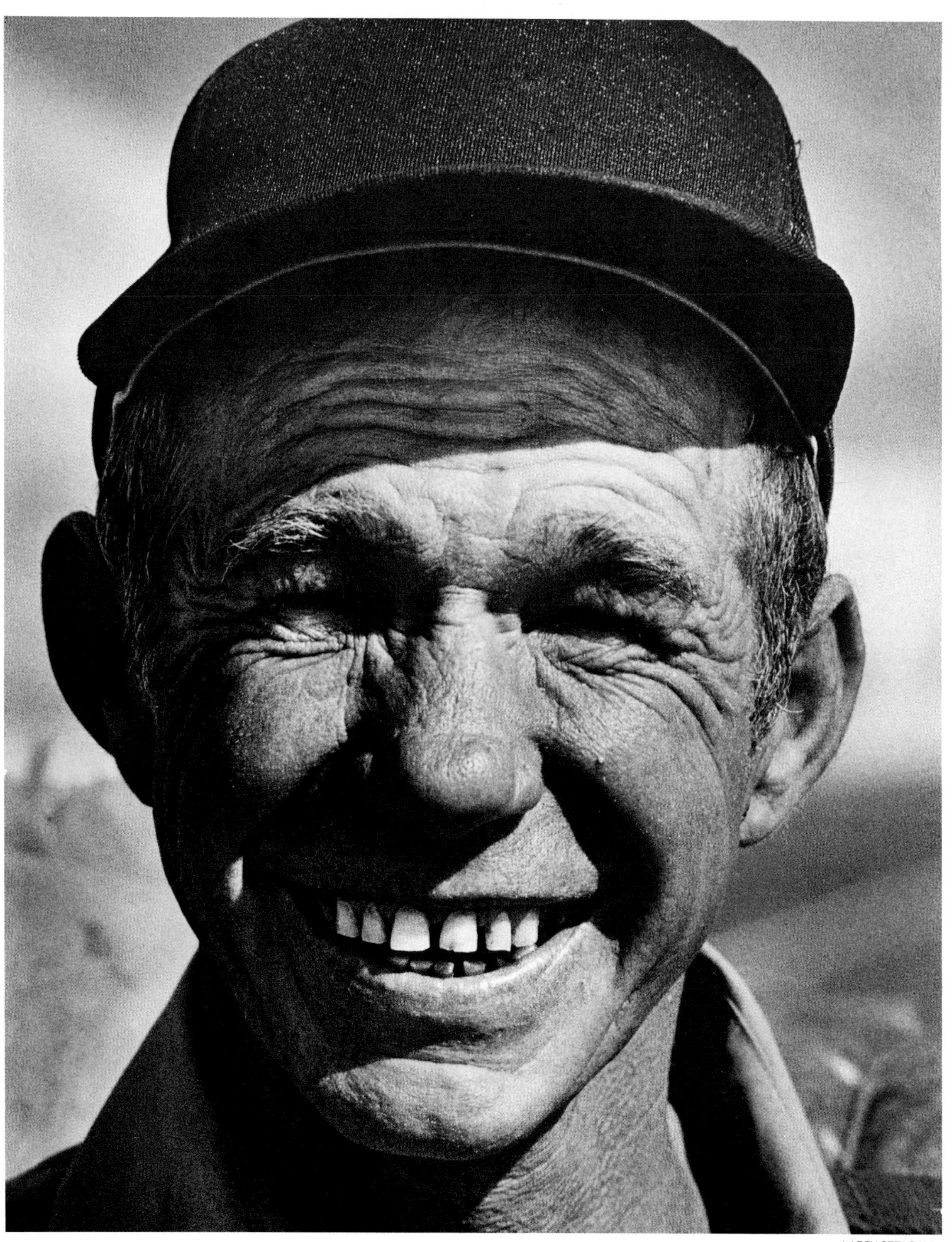

LARRY STEAGALL

Hitchhiker Donald Walster on the road outside Yakima.

Preface

"Photography combines those elements of spontaneity and immediacy that say, 'this is happening, this is real,' and creates an image through a curious alchemy that will live and grow and become more meaningful in a historical perspective." –DAN WEINER

In May of 1983, the regional directors of the National Press Photographers Association initiated a photographic project to document life in Washington and preserve the images of our culture as we enter the mid-eighties. To that end, this book is dedicated to the ideals of photojournalism and documentary photography.

The organizers recruited photographers from the NPPA, the American Society of Magazine Photographers and freelancers to participate in a 24-hour "Dayshoot."

The intent of the project was twofold: to produce and preserve a visual record of the day, and to present the work of our state's photojournalists. The Museum of History and Industry in Seattle agreed to exhibit the work and store the collected images in their archives.

The date of the shoot was September 23, 1983. On that day, 122 still and video photographers from 41 newspapers and 17 TV stations set out to capture one 24-hour period. They had agreed to think of themselves as documenters of life in our time and to look for the ordinary occurrences of everyday life that might take on larger significance in an historical perspective.

All the photographers paid their own expenses for film and materials, and donated their time, talent and vision to make this project work. Many of them did double duty on that day, having to work their regular shifts at their jobs and setting out before or after work to photograph subjects that particularly interested them.

Governor John Spellman proclaimed September 23rd as "Photojournalism Day," fitting recognition for the contribution of these photojournalists to our state's historical record.

The idea of "One Day in the Life" has its own history. The first project of this sort was published in 1970, when Life Magazine made photographic history with its "One Day in the Life of America." Since then the concept has been repeated all over the world, including the notable "Day in the Life of Australia." It's an idea that has captured the imaginations of thousands of people as we seek to preserve the record of who we are and how we live.

The members of NPPA are particularly well suited for this ambitious venture. As press photographers, we are constantly using our camera to immortalize the lives of ordinary people. We are realists rather than romanticists, and find it exciting and worthwhile to inform, enlighten, convince and persuade with our photographs. We hope we have accomplished at least some of these things with this book.

The Dayshoot never could have been a success without the involvement and hard work of so many photographers, and thanks to each and every one of them.

I also appreciate the support of the newspapers in the state who lent their people to this project, especially the *Seattle Post-Intelligencer,* the *Seattle Times,* the *Bremerton Sun* and Valley Newspapers.

For her constant encouragement and unwavering enthusiasm, a very special thanks to Theresa Aubin.

Thanks to Steve Small and Phil Webber for patience and support throughout the long process of putting this together; to Ned Ahrens for his help with prints and other aspects of production; to Bill Kuykendall for his advice and inspiration, and to Stuart Grover and the staff of the Museum of History and Industry.

A special thanks to my husband, Lansing Jones, for his help and encouragement. I would also like to express my deep gratitude to Bill Speidel for helping make this book possible.

JENNIFER WERNER
PROJECT DIRECTOR

KURT SMITH

One Day

No two days are alike, and September 23, 1983, was unlike any other day in the annals of Washington state. It was not like April 13, 1949, when our earth trembled and shook from the force of an earthquake and eight people died. Or November 7, 1940, when the Tacoma Narrows Bridge, old "Galloping Gertie," did a bellyflop in a 50-mile-an-hour wind. Certainly it was not like May 18, 1980, when Mount St. Helens erupted and sent a plume of ash into the air that made its way around planet Earth.

Those dates belong in history books. September 23, 1983, produced a picture book. At one tick of the clock past midnight, 122 still and television photographers officially were banded together for the first Washington Dayshoot—to record for posterity what they and their cameras saw during a 24-hour slice of Washington time.

Twenty-four hours is an eternity if one is seated in a stuffy classroom on a June day, waiting for the beginning of summer vacation. But it's only 1/27,000th of the average human lifespan, a tiny grain of sand in the hourglass of the universe. The photographers didn't catch everything that happened to the 4.3 million residents of the smallest state west of Minnesota, the most northwesterly in the continental United States, the only one named after a president. But they did preserve some of its wonders and its wackiness, its victories and its defeats, and its plain ordinariness.

One of the joys of peeking into old photo albums is to see what kind of car mom or dad drove, what kind of hats and dresses the women wore, what the hairstyles were and what the stores looked like. We don't always use big words like "social commentary," but that's what those old photographs are.

A roadside chapel near Marblemount in morning fog.

And that's what this book is — a documentary of our times. Because professional photographers do a lot less posing of their subjects than they once did, and because they grow angry at the suggestion that they do a little touchup, pictures today are a truer reflection of our life than ever before.

The split-second timing of a camera freezes people and scenic grandeur in a way that frequently defies written description. Writers can interpret, but often their words simply cannot paint the scene as well as a camera in the right hands.

At 6:44 a.m., from 93 million miles away, the great lightbulb we call sun washed over the rolling brown hills of Eastern Washington, splashing them with orange and purple. It swept over the mighty Columbia and sped across wheat fields and cattle ranches, sweet-scented pine forests and fruit orchards, and took the chill from sagebrush and prairie.

With a single stride, it leaped the Cascade Mountains, drove shafts of light through dense forests of fir, hemlock and cedar, and began burning the fog from Western Washington's fertile valleys. It cast a pink sky over concrete, steel and glass, and showered jewels on Puget Sound and Hood Canal. It skipped quickly over the Olympics and lightly touched bleached driftwood and the tops of creaming waves on Pacific sands.

In 30 minutes, Washington, the Evergreen State, was awash with light from Chewelah to Walla Walla, from Neah Bay to Ilwaco.

At newspaper, radio and TV newsrooms, early arrivals scanned the wires: War in Lebanon; 112 dead in an Arabian airplane crash; a riot in the Philippines; the president's daughter calling for James Watt to resign; digging of the I-90 tunnel about to start; Curt Warner and John Riggins to match running skills in Sunday's Seahawks-Redskins NFL football

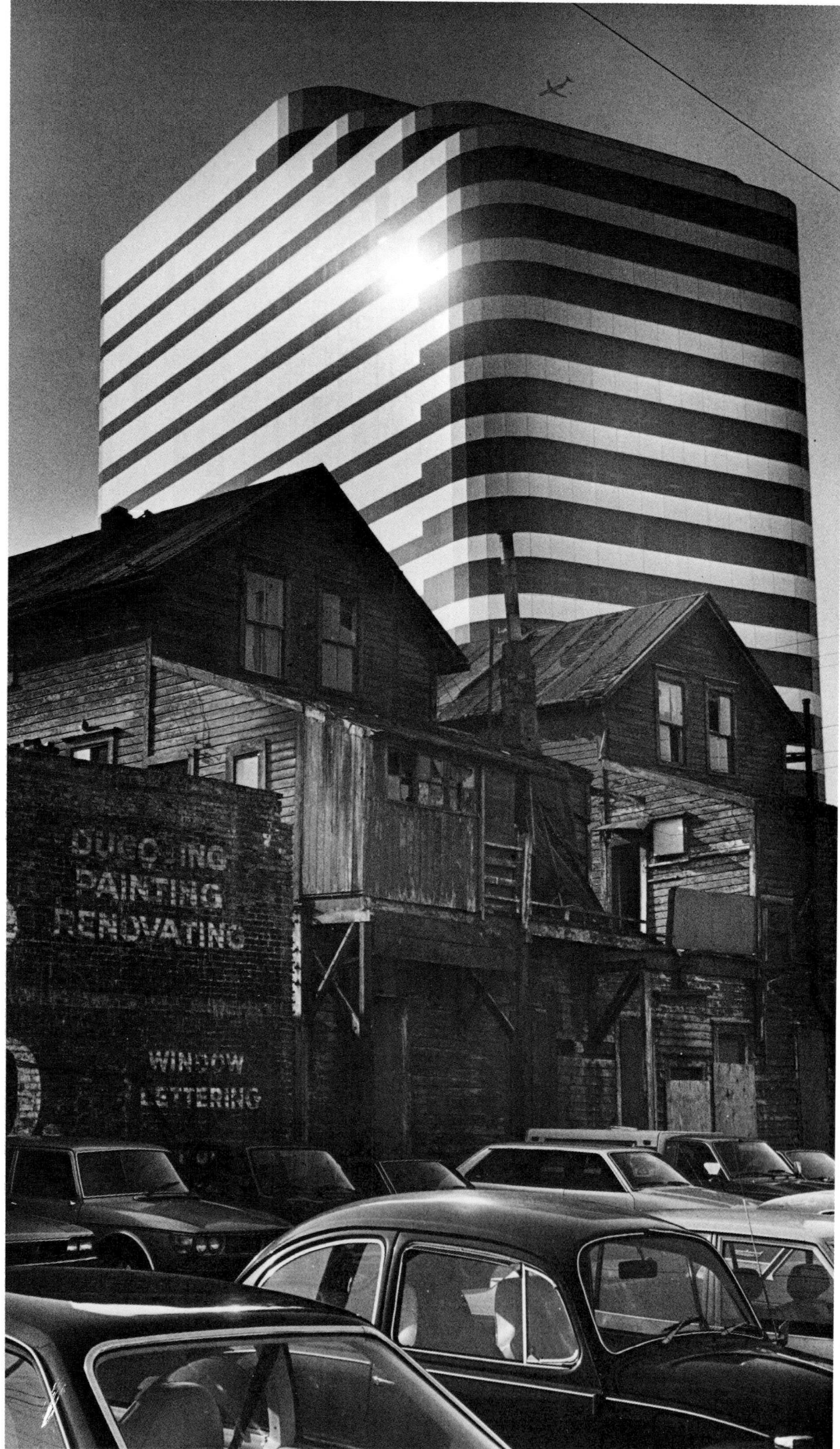

Old and new in downtown Seattle.

ALAN BERNER

MERRILL OLIVER

Grain silos south of Kennewick.

game. Print editors soon would determine lead stories, TV editors would decide how best to employ helicopters to get there first and be back with the best.

By 7 o'clock, maybe earlier, many of us had been roused by electric alarm clocks, the signal to shower in water heated by electricity or gas and get ready for another day. Newspapers thudded on front porches. Coffee was brewed. Radios were turned on, because we always need an outside voice to confirm our suspicion that nothing really important happened while we snoozed.

The day couldn't have been nicer. In a state famous for airplanes, apples, mountains, trees, wheat and rain, in no particular order, we had everything except the rain. Skies were clear, the moon was full and daytime temperatures were in the mid-70s.

It was a perfect day for a shoot. And shoot these photographers did, more than 100,000 frames. One photographer admitted to shooting up 100 rolls of film, at 32 frames to the roll.

While most of us followed our familiar routines, the press photographers and their freelance partners in the Dayshoot pursued shapes, shadows, light and color. If someone asked for one grand portrait of Washington state on September 23, 1983, no single photographer could deliver it. That portrait would be a mosaic of everything shot by all Dayshoot participants, as well as the thousands of times they almost clicked the shutter and didn't.

But basically, any portrait of the state named for George would show an honest, kindly face, with little laugh lines around the eyes. And that's what this book preserves.

It shows that in the fall of '83, there were a lot of traditional families doing the things they've always done. It also shows there were plenty of people doing whatever they wanted to do, that the age of Do Your Own Thing is alive and well.

We are increasingly concerned about our bodies and our looks. We run and stretch and cycle and "pump iron" to keep trim, and some sit under tanning lamps to accomplish what our weather doesn't do naturally.

We work hard, in businesses that are high-tech, those that demand muscle, and in those that rely on the natural resources we get from forest, field and water.

We play just as hard as we work. There are fish to catch, football games to see, card games to play and streets to cruise. There are oceans to explore and mountains to climb.

Since Washington state always has enjoyed a reputation for being a bit of a maverick on the national scene, it is no surprise that we have more than our share of characters. It is important to the survival of our independence that the elderly inventor in Coulee City can still sit on his front steps and honk at the cars that pass by, that the Hutterites continue to follow the conservative lifestyle dictated by their religion. It is just as important that we see the joy on the face of a roller-skating nun, that a small child can climb on a fence and peer in at the grave markers of a Port Gamble cemetery.

There was drama all around us on September 23rd, but most of it didn't make the paper. There was no headline in the elderly man playing the guitar for his 107-year-old mom, for the around-the-clock effort at Children's Orthopedic Hospital to save the life of little Crystal Dietiker. The 5 o'clock News didn't mention the Indian boy grinning from a teepee, the ferryboat that landed at the dock without wiping it out, the bartender who has hundreds of baseball caps stapled to his ceiling.

In truth, for those who like to know such things, it was not a great day for hard news. Gaylord Perry, a 314-game winner and likely Hall of Famer, announced his retirement. Pierce County deputies arrested a man wanted for eight bank robberies and a murder in the past 18 months. In late afternoon, two fires—one in a loft at West Seattle High School and the other in a University District home—attracted attention. At the school, two propane tanks exploded,

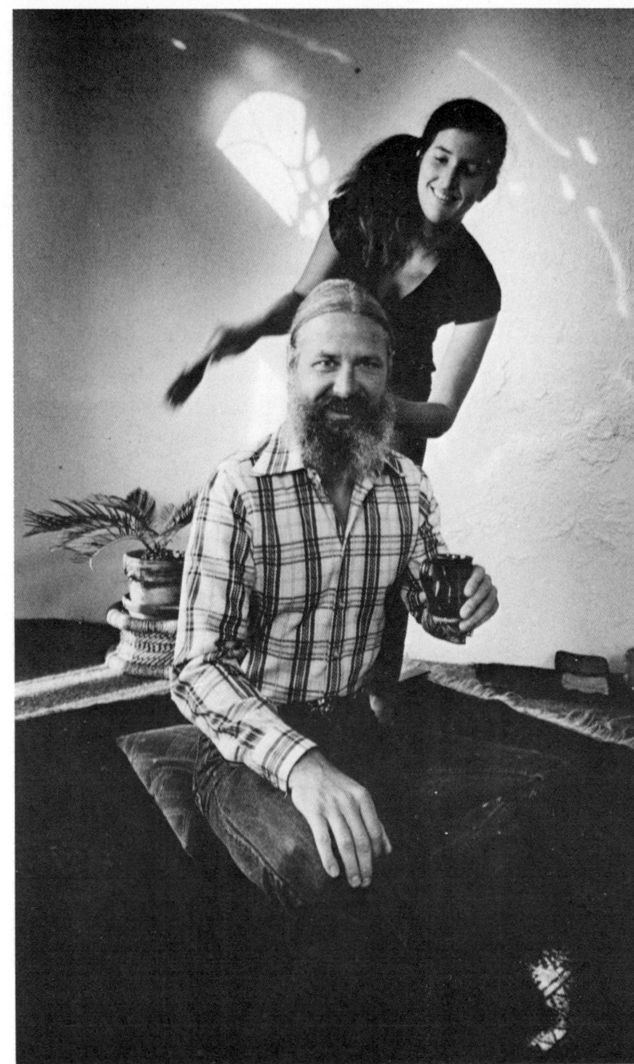

JENNIFER WERNER

Love Israel, leader of a religious sect on Seattle's Queen Anne Hill, has his hair brushed and braided in a ponytail by one of his followers.

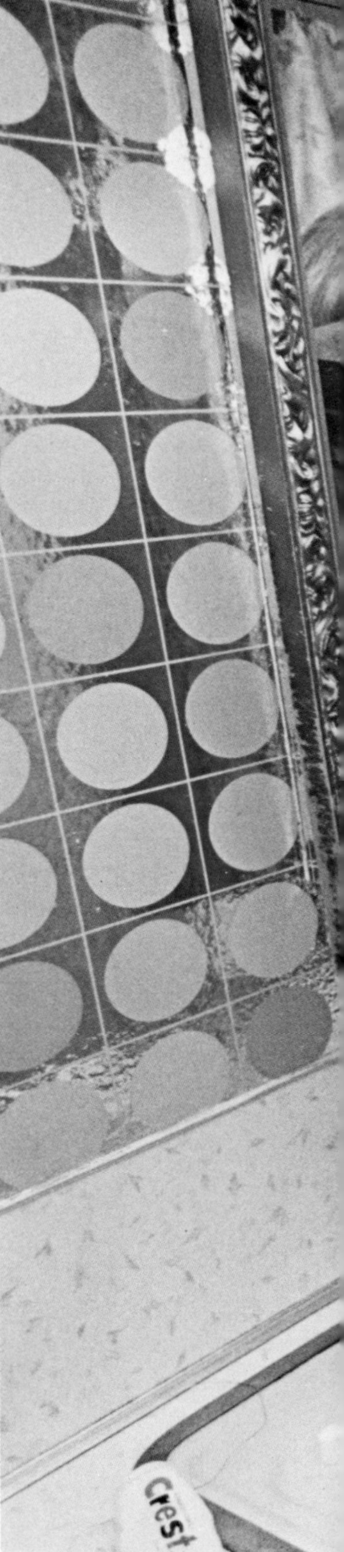

Mary Haller of Lynnwood combs the snarls from her daughter Rory's hair.

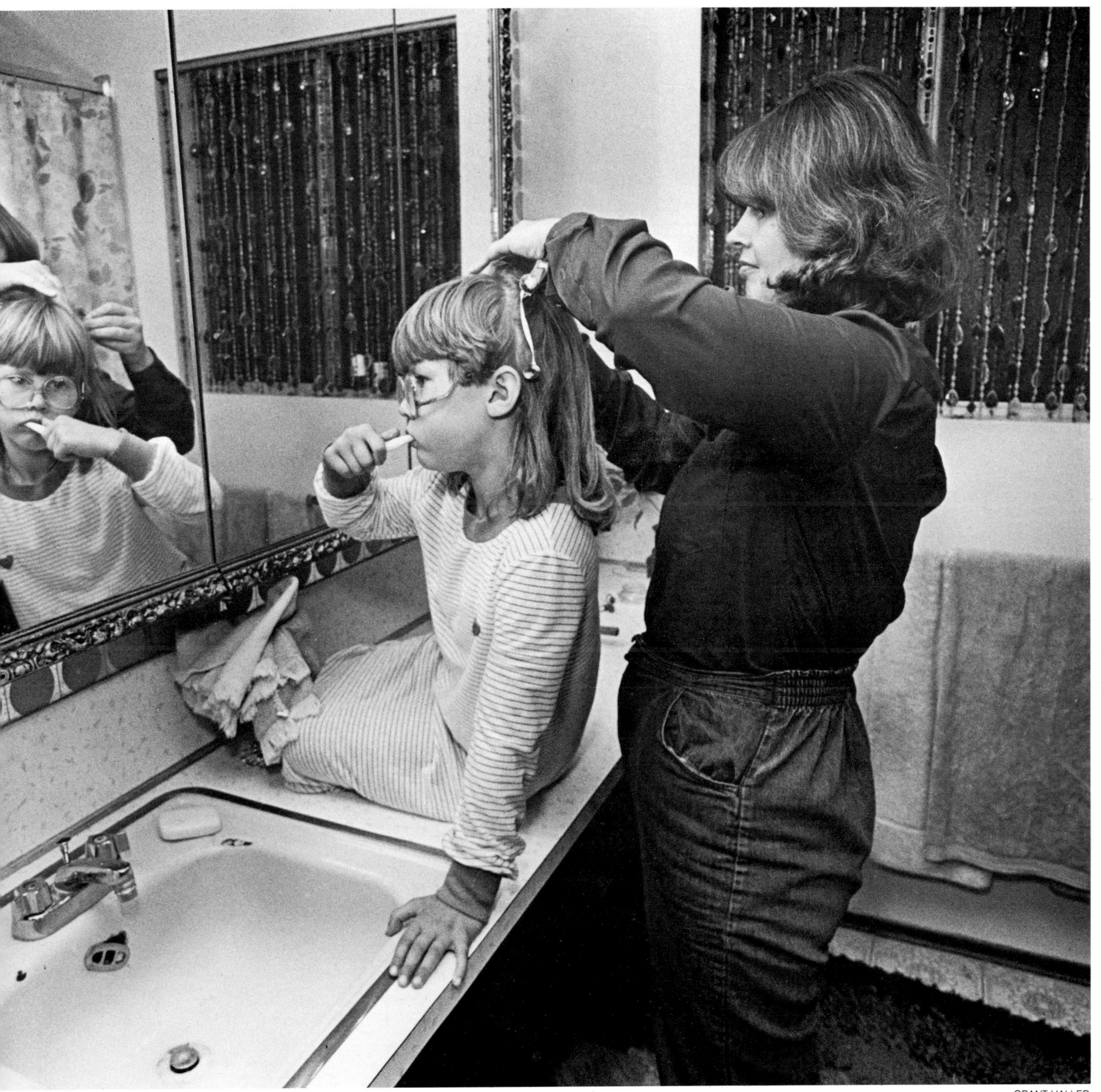

GRANT HALLER

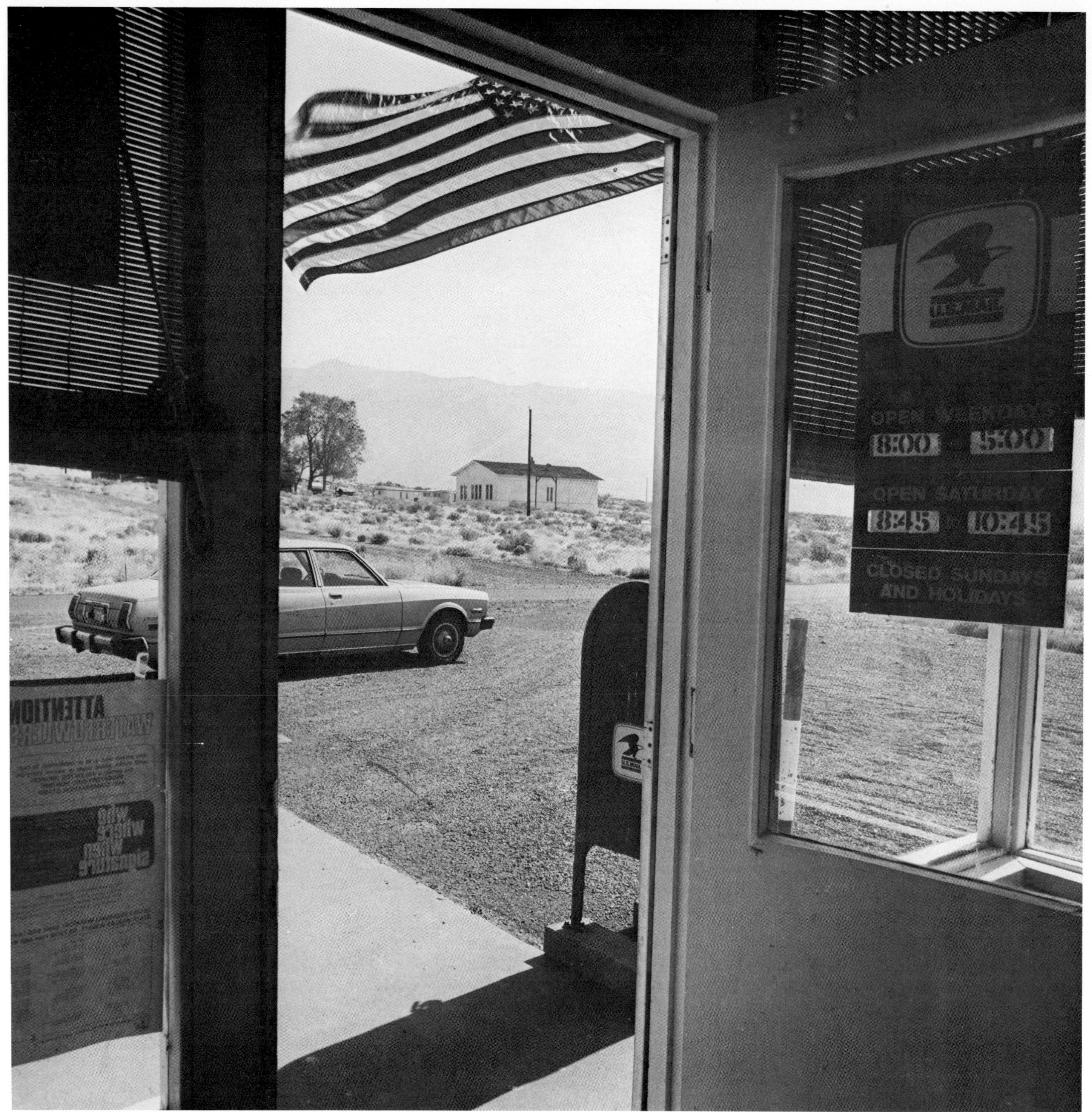

PHOTOS BY DON NORMARK

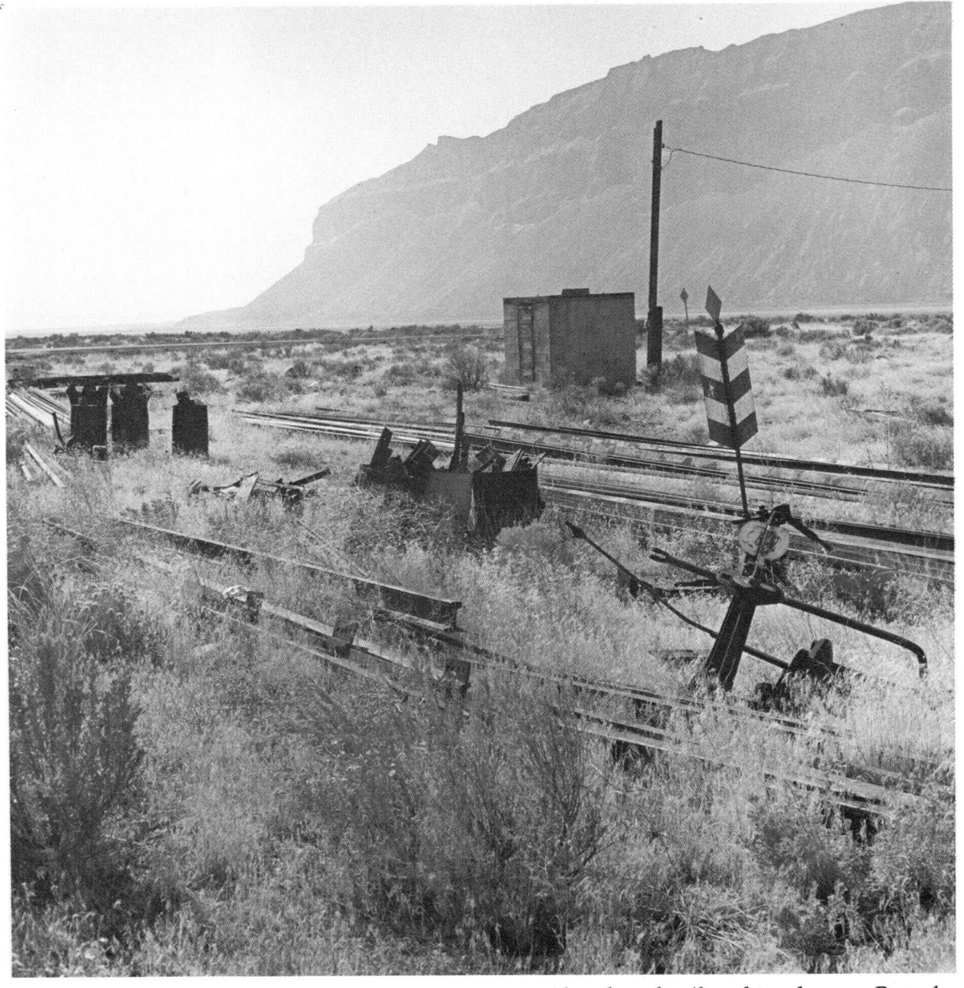

Abandoned railroad tracks near Beverly.

The self-service post office in Beverly, Grant County.

Following pages: *After buying a houseboat from an evicted tenant, Craig and Linda Boring set out across Seattle's Lake Union in search of a berth.*
CARY TOLMAN

sending their fiery contents skyward, causing damage estimated at $35,000. At the home, where a young man left a cheese sandwich in a broiler and went hiking, damage was estimated at $69,000 and three firefighters were overcome by exhaustion.

That only one of those stories is represented by a photograph in this book is of little importance. These photographers were looking for things that told their own story, a drama of a different sort.

They went to little hamlets, wide spots in the road that look pretty much the same as they did in the quiet Eisenhower '50s. They went to farms that have been in one family for nearly a century. And they saw a choker-setter in the woods of the Olympic Peninsula who might have stepped out of one of those old glass-plate photographs of loggers standing on platforms to fell a giant Douglas fir.

For all the super high-rises sprouting in our cities, including the Columbia Seafirst Center that will, by golly, be the tallest west of the Mississippi, it was nice that the camera's lens focused on old wooden structures and on those, like the service station in the shape of cowboy boots and hat, that show our state is not all look-alike glass-and-steel towers.

Ask the photographers why they took the time to participate in the Dayshoot and they put aside talk about film speeds and f/stops and wax philosophical. For many, it was a chance to explore something that interested them, not what some editor thought should be on the front page or lead off the evening news.

Robert Harbison of Federal Way did double duty, taking "deadline photographs" for Robinson Newspapers and doing Dayshoot photographs before and after his job. He was out watching his son deliver newspapers at 6 a.m. Before going to work, he got some excellent photographs at a school and of a free car wash. And from 8 p.m. until 2 a.m. the next day, he rode with a King County K-9 unit. Near the end, he was so tired that he fell asleep in the K-9 unit car.

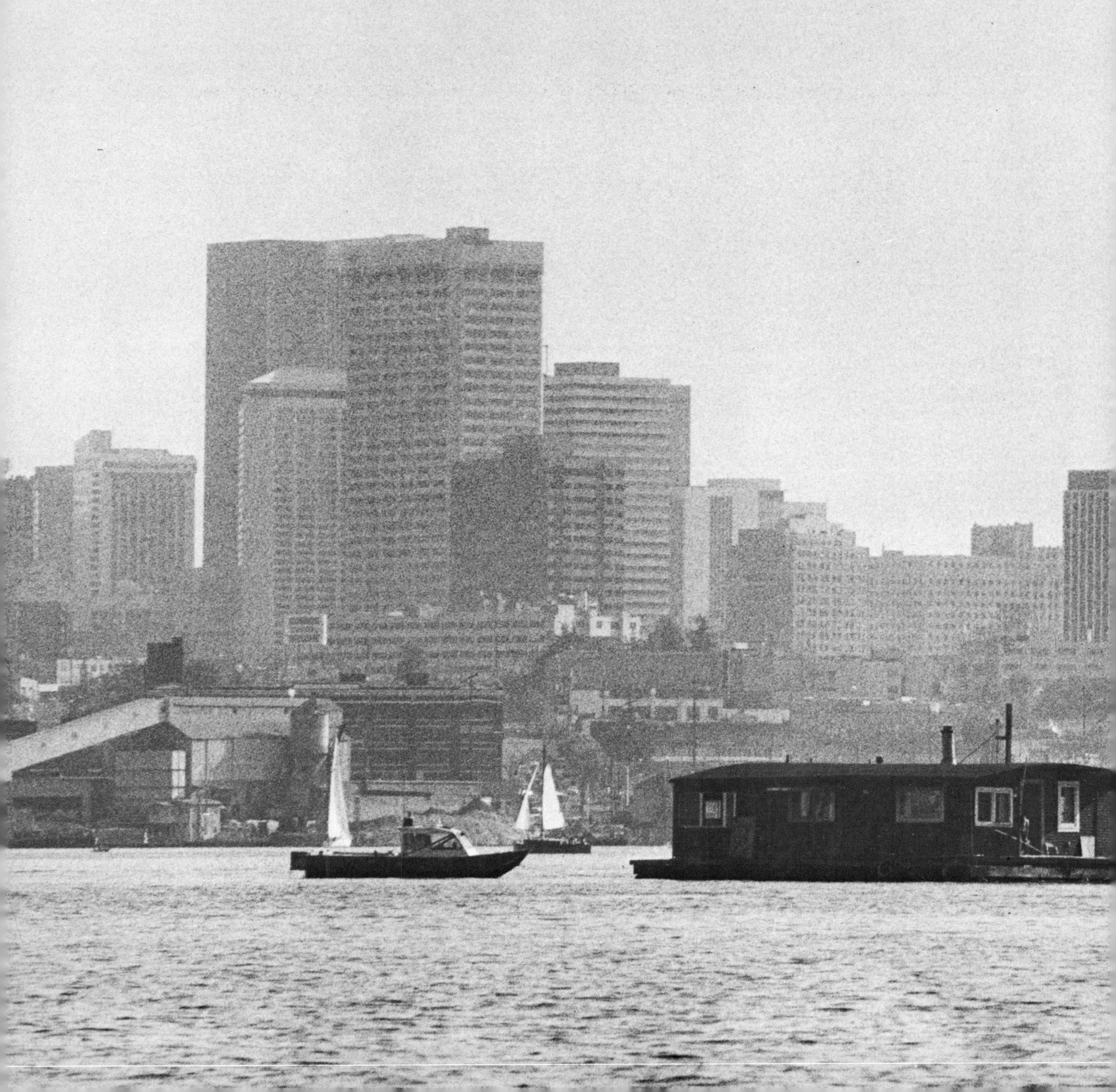

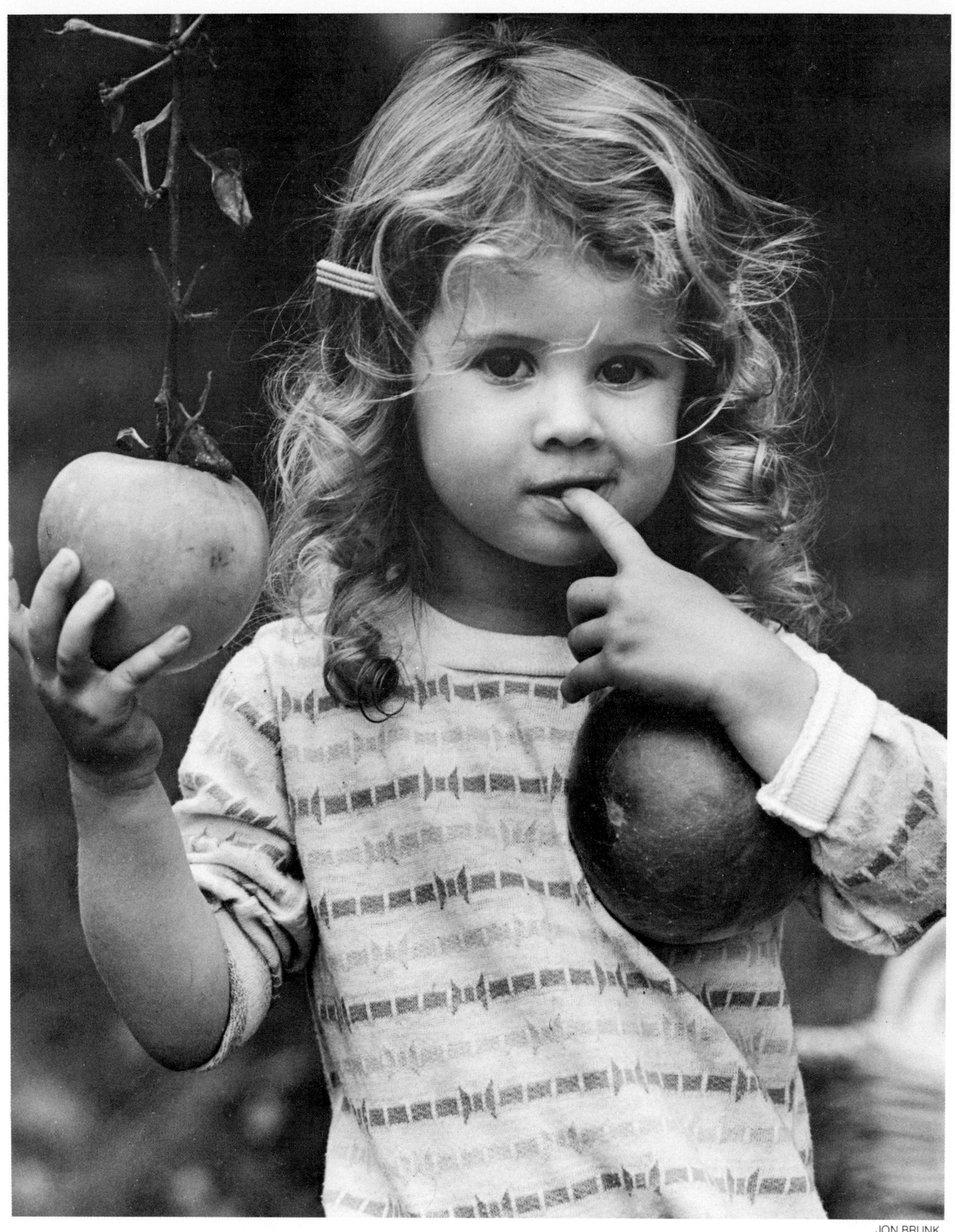

Sarah Gwen Shifflet of Lyman, Skagit County.

JON BRUNK

Art and Emily Grice are a photographic team, and they set out for the Deception Pass area with the whole family, because the Samish Indians were going to raise a totem pole and the chief is a friend of theirs. "It was," says Emily Grice, "the first time the family had gone camping all year, and it was one of the last times we were with Art's dad before he died. It was a magical day, of sun and mist and family spirit."

Bruce Carroll elected to do Seattle's inner city and what used to be called the tenderloin district, where the down-and-outers mingle with those in three-piece suits. Carroll was "impressed with how quickly the city comes alive, between 5:30 and 6:30 in the morning, and how fast it goes back to sleep, between 6:30 and 7:30." And, keeping his distance to shoot candid shots, he noticed the "territorial imperative" of the human race—"the high-powered business executives and the destitute bums on the same street, but always keeping an exact and proper distance from each other."

James Johnson, a photographer for the Citizen Newspapers, found himself in Eastern Washington, taking photographs of the Hutterites, a religious sect "that never left the past... that isn't concerned about war or our modern-day drug problems, or whether appliances work." And from there he went to see the old inventor in Coulee City who came over from Greece on the Titanic and survived the sinking.

Jim Stuart, a freelander, got into a Cessna airplane piloted by a Seattle Post-Intelligencer reporter, John O'Ryan, and they went all over Western Washington taking aerial photographs. "From up there, you get all those neat patterns you can't see from the ground."

Jimi Lott, a photographer for the Spokane Spokesman Review, was so ill the morning of the Dayshoot that he felt like "bagging the whole idea." But he went out anyway, "to see if I could catch little unorchestrated moments, the unplanned things that make life interesting." He captured quite a few, including a wonderful shot of a little girl, glasses down on her nose, who had just written the date ("23") on the blackboard.

Don Normark, a Seattle freelancer, spent his time close to the Eastern Washington soil, "and when the day ended, I felt I had failed utterly... it wasn't until a few weeks later that I could bring myself to develop and print, and then I remembered, with fondness, some of the things that had happened." Like the trucker bogged down at a rest stop with a flat tire who got a ride from a young woman. Like the surveyor on a Columbia Basin irrigation project who said that water eventually would be brought to thousands more acres "and this sagebrush here, it'll all be green."

Grant Haller, Post-Intelligencer photographer and an organizer of the Dayshoot, found it "an escape from our daily newspaper life." During the shoot, in an Issaquah restaurant, Haller saw on the wall some 1880-1890 logging photographs "and I thought how neat they were and how important our own project might someday be to history. Maybe some guy getting $20 from a bank cash machine will be astounding to people 100 years from now... maybe they'll look at our shoes and be amazed."

September 23rd wound down the way most fall Fridays do. Leaves turning red and brown, the sun sliding low in the sky in the late afternoon were reminders that Indian summer couldn't last much longer, that the familiar overcast skies and drizzle would soon be upon us. Going-home traffic was the usual mess in the big cities. Many headed out of town for one last fling at summer cottages at the seashore or mountains.

In Spokane, the sun set officially at 6:38 p.m. Street lights and house lights began flashing on, moving west until people from La

Push to Oysterville saw the blood-red wafer that had warmed them dip below the curve of the Pacific.

For some, the workday was just beginning. They waited on restaurant tables, steered jet pilots from radar screens, drove police cars, pumped gas and ministered to the ill.

The young, and the young at heart, flocked to theaters. They cheered at high school football games under lights and they engaged in the age-old mating games.

Mothers and fathers tucked youngsters between white sheets, read them bedtime stories, said prayers and kissed them before turning out the lights. Then they flipped the switches on TV sets, opened newspapers or, because this is one of the readingest areas in the United States, turned the pages of a good book.

Midnight arrived before many of the Dayshoot photographers realized what time it was. Ahead were hours in the darkroom and rigorous culling of finished prints.

The result is a lively still life of one day in a state so young its 100th birthday still is a few years away. Maybe this picture book will turn out to be a history book after all.

DON DUNCAN

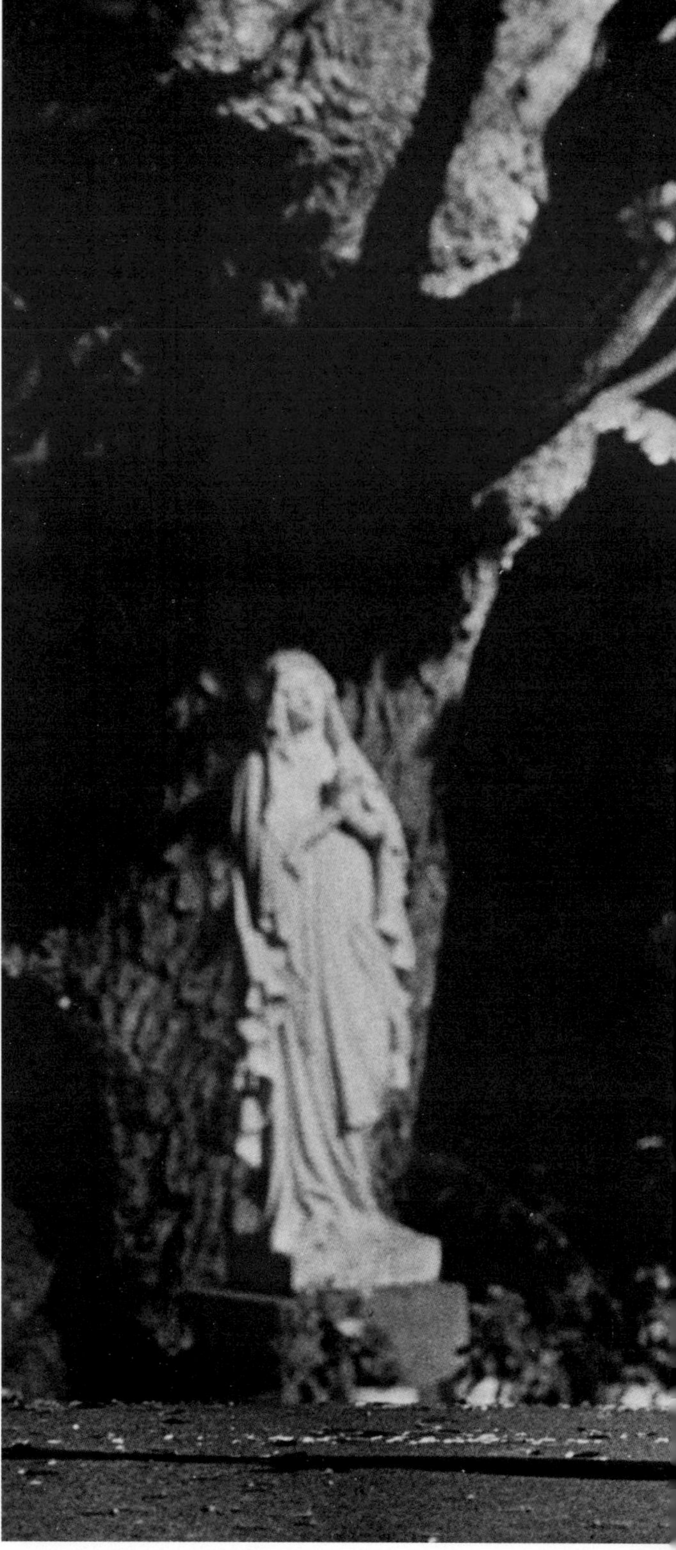

Sister Francis Bitterman of the Sisters of Visitation in Dash Point, Pierce County.

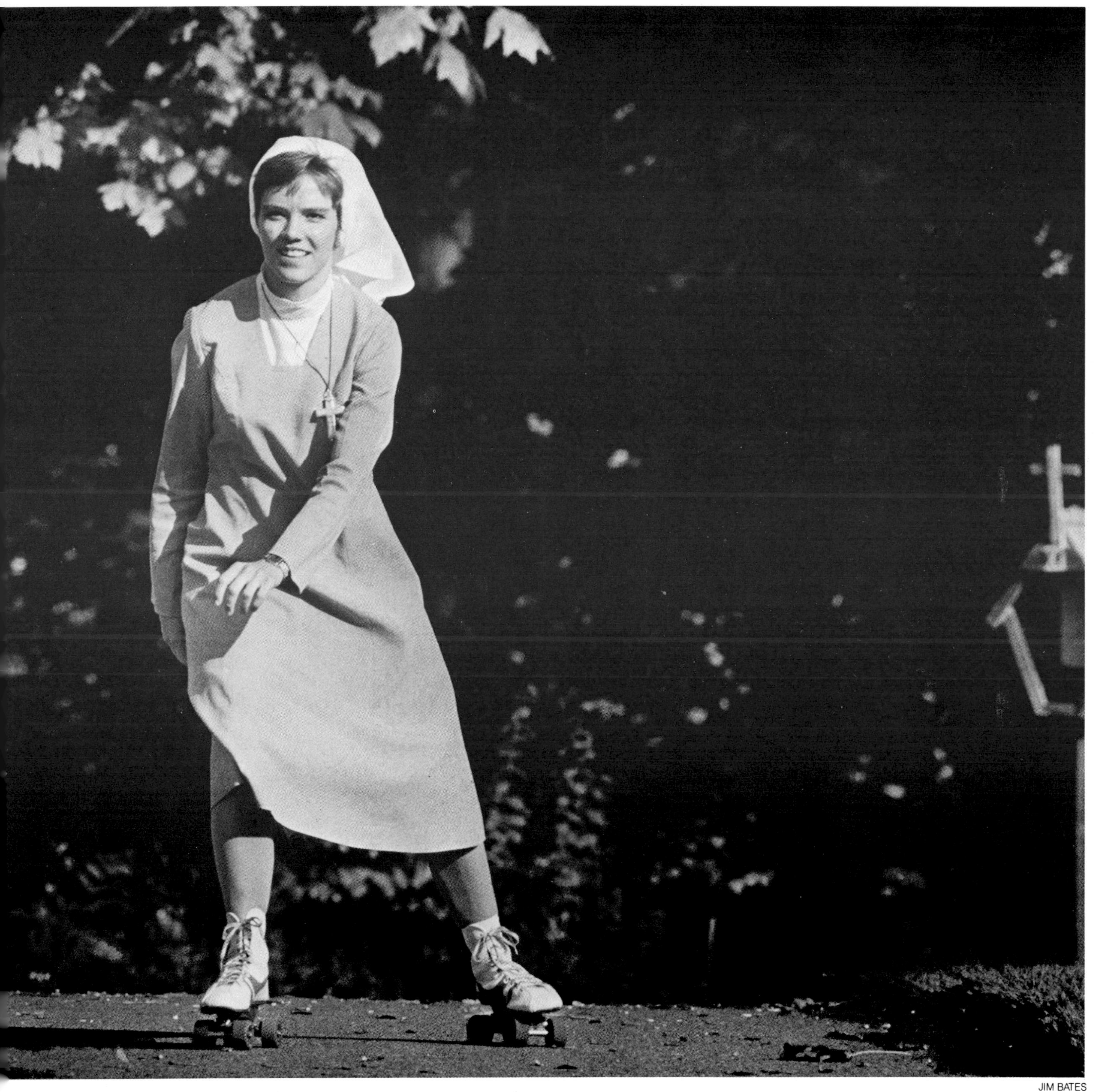

JIM BATES

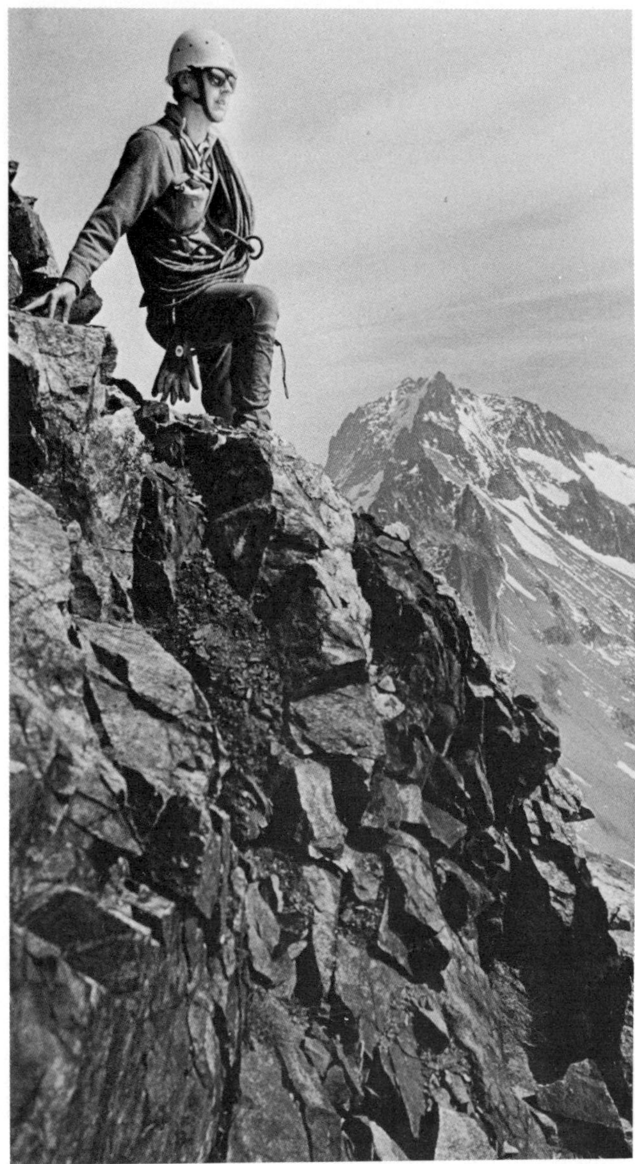

KURT SMITH

Dick Buck at the top of Sahalee Peak in the North Cascades.

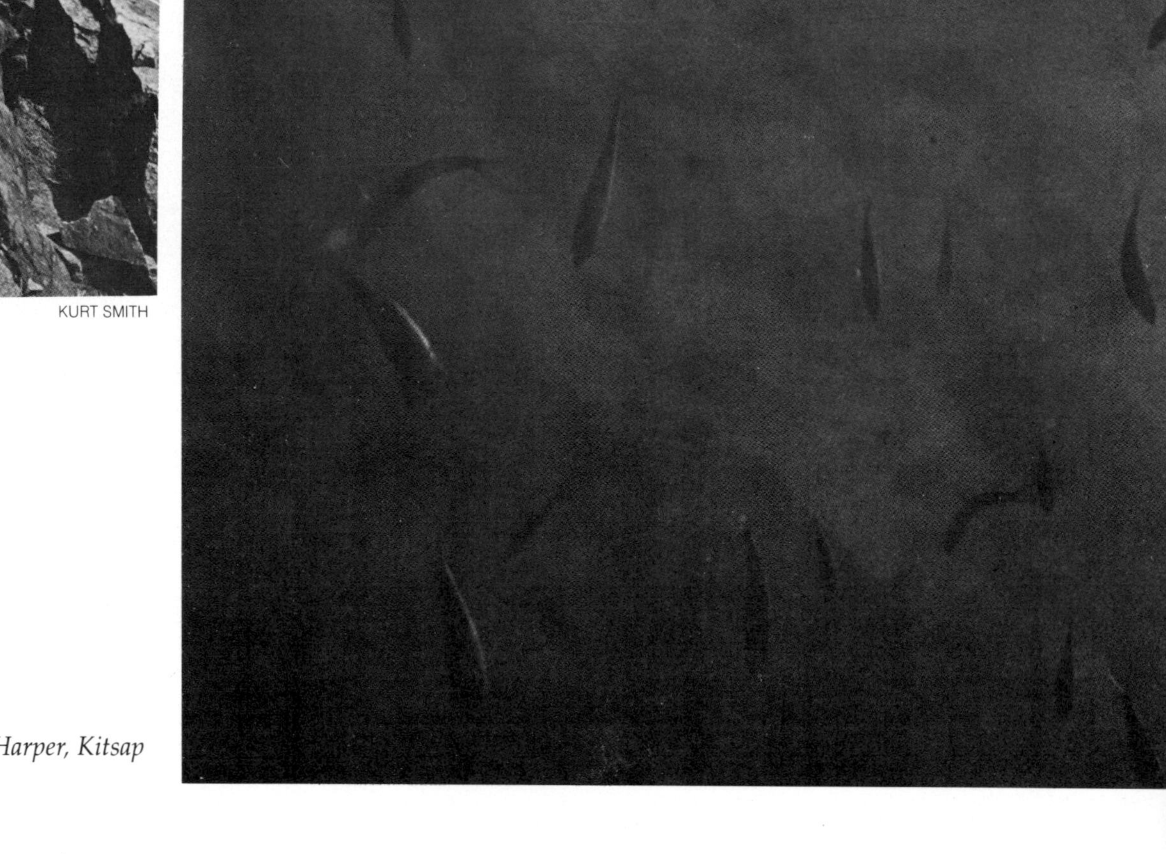

Steve Wojcik in the deep at Harper, Kitsap County.

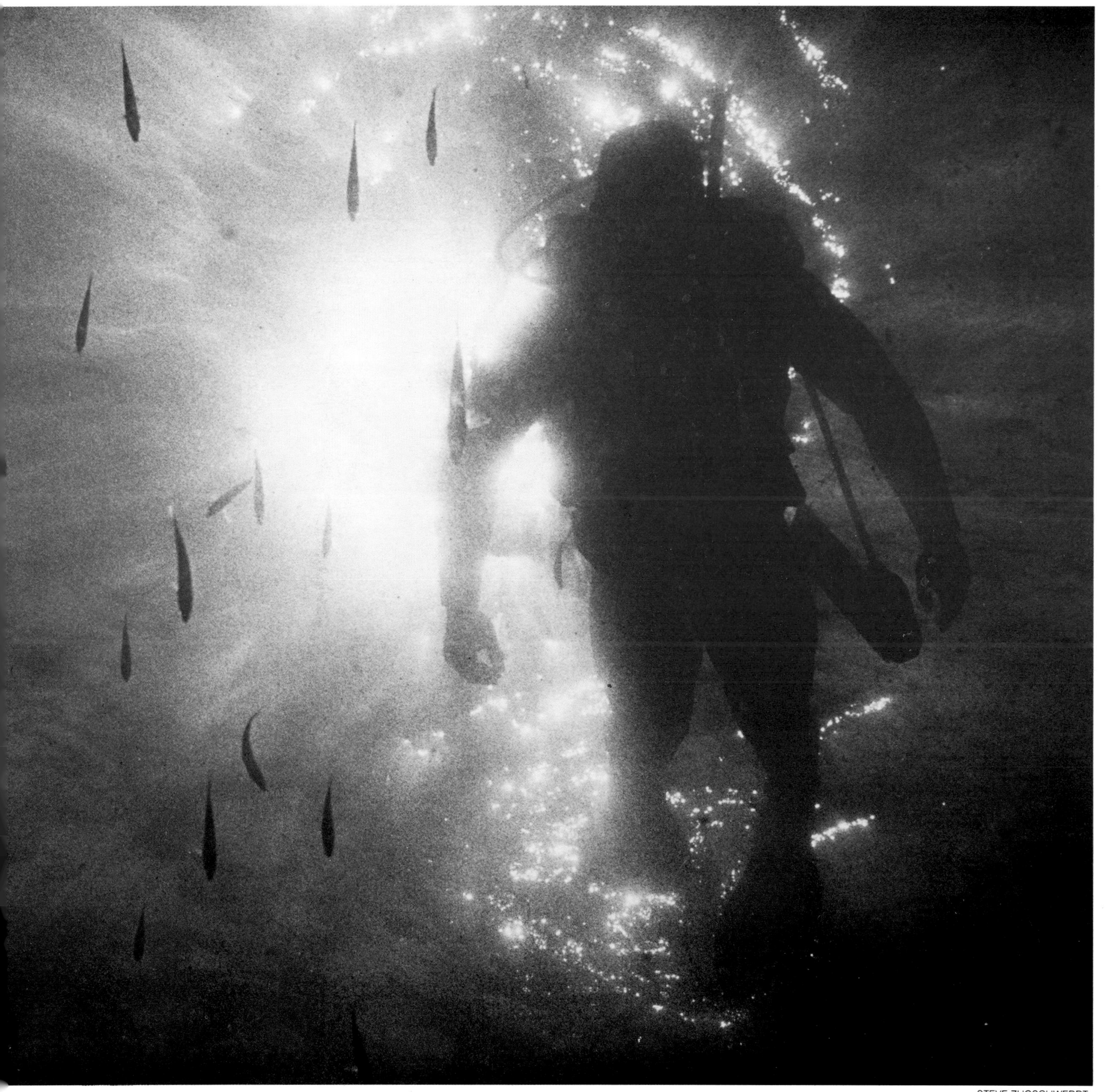

STEVE ZUGSCHWERDT

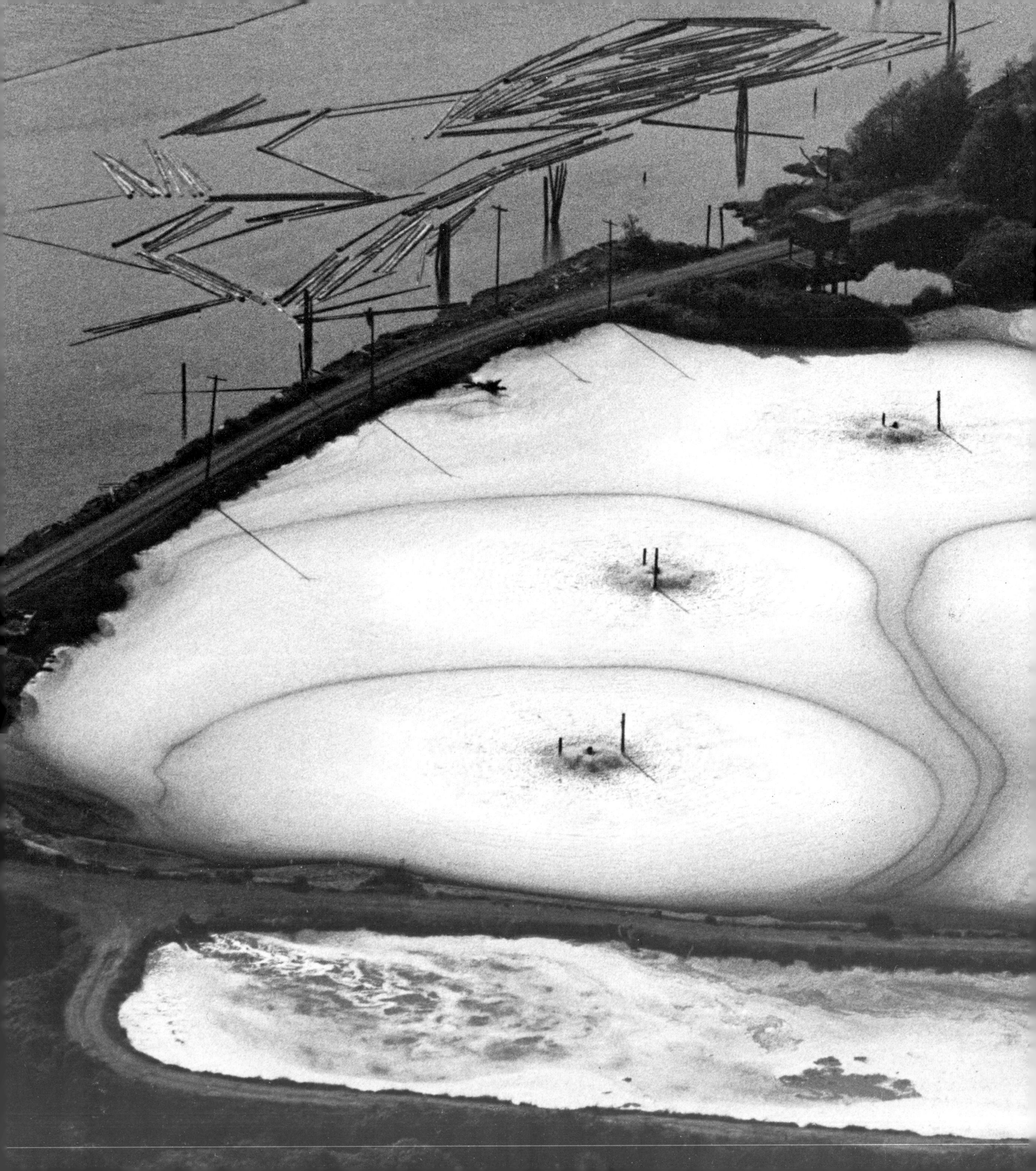

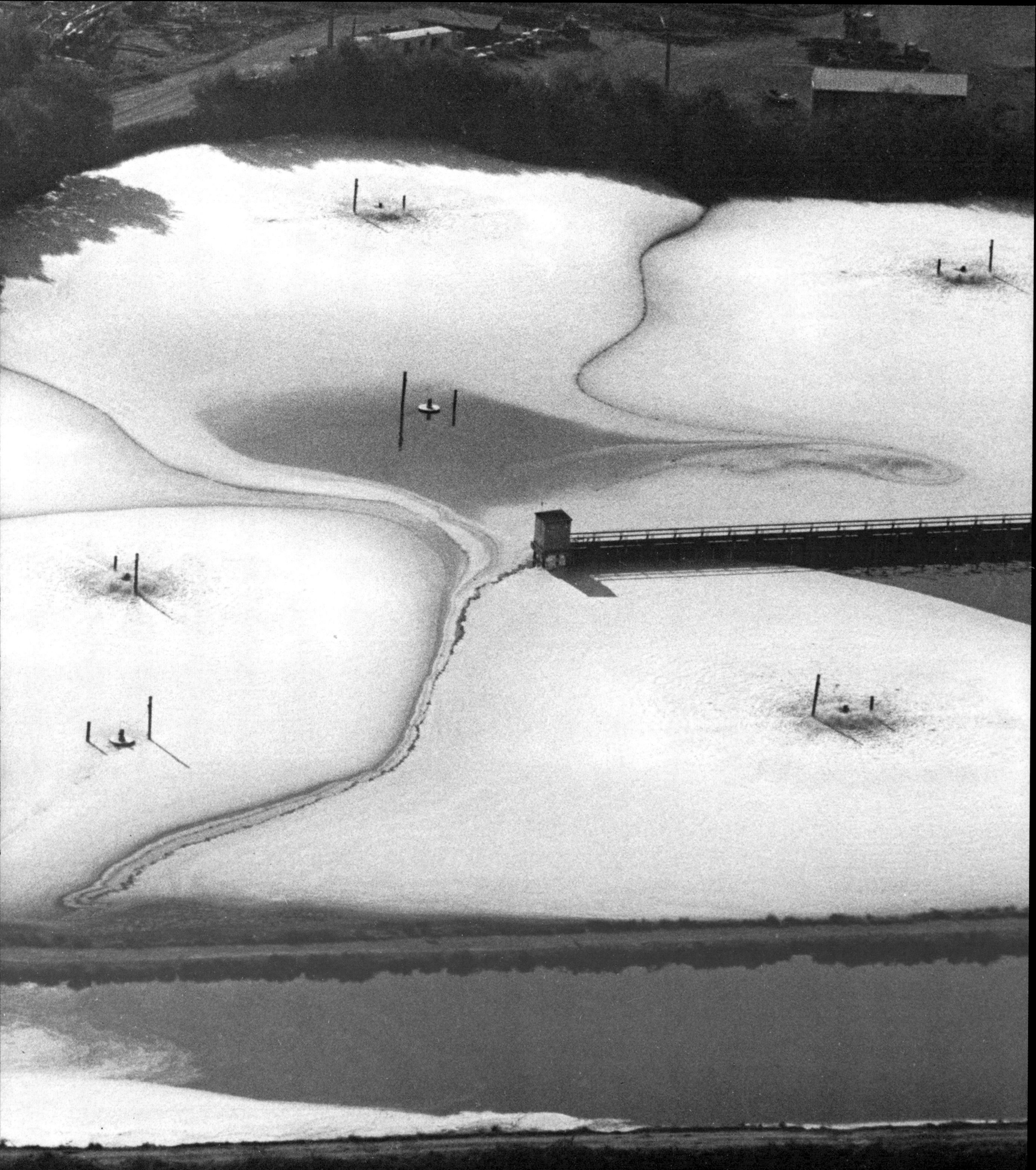

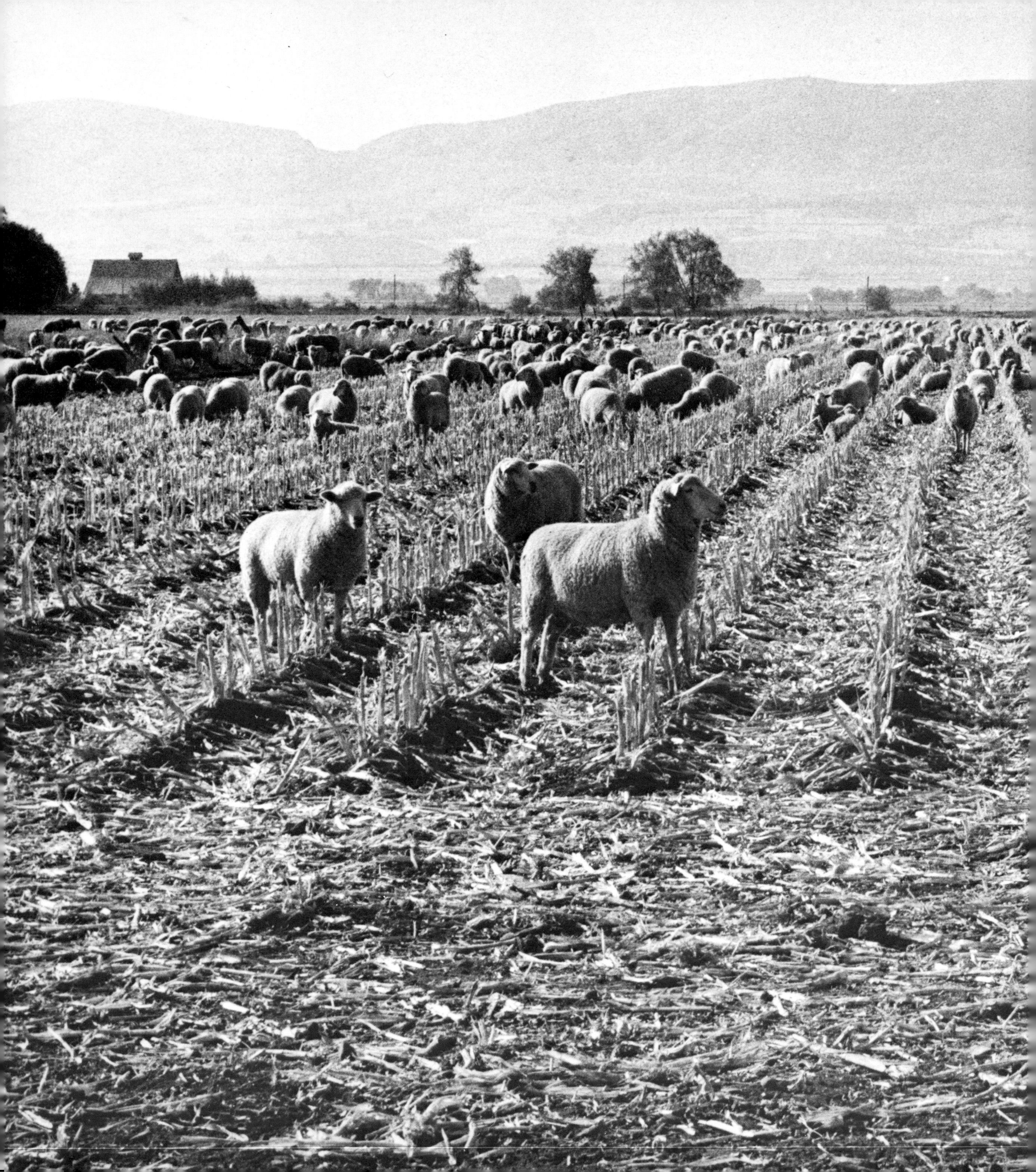

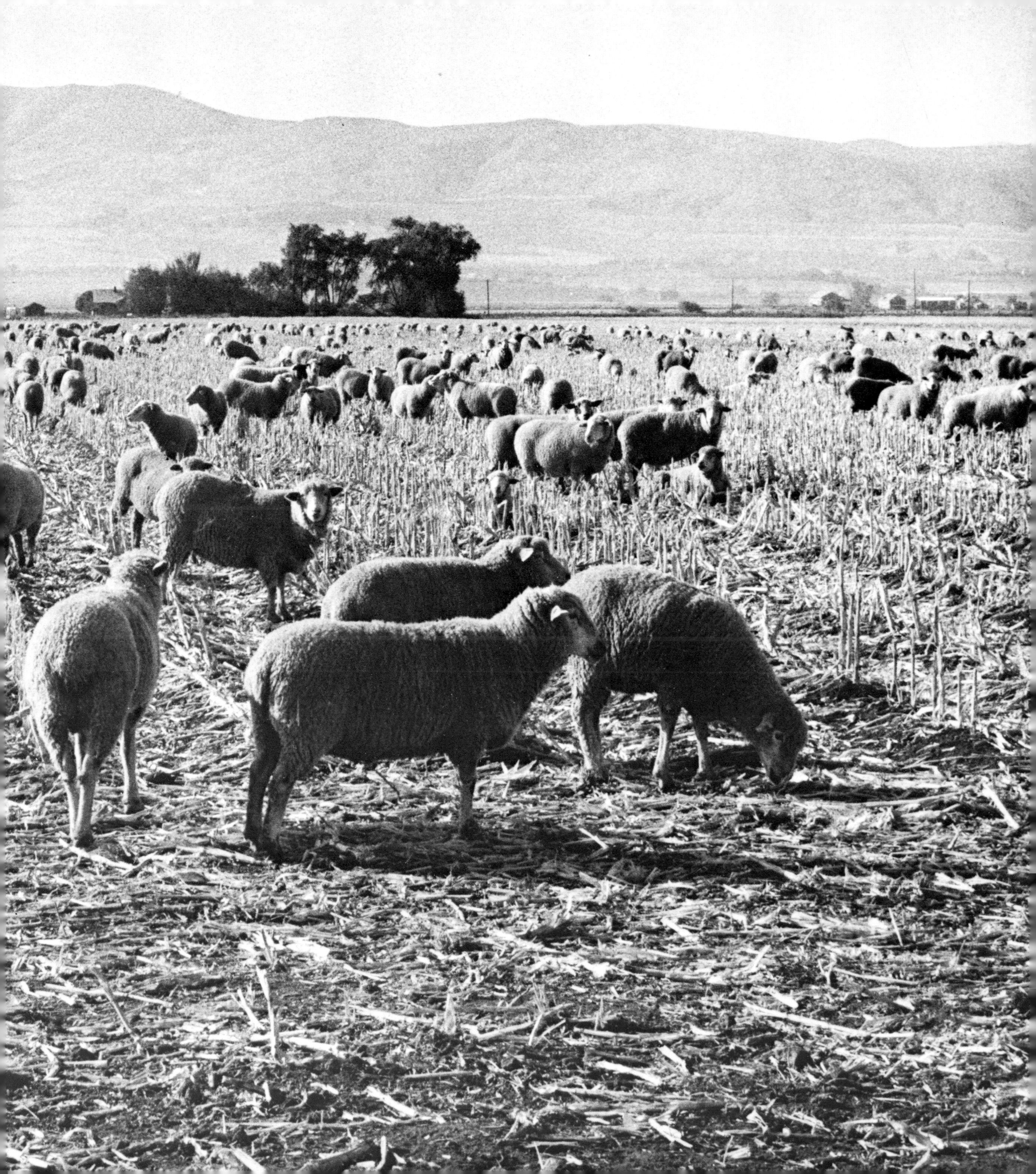

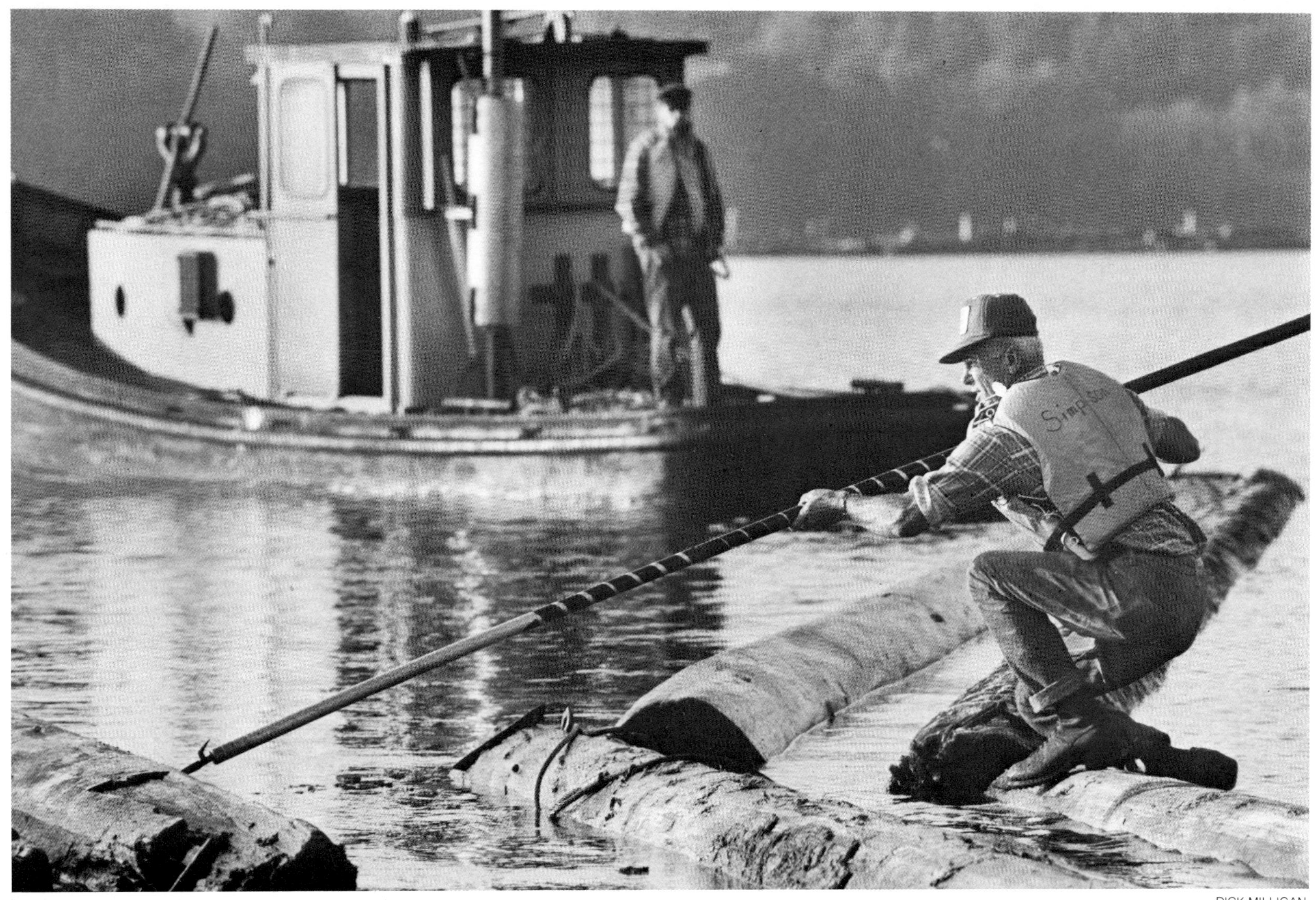

DICK MILLIGAN

Chuck Ellis watches Donald "Tuffy" Bina make up a log raft at the Simpson millpond in Oakland Bay, Shelton.

Preceding pages:

26-27, *Waste-water treatment ponds at Everett.*
JAMES STUART

28-29, *Near Kittitas in the morning.*
DON NORMARK

30-31, *Long Beach in Pacific County.*
KURT WILSON

Right: *Sam Zorich, 70, on his boat* The Gillnetter *in the early morning at Fishermen's Terminal, Seattle.*
NATALIE FOBES

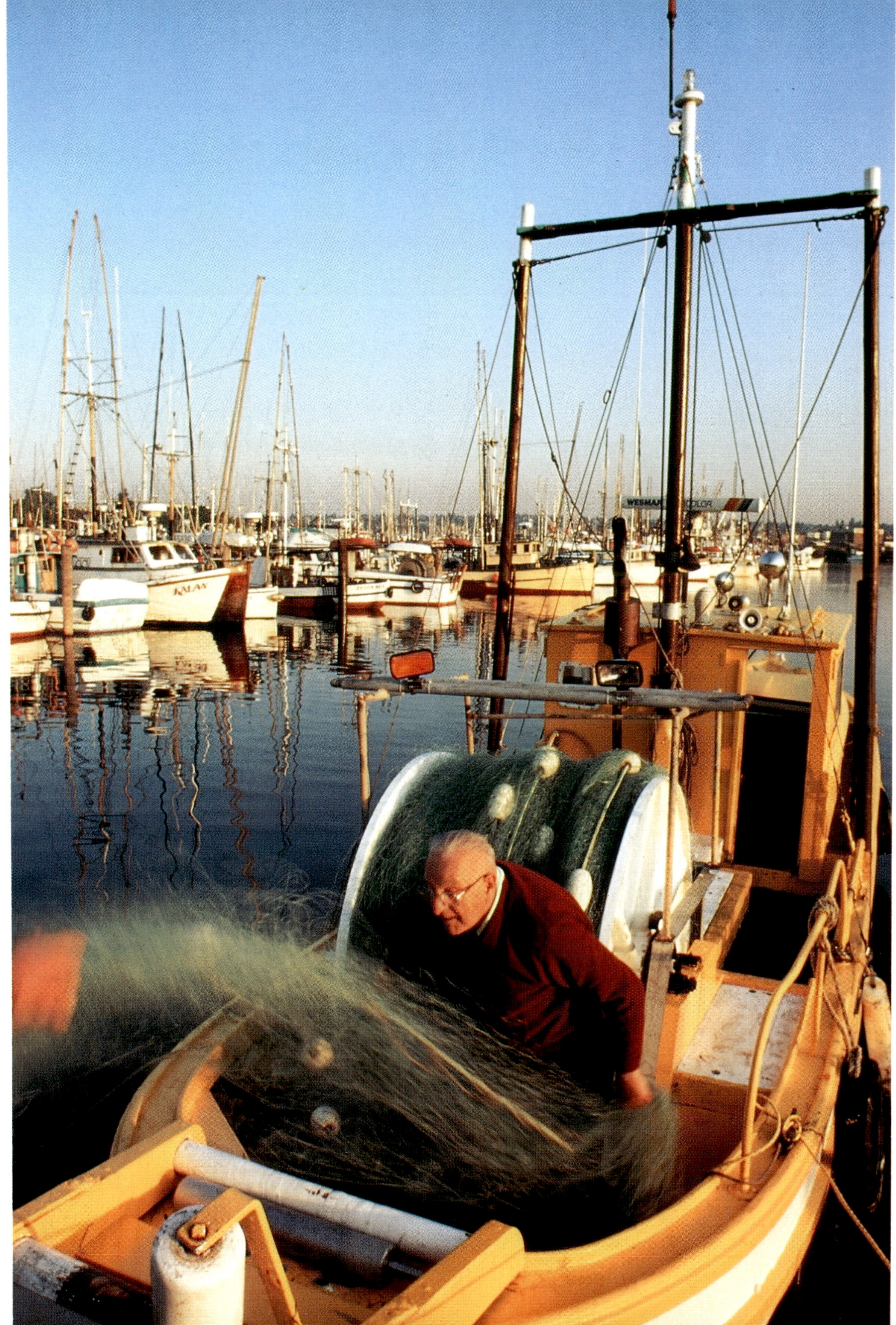
WESMAR
COLOR

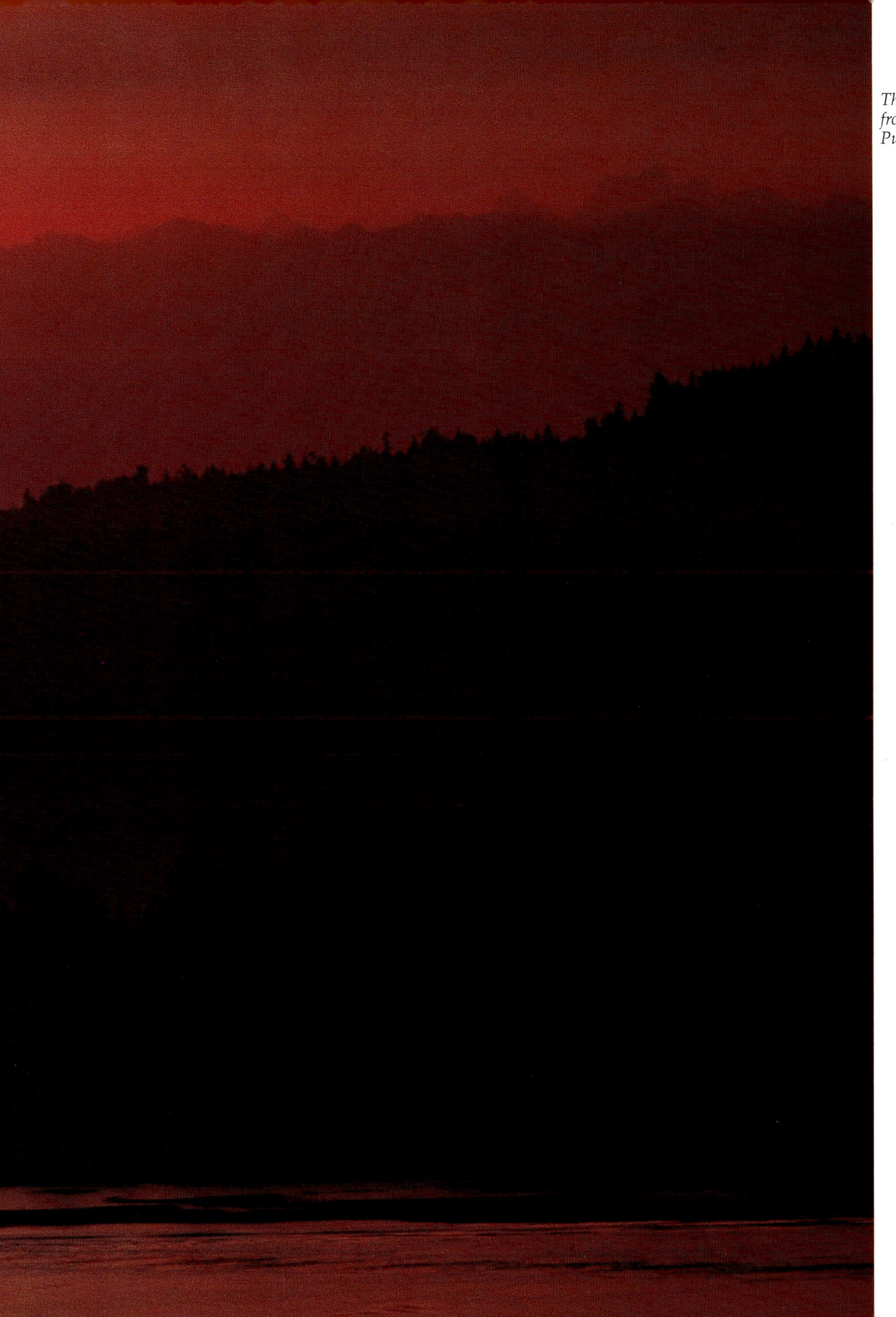

Through Rich Passage from Sinclair Inlet to Puget Sound.
THERESA AUBIN

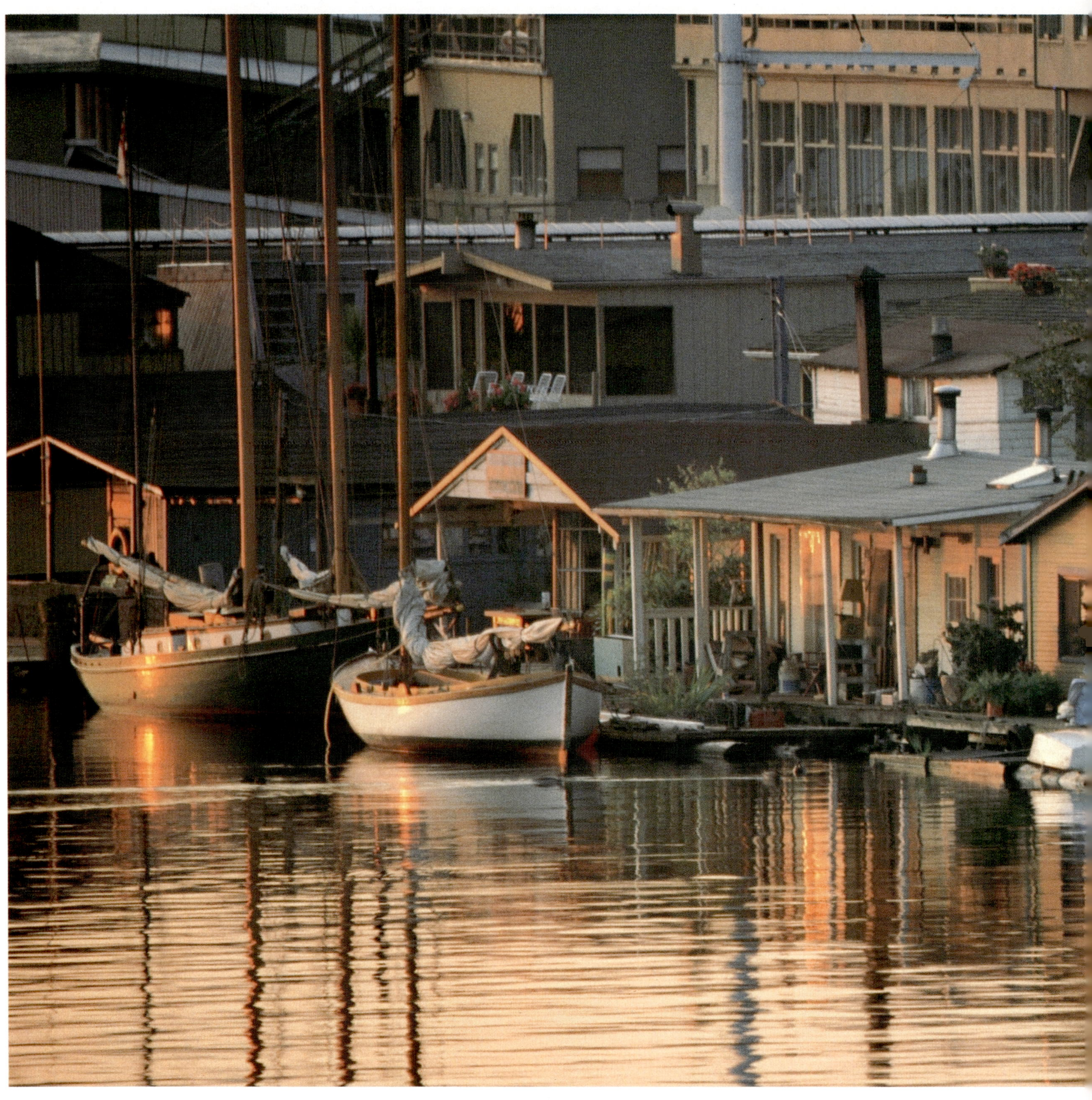

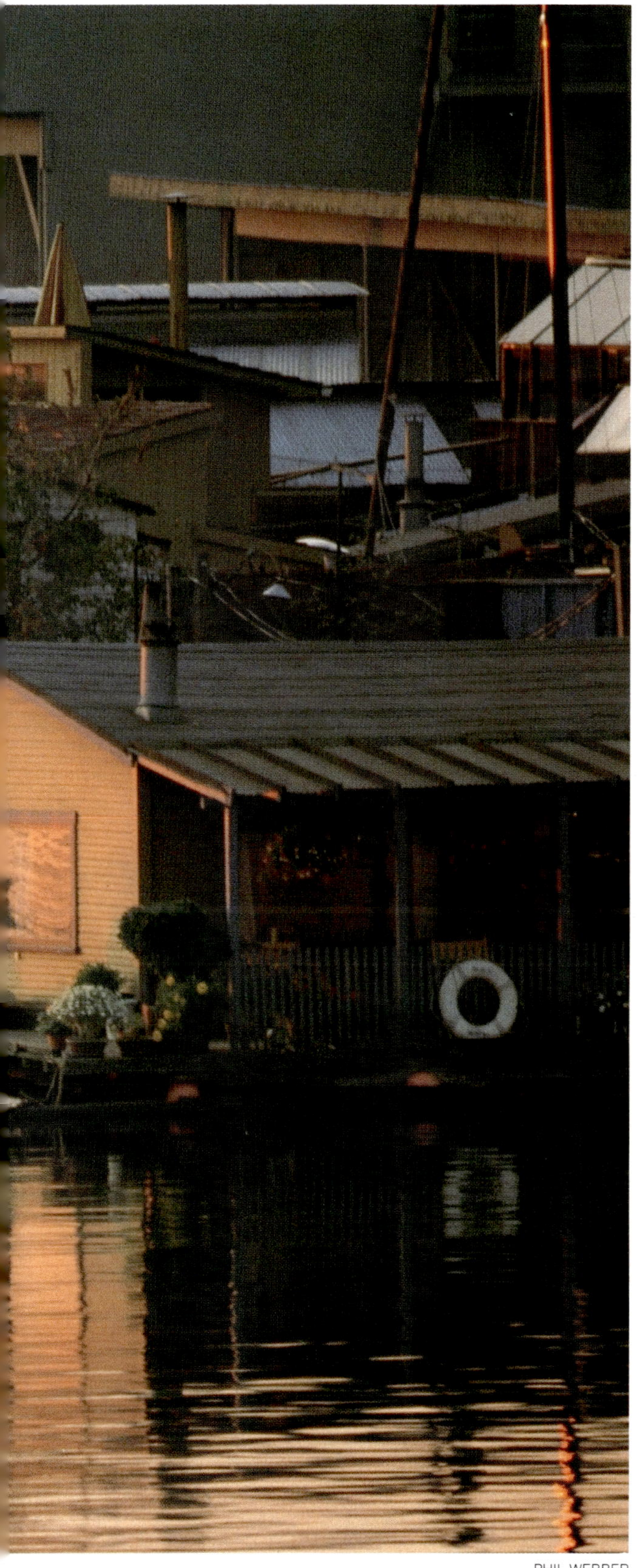

PHIL WEBBER

On Lake Union near the Fremont Bridge, Seattle.

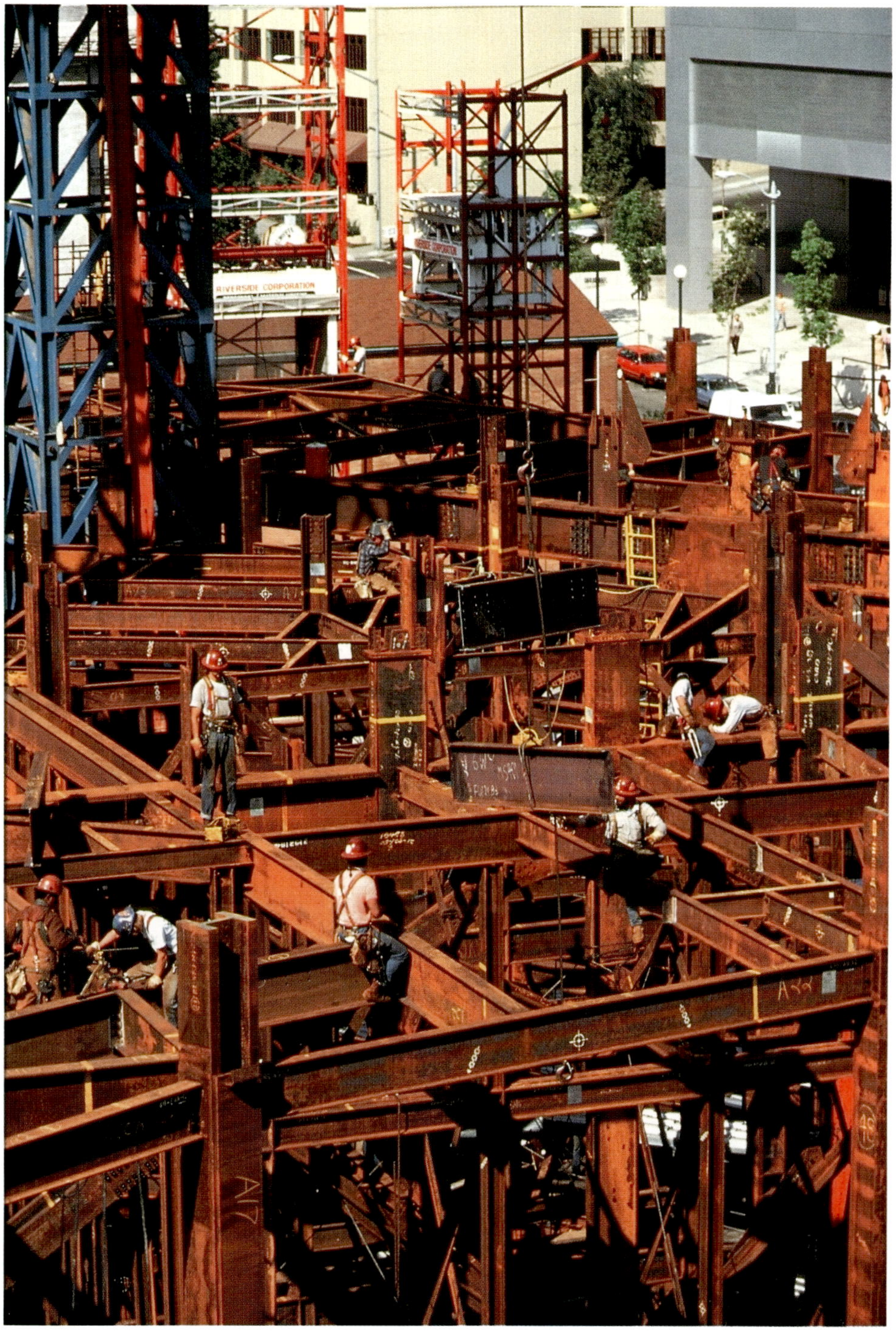

CHARLES GORDON

The Columbia Center goes up in Seattle.

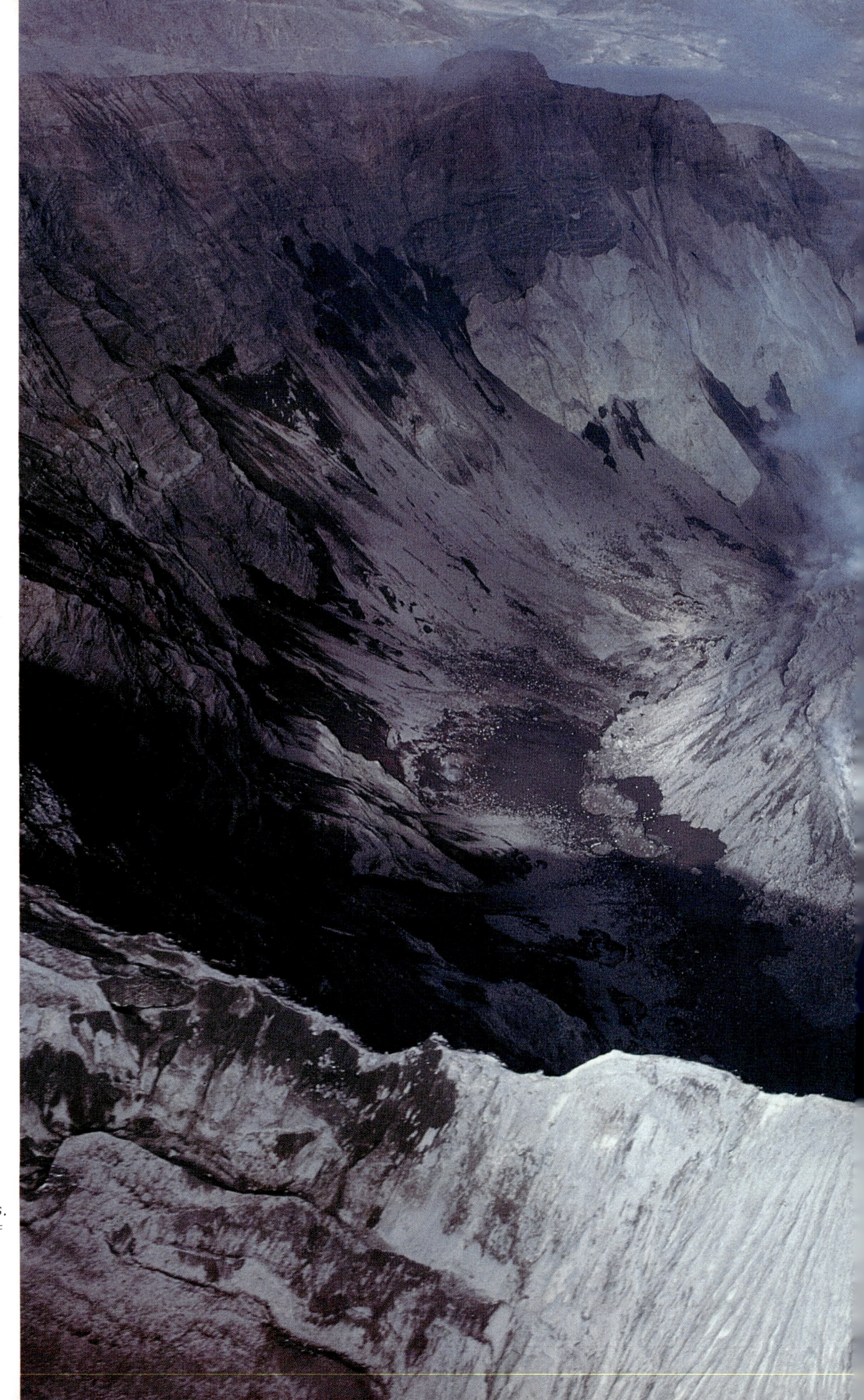

Mount St. Helens.
ED VIDINGHOFF

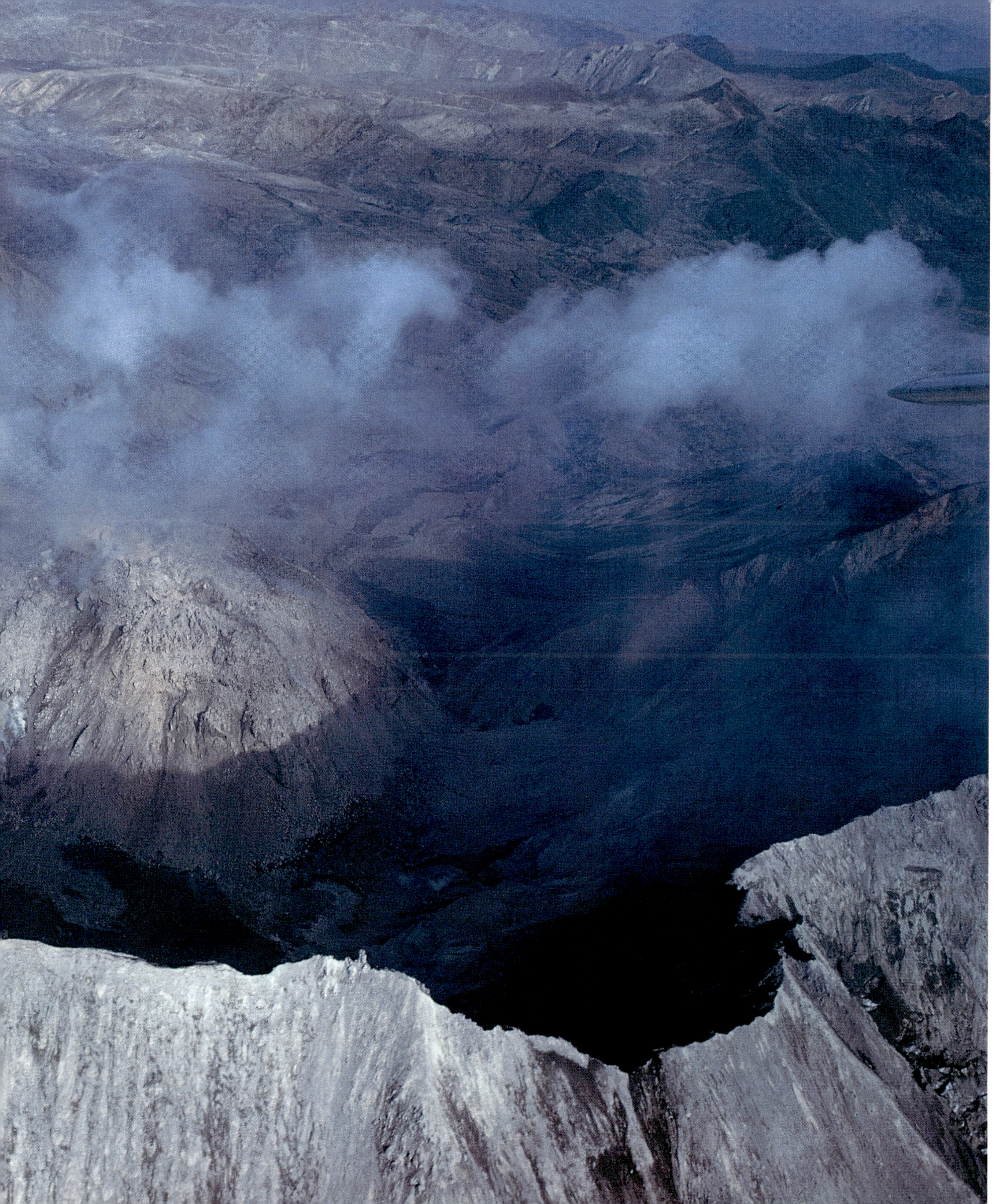

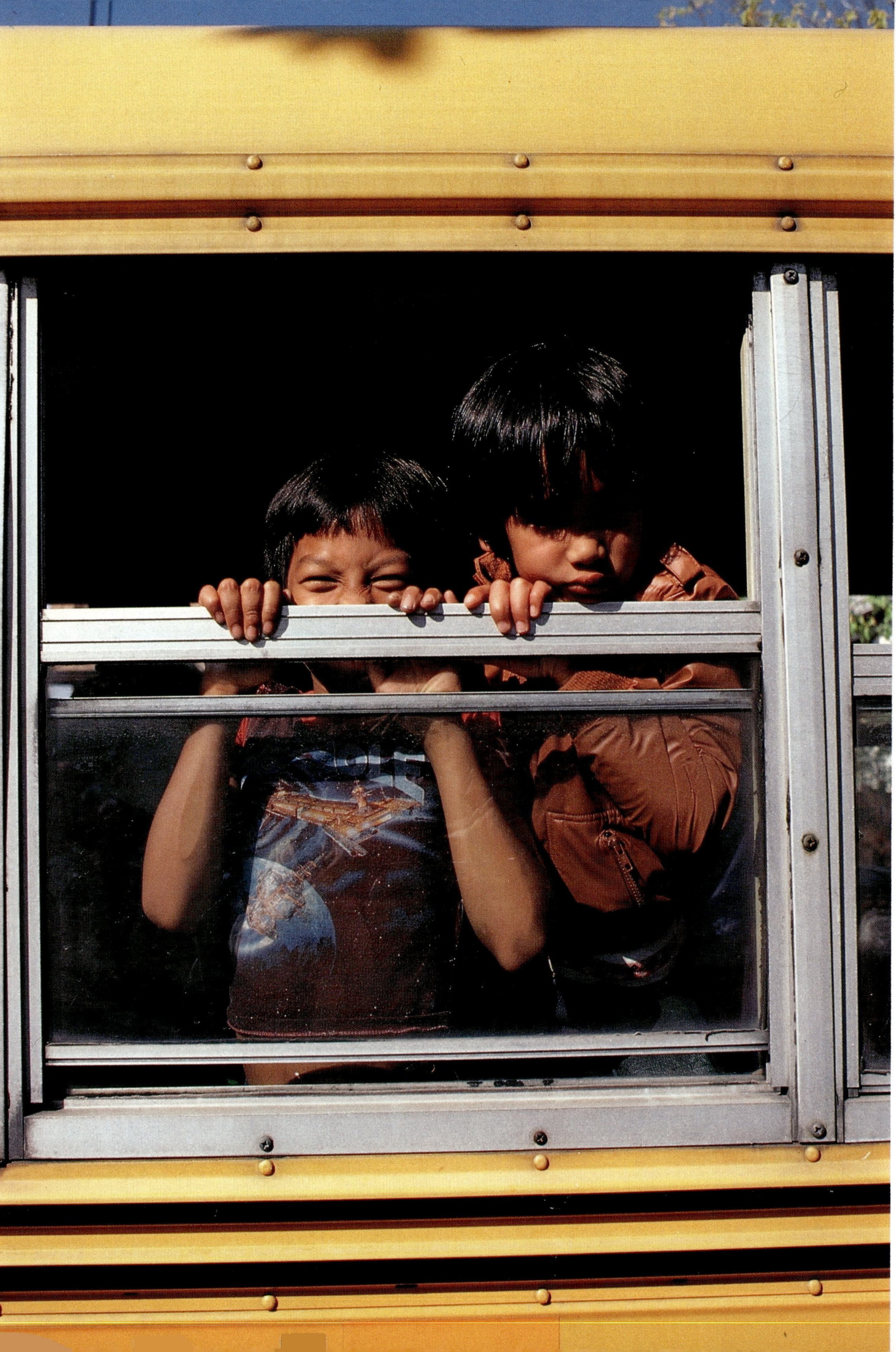

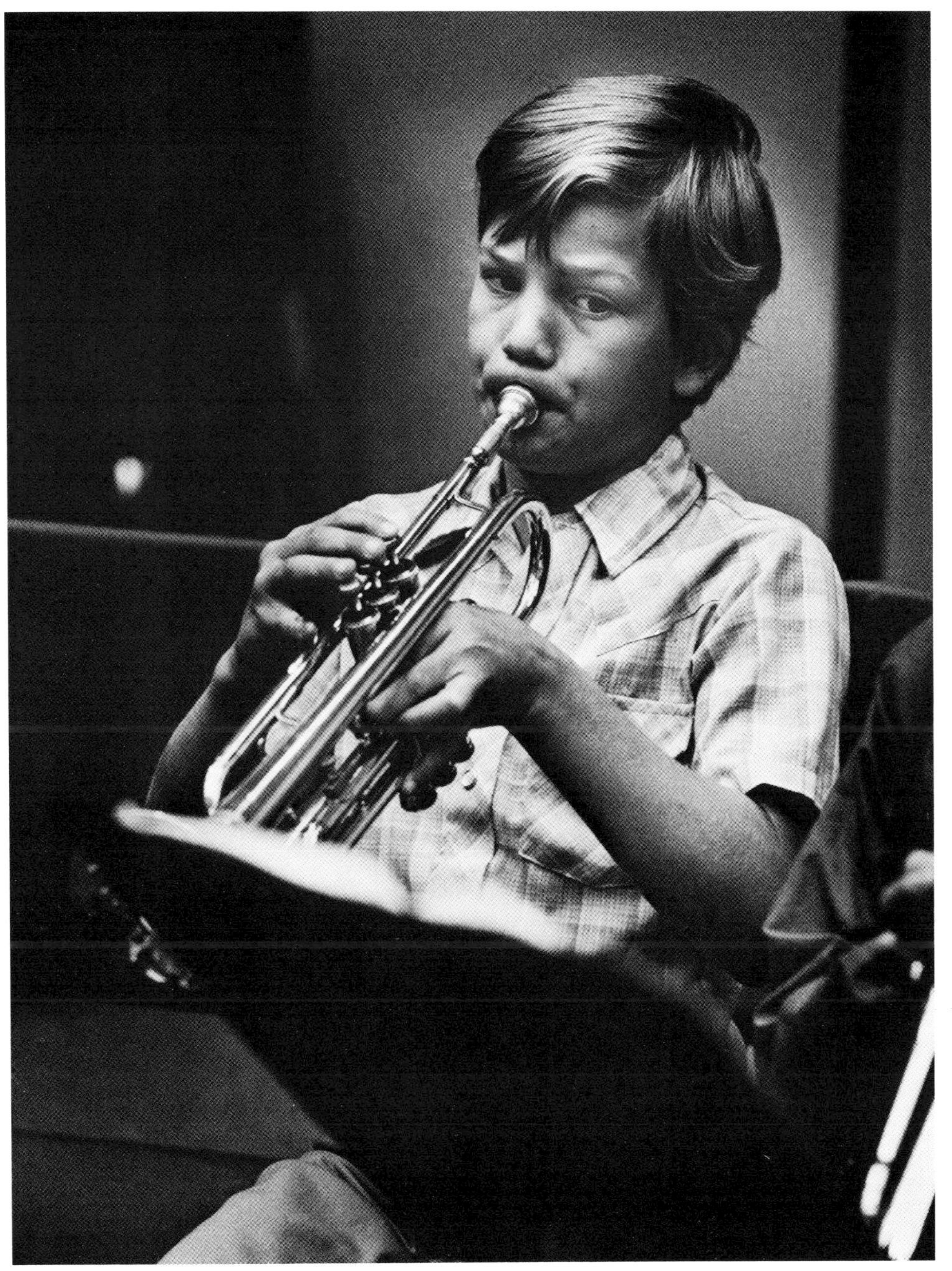

RICH SCHWEINHART
Jeff Pferffer at band practice in Bothell's Maywood Hills Elementary School.

Left: *Students from the Bilingual Center at Greenwood School, Seattle.*
BOKMON DONG

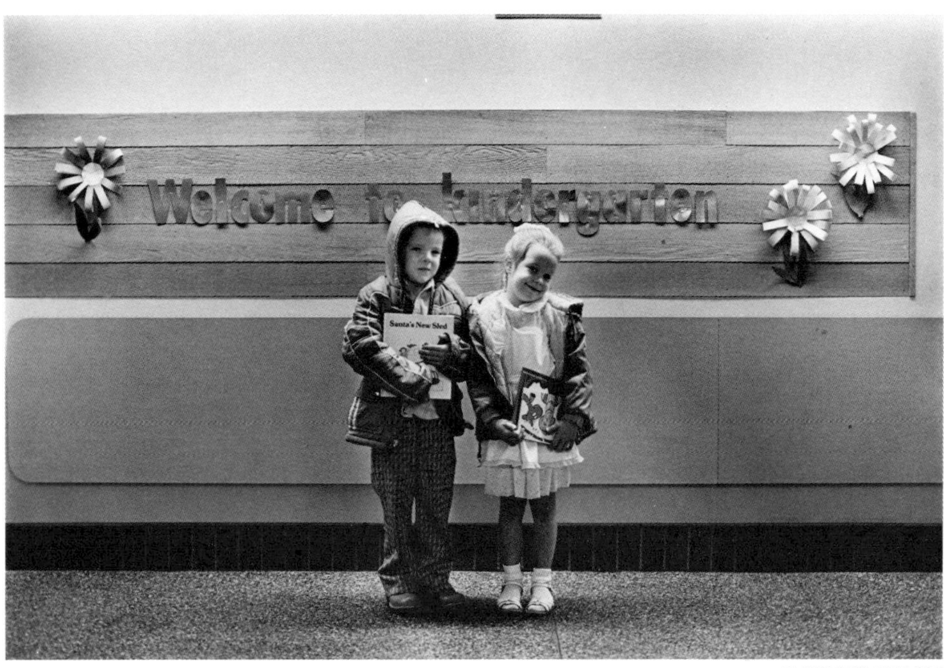

PHOTOS BY JIMI LOTT

Late arrivals at Sheridan Elementary School in Spokane.

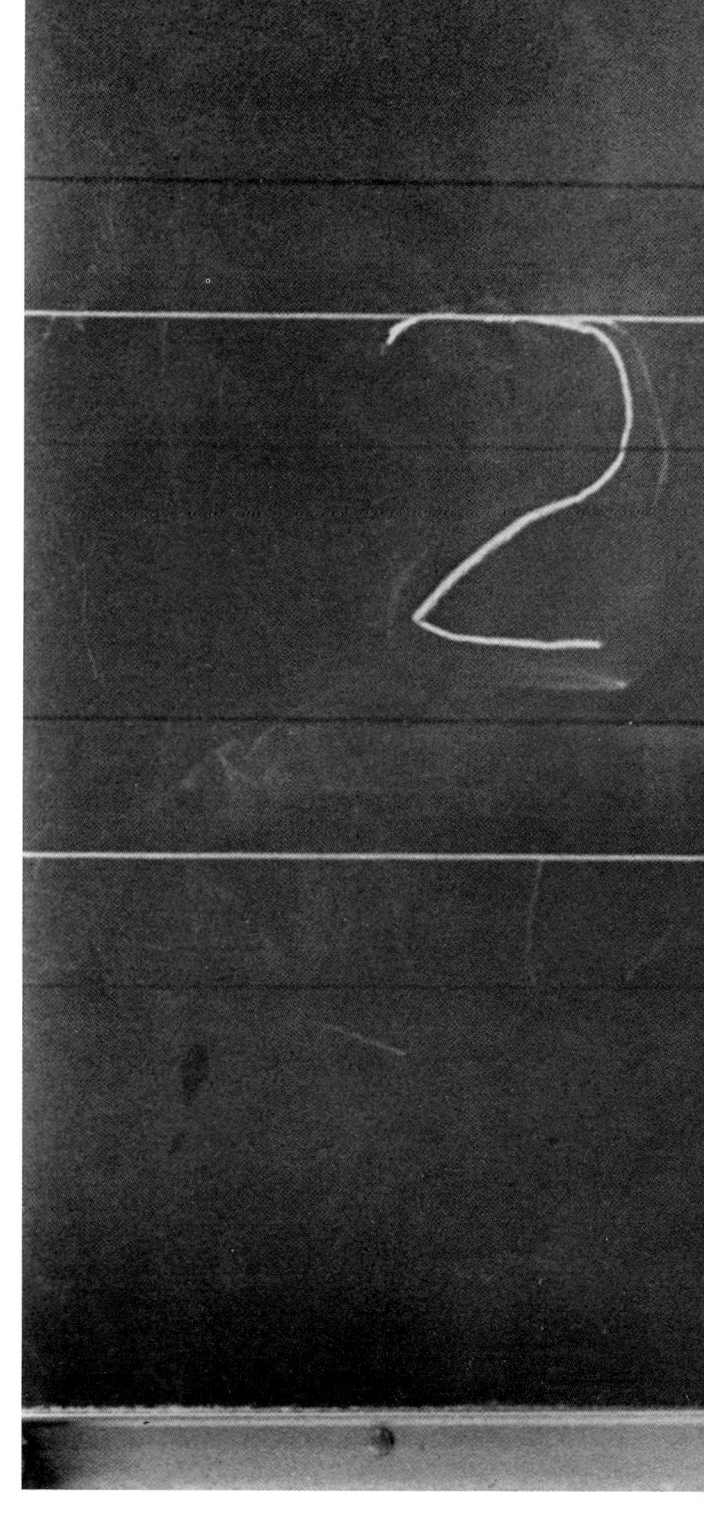

Teressa Klump, first-grade date monitor at Sheridan.

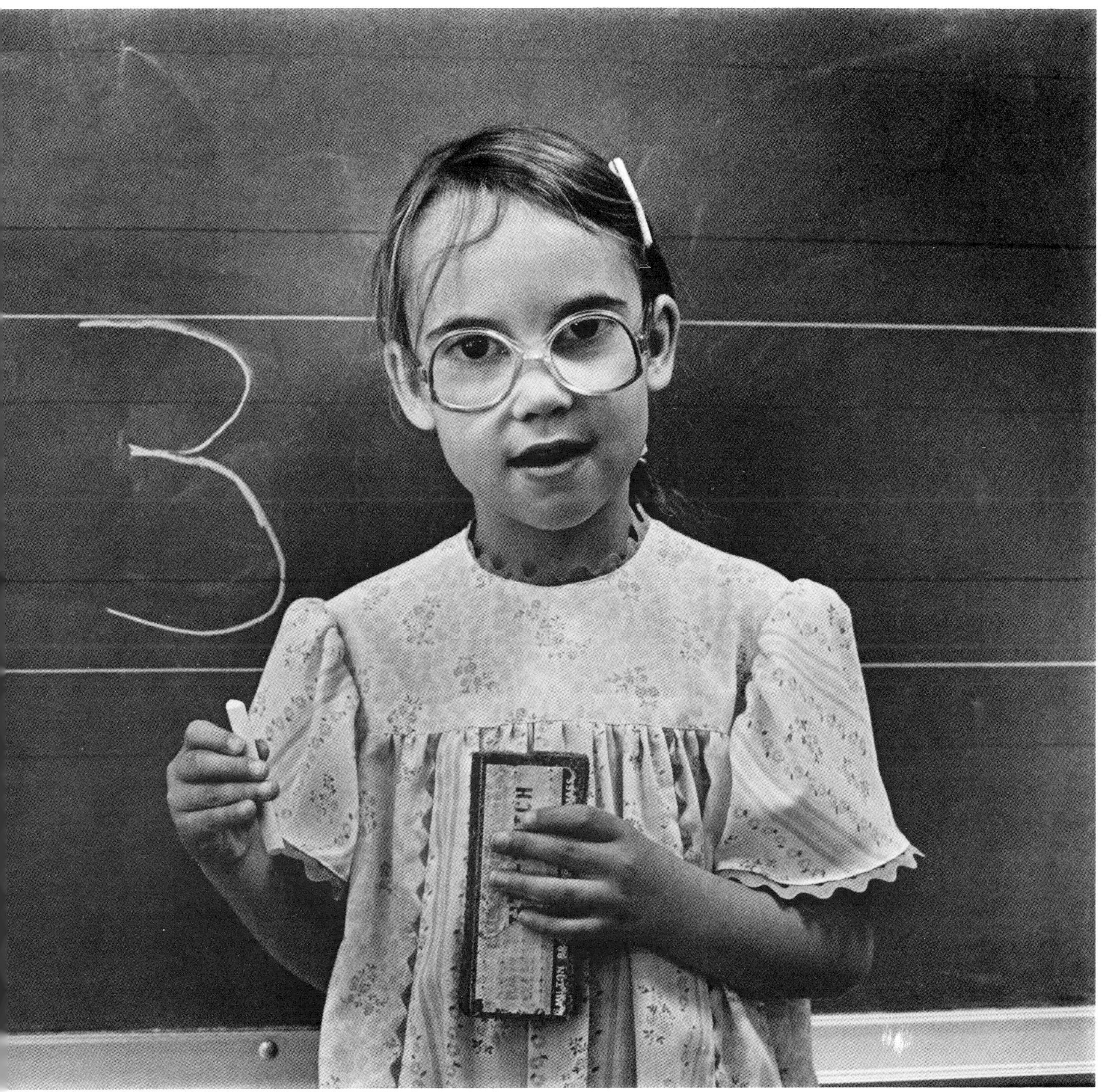

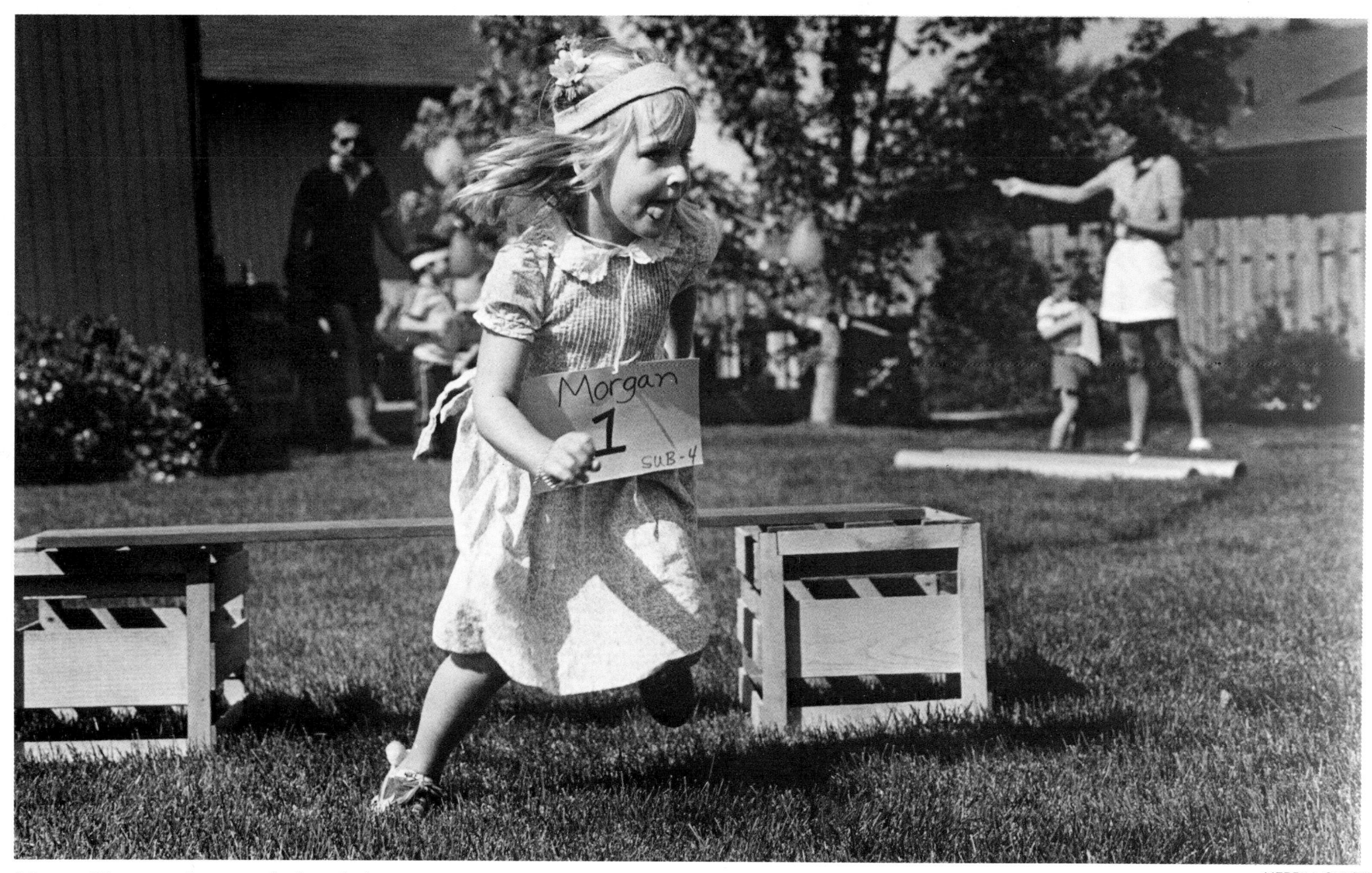

Morgan Wynne at the party for her sixth birthday in the backyard of her Tri-Cities home.

MERRILL OLIVER

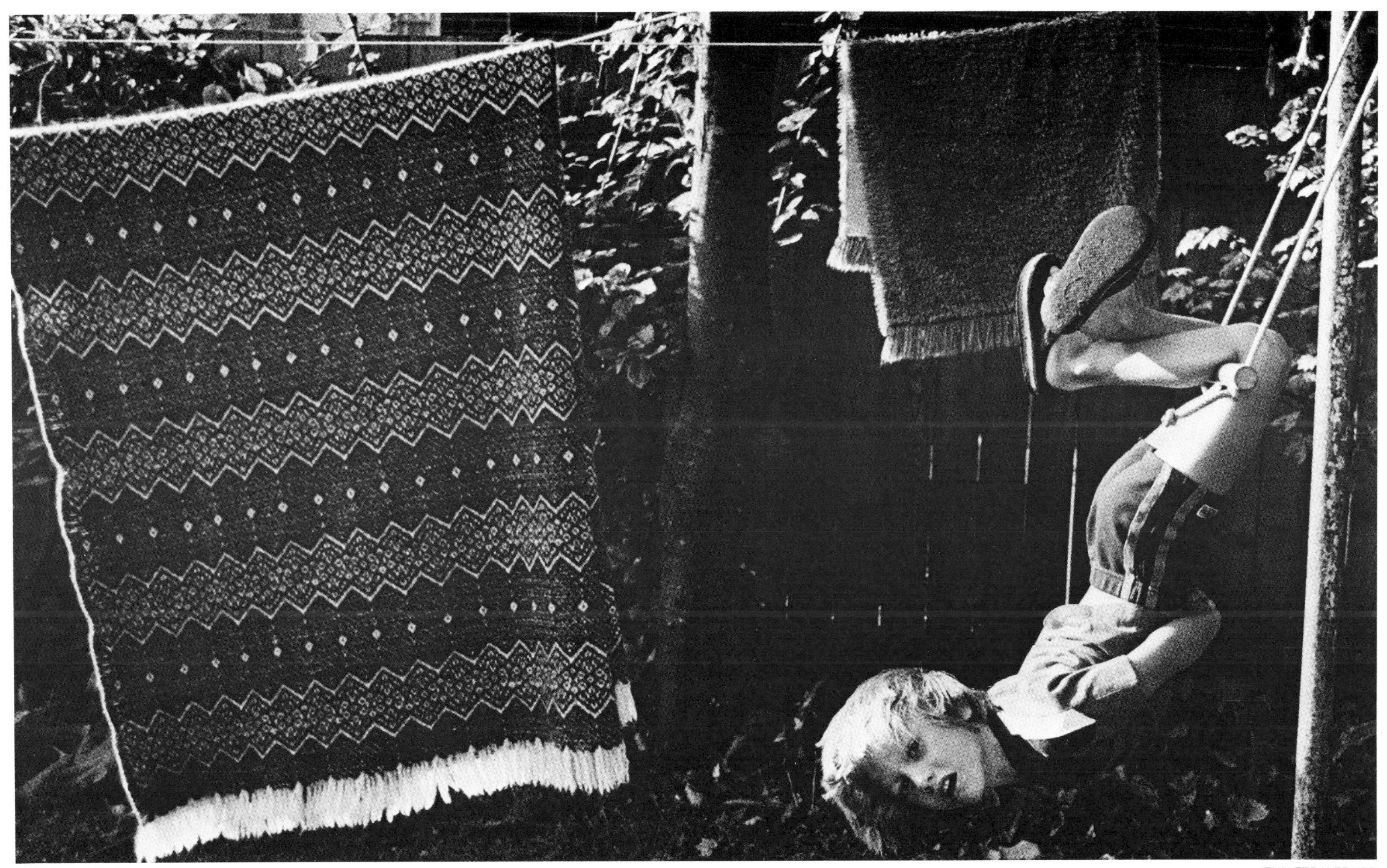

Justice Israel of the Love Israel family.

JENNIFER WERNER

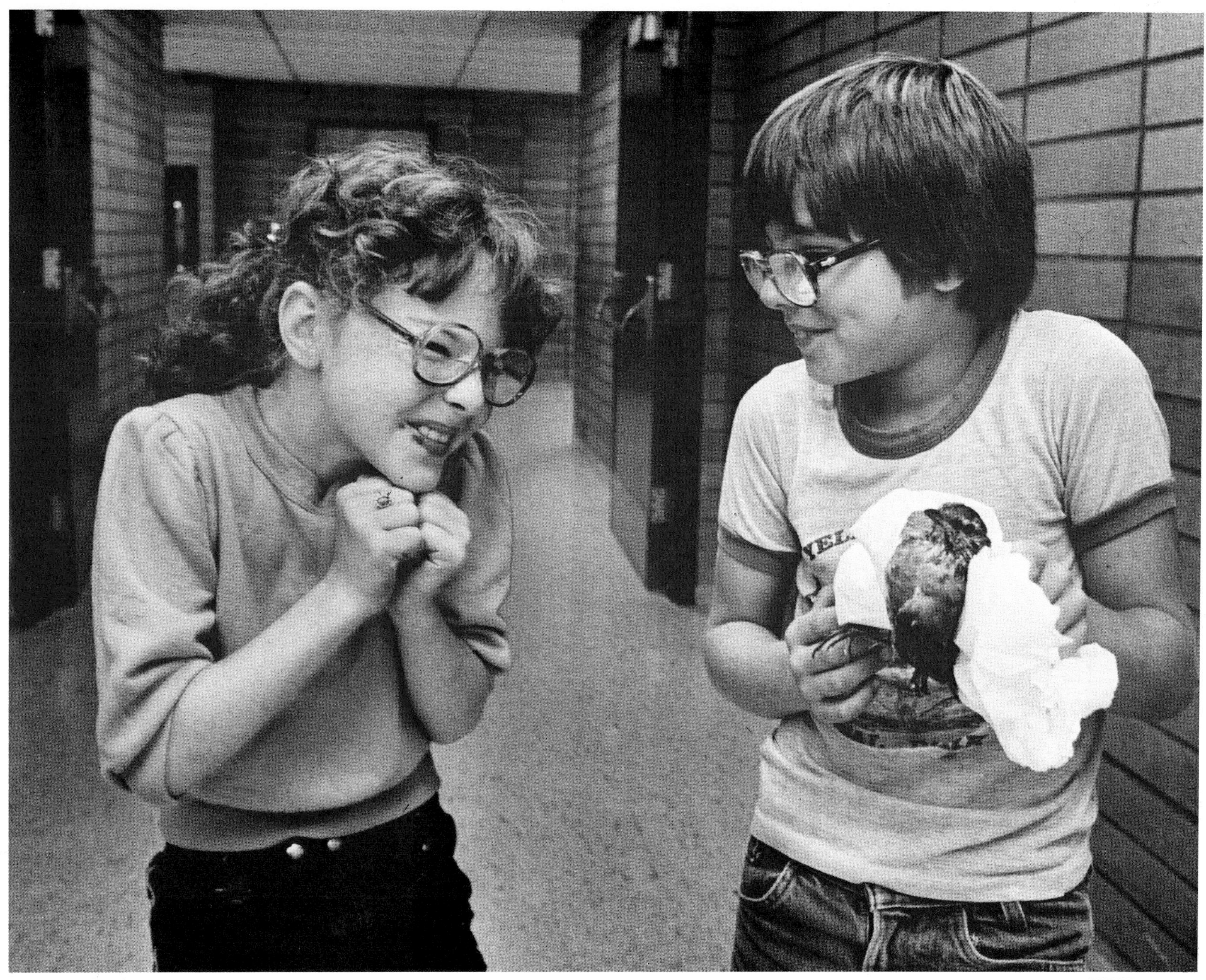

ROBERT HARBISON

Del Smith shows Heidi Beach a robin with a broken wing in a hallway at Wildwood Elementary School, Federal Way.

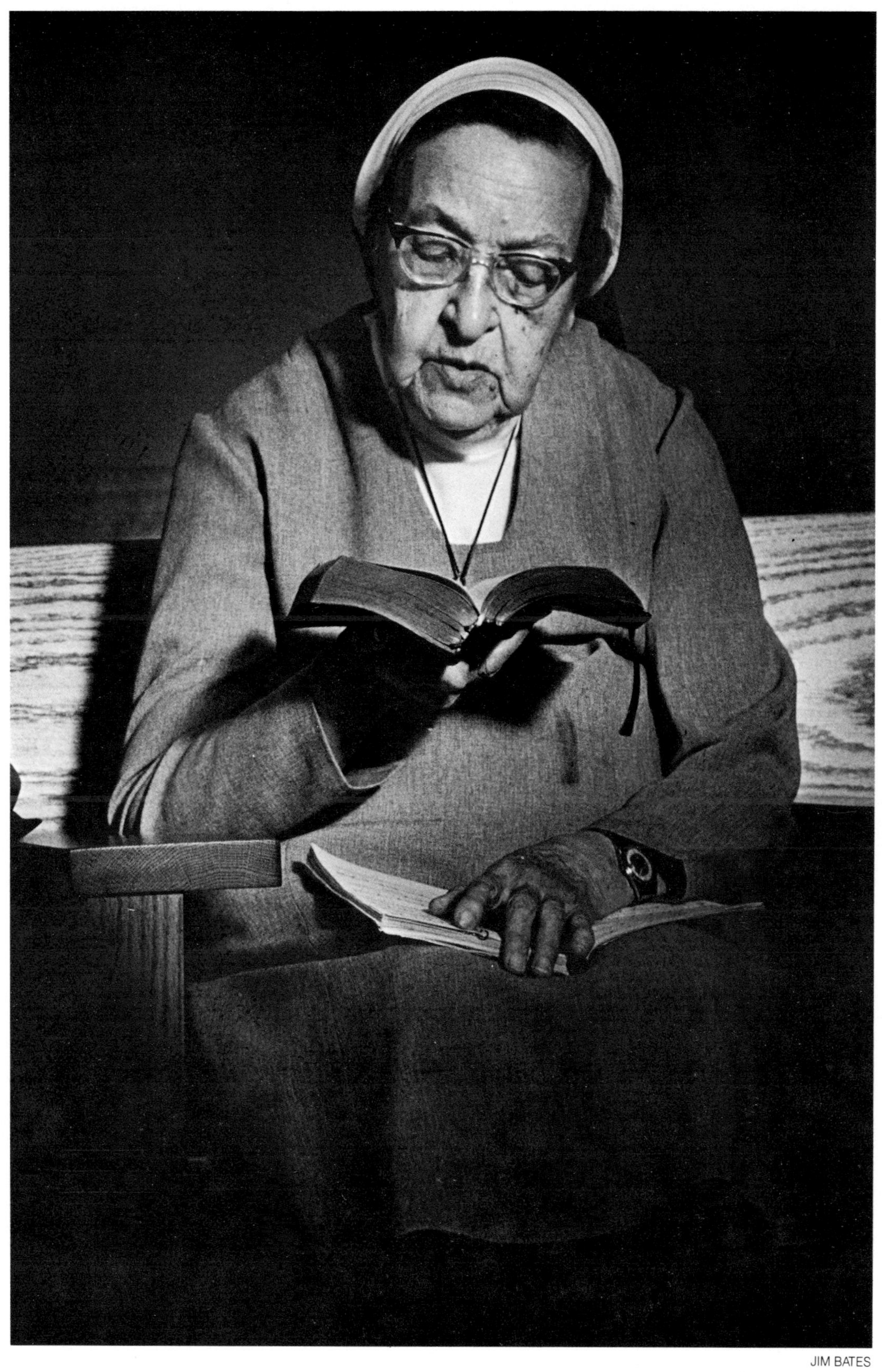

JIM BATES

Sister Regina Delaney of the Sisters of Visitation.

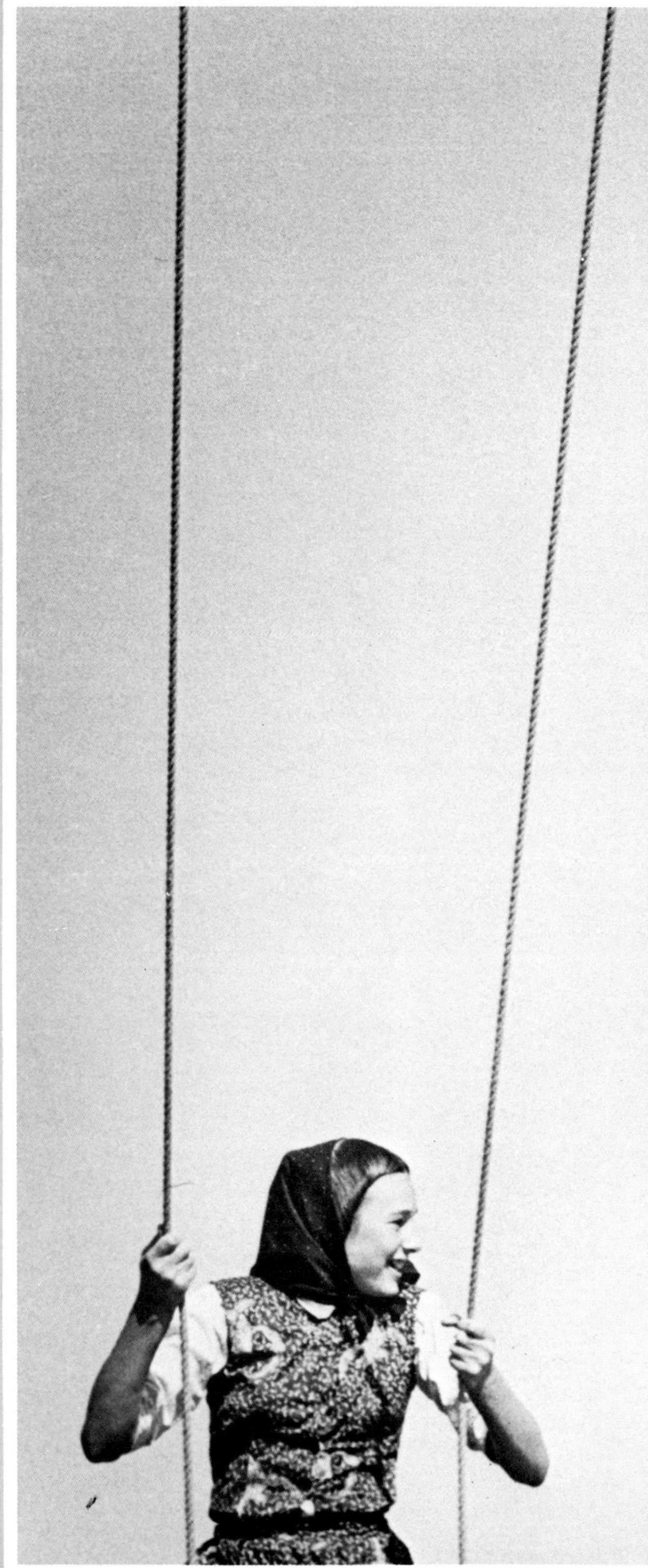

In a world of high-tech and permissiveness, members of a Hutterite colony at Espanola, east of Reardon, lead a life that is a throwback to much simpler times.

Hutterites —they're all named Gross in this colony —do not have television or modern appliances. Children eat separately from adults ("children should be seen, not heard") and they do their own dishes to learn responsibility.

The children are taught by a teacher hired from "outside." Classes are in a one-room schoolhouse that includes grades 1 through 7.

But Hutterites don't entirely ignore America in the 1980s. The elder of the Gross colony confessed to Dayshoot photographer James Johnson that he went to a neighbor's home to watch a Seattle Seahawks' professional football game.

"It was OK," Johnson says, "because the TV wasn't in his house."

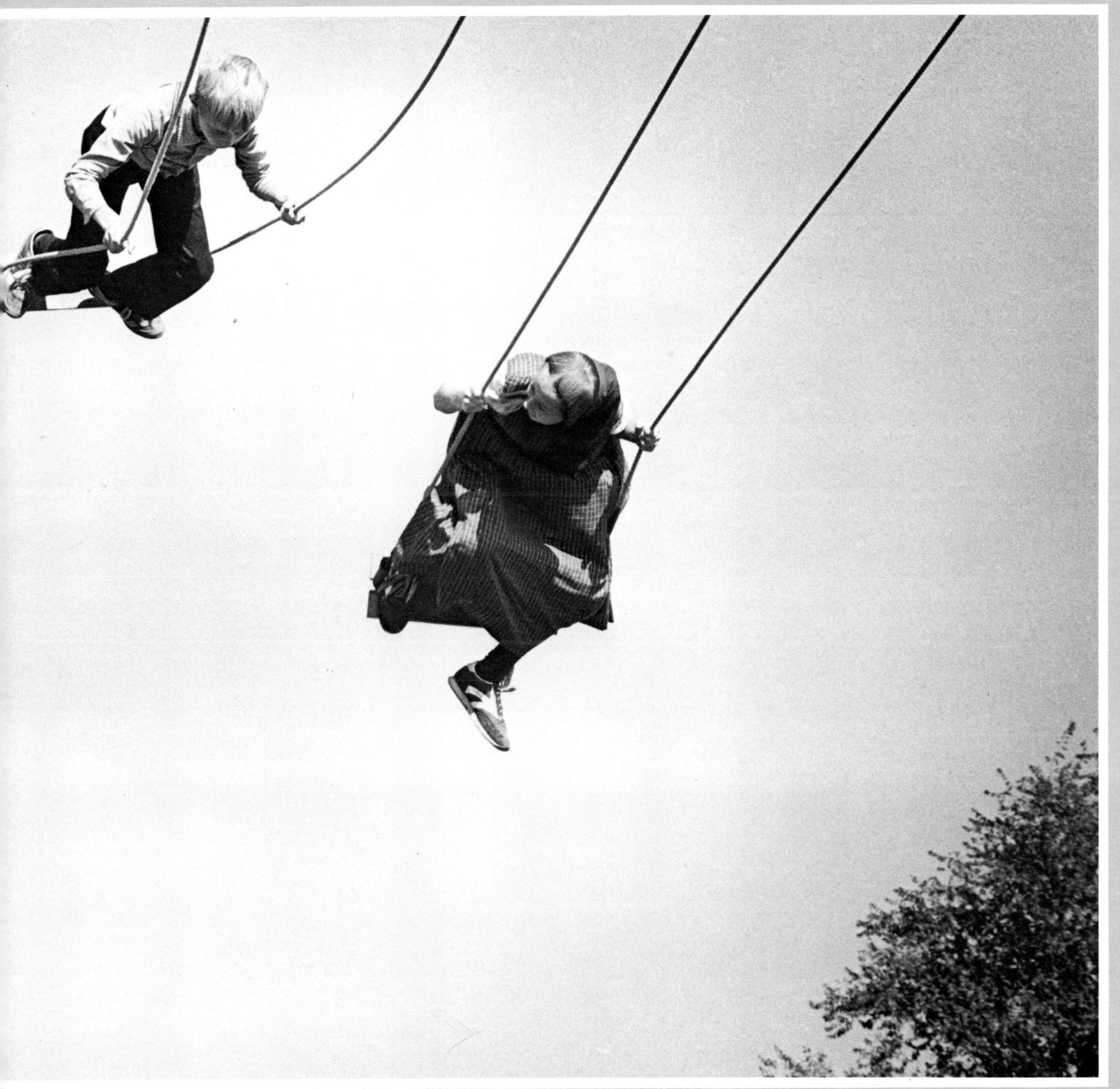

JAMES JOHNSON

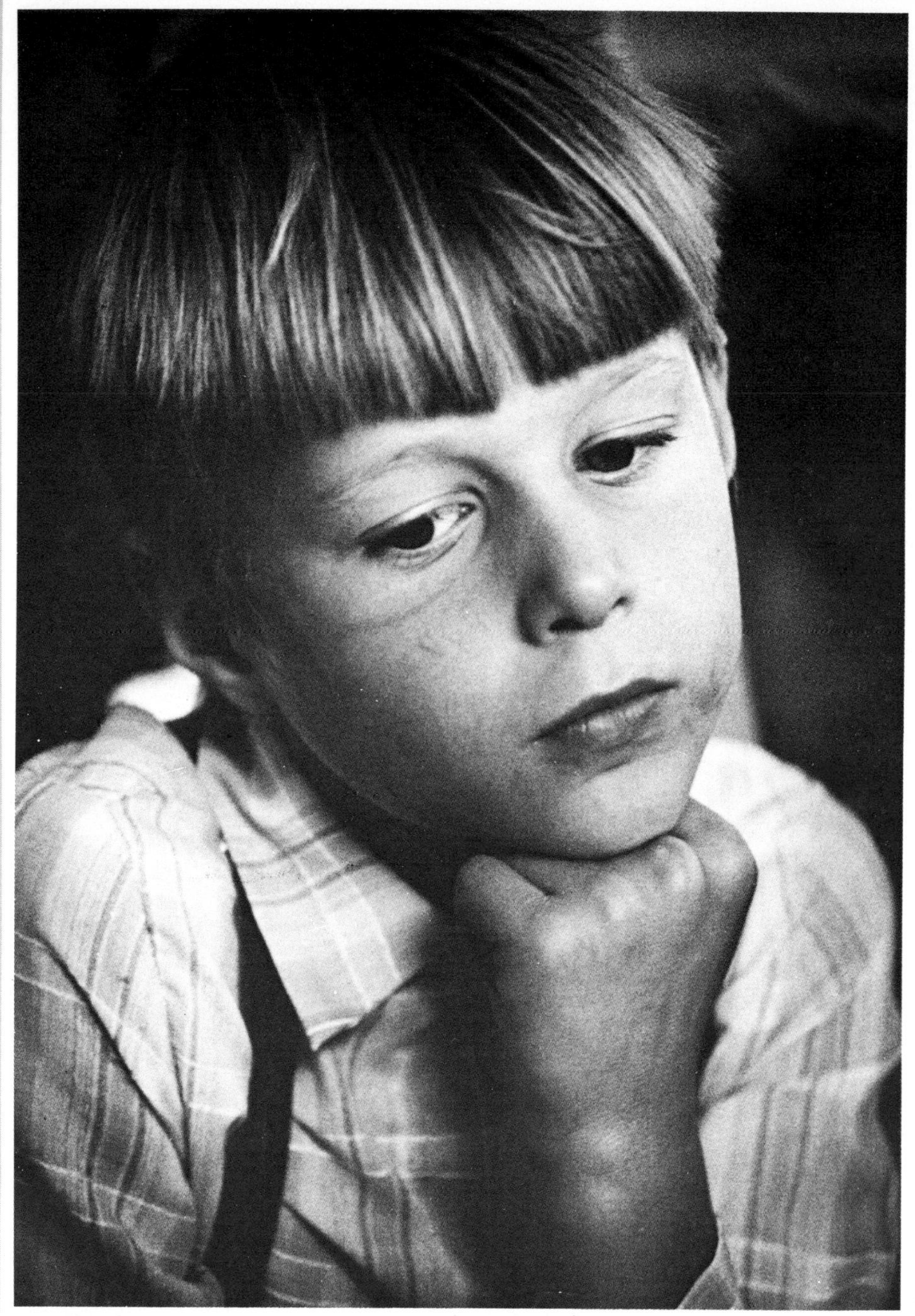

PHOTOS BY JAMES JOHNSON

David Gross.

Rachel and Sarah Ann Gross.

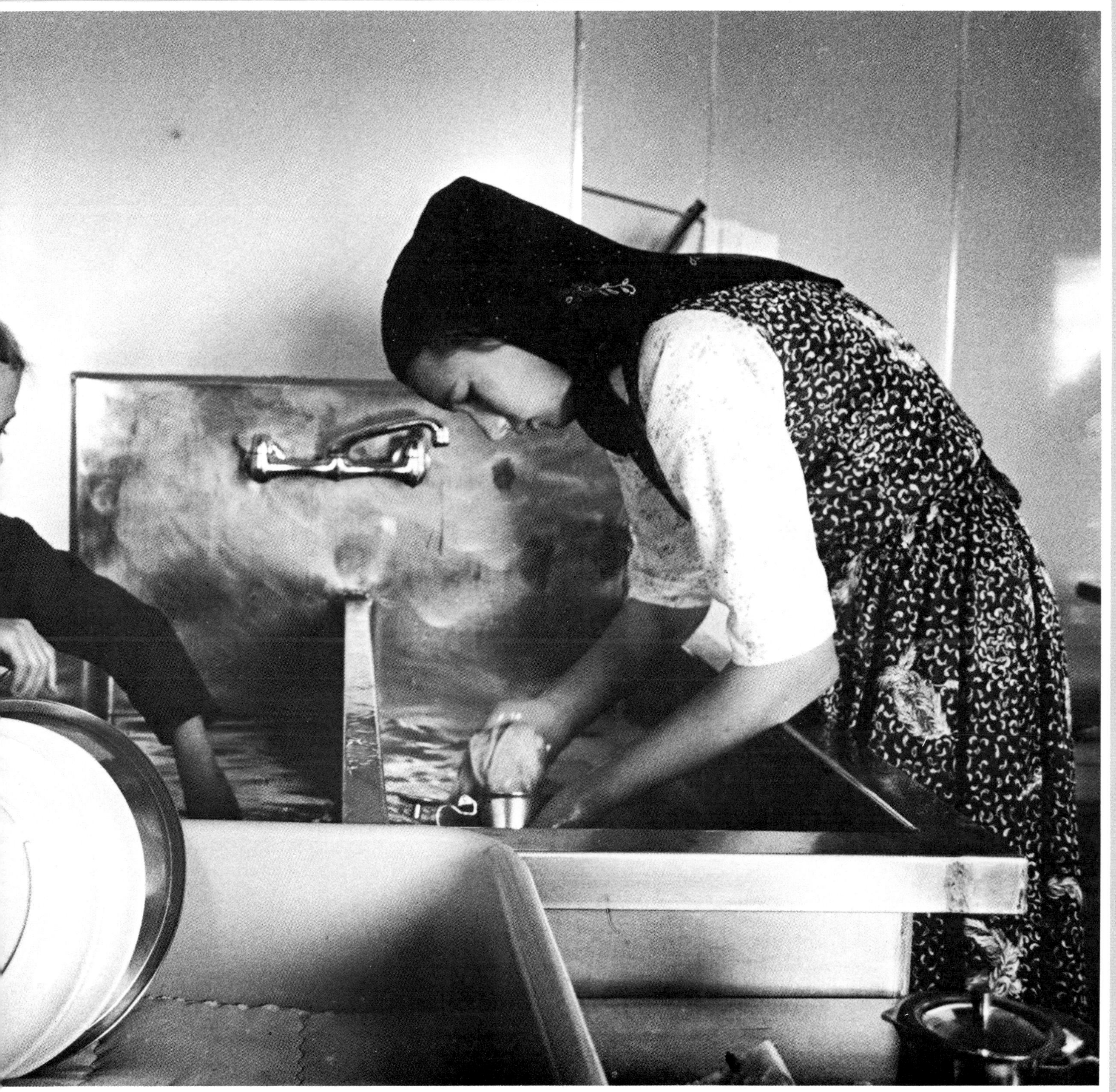

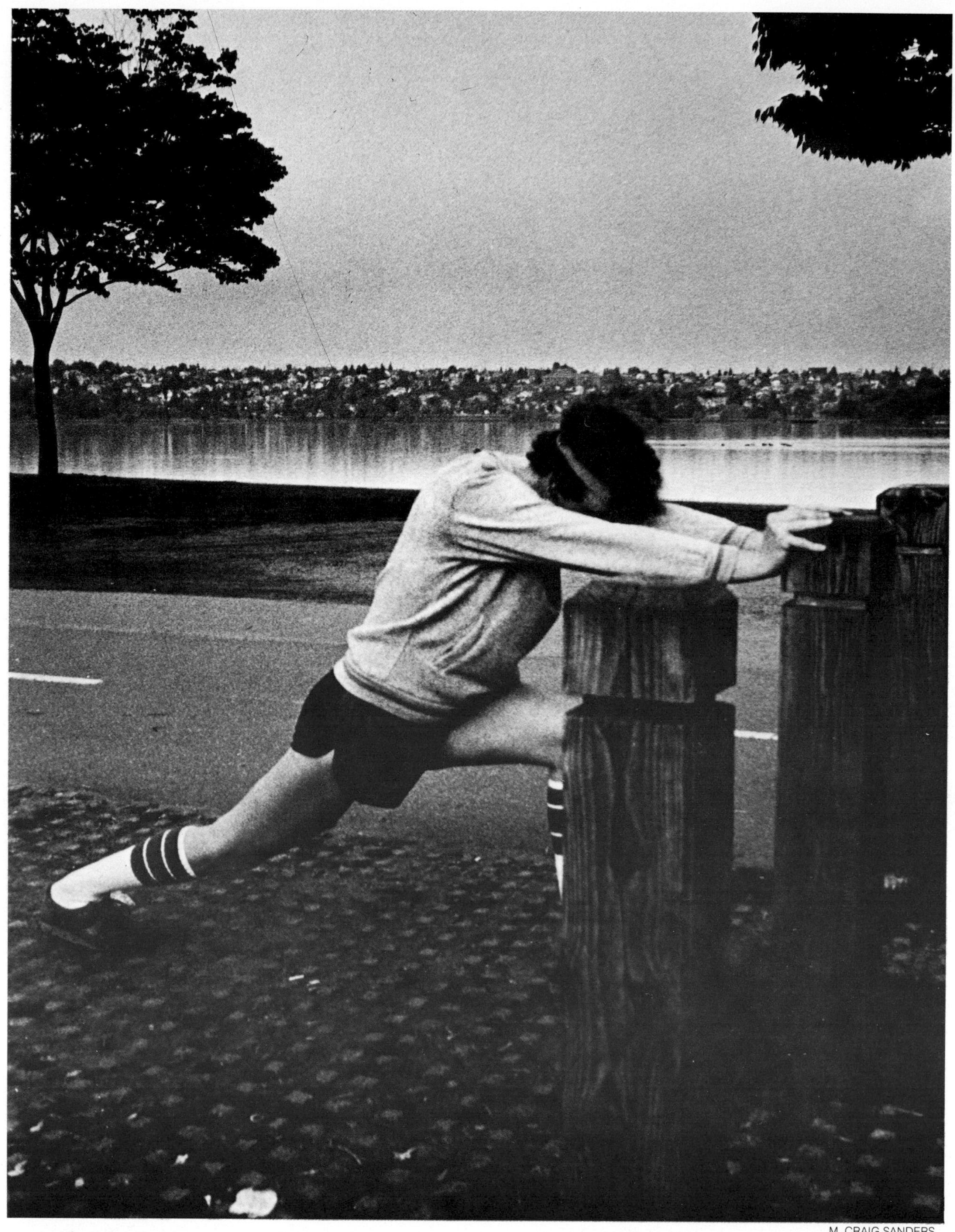

M. CRAIG SANDERS

A jogger stretches his muscles during a morning run at Seattle's Green Lake.

Boeing workers exercise at Renton Stadium during their lunch break.

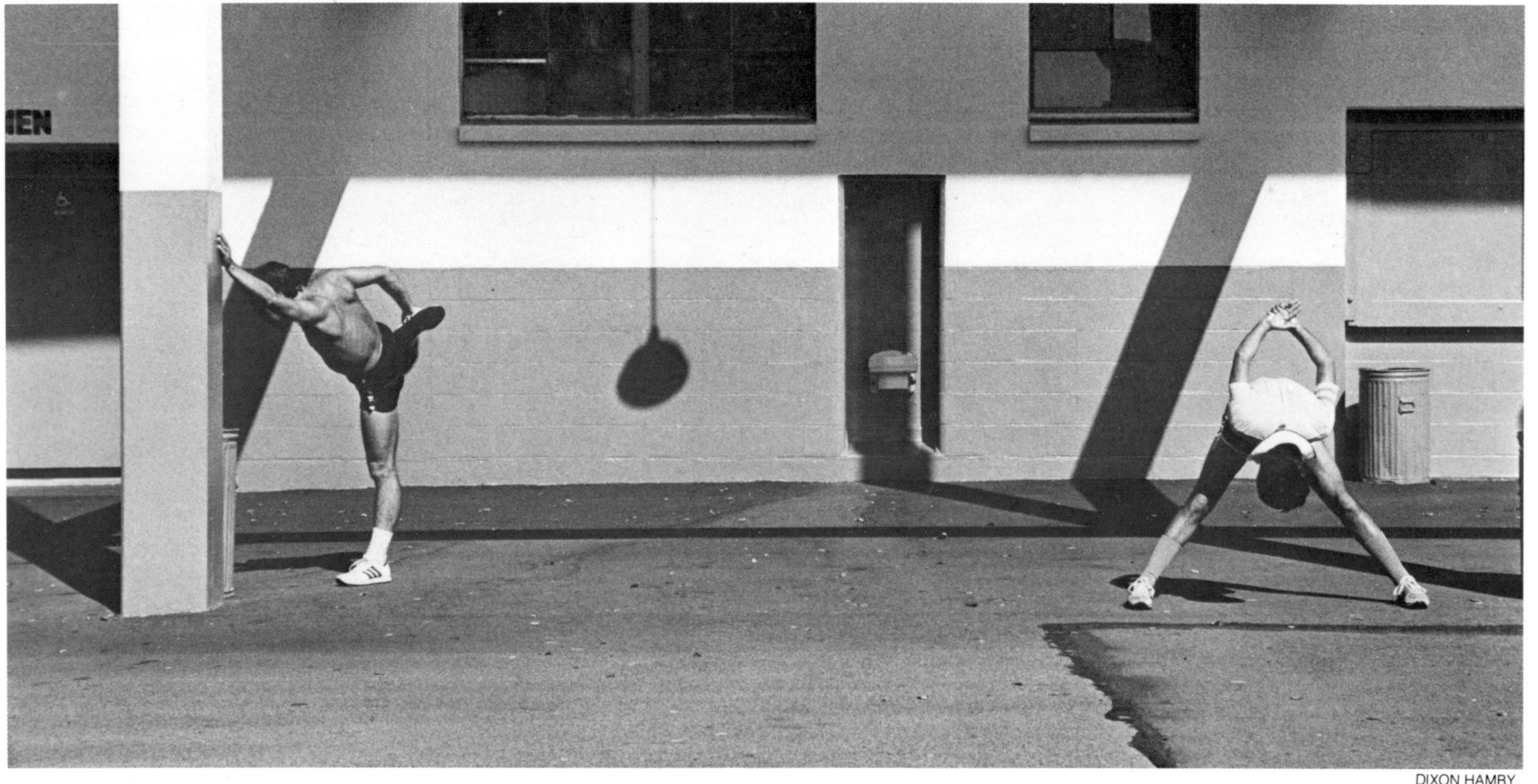

DIXON HAMBY

A newspaper hawker makes the round of motorists waiting for the Winslow ferry at Colman Dock.

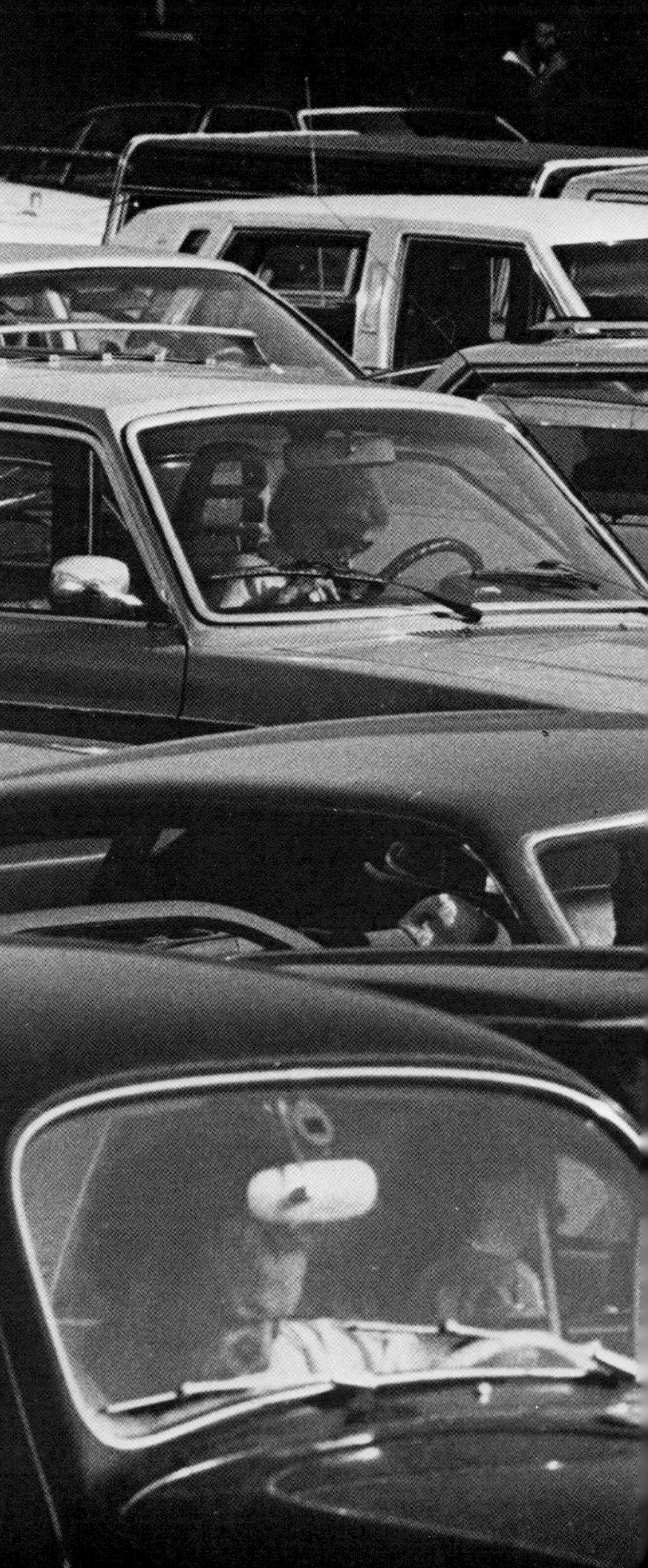

Mark Baze unwinds with his guitar on the ferryboat to Kingston, Kitsap County.

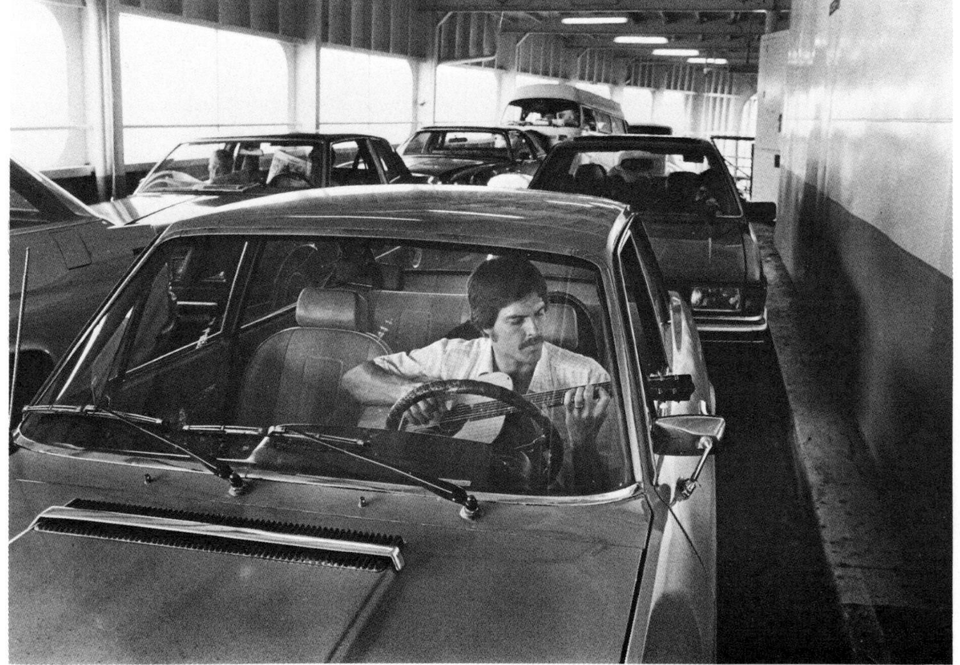

PHOTOS BY DALE BLINDHEIM

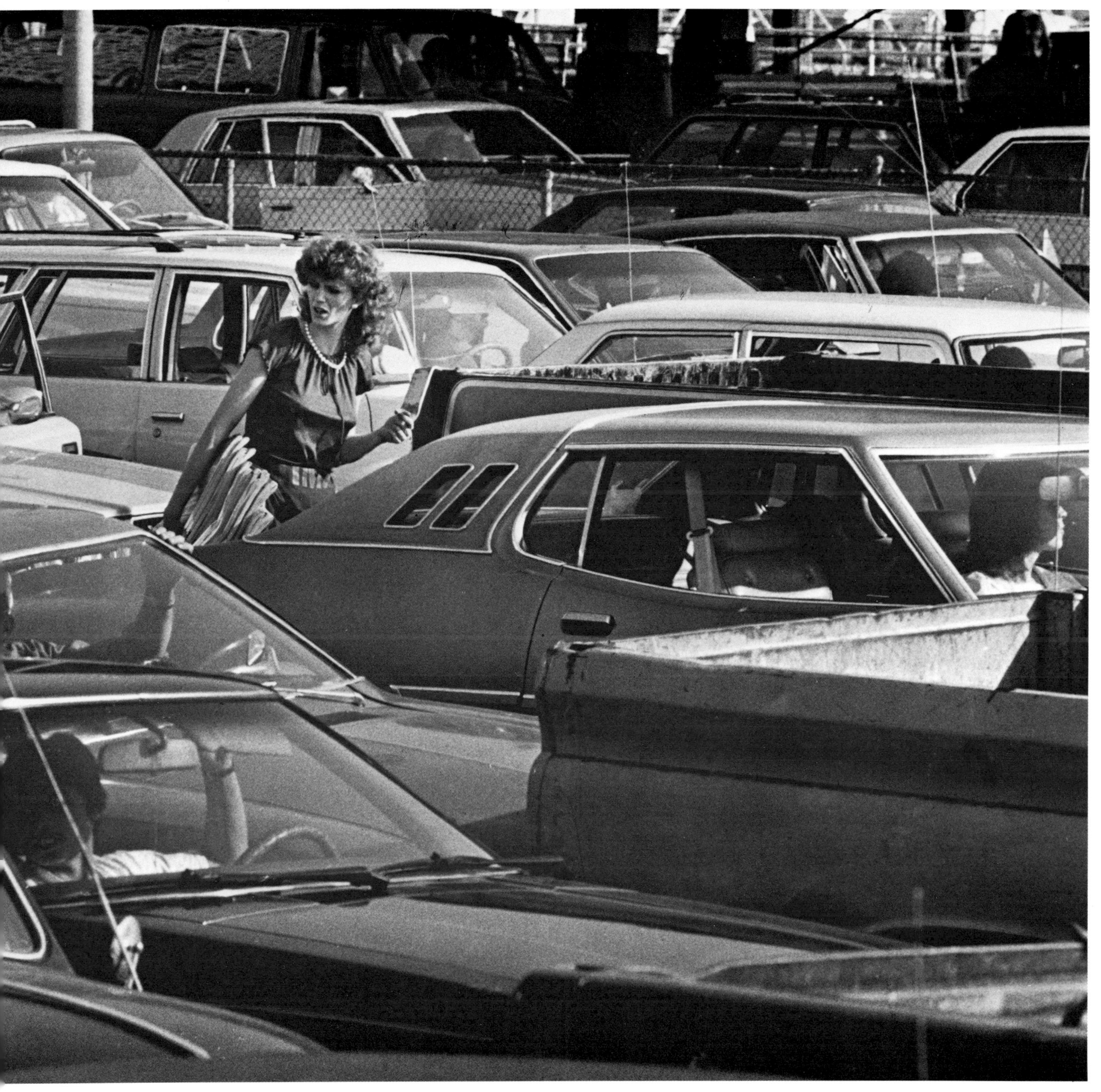

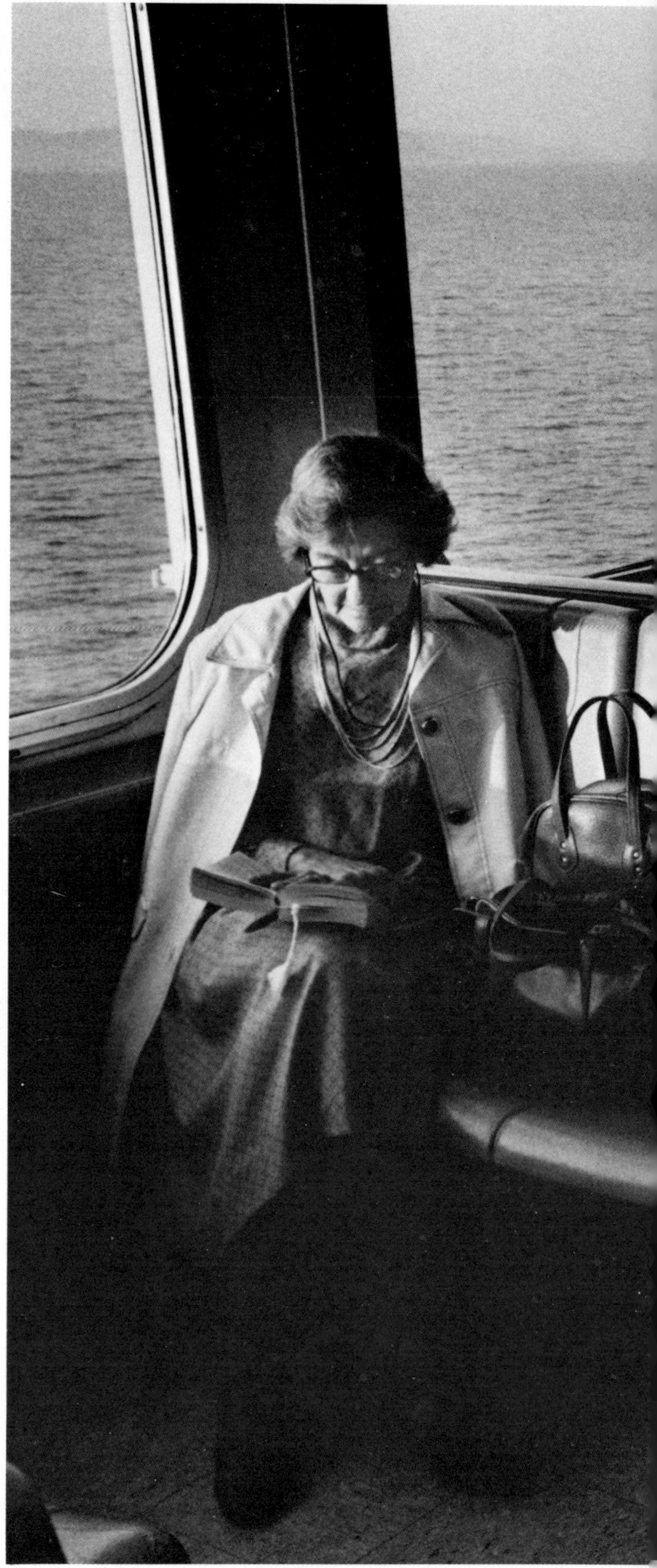

The 6:55 A.M. *run from Bremerton to Seattle.*

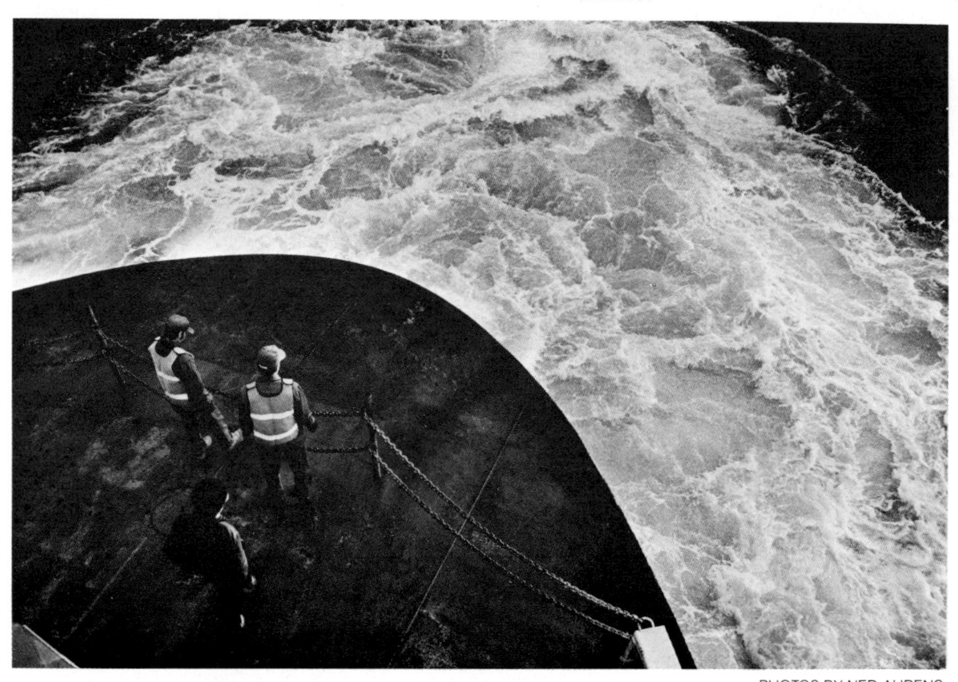

PHOTOS BY NED AHRENS

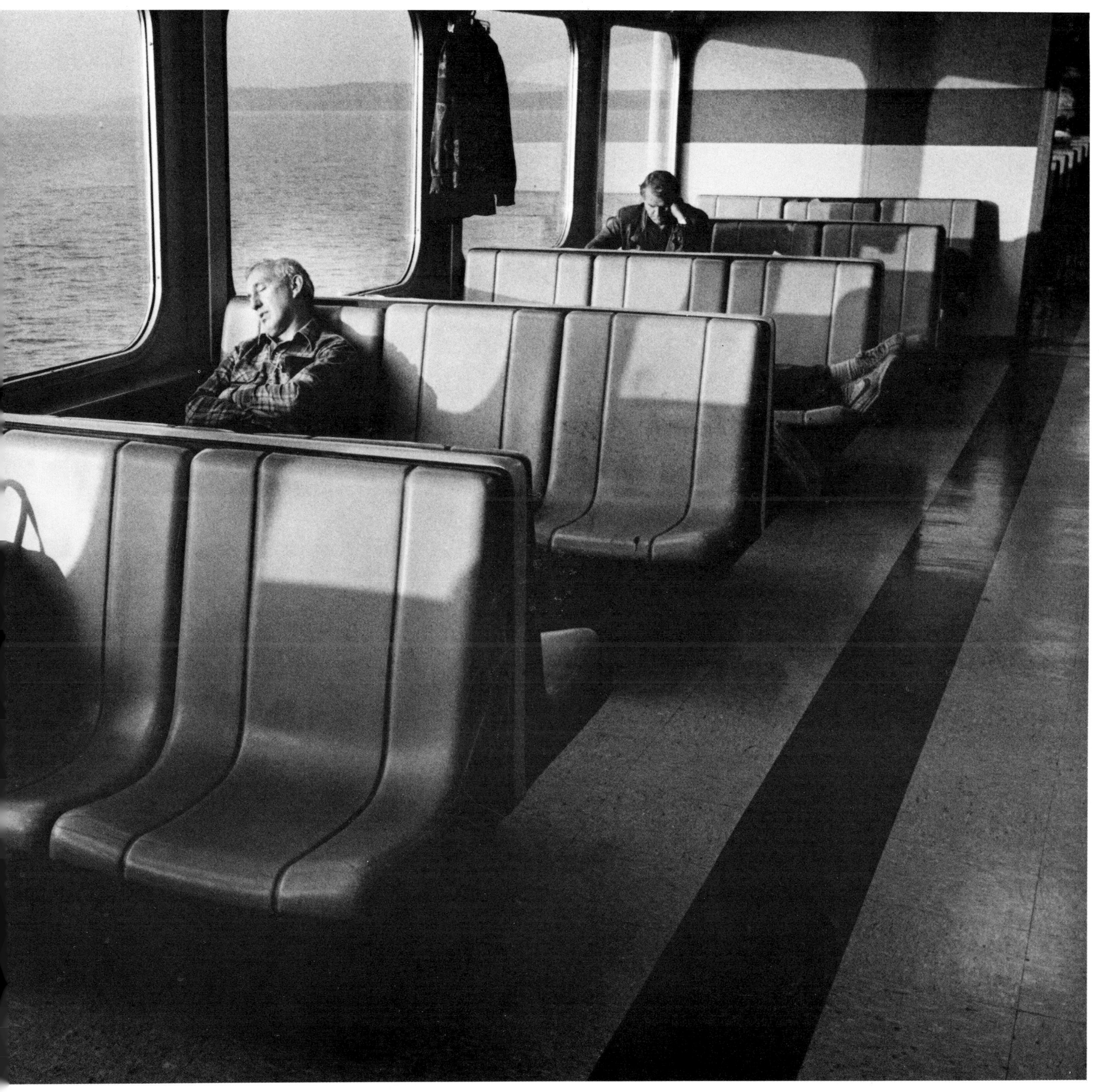

Right: *A Port Angeles trucker and friend.*

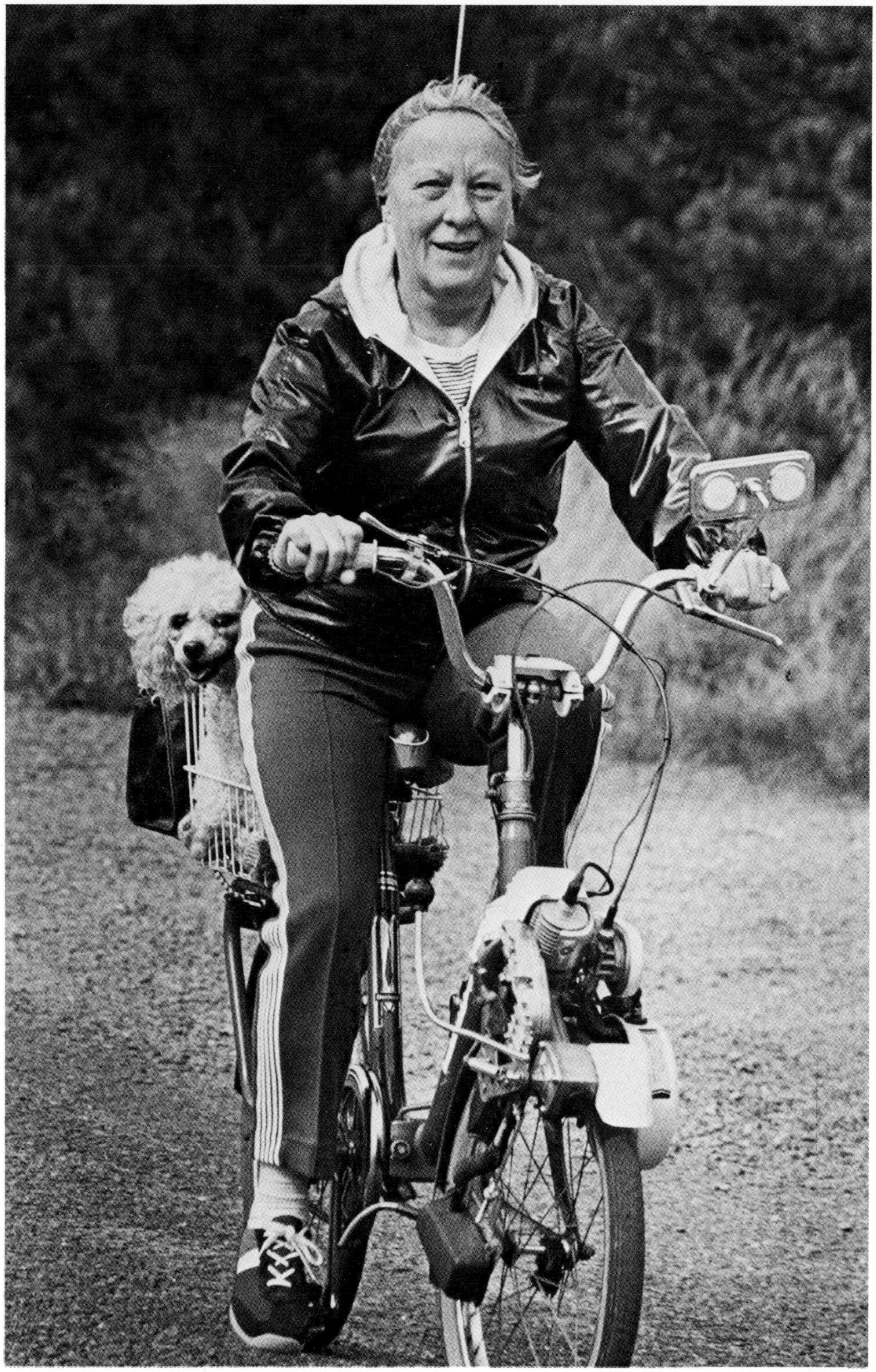

Verna Johansson of Kent and her dog, Pojke.

KATHY QUIGG

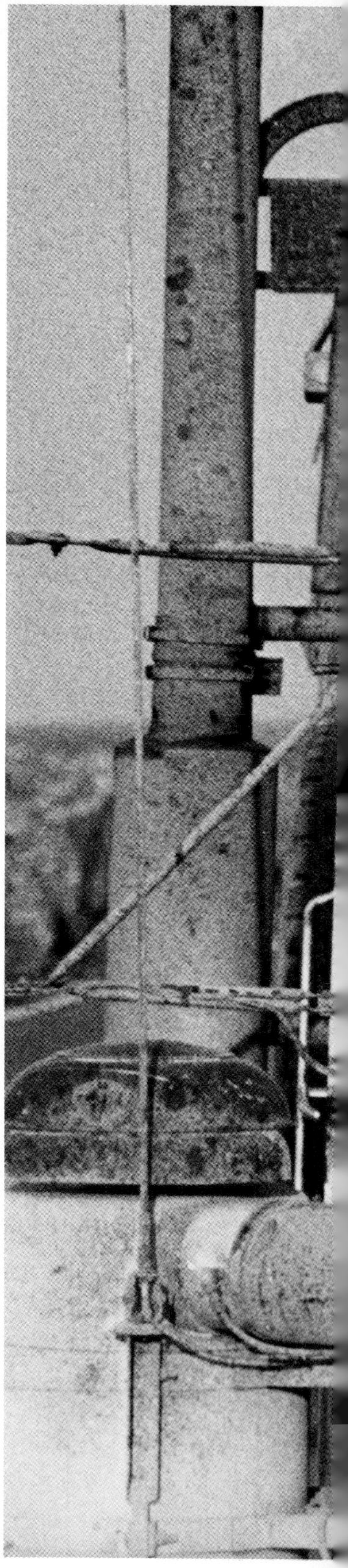

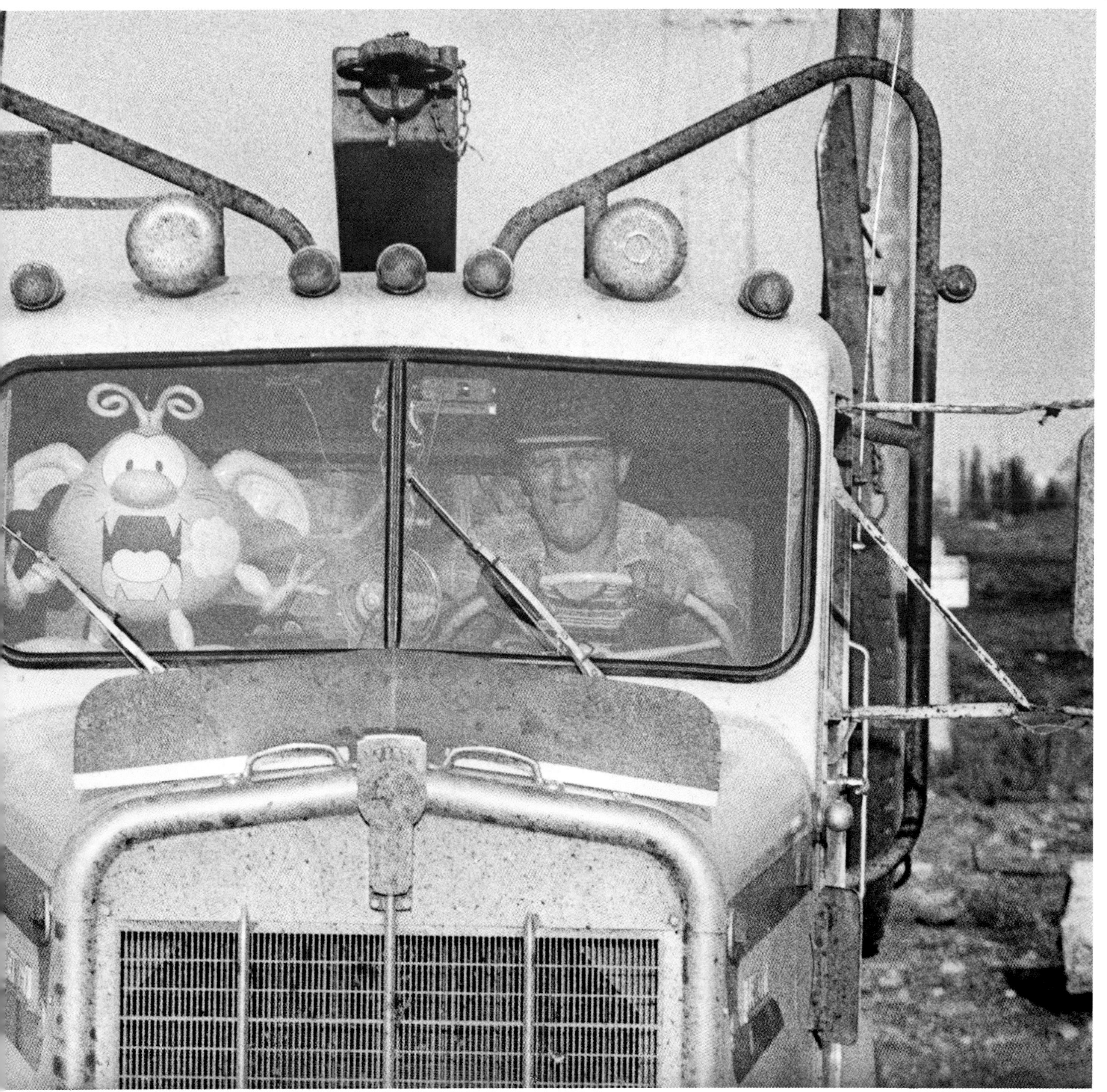

TOM THOMPSON

MUSEUM
PETRIFIED WOOD
INDIAN ARTIFACTS
FREE ADMISSION
GIFT SHOP
PETRIFIED FOREST
JEWELRY SOUVENIRS
CHINA NOVELTIES
WEST WIND
GIFT SHOP
MUSEUM
CHRYSLER
ERU 815
ARCO Unleaded
supreme

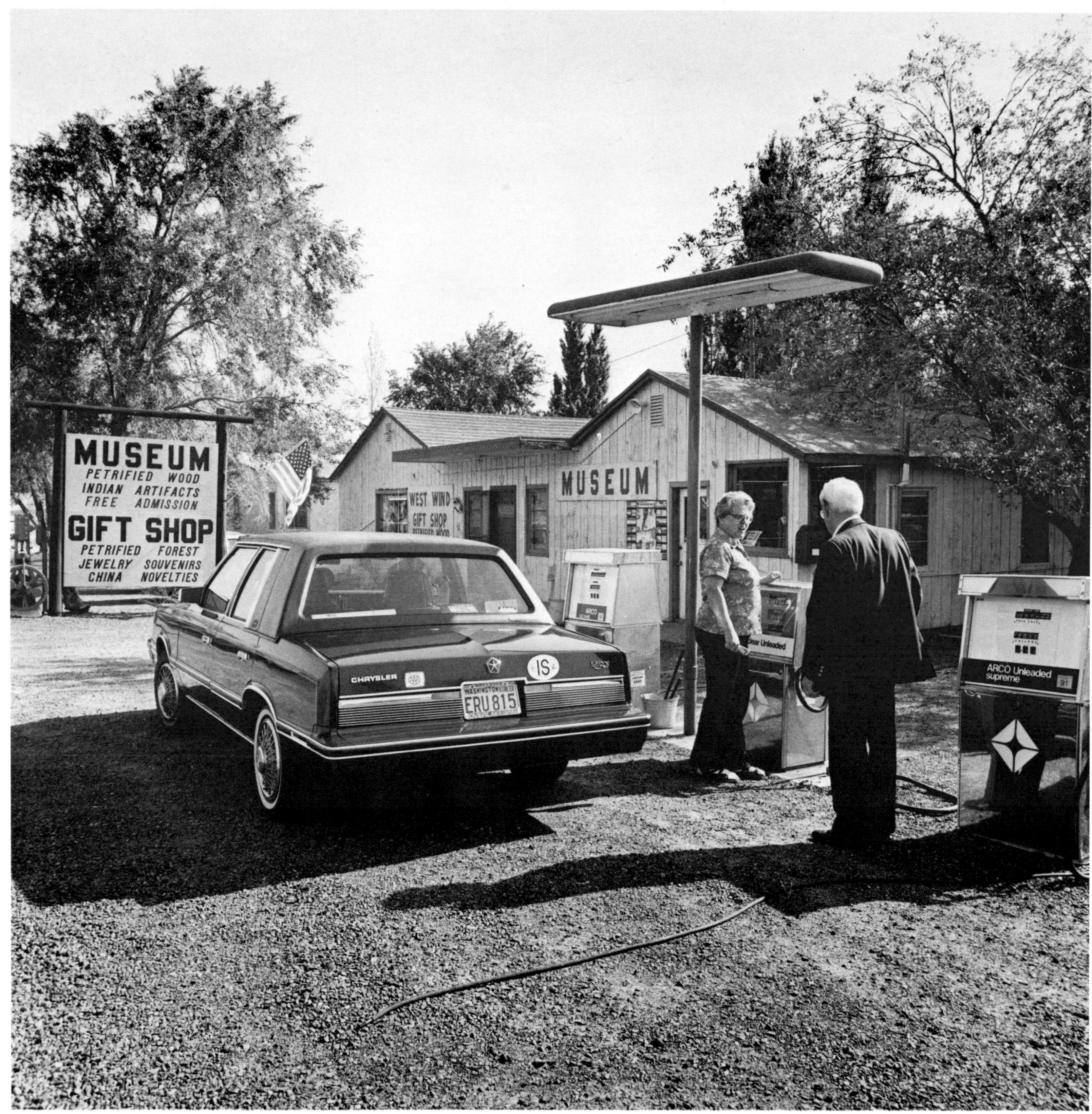

DON NORMARK

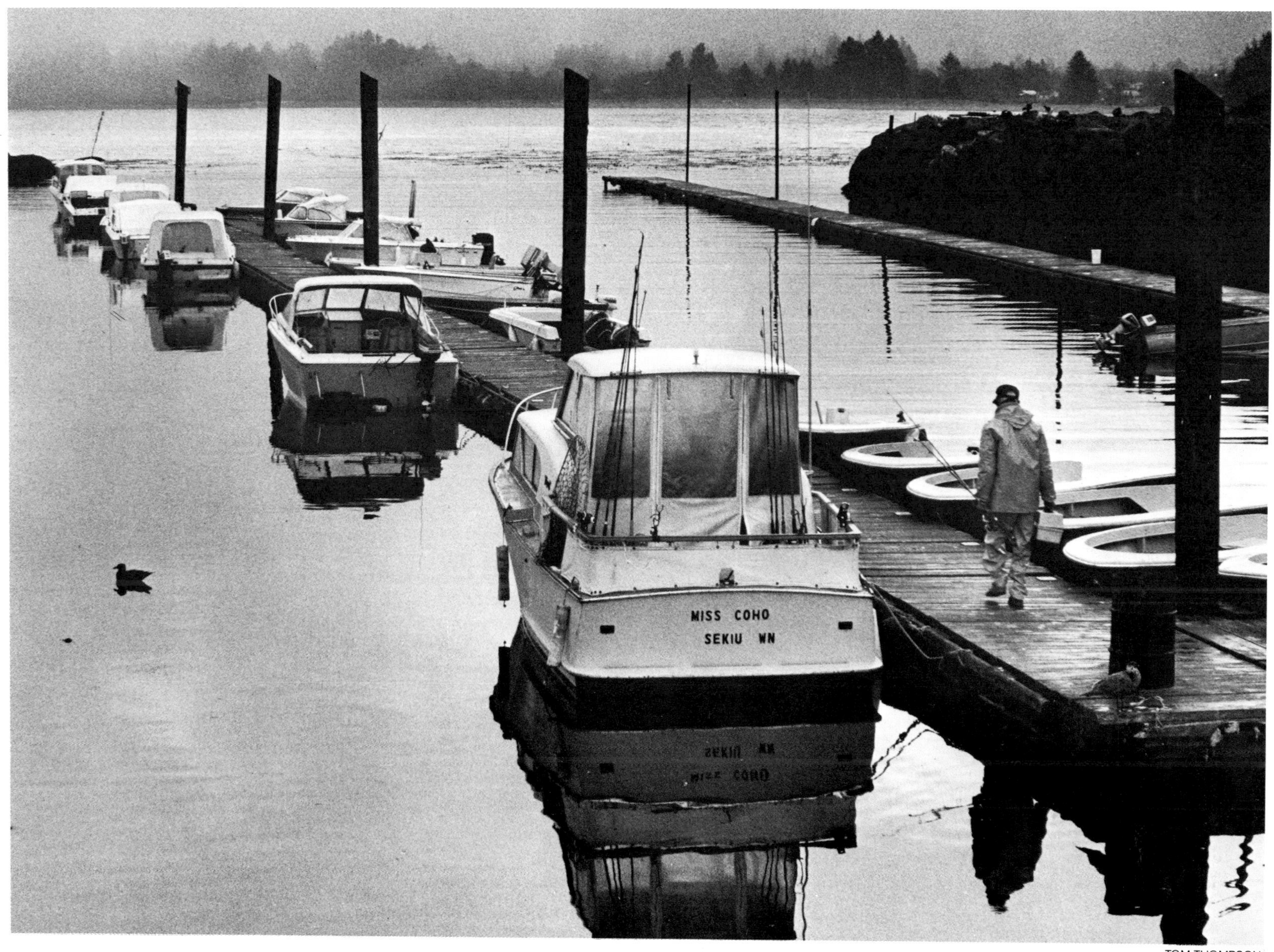

TOM THOMPSON
Heading out for sunrise fishing at Sekiu, Clallam County.

A combination gas station-museum-gift shop at Vantage, near Gingko State Park.

Following pages: *The Holtcamp farm in Sedro Woolley.*

BILL STALEY

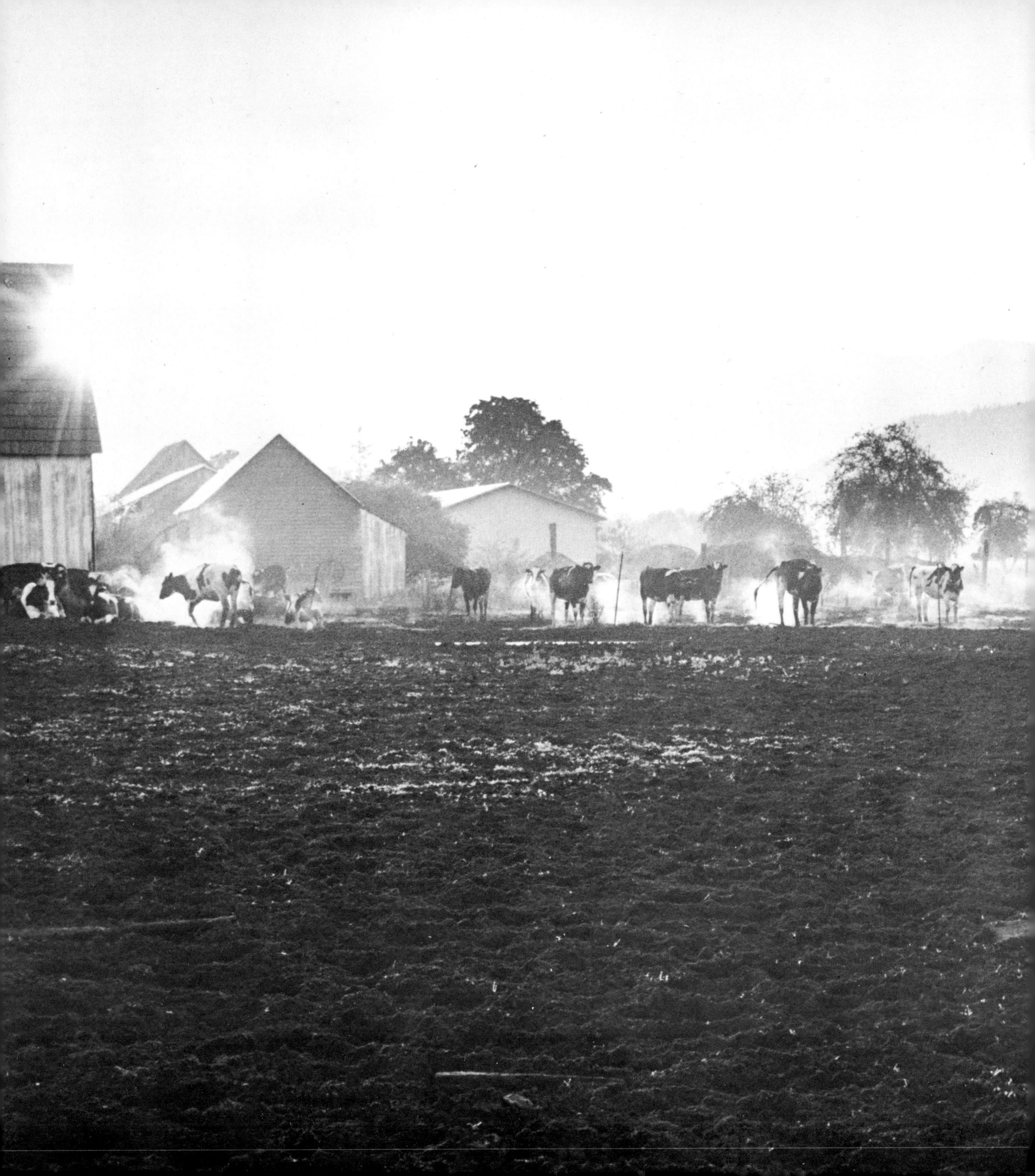

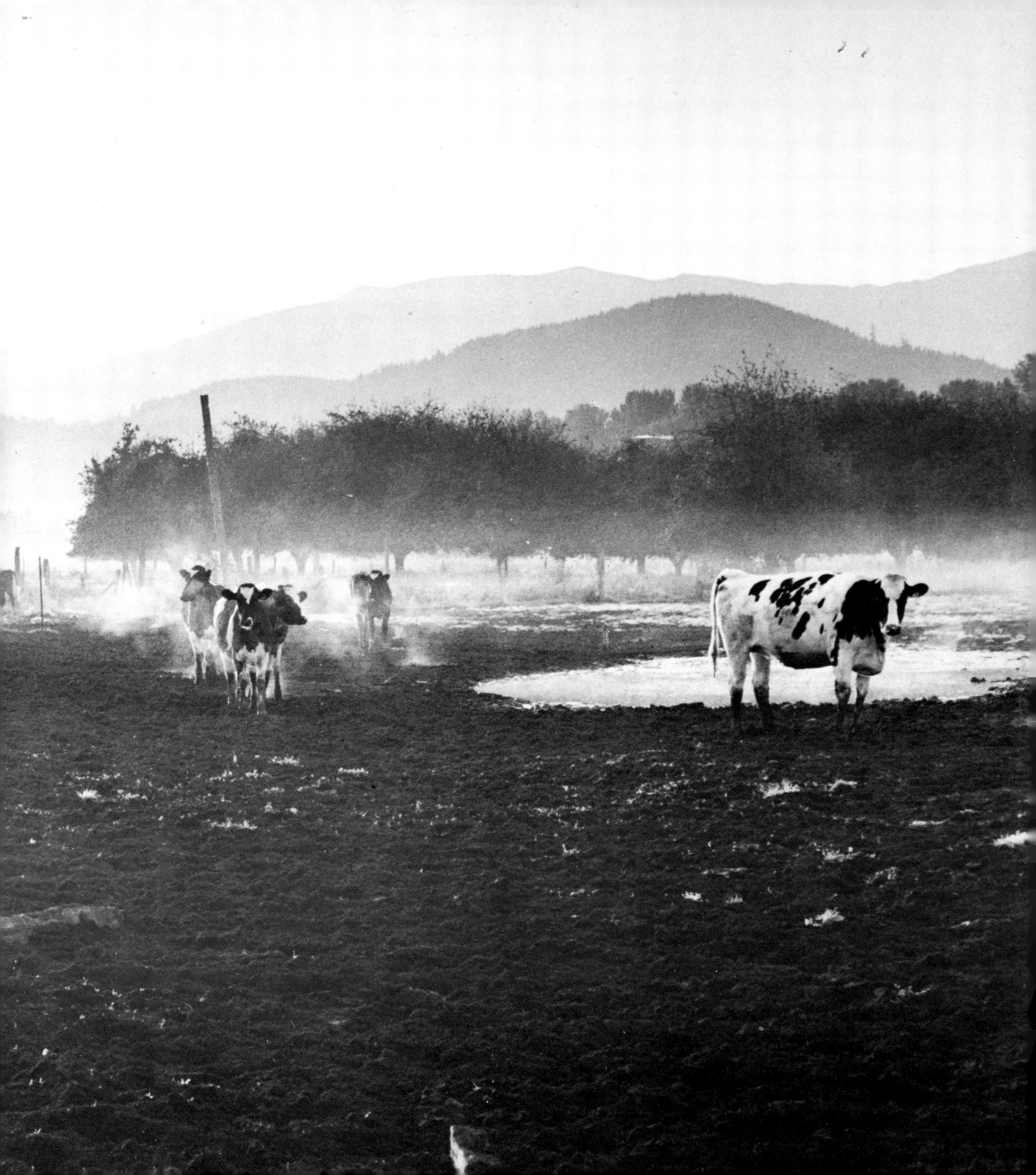

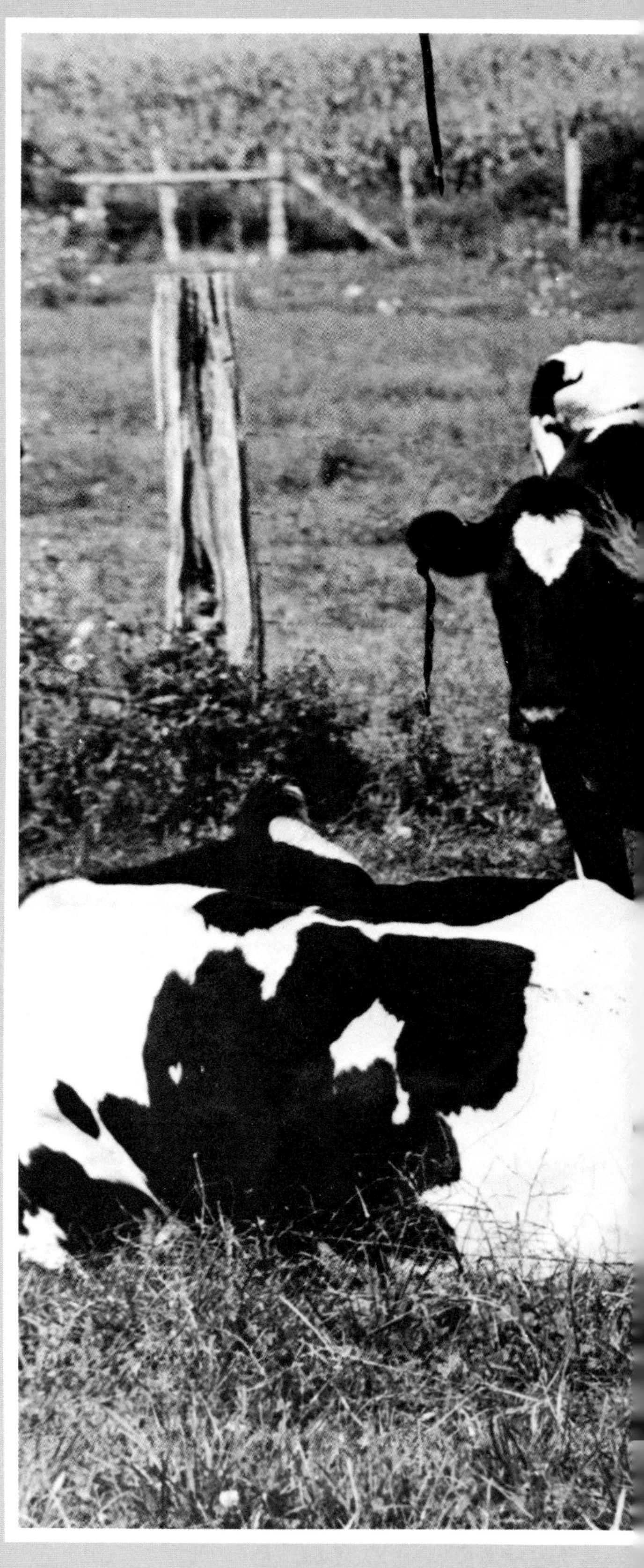

Tom Holtcamp helps deliver a calf, tying a smooth chain to the calf's hooves and pulling.

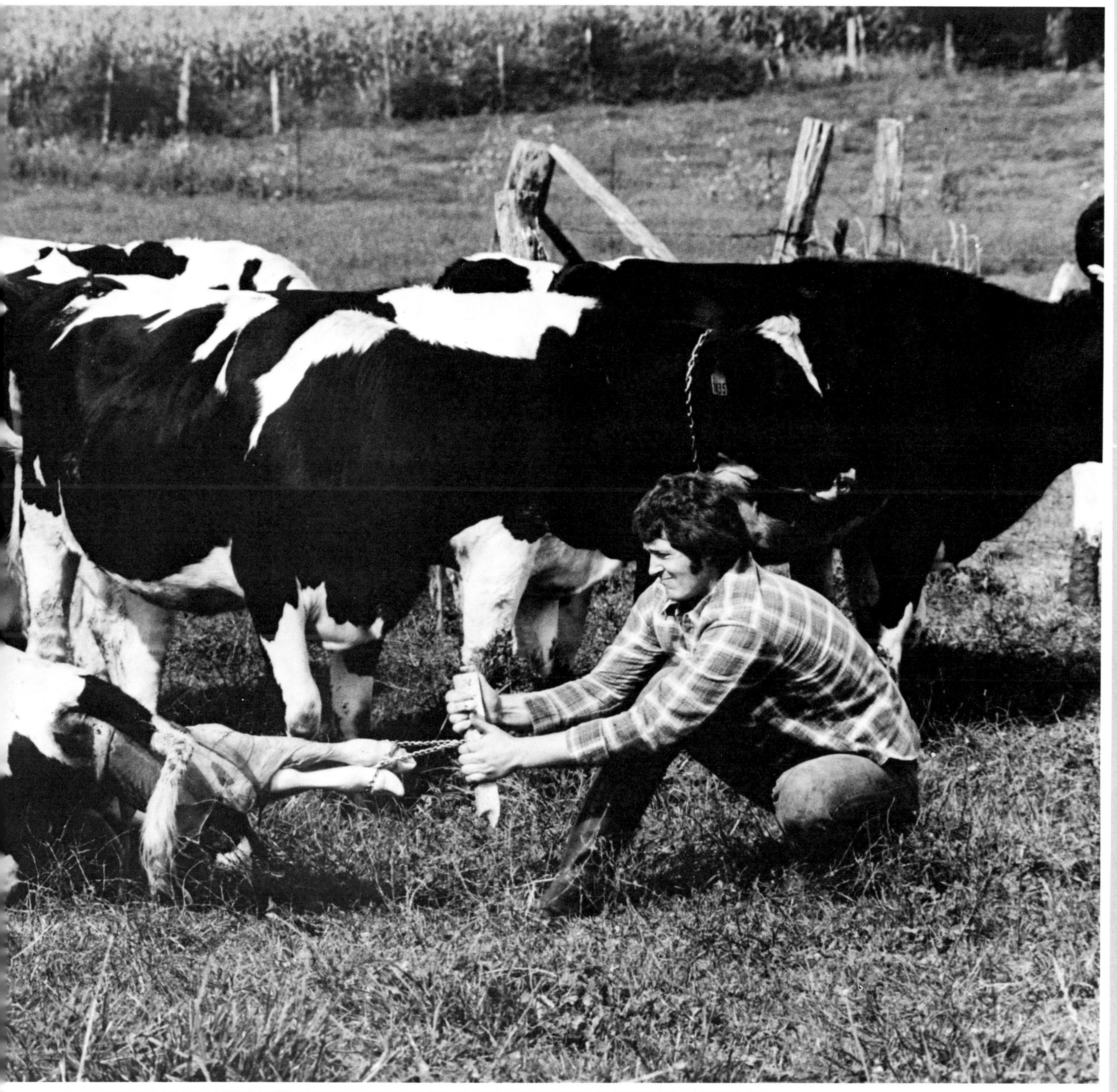

BILL STALEY

Joe Holtcamp, 12, and Gretchen Holtcamp, 14, in the hayloft.

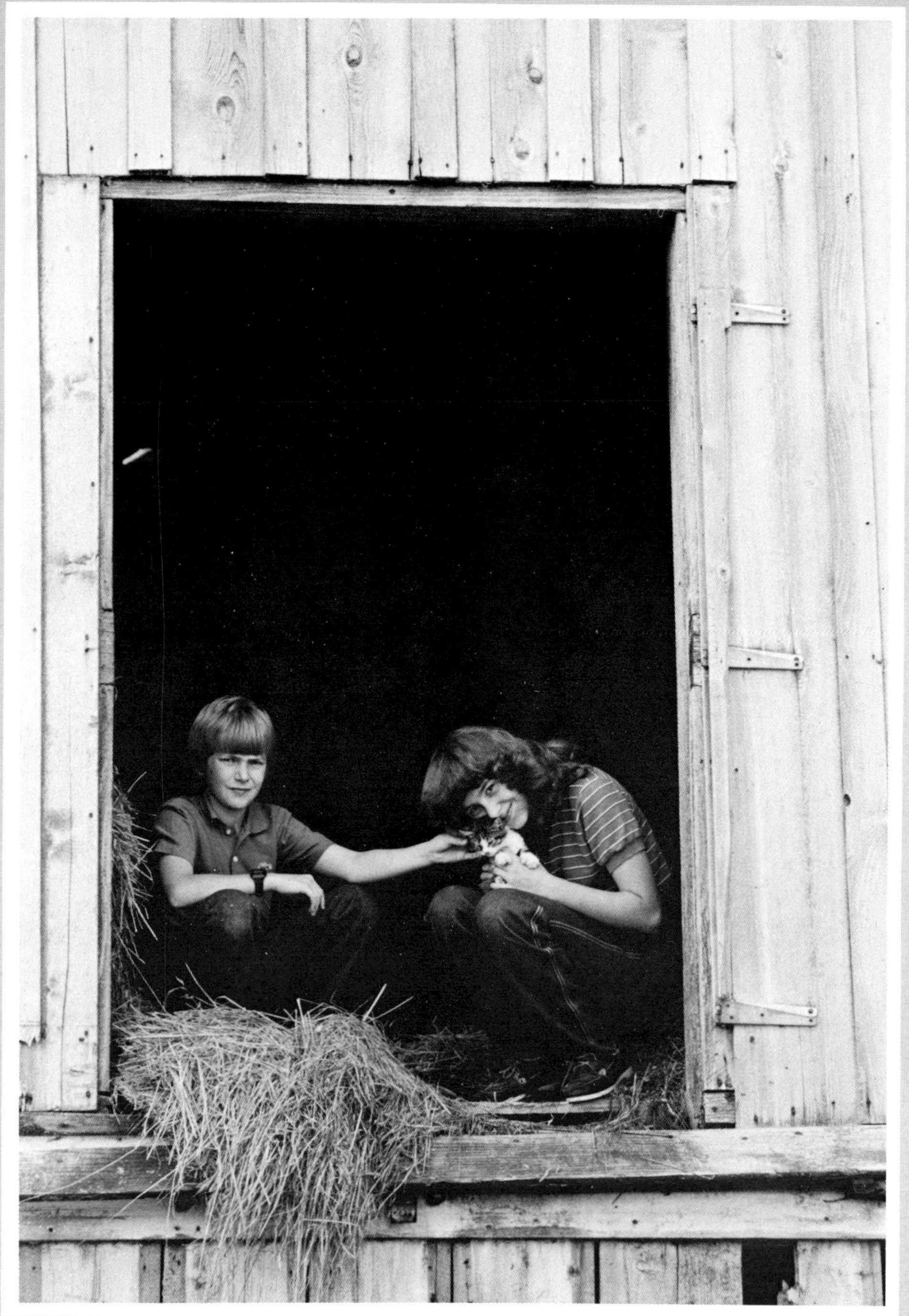

PHOTOS BY BILL STALEY

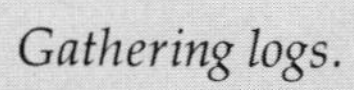

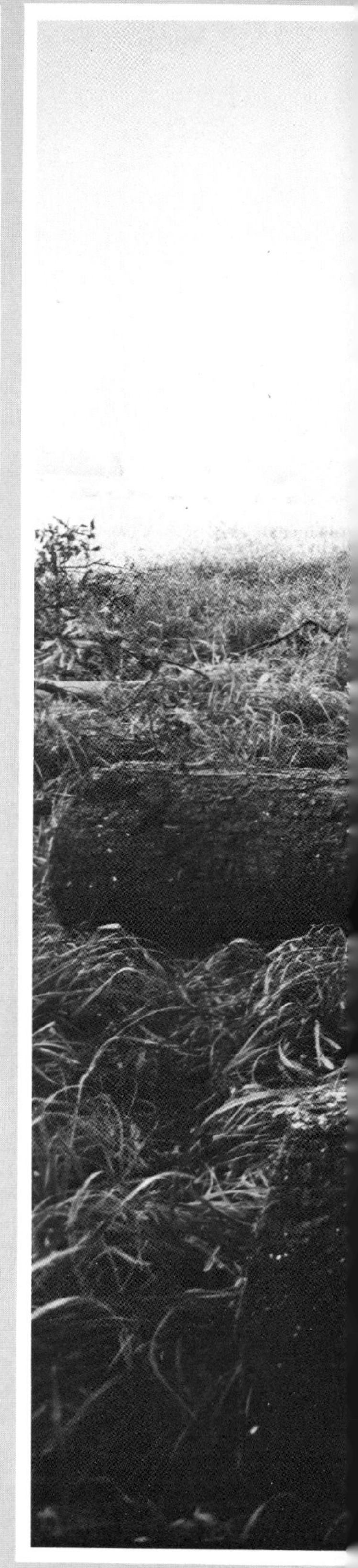

Gathering logs.

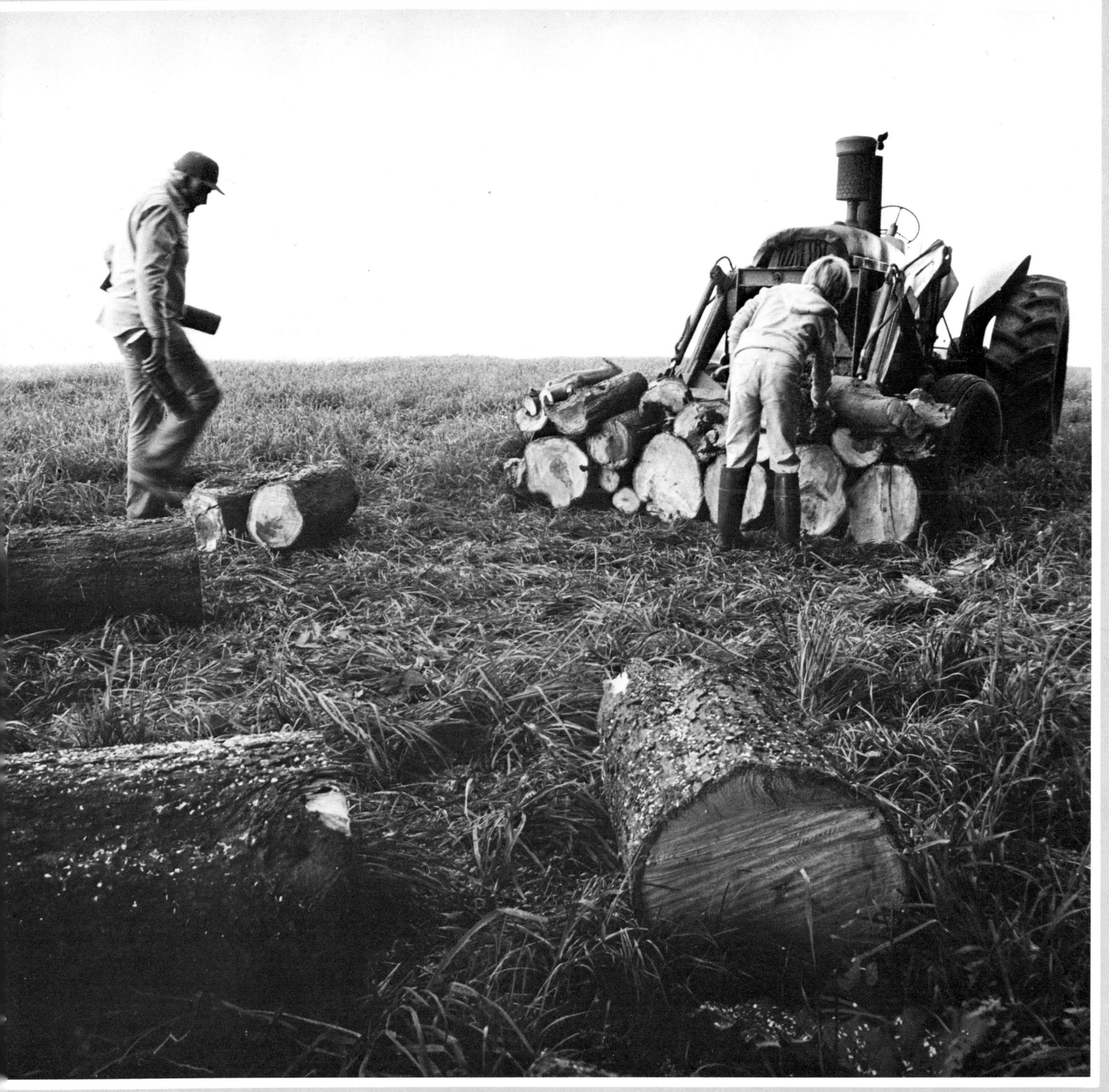

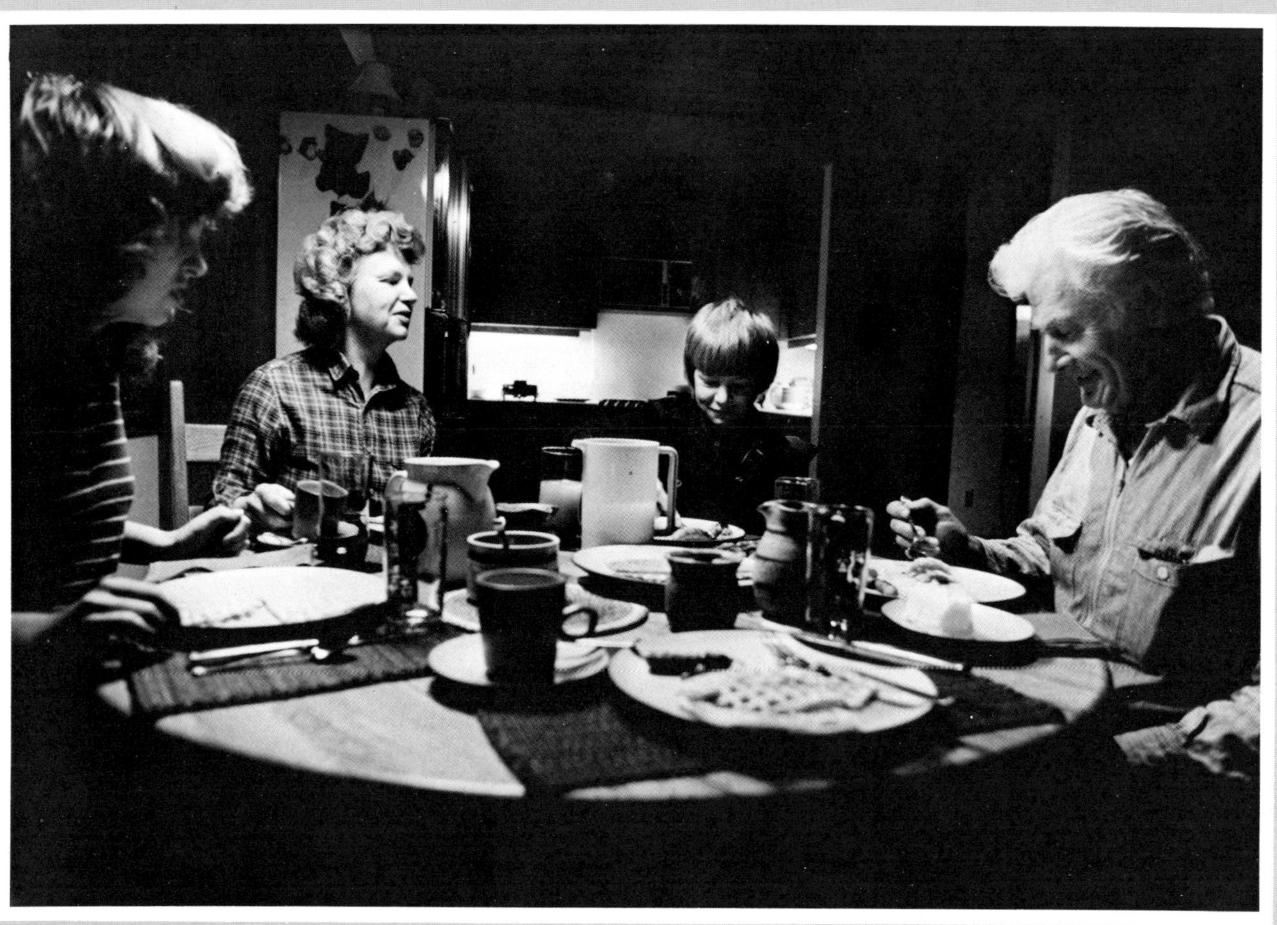

PHOTOS BY BILL STALEY

Long before the sun comes up over the 300-acre dairy farm, the Holtcamps sit down to breakfast. There are 150 to 160 cows to milk, and there are 200 new calves born every year.

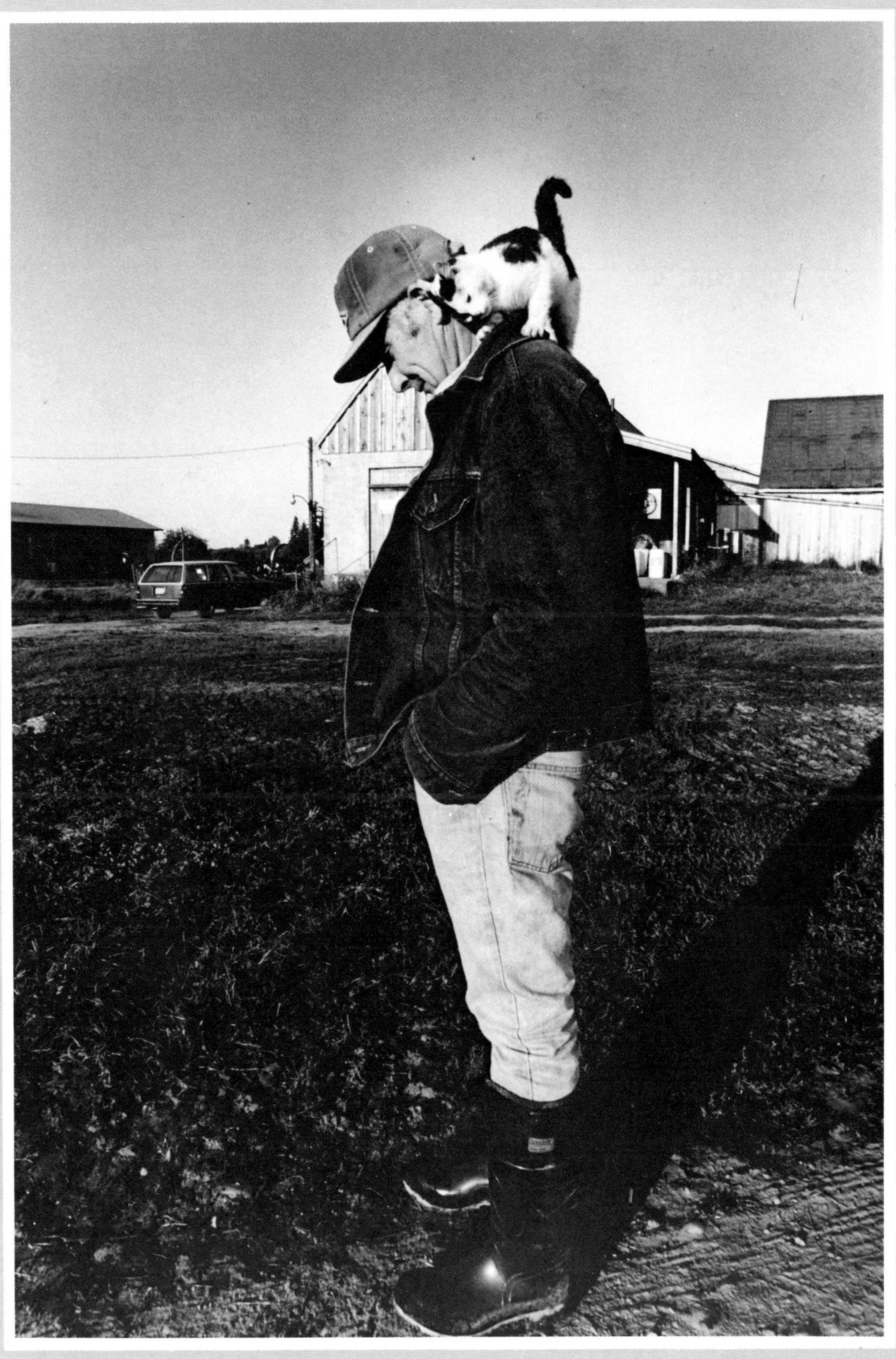

William Holtcamp's German-born grandfather homesteaded the land in the late 1800s.

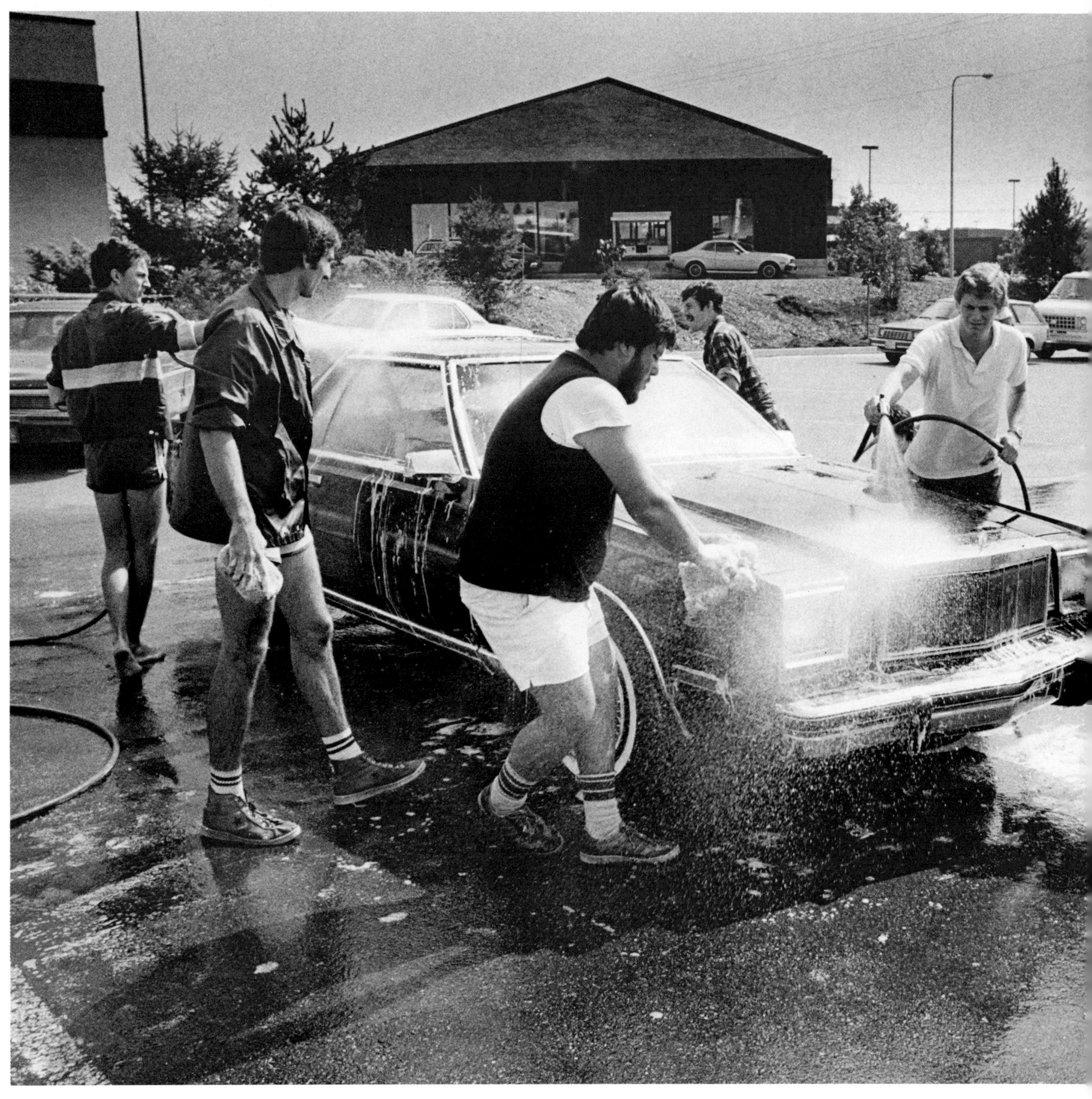

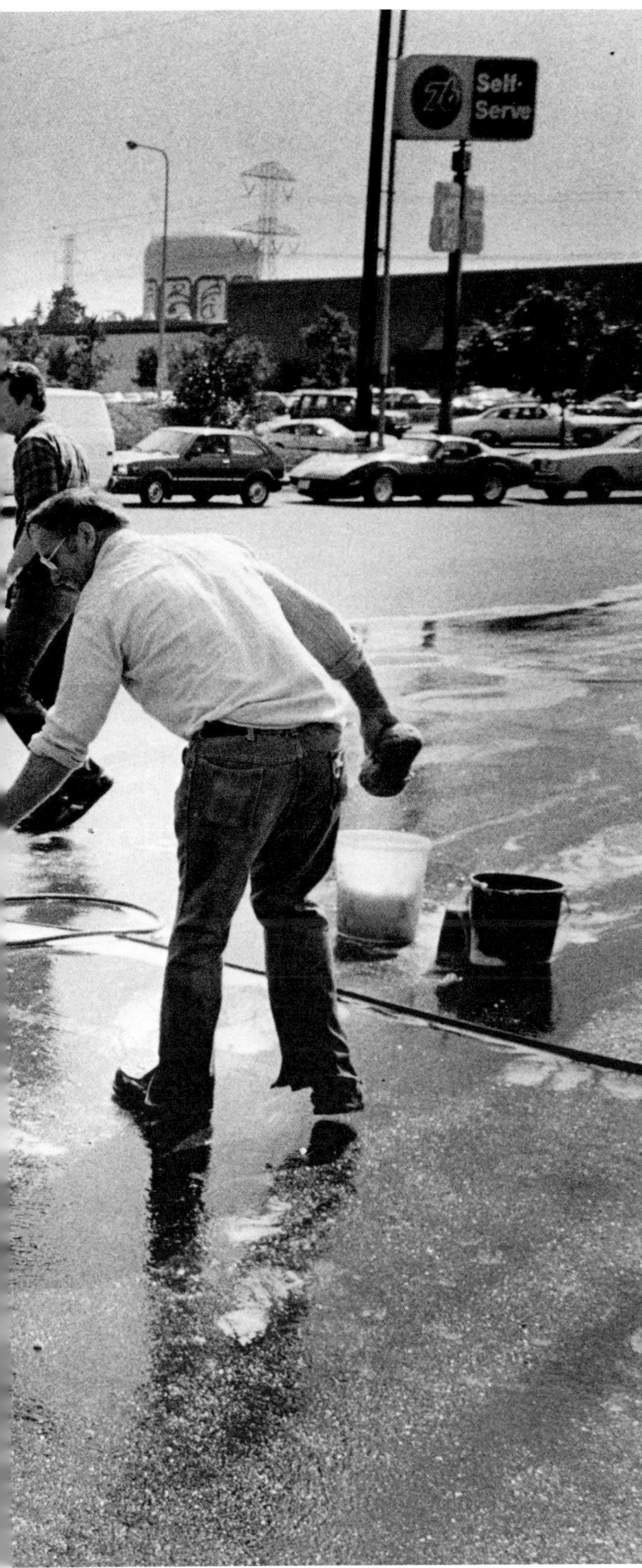

ROBERT HARBISON

The "Agape Force Free Car Wash," sponsored by Federal Way Merchants.

A cooling scrub after a morning workout at Longacres Race Track.

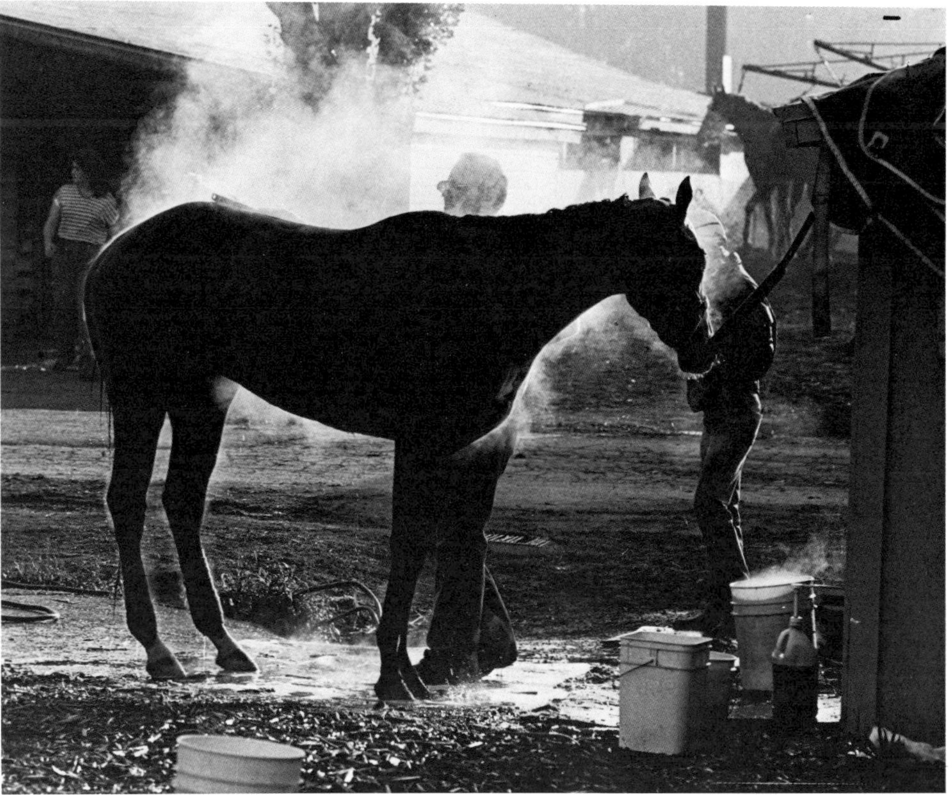

JERRY CLARK

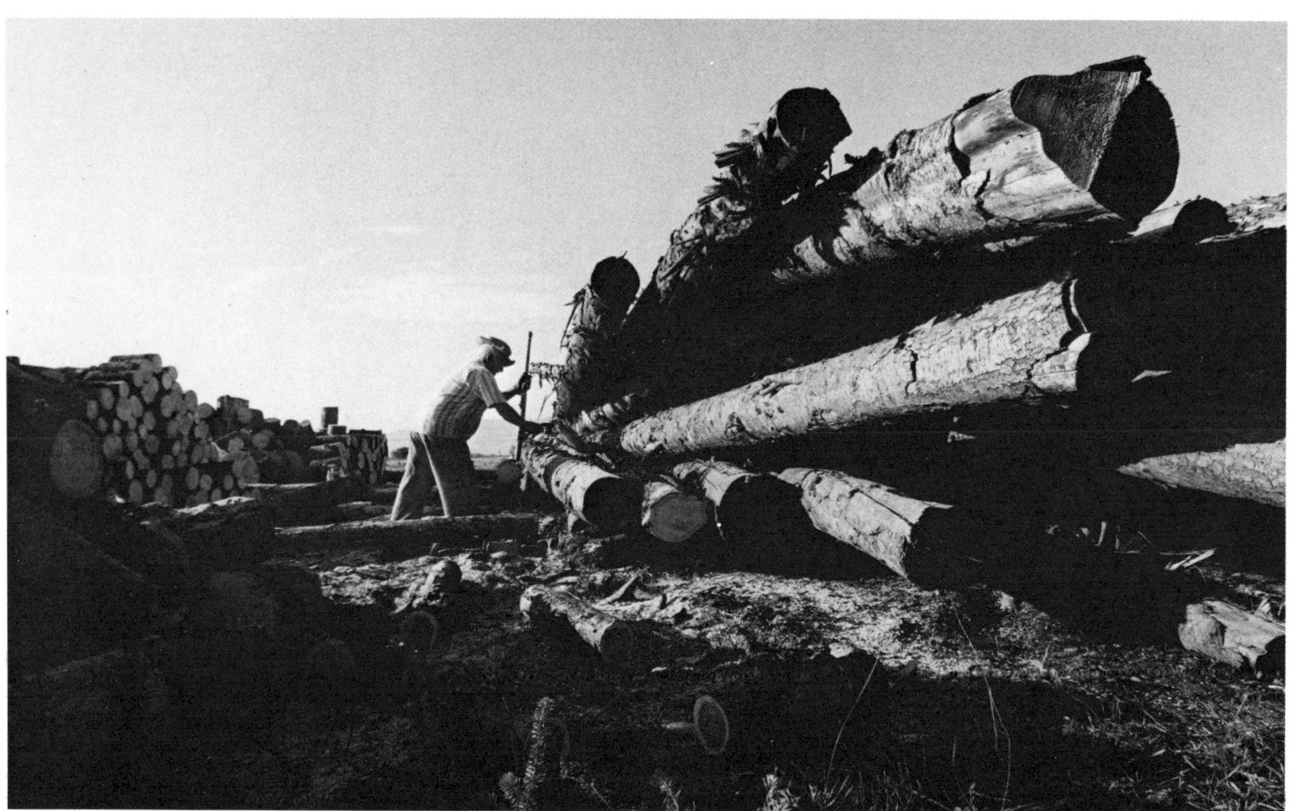

Mr. Godfrey, a woodcutter near Kittitas, is a retired ironworker from Seattle.

DON NORMARK

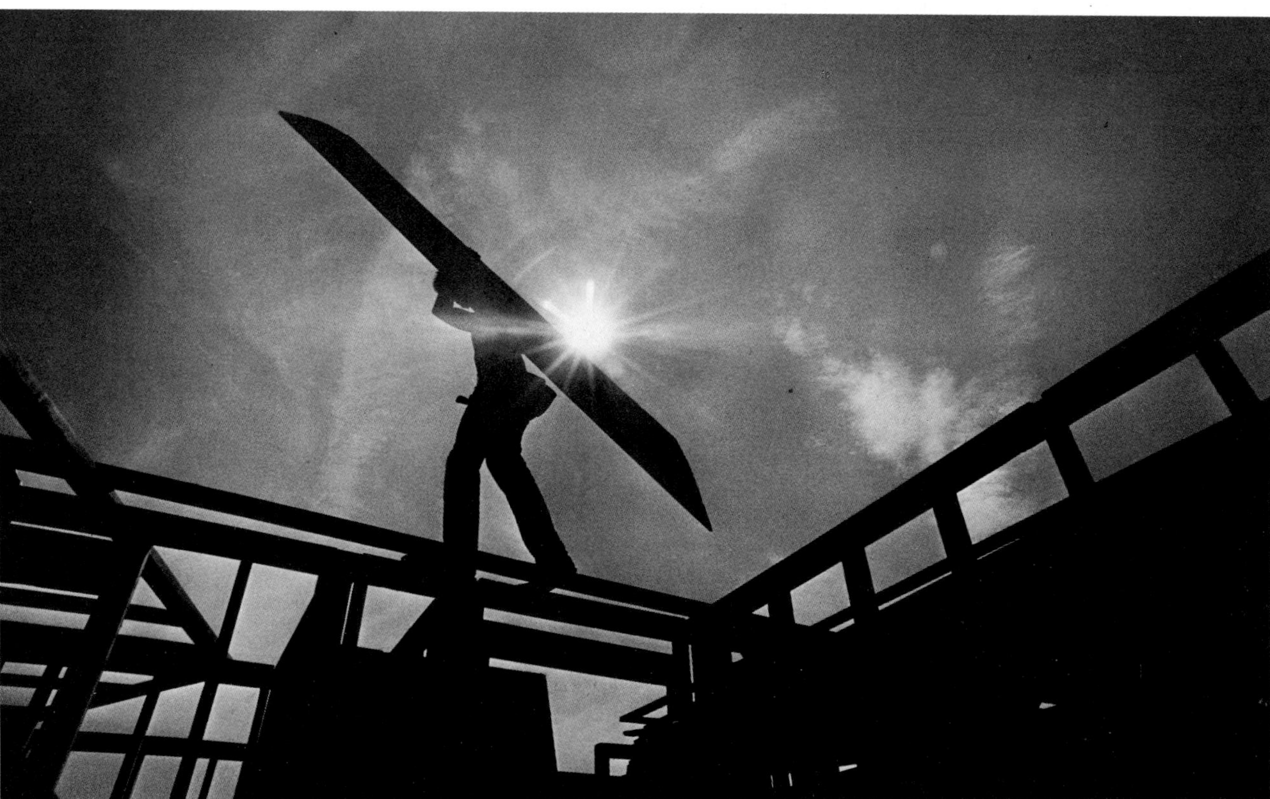

Tim Spencer, a framer on an apartment house construction job in Enumclaw.

MARK MORRIS

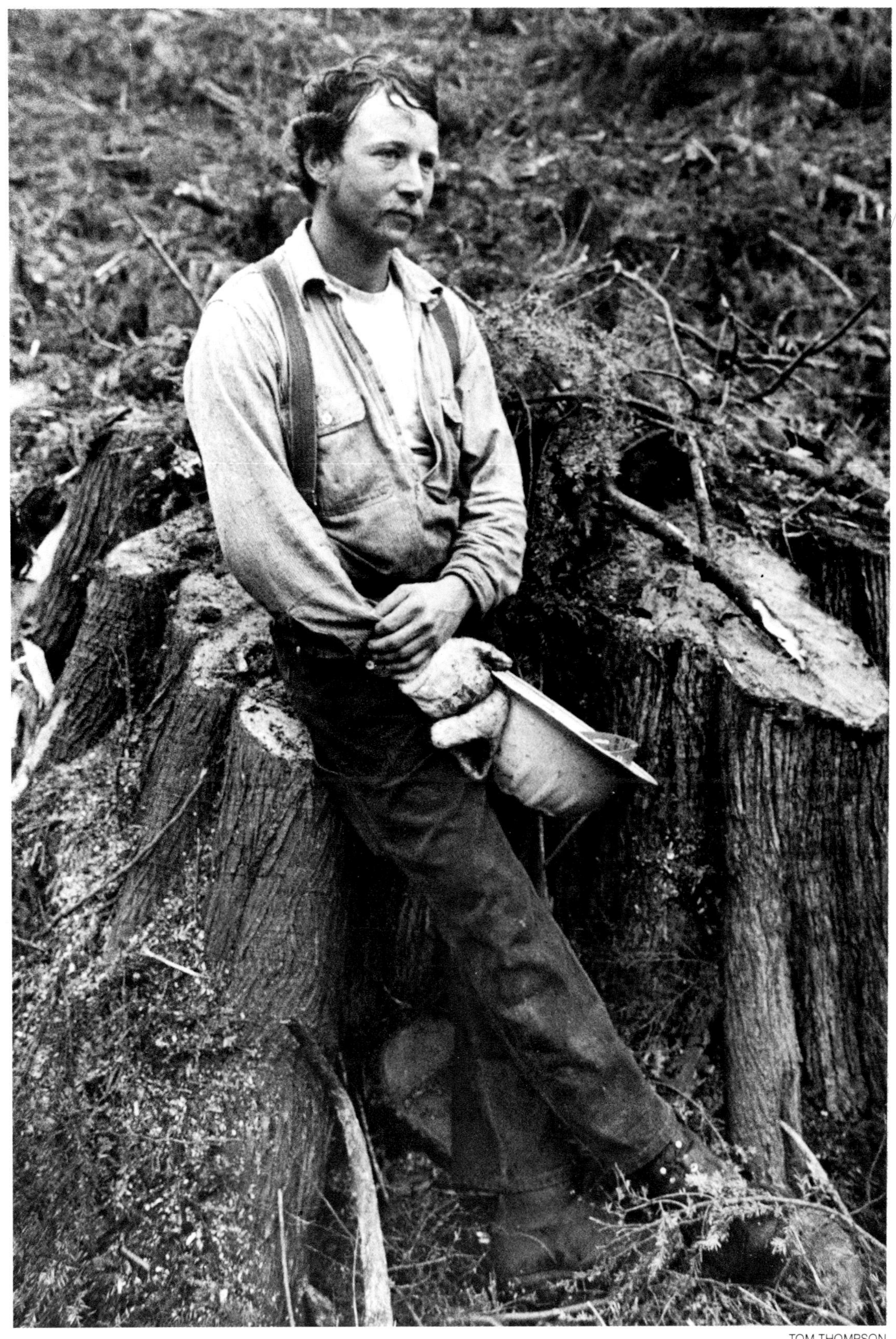

TOM THOMPSON

A logger on the Olympic Peninsula.

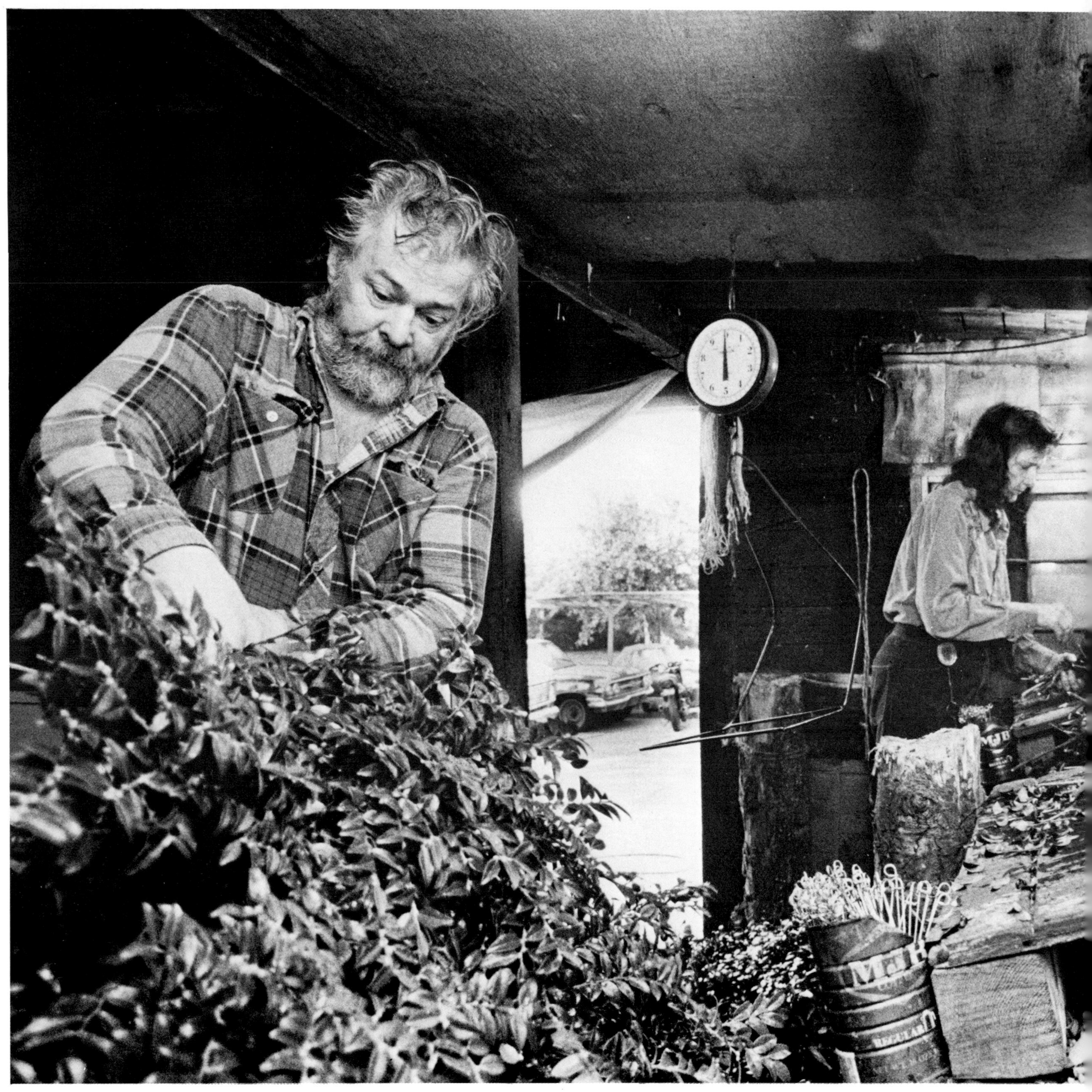
MJB

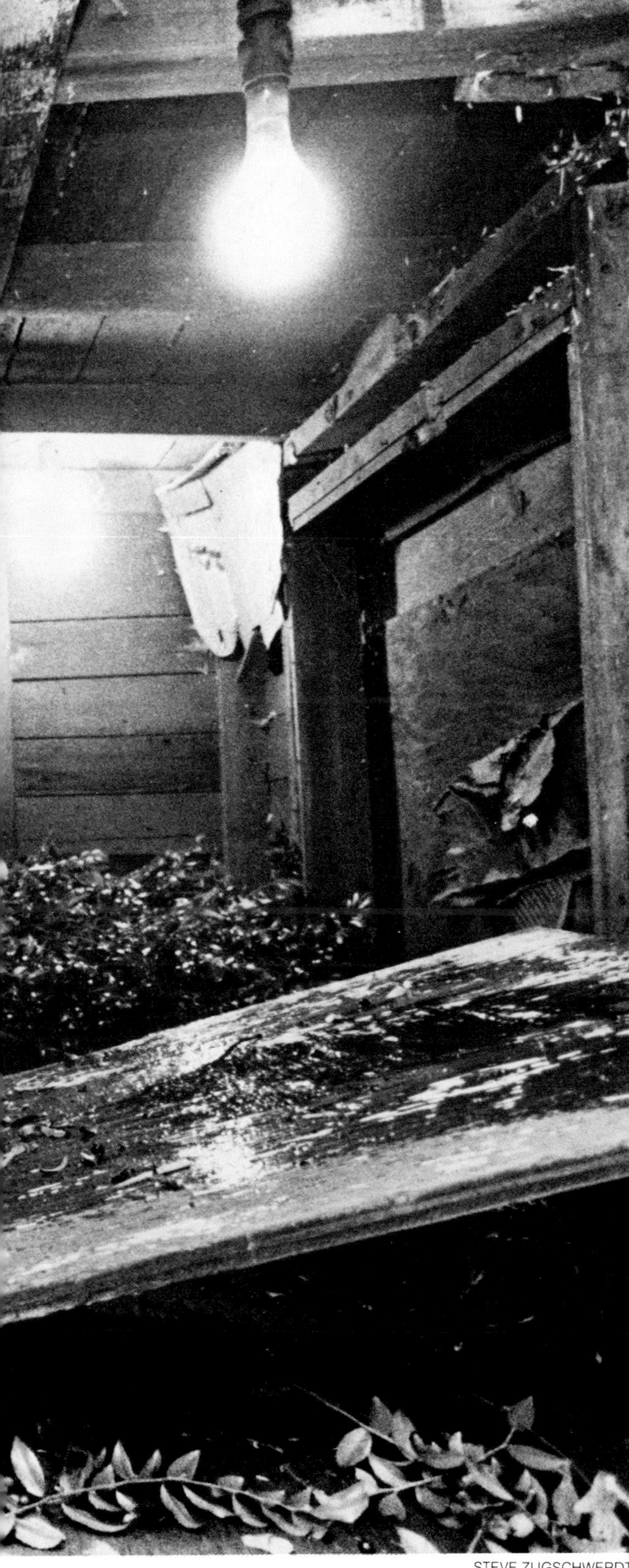

STEVE ZUGSCHWERDT

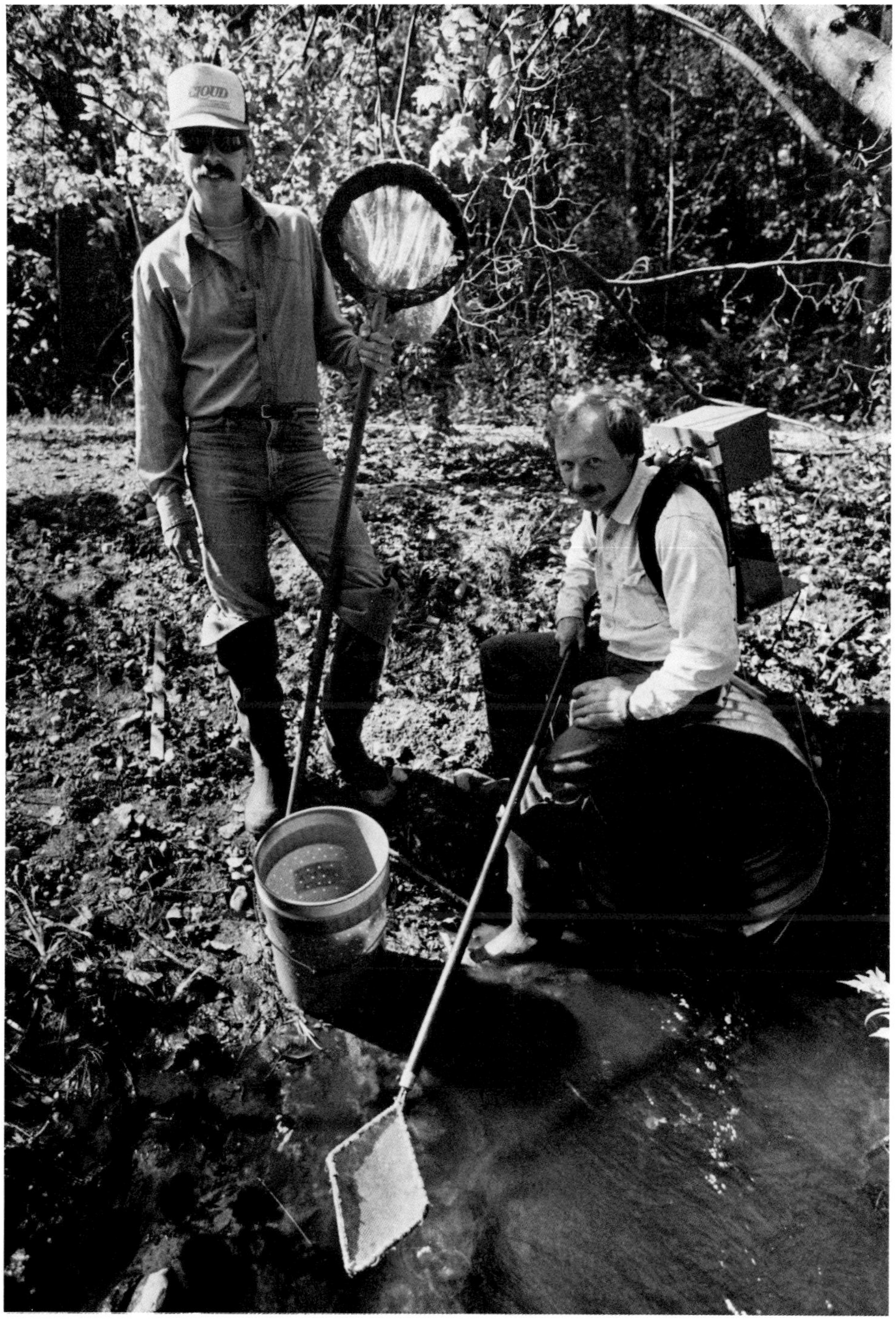

Smokey and Ardie McCartney pick brush around Belfair, Mason County, for use by floral arrangers as far away as Germany.

NED AHRENS

Dale Anderson and Rob Morrice, water quality technicians, in East King County.

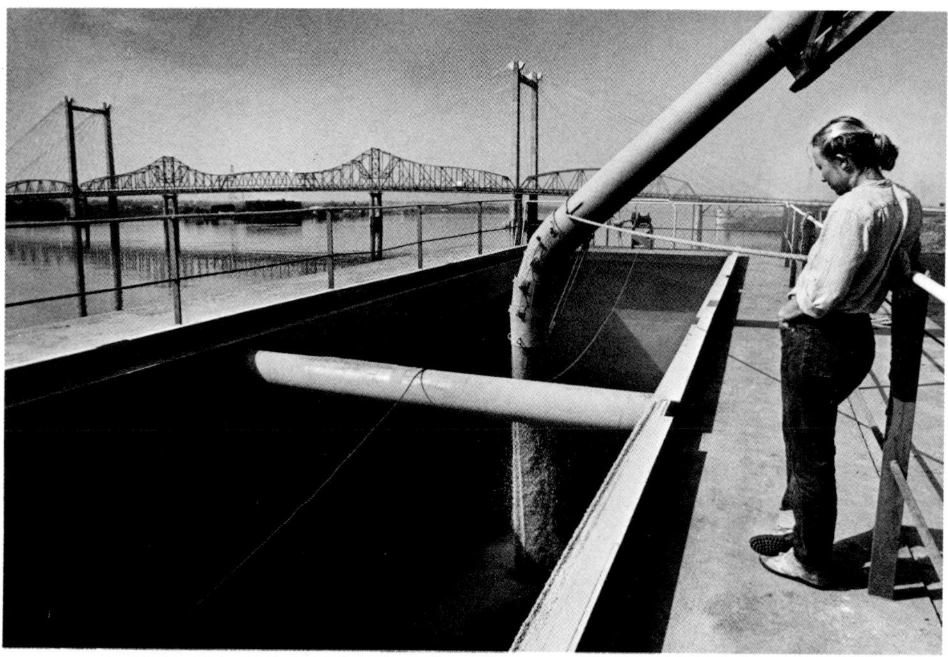

MERRILL OLIVER

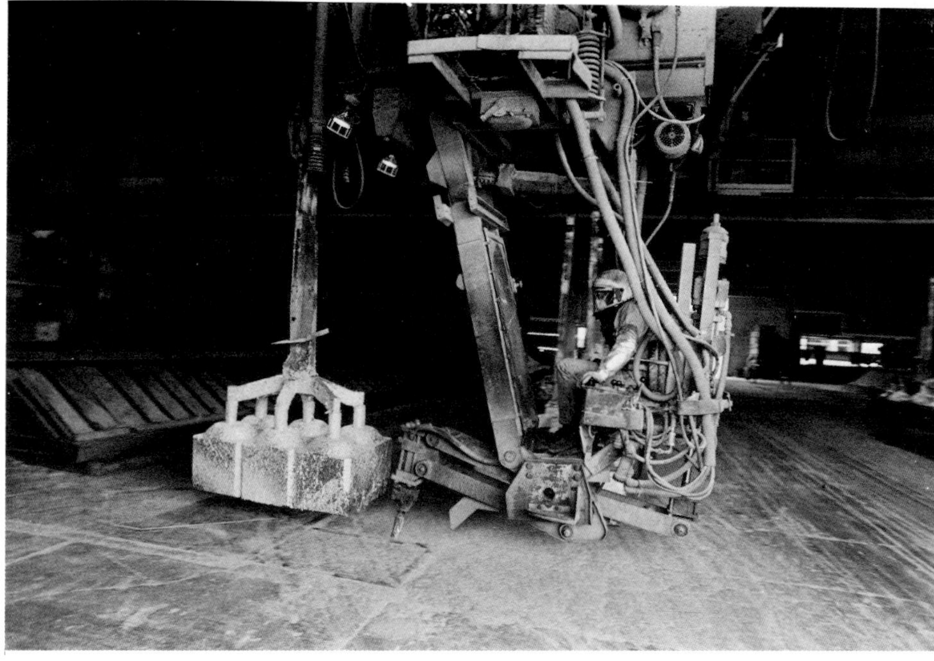

MARTIN WAIDELICH

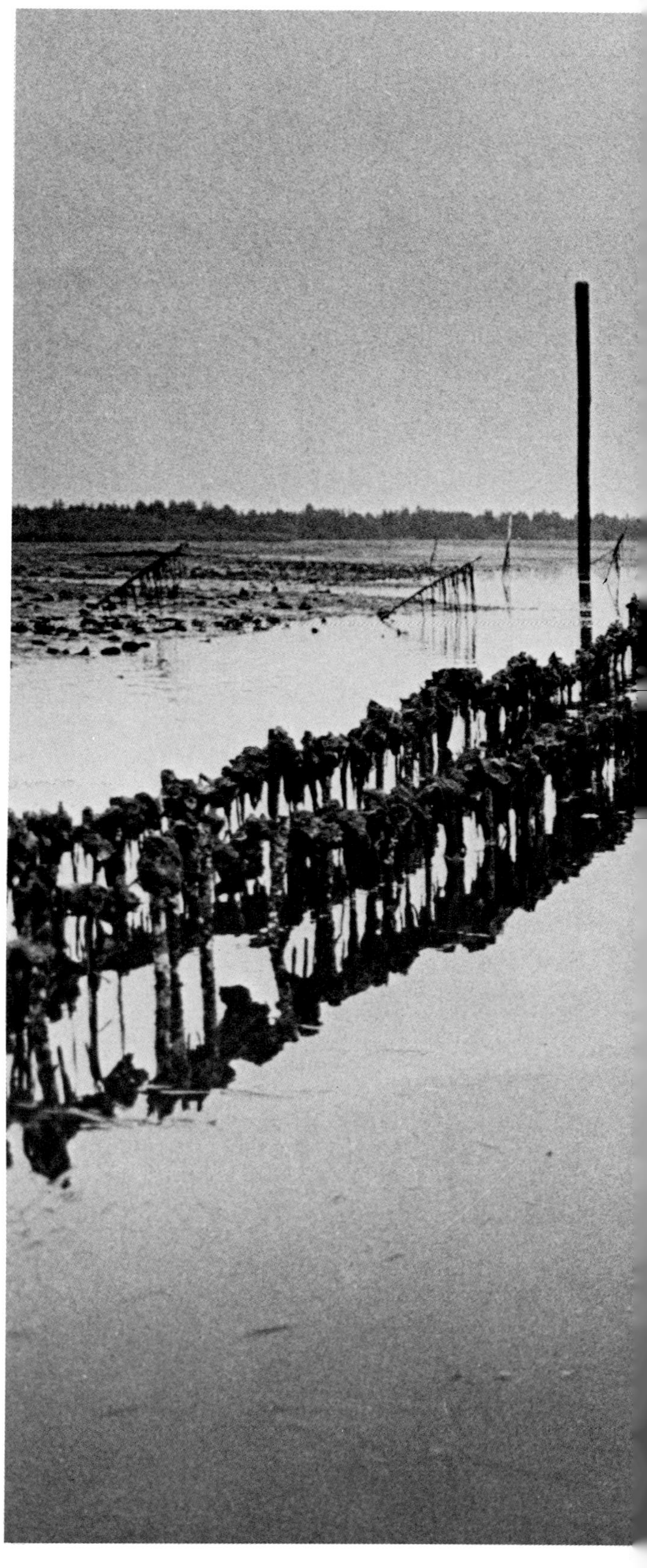

Top: *Grain barge on Columbia River.*

Above: *Intalco aluminum plant.*

Right: *Harvesting oysters.*

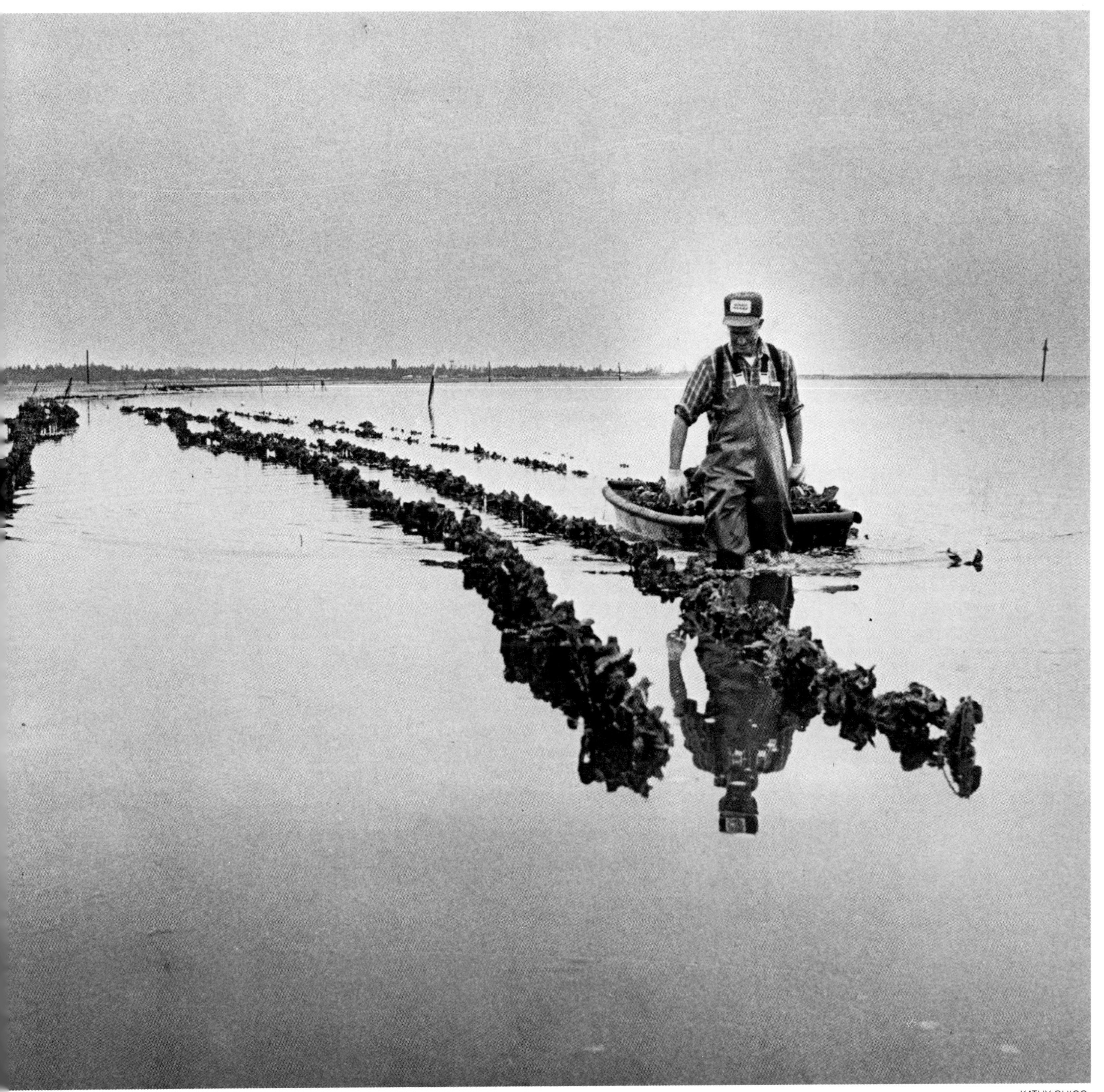

KATHY QUIGG

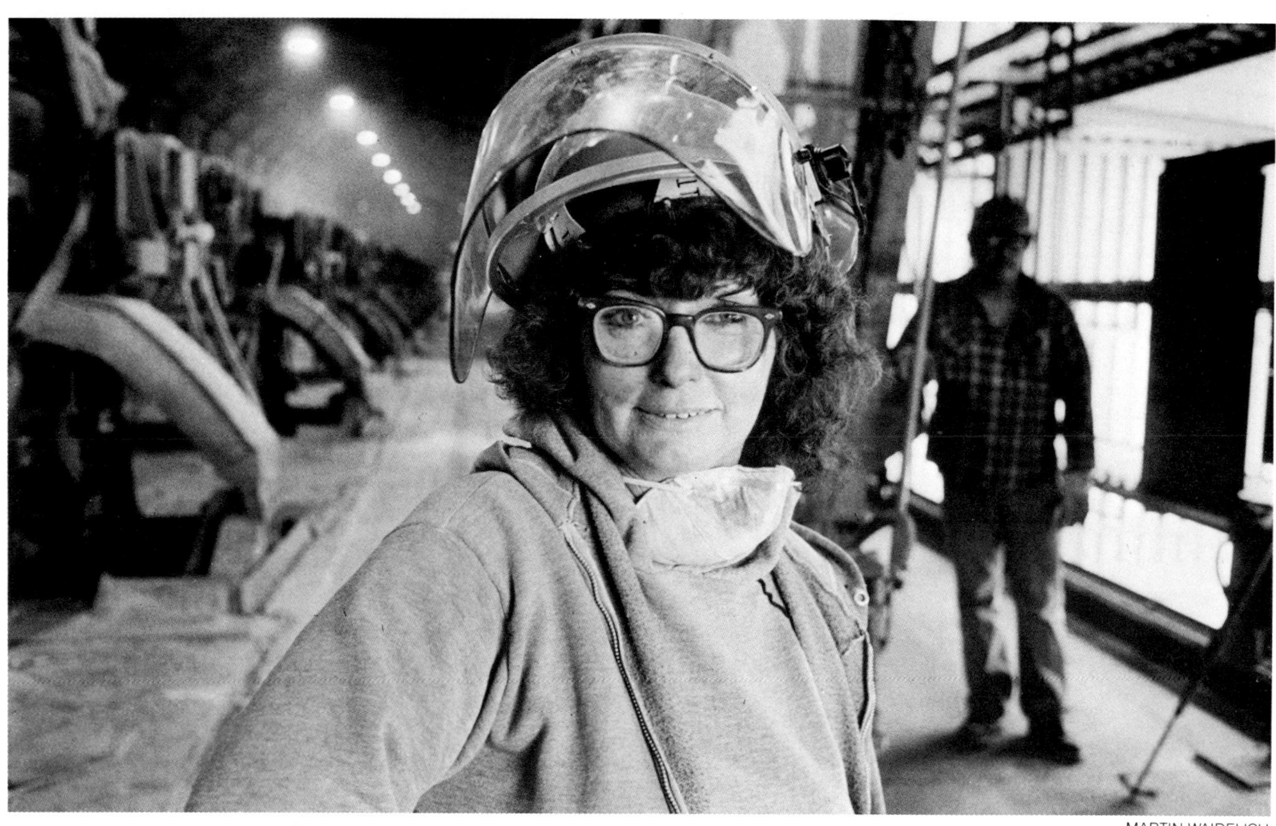

MARTIN WAIDELICH

Imogene Wilson, potline worker for Intalco in Bellingham.

City maintenance worker Dorothy Gile in Pioneer Square, Seattle.

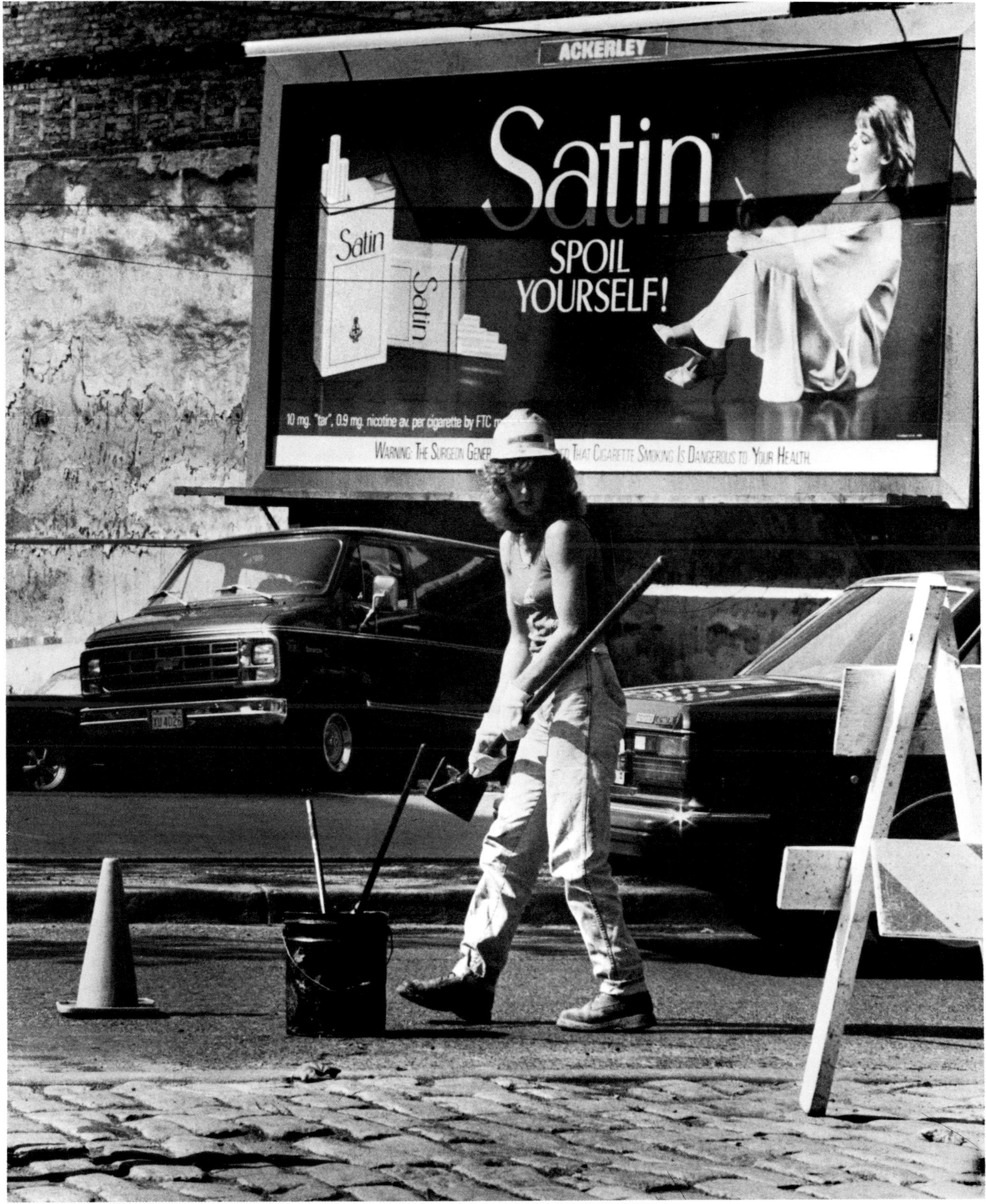

BRUCE CARROLL

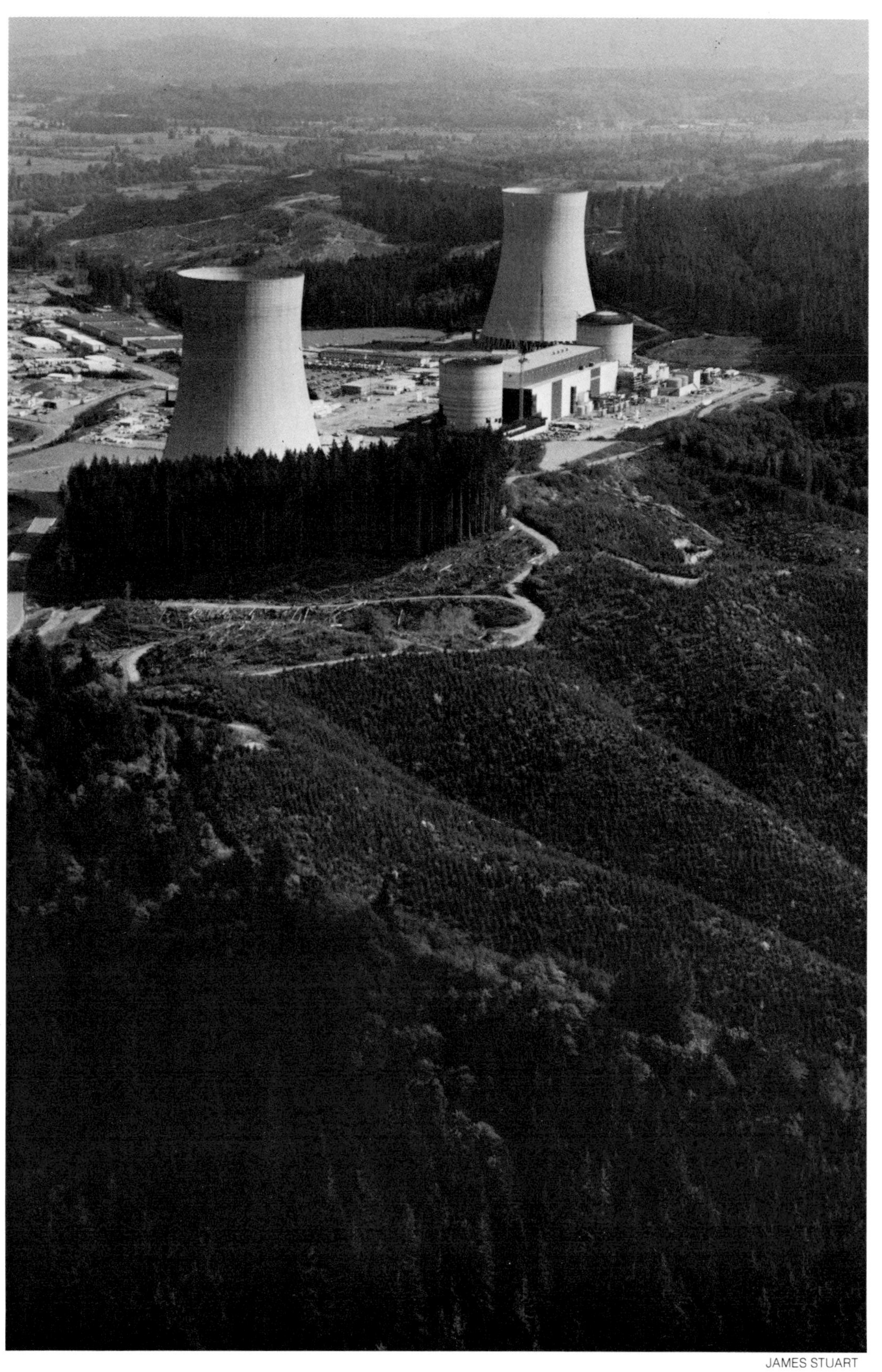

JAMES STUART

The Washington Public Power Supply System's two nuclear power plant projects at Satsop.

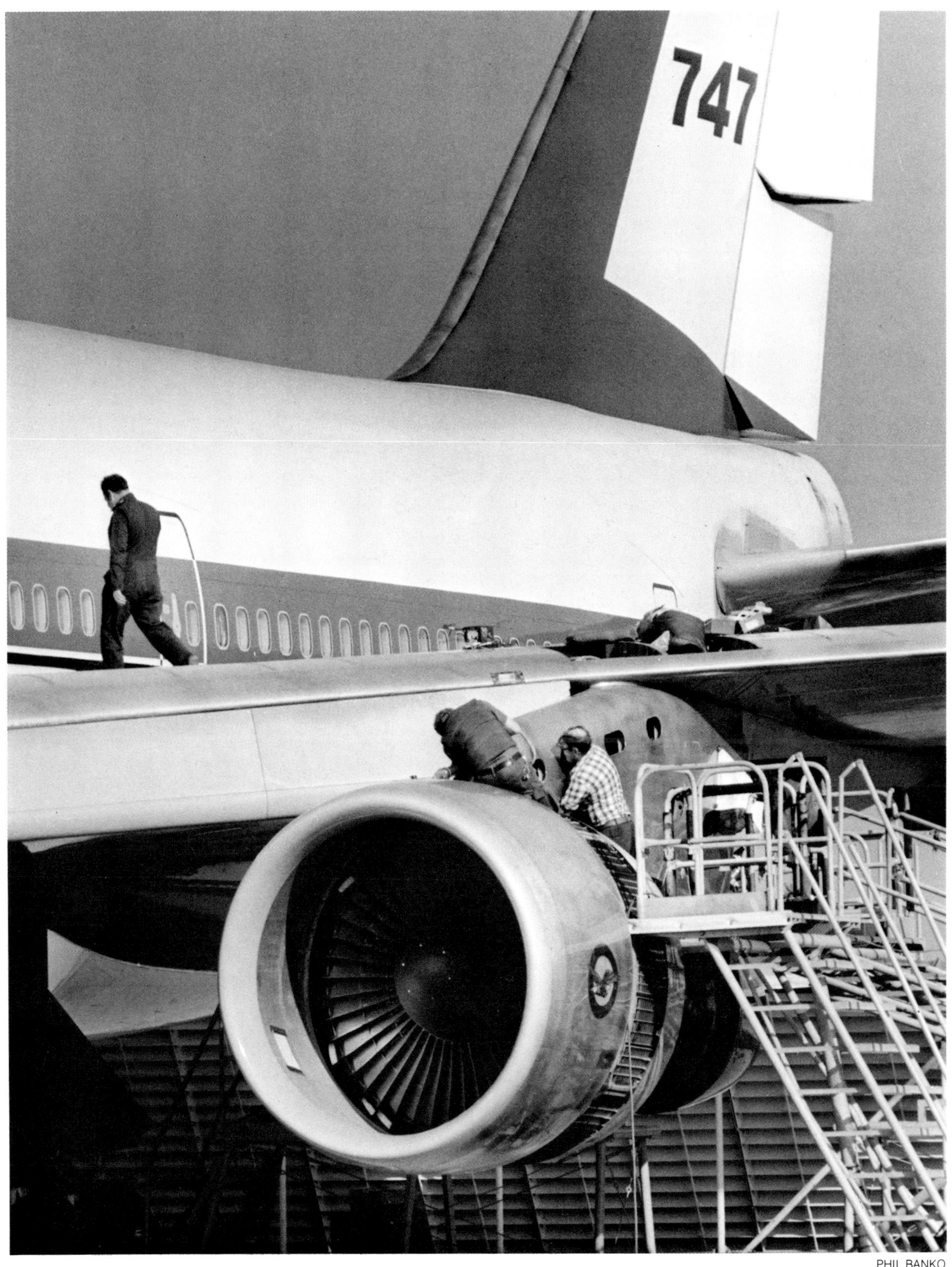

PHIL BANKO

Boeing workers check out the engine of a 747.

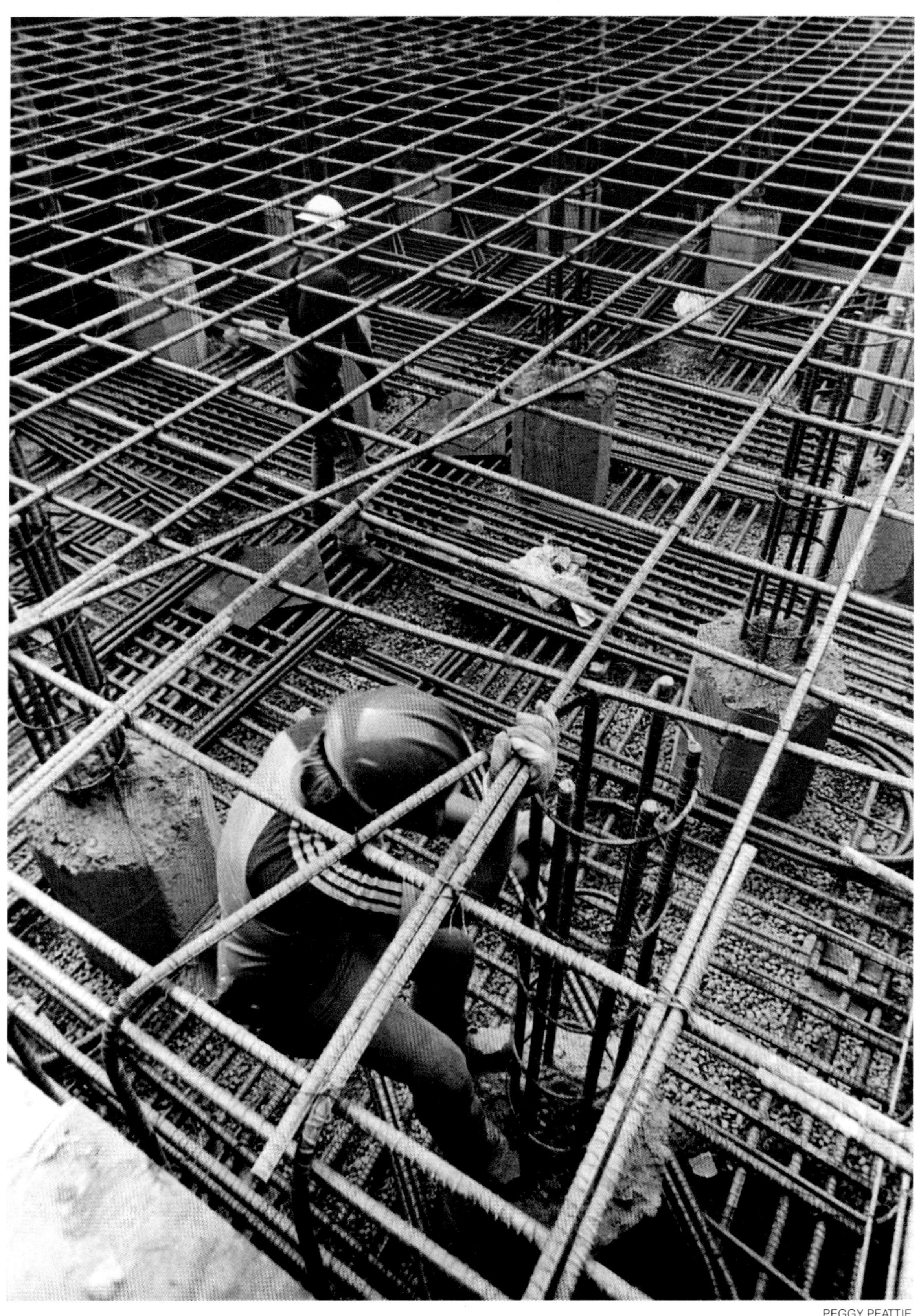

PEGGY PEATTIE

Installing metal rods for the concrete sections of the new high-rise West Seattle bridge across the Duwamish River.

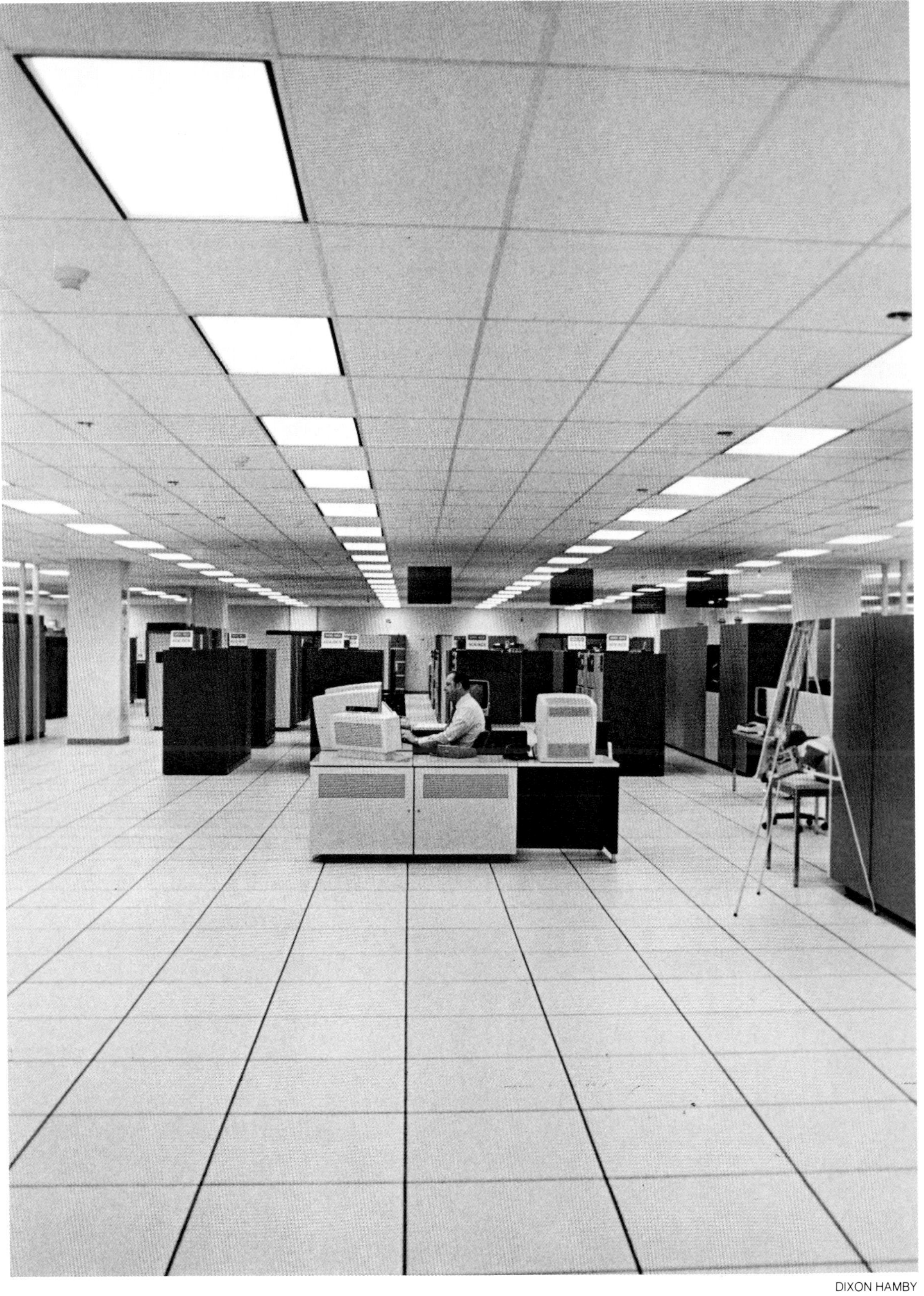

DIXON HAMBY

Boeing's computer services plant in Bellevue.

Following pages: *Brad Ver Hoef tanning at Bronzage Rapide in Seattle.*

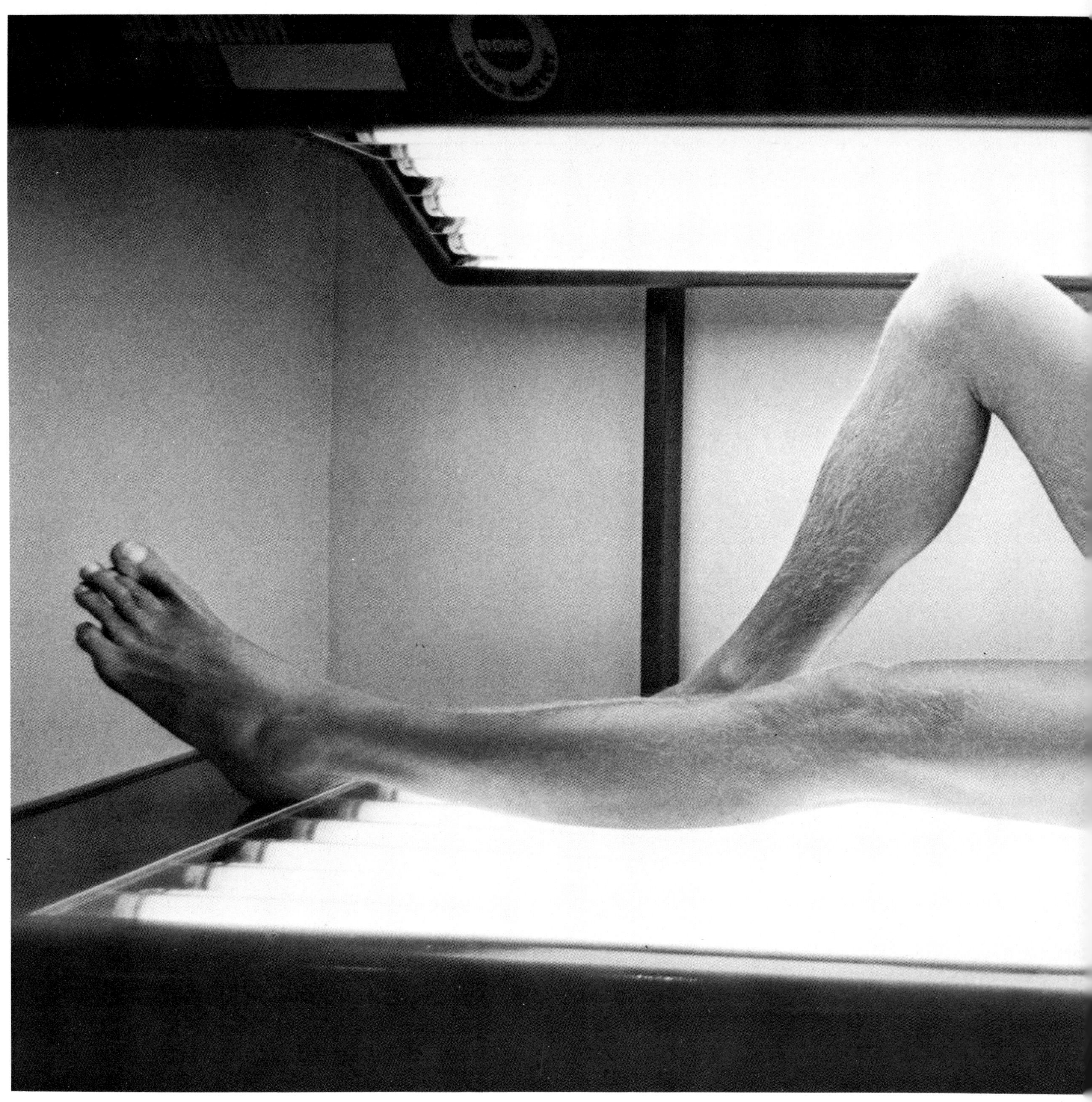

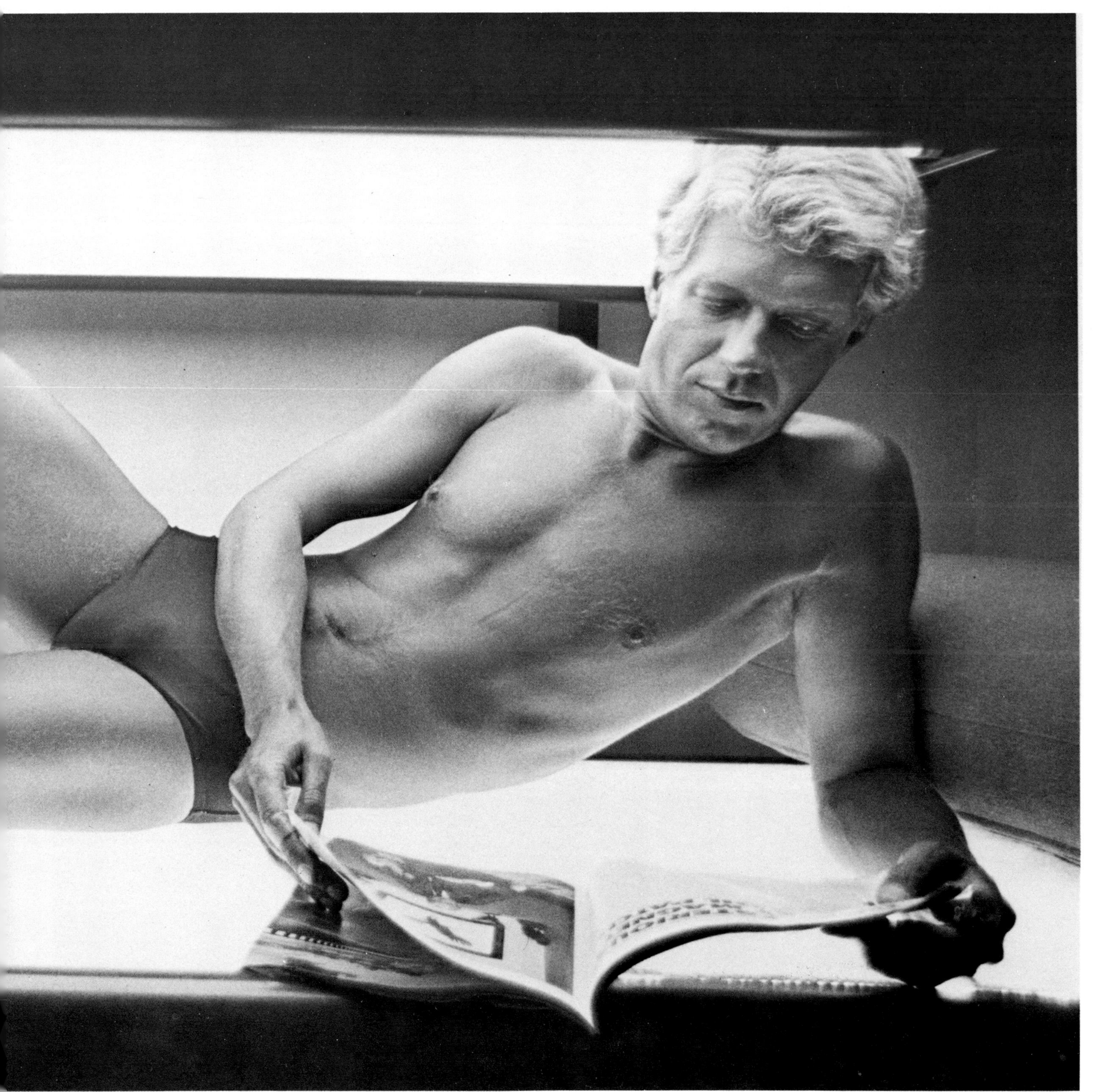

BENJAMIN BENSCHNEIDER

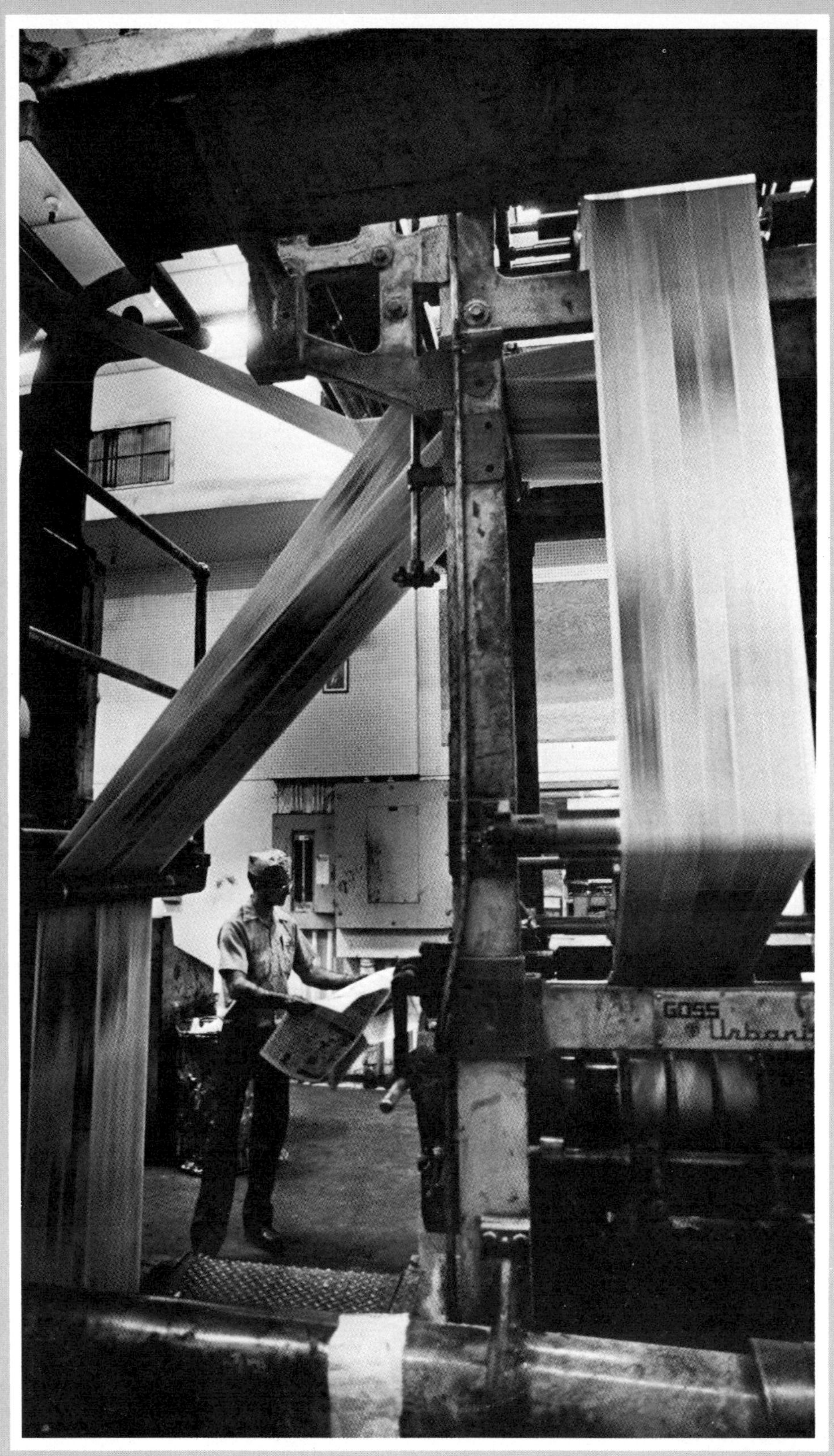

JIM BATES

Pressman Dick Tracy of Valley Newspapers checks the first edition of the Auburn Globe News.

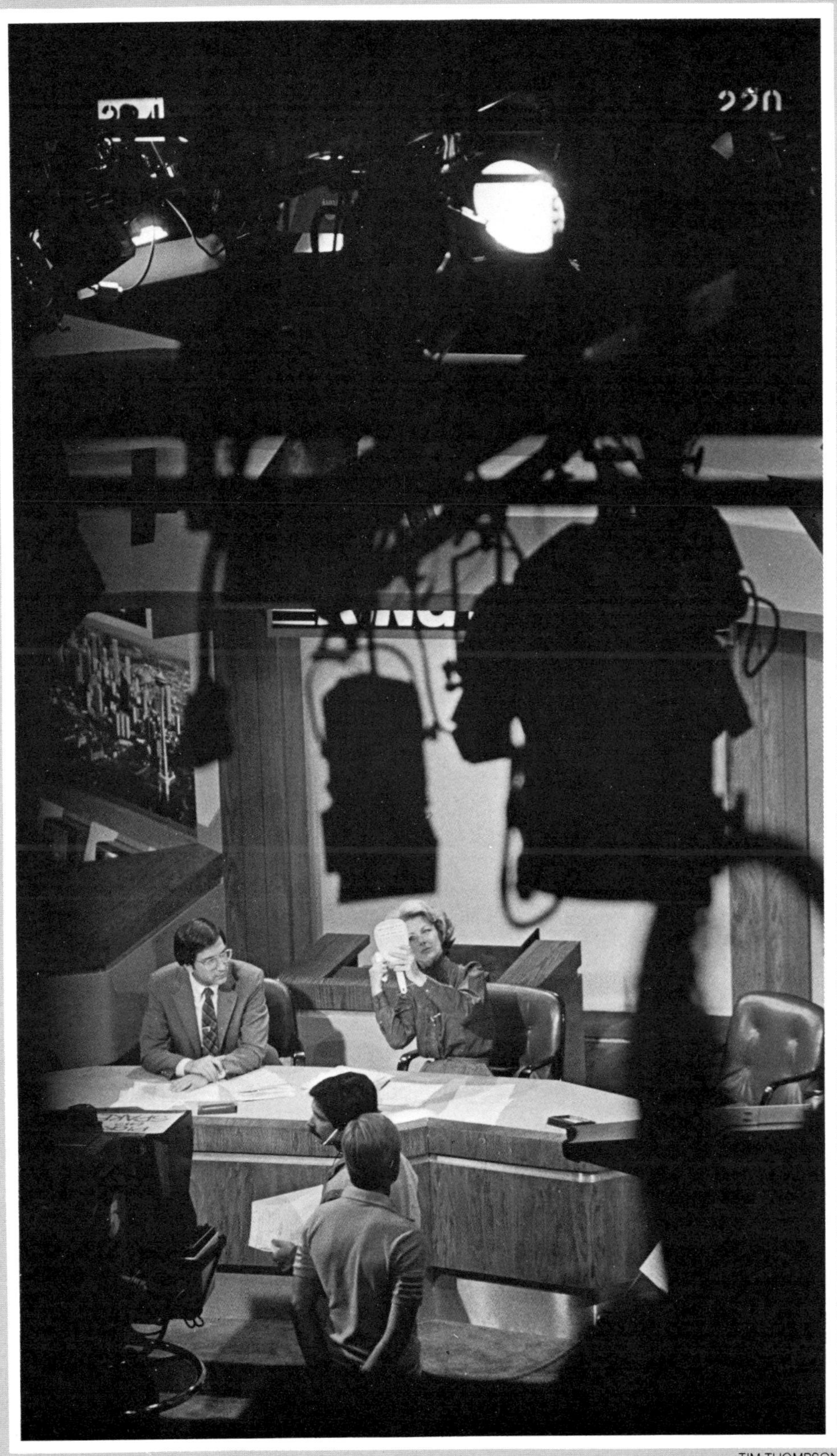

TIM THOMPSON

Getting ready for the 5 o'clock news, KING-TV's Aaron Brown and Jean Enersen.

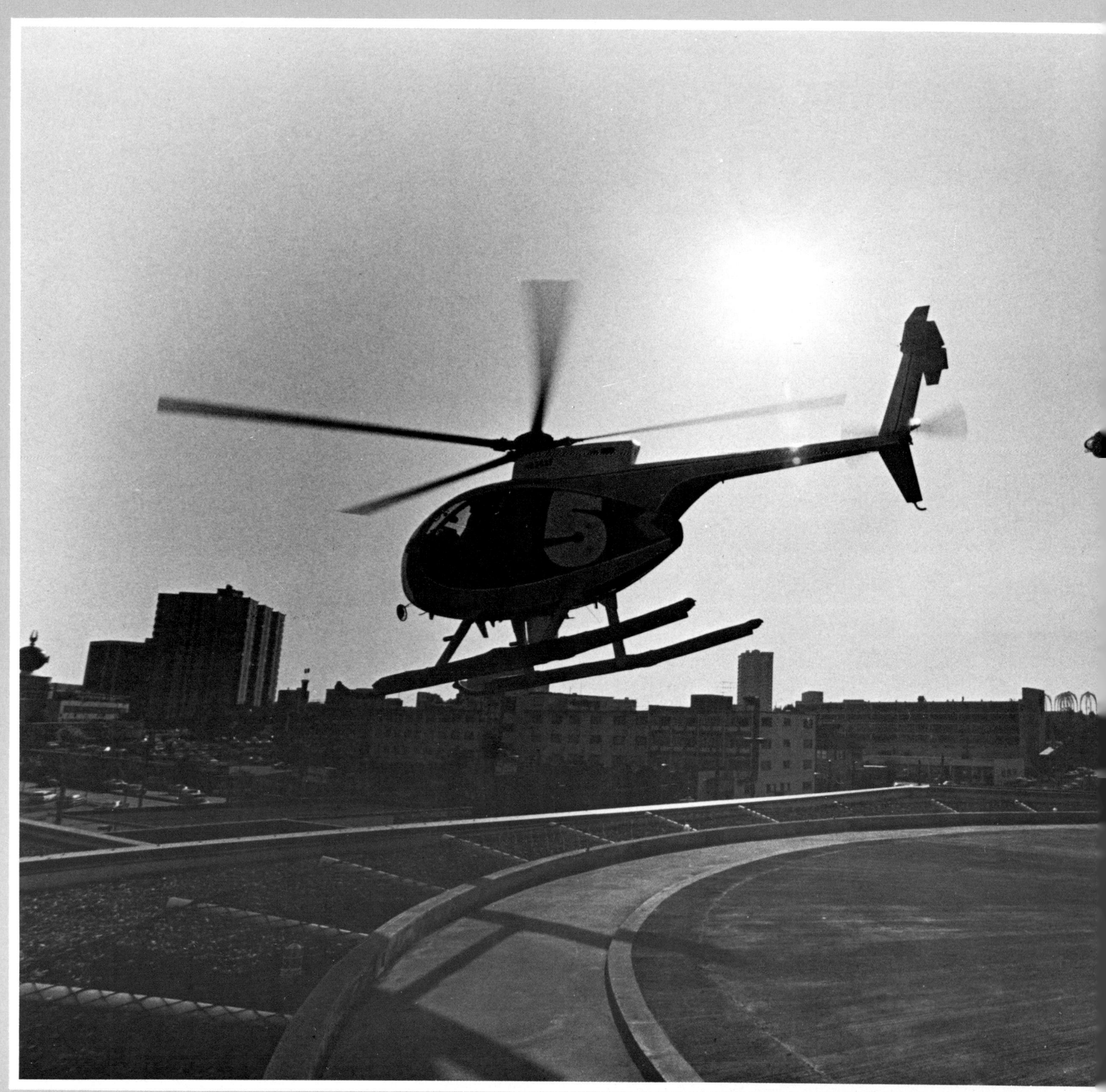

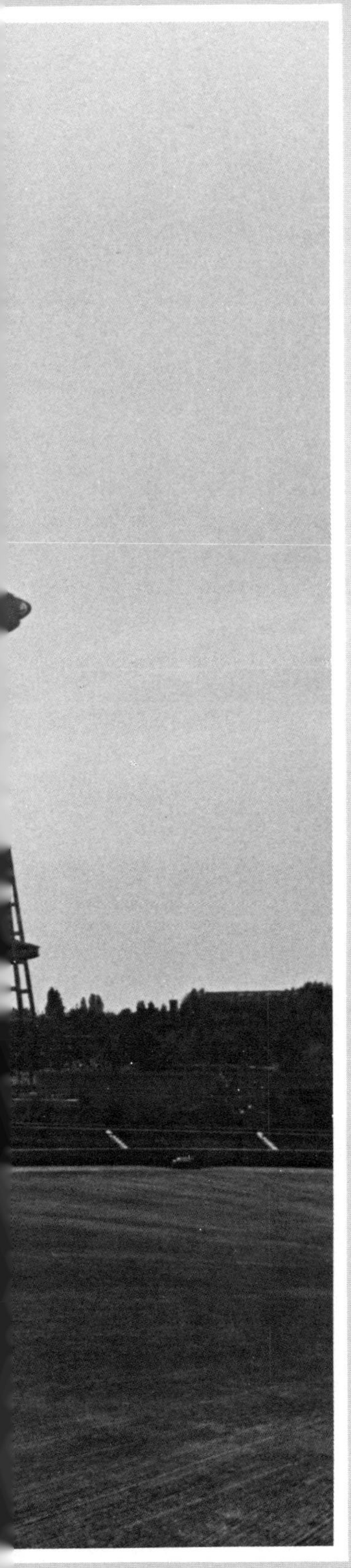

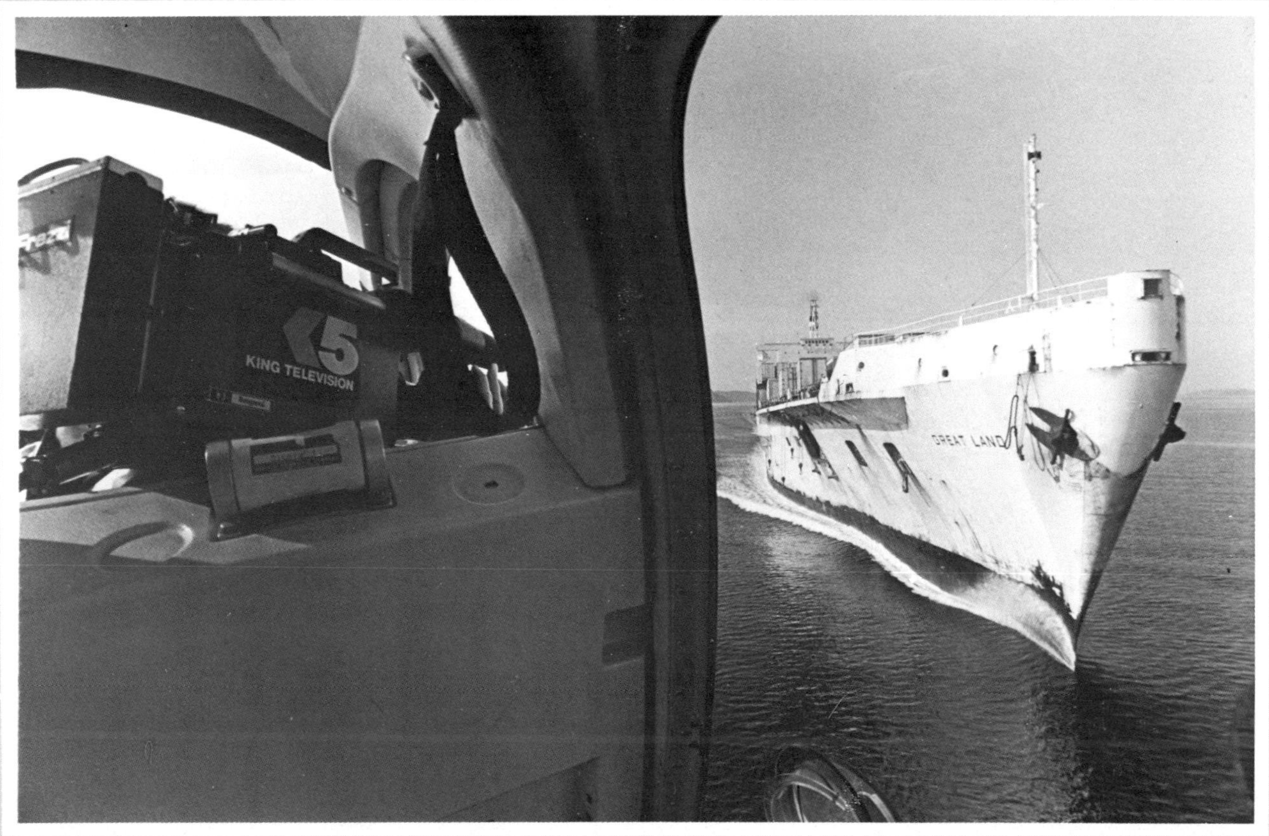

TV news helicopters race to beat the opposition.

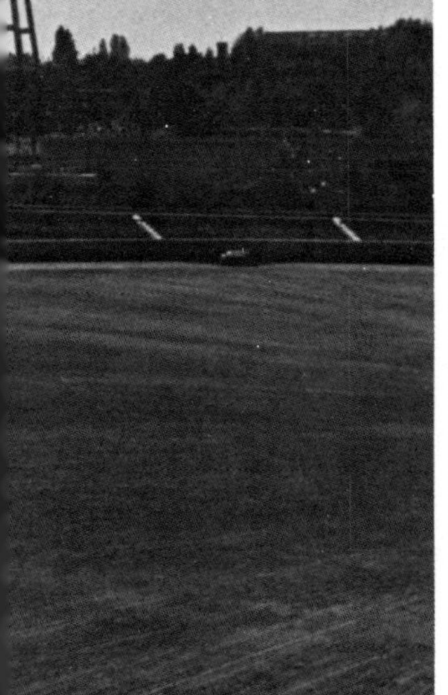

PHOTOS BY TIM THOMPSON

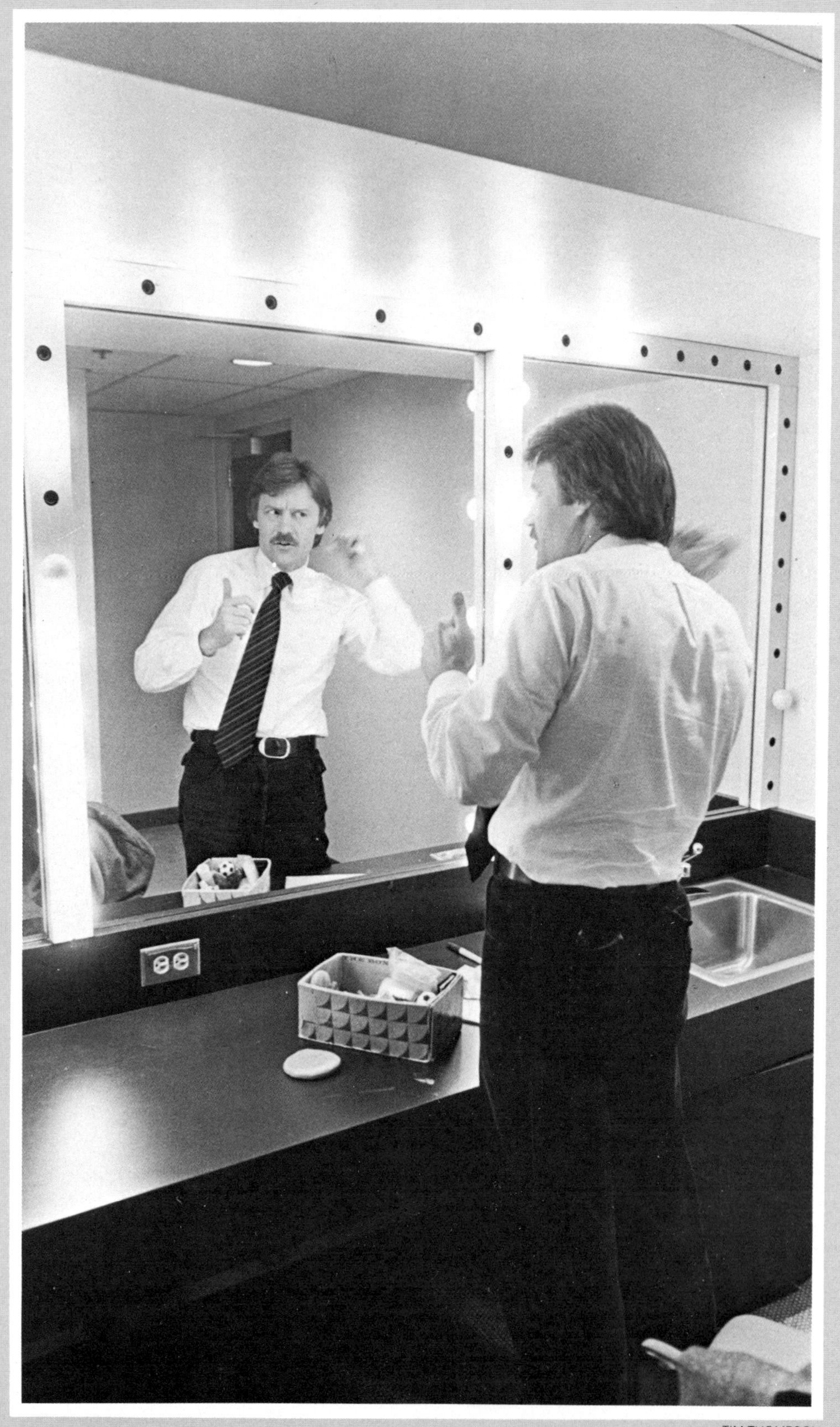

KING-TV's Mike James getting ready for "Top Story."

TIM THOMPSON

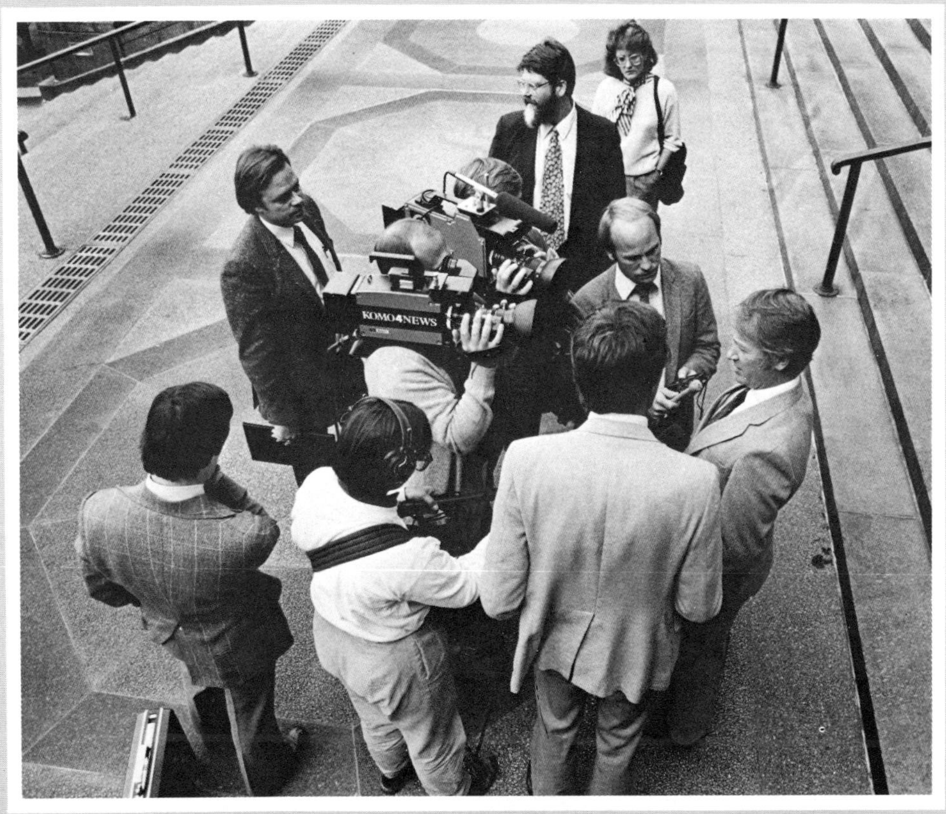

GILBERT ARIAS

Attorney Joe McCray takes questions.

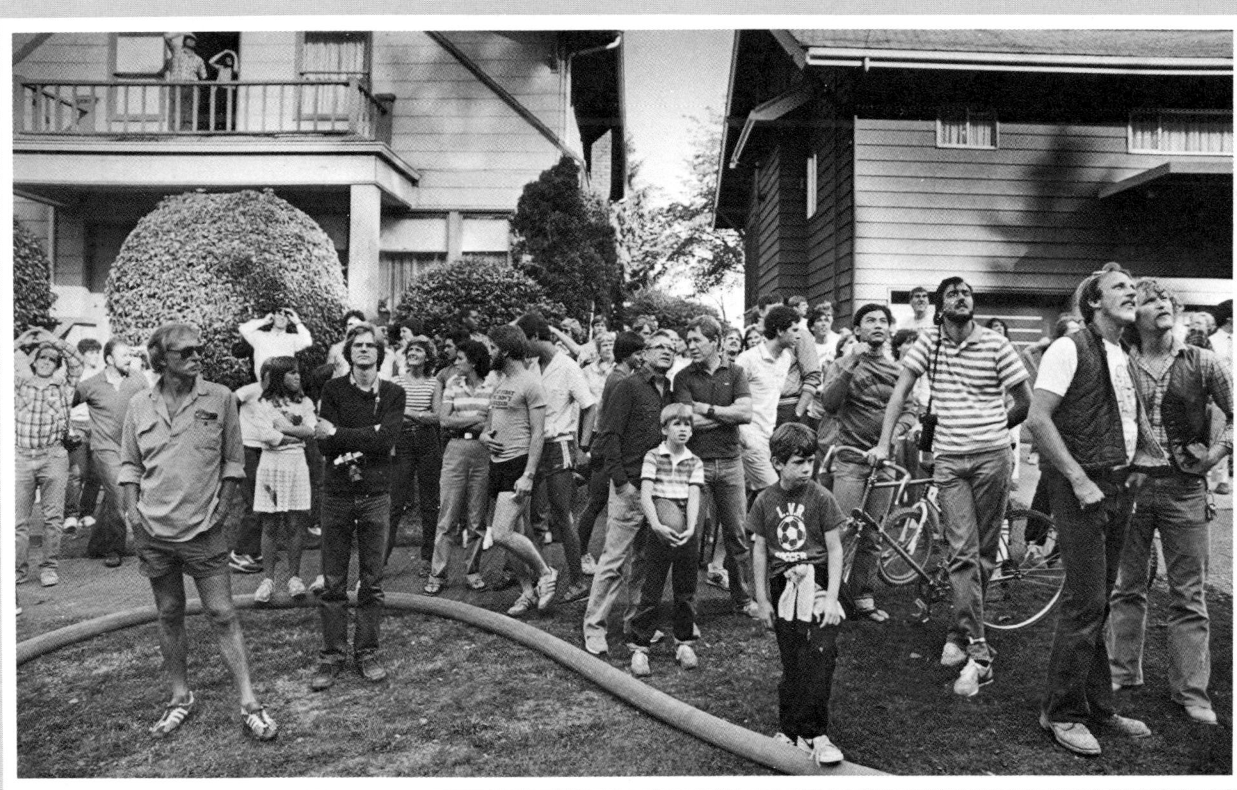

NATALIE FOBES

A house fire in Seattle's University District draws a crowd.

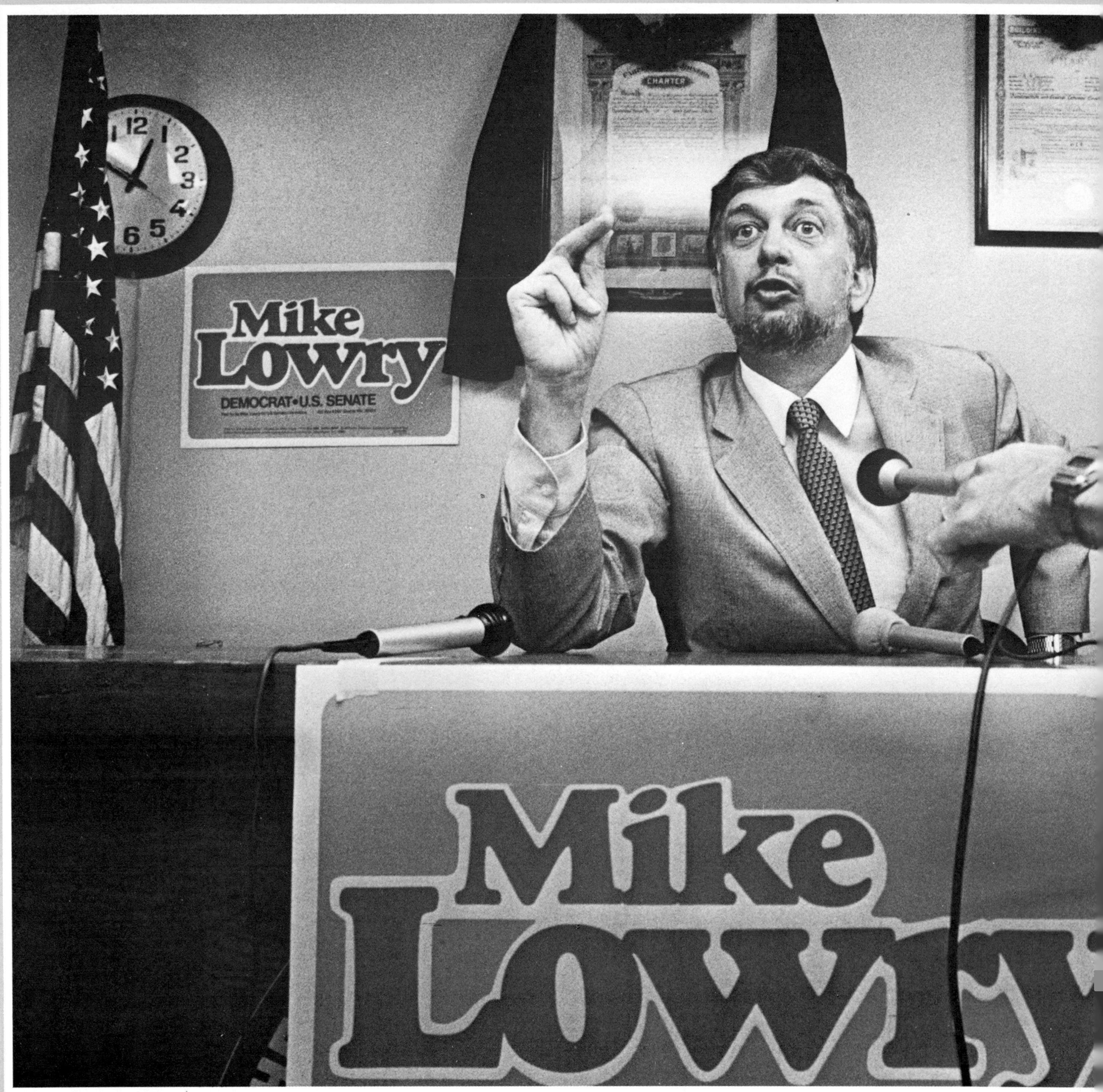
CHARTER
Mike
Lowry
DEMOCRAT•U.S. SENATE
Mike

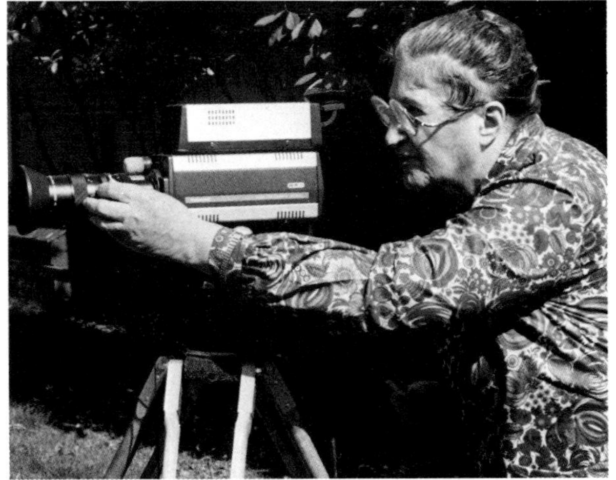

DOT STENNING

Virginia Brookbush filming for Community Access Television.

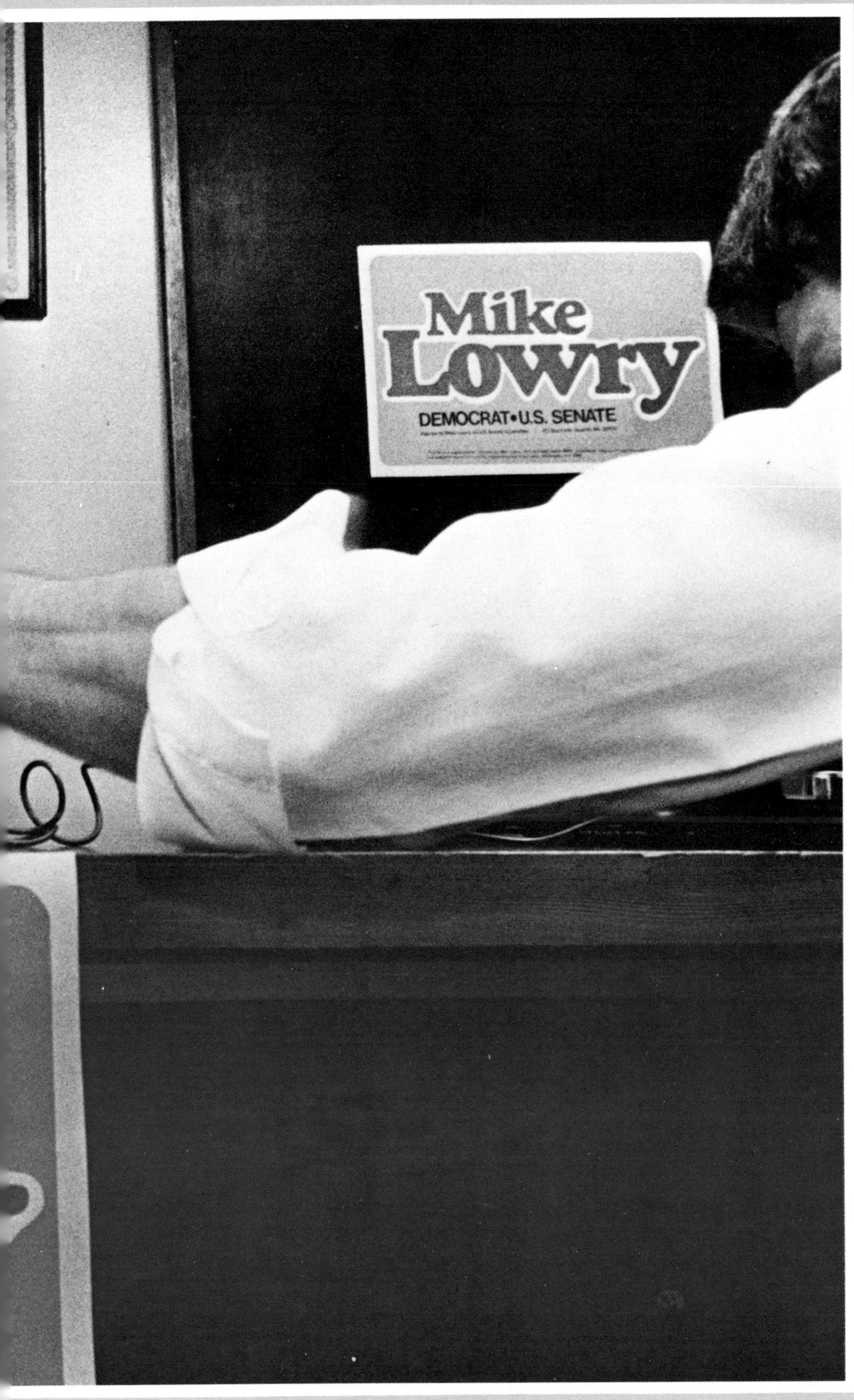

Congressman Mike Lowry campaigns for the U.S. Senate in the Carpenter's Union Hall in Yakima.

TOM TOTH

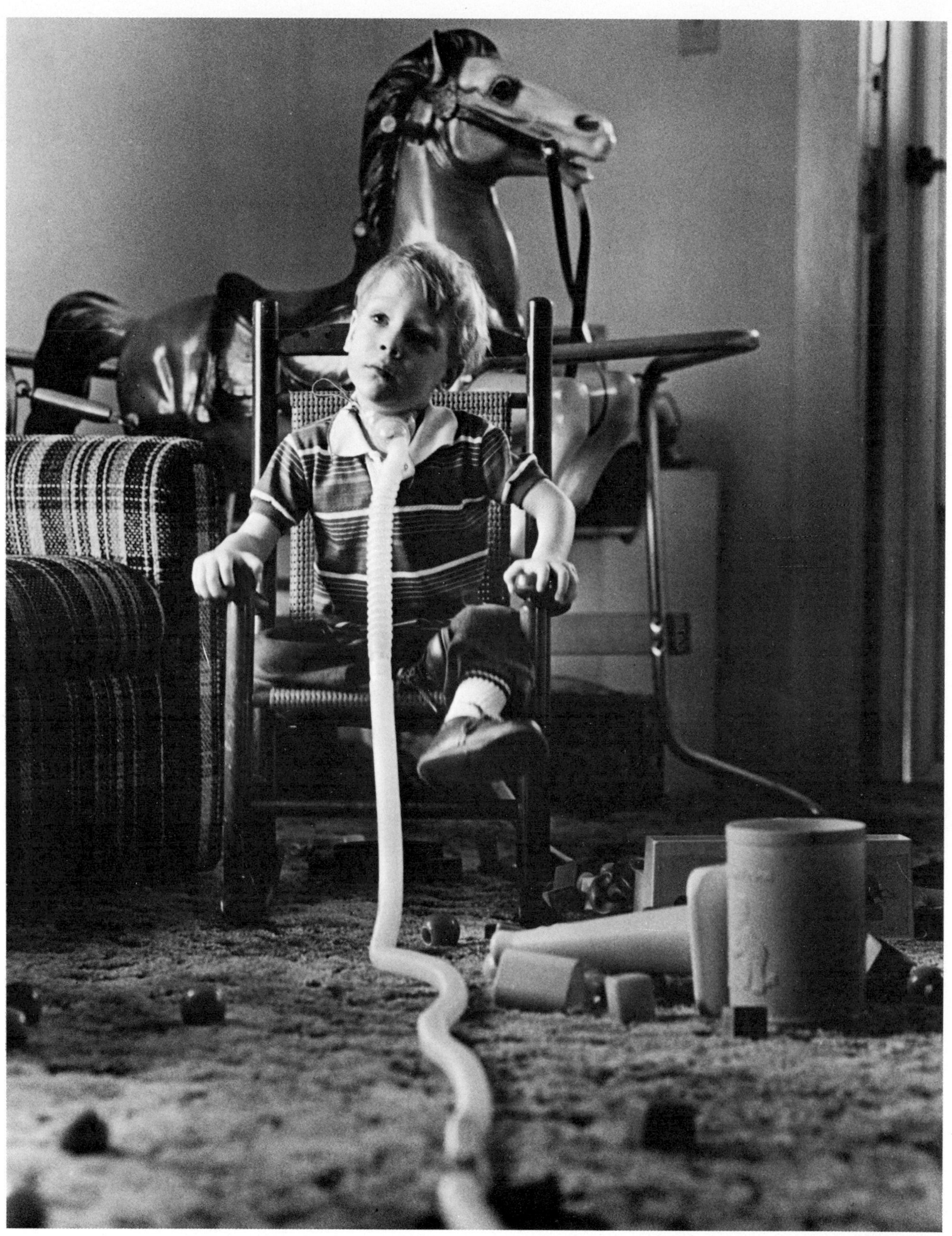

GRANT HALLER

Jonathan Long, 3½, with a chronic lung disease, sits listening to music.

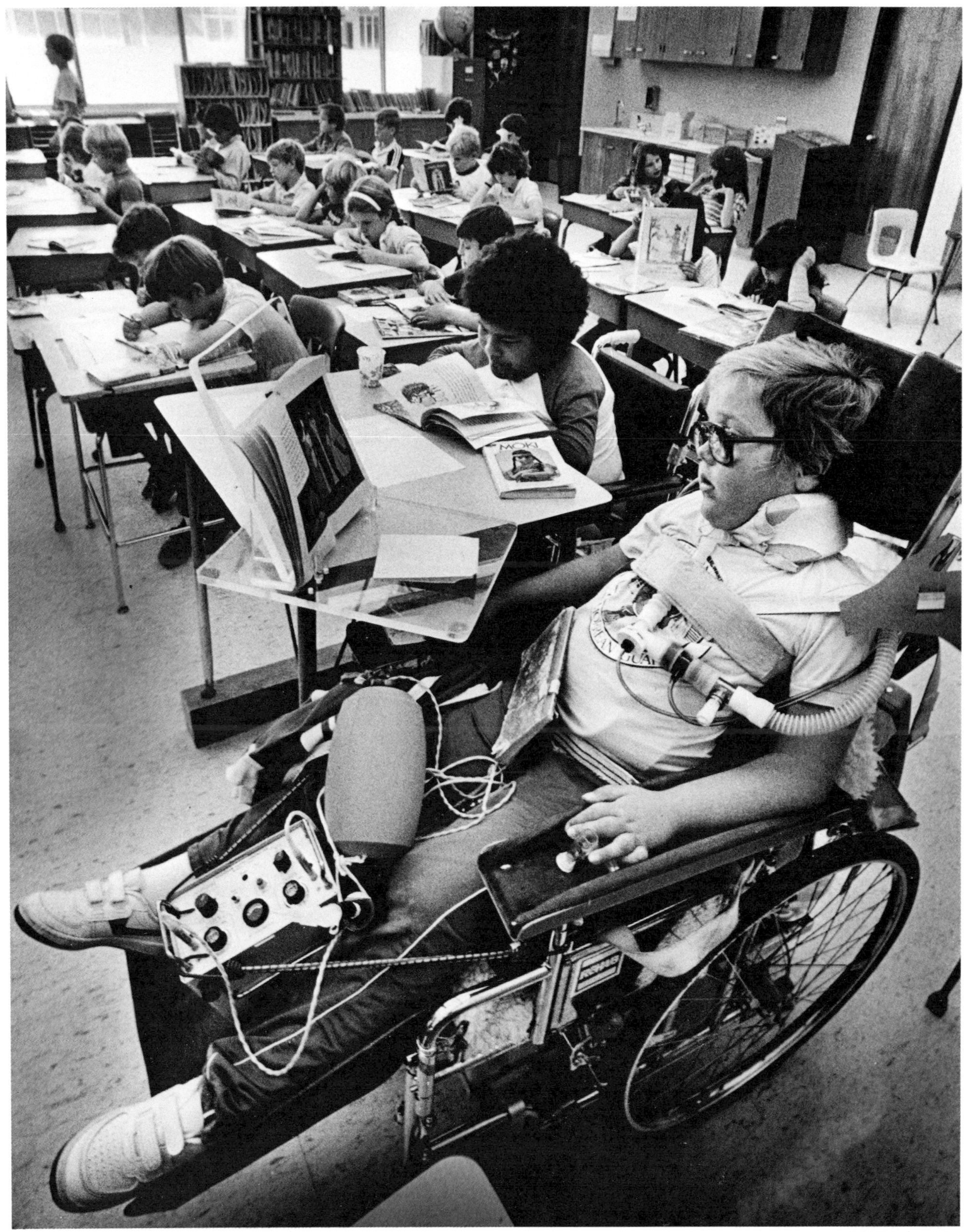

ROBERT HARBISON

Jimmy Akehurst studies with other fourth-graders in Steve Orbeck's class at Wildwood Elementary School, Federal Way.

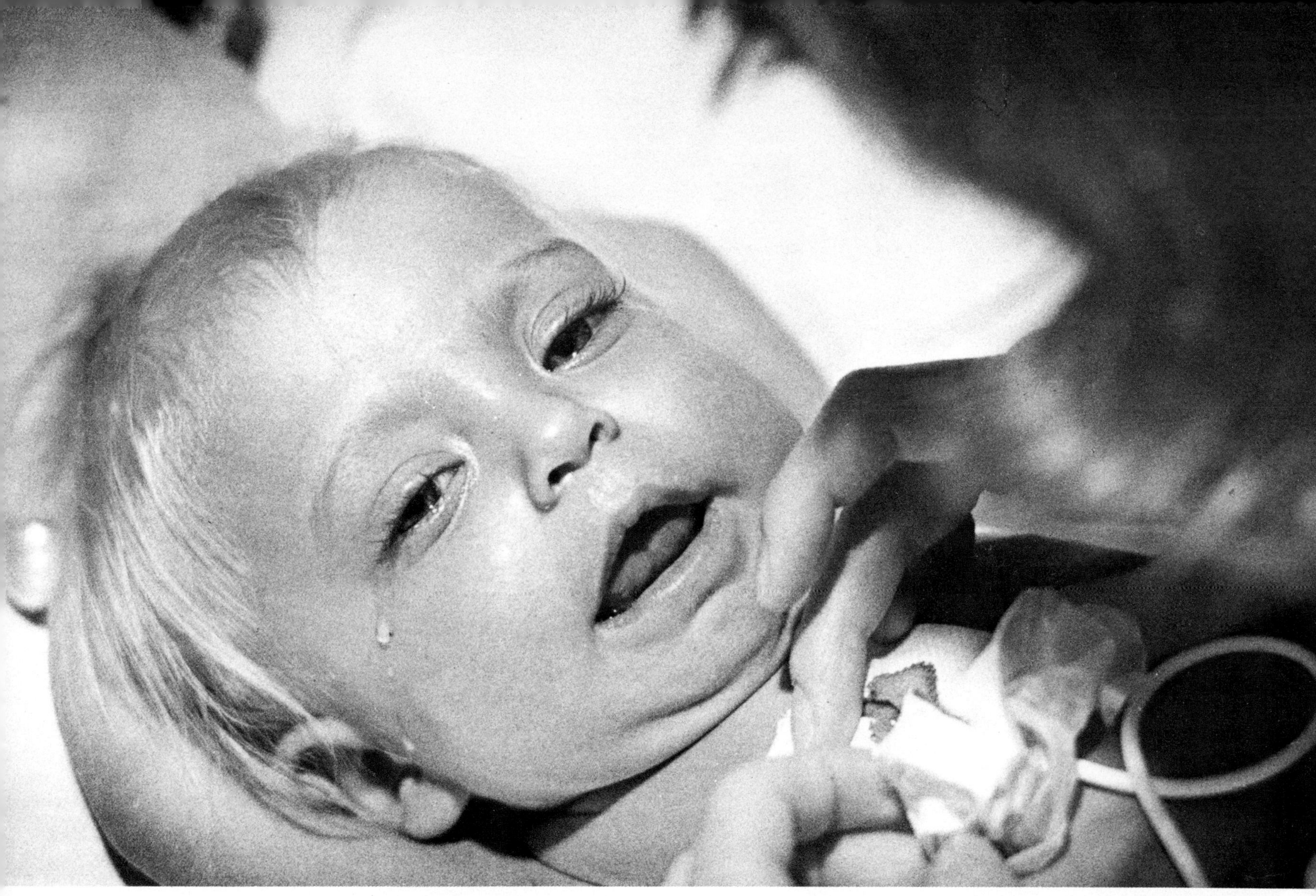

PHOTOS BY JENNIFER WERNER

Crystal Dietiker, 14 months old, with her mother Cheryl, awaits a donor for a kidney transplant at Seattle's Children's Orthopedic Hospital.

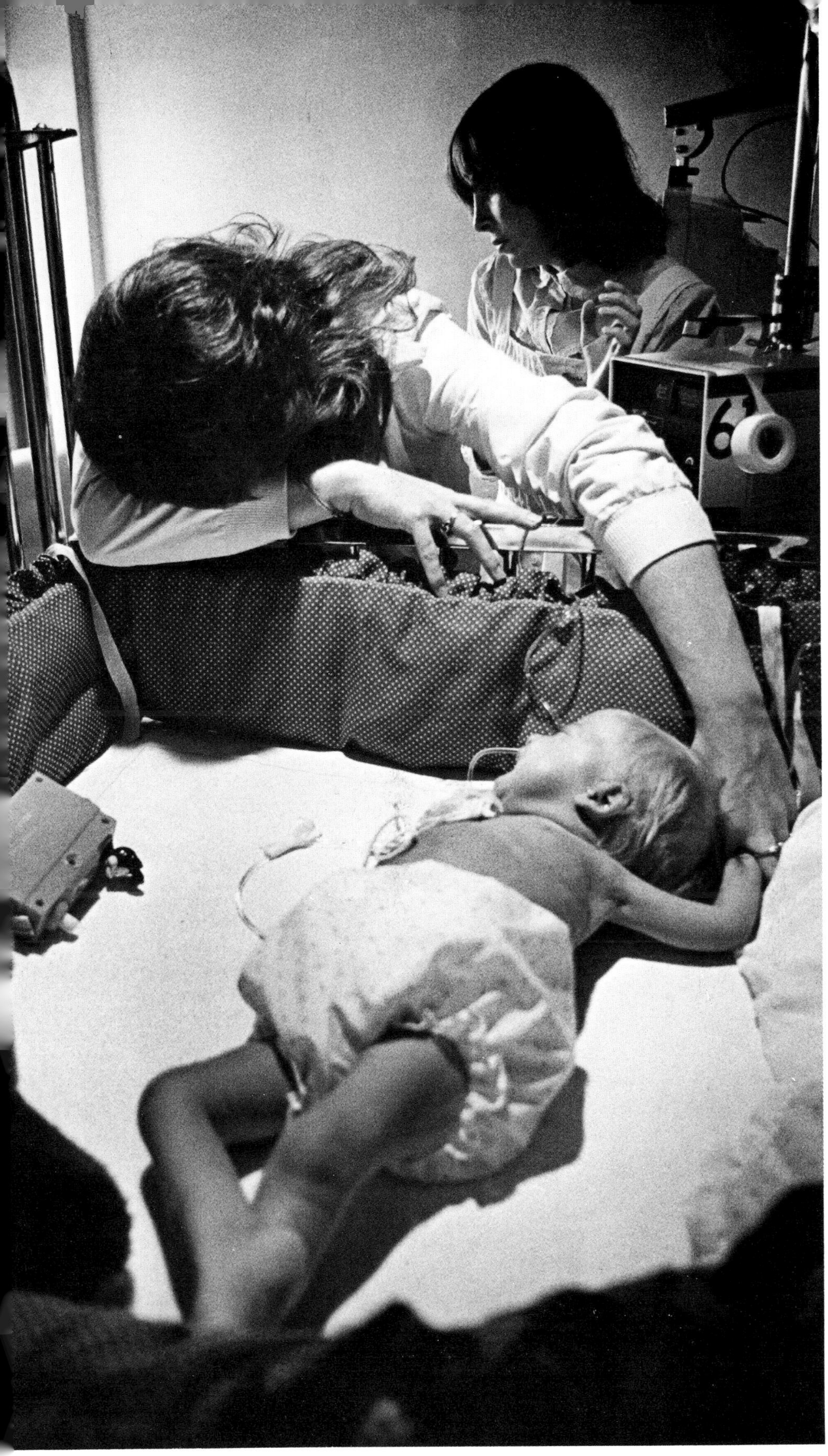

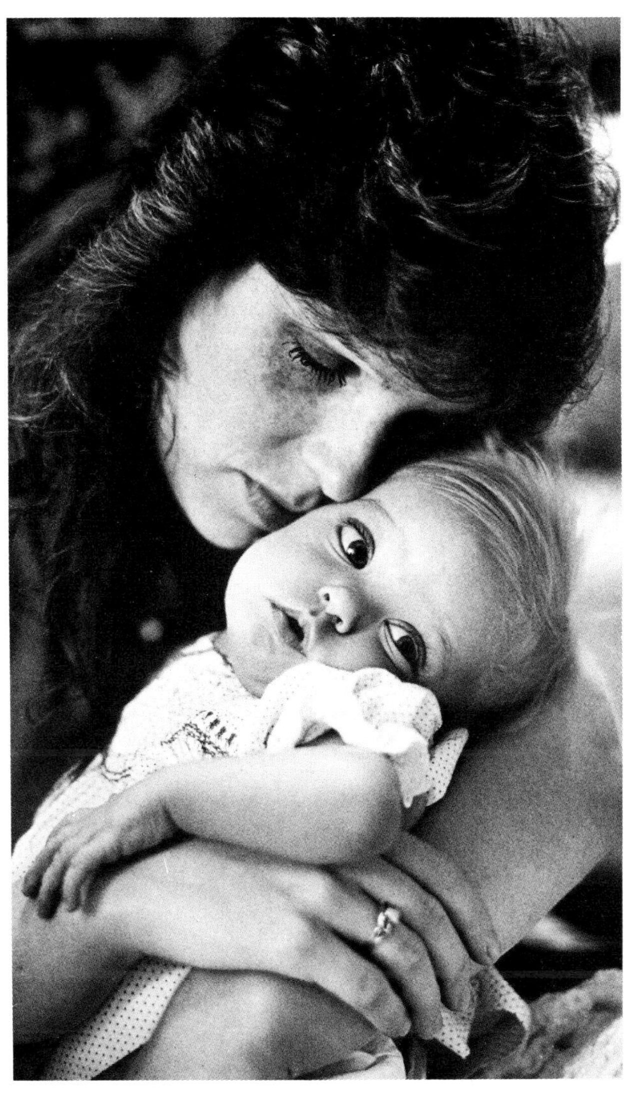

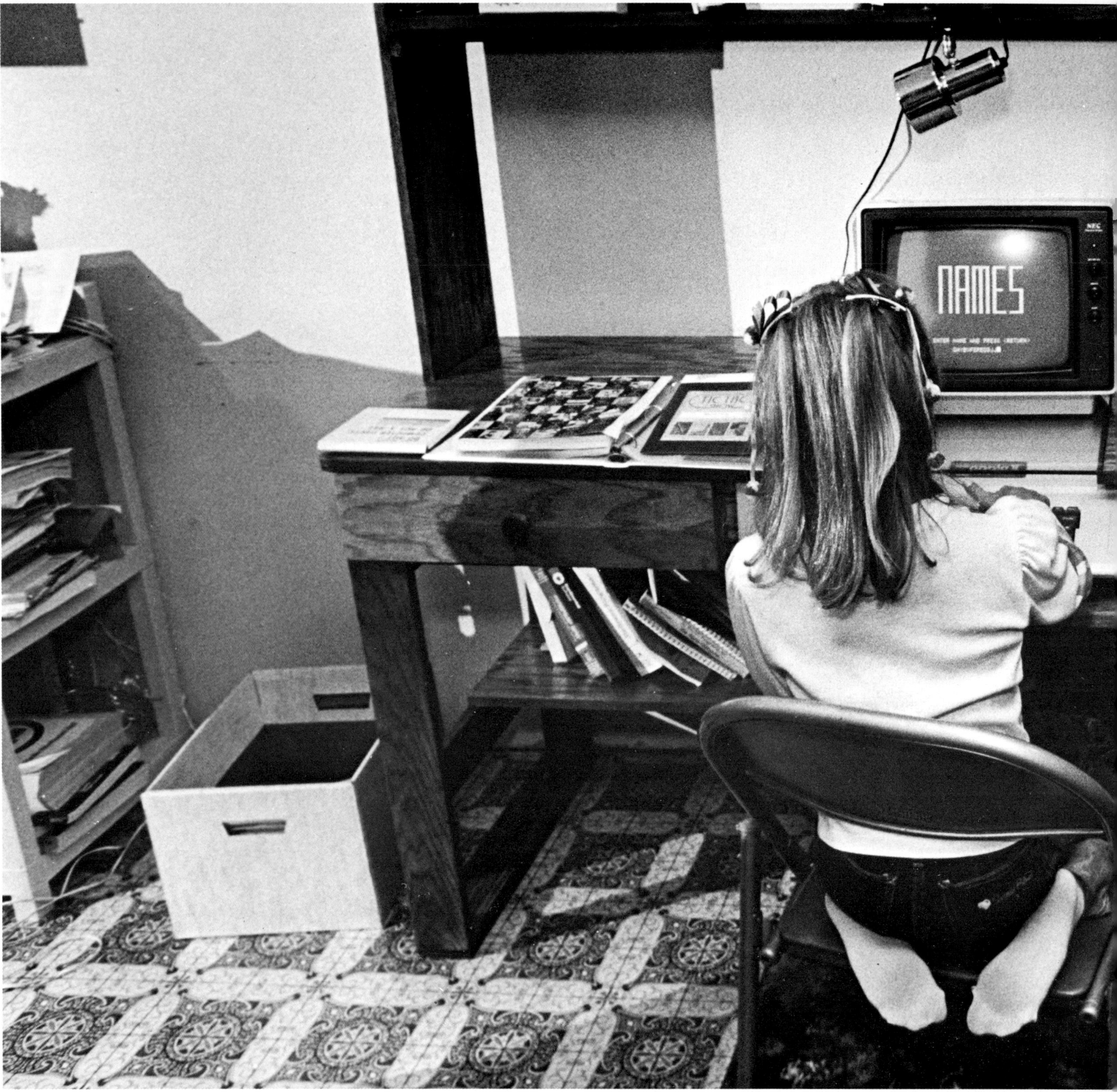
NAMES

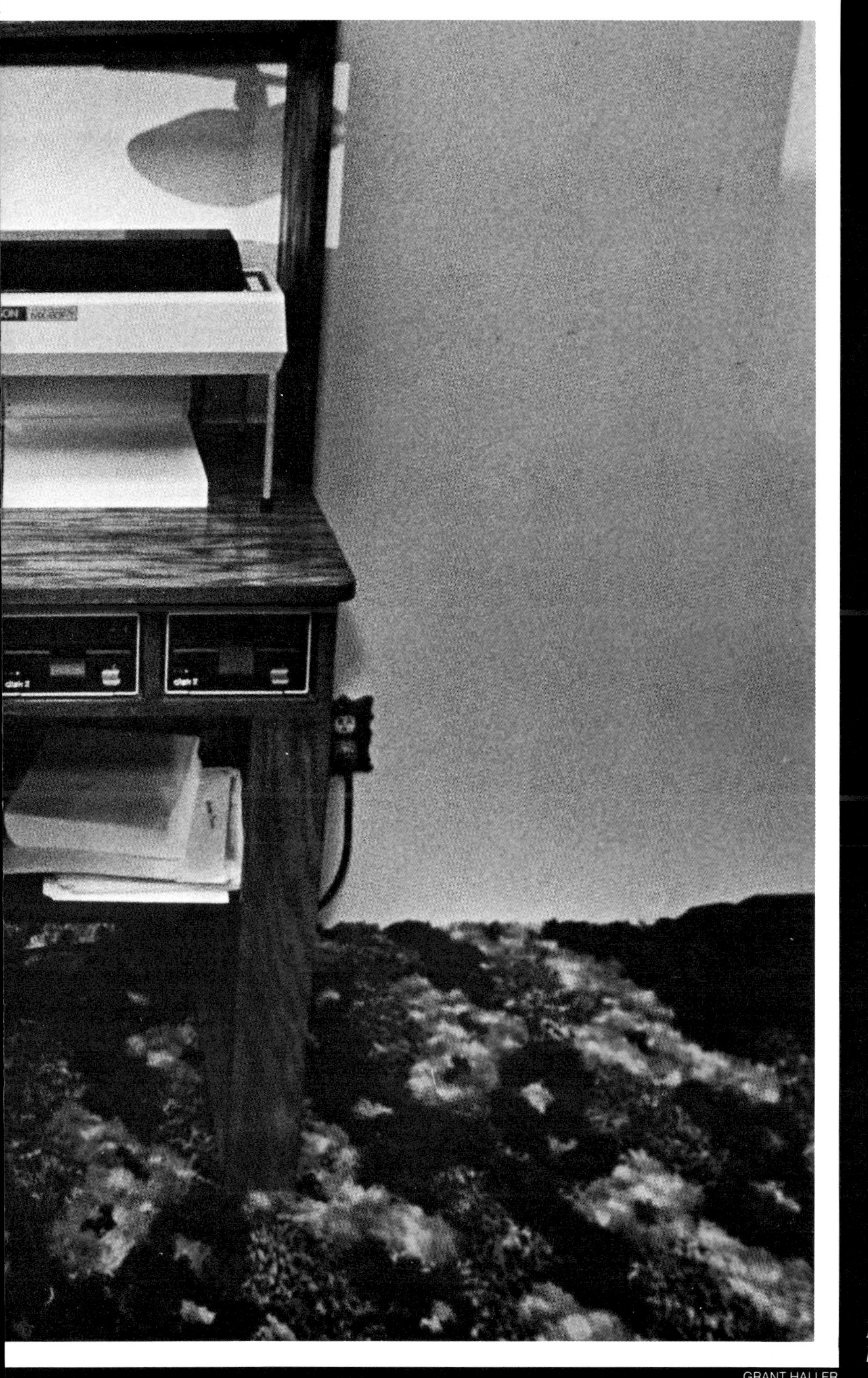

GRANT HALLER

Rory Haller, 6, plays a computer game in her Lynnwood home.

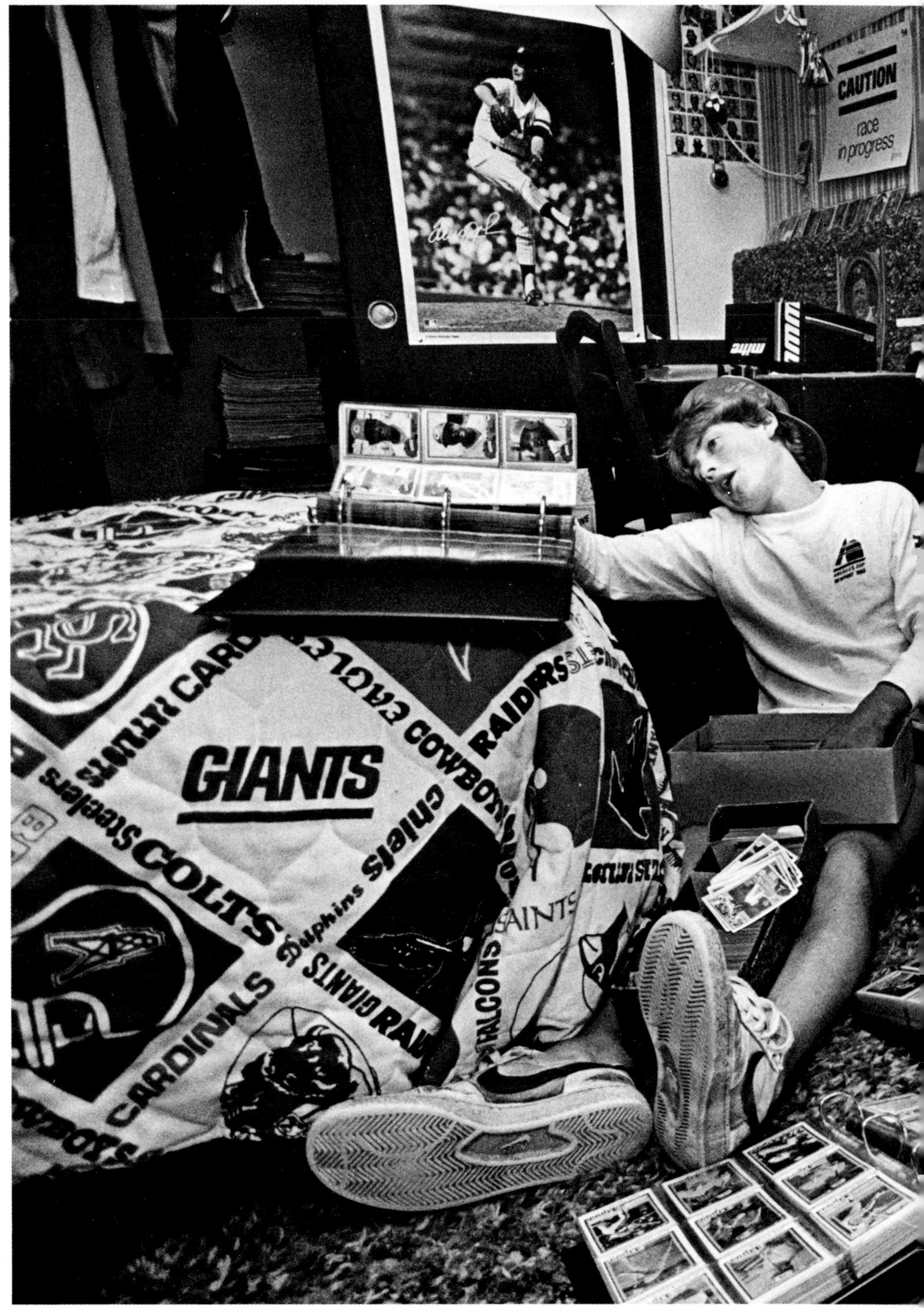
CAUTION
race
in progress
GIANTS
COLTS
CARDINALS
Steelers
chiefs
Dolphins
COWBOYS
RAIDERS
SAINTS
FALCONS
mite

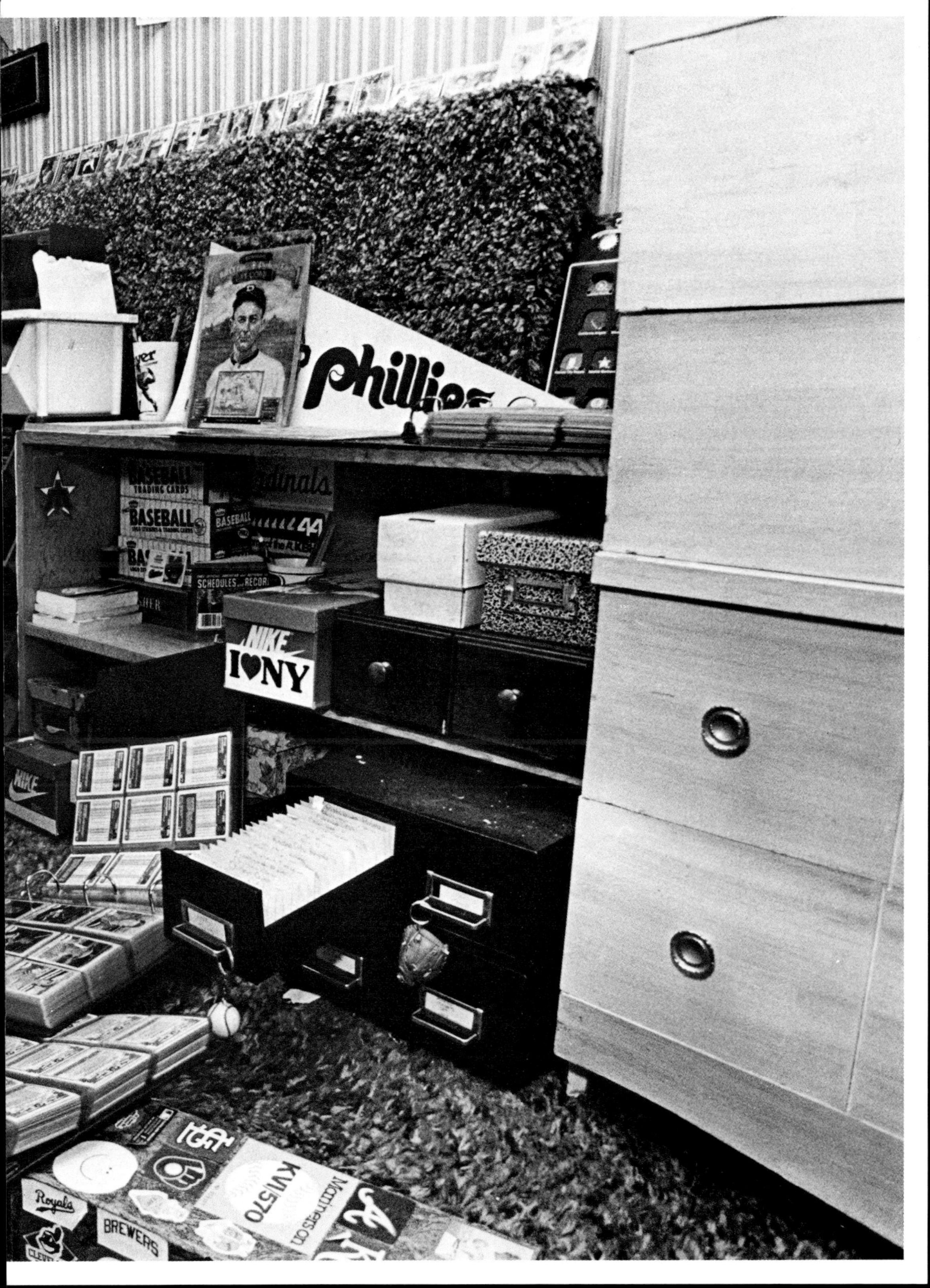

GRANT HALLER

Fourteen-year-old Patrick Haller has 11,000 baseball cards, and his favorite player is Pete Rose.

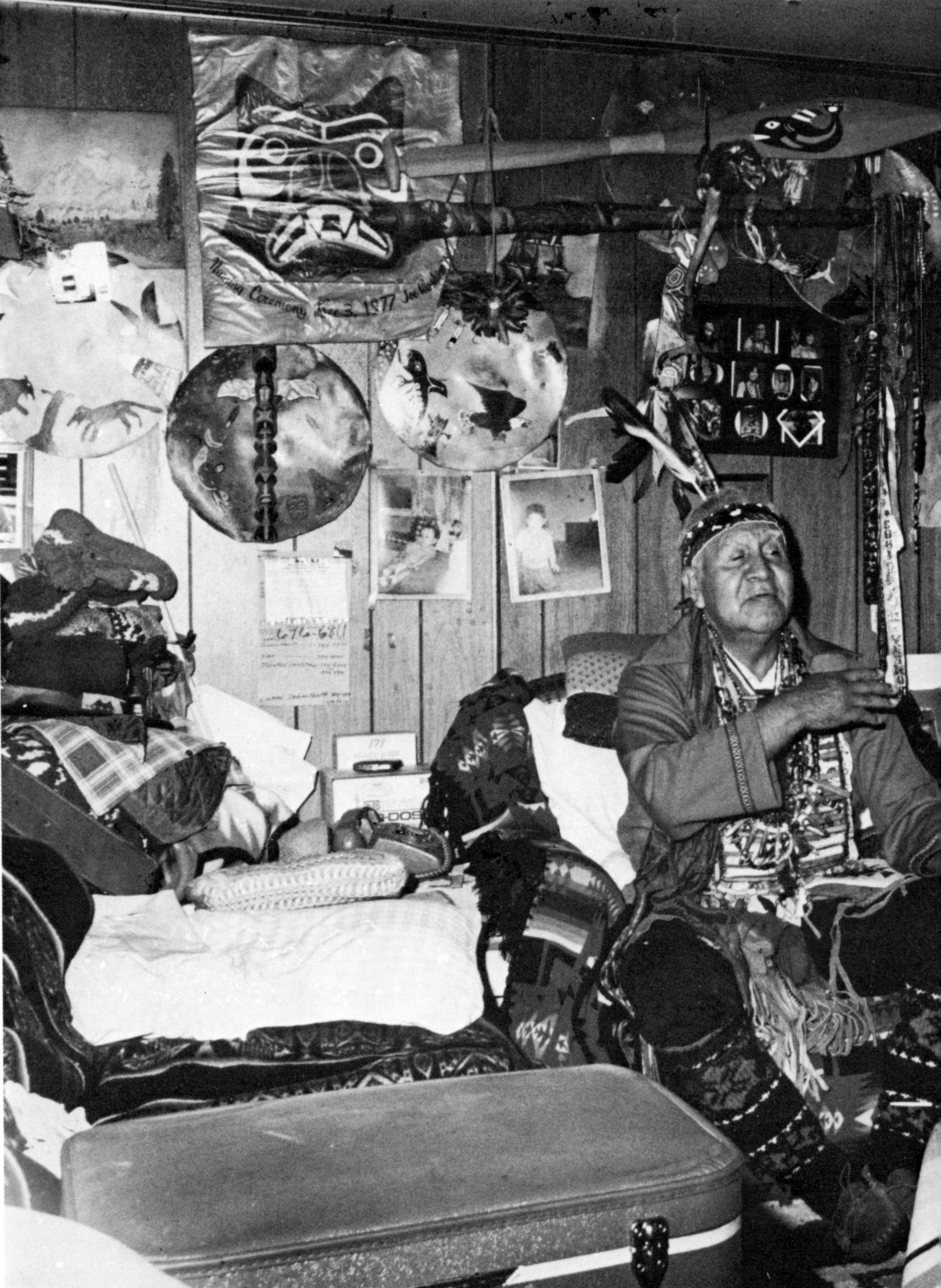
Ceremony 1977
676-6811

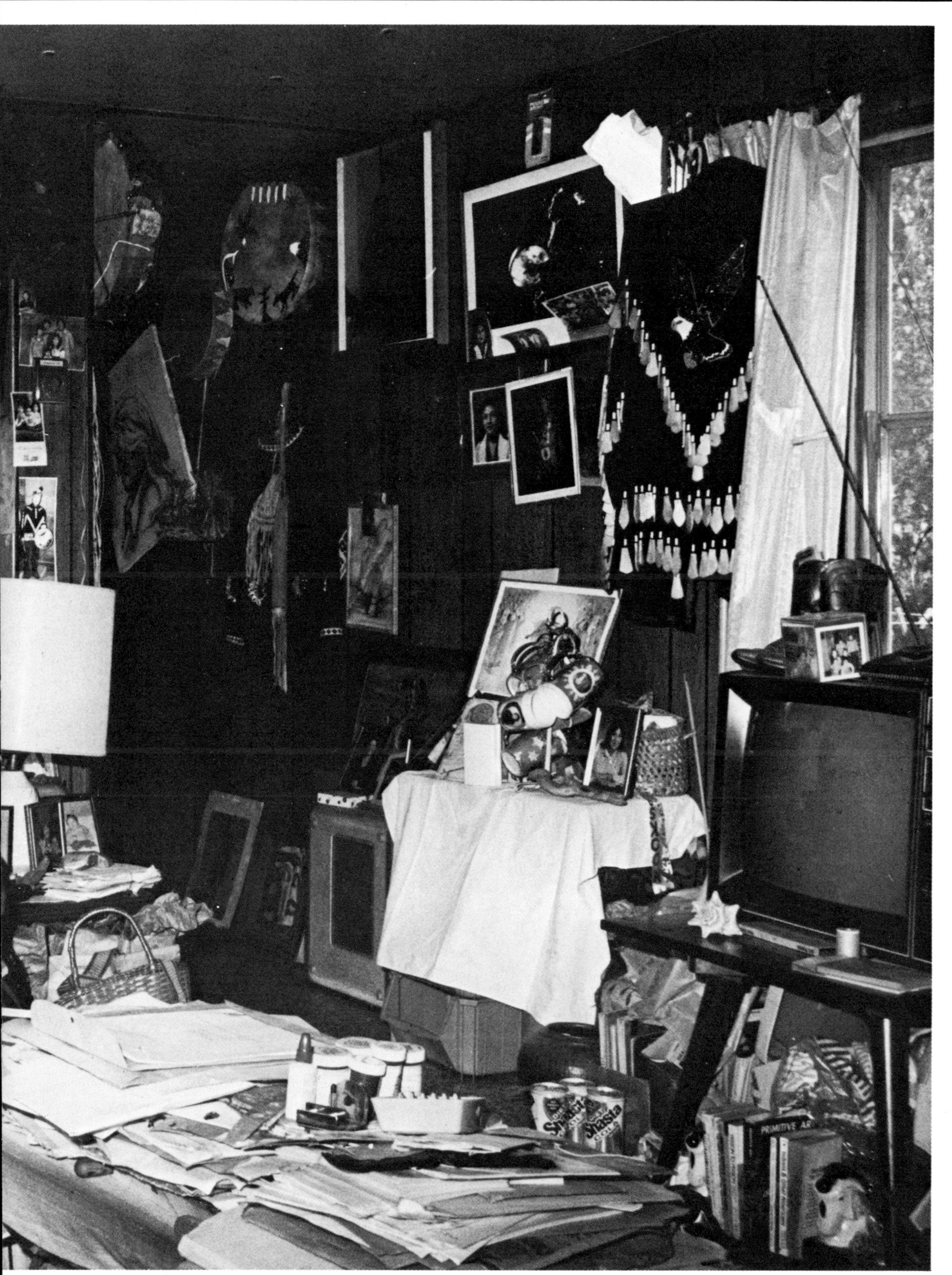

MARIA MAYER

Joe Washington, a leader of the Lummi Indian tribe in Whatcom County.

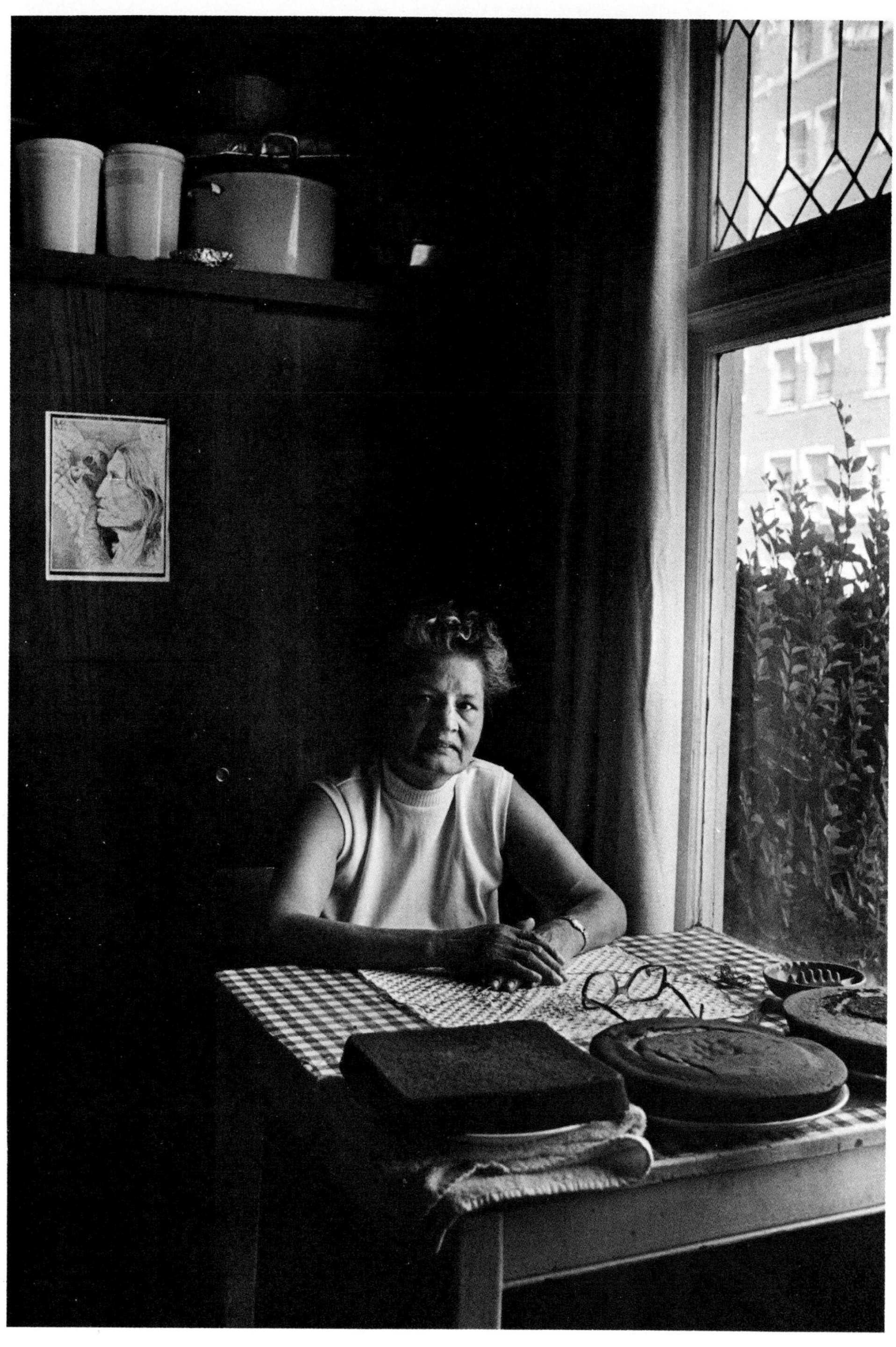

DIANNE HAGAMAN

Elaine Dominic sits in her room at Seattle's Benson House.

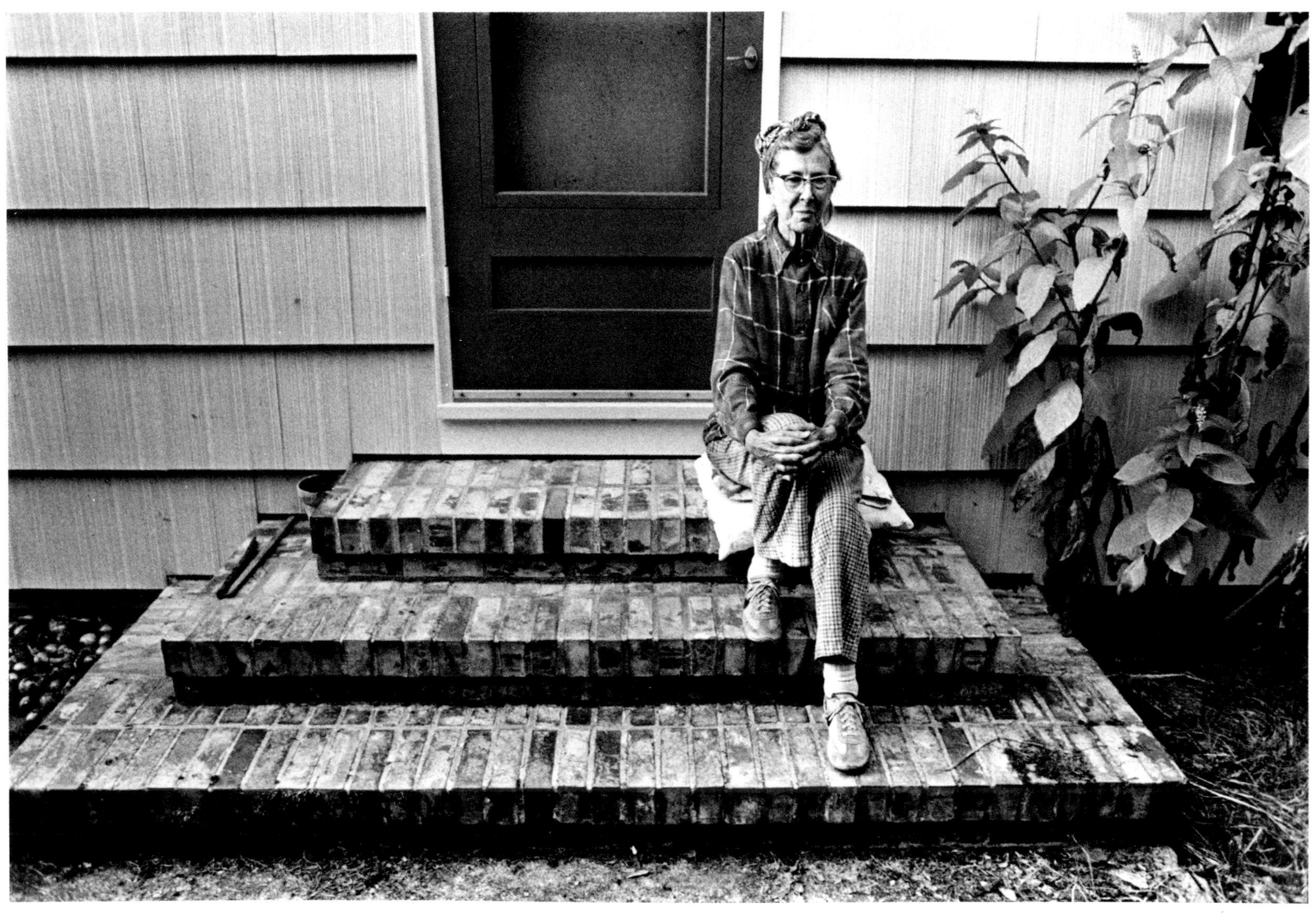

DALE BLINDHEIM

Lois Pratt sits on the back porch while husband Henry watches the McNeil-Lehrer Report.

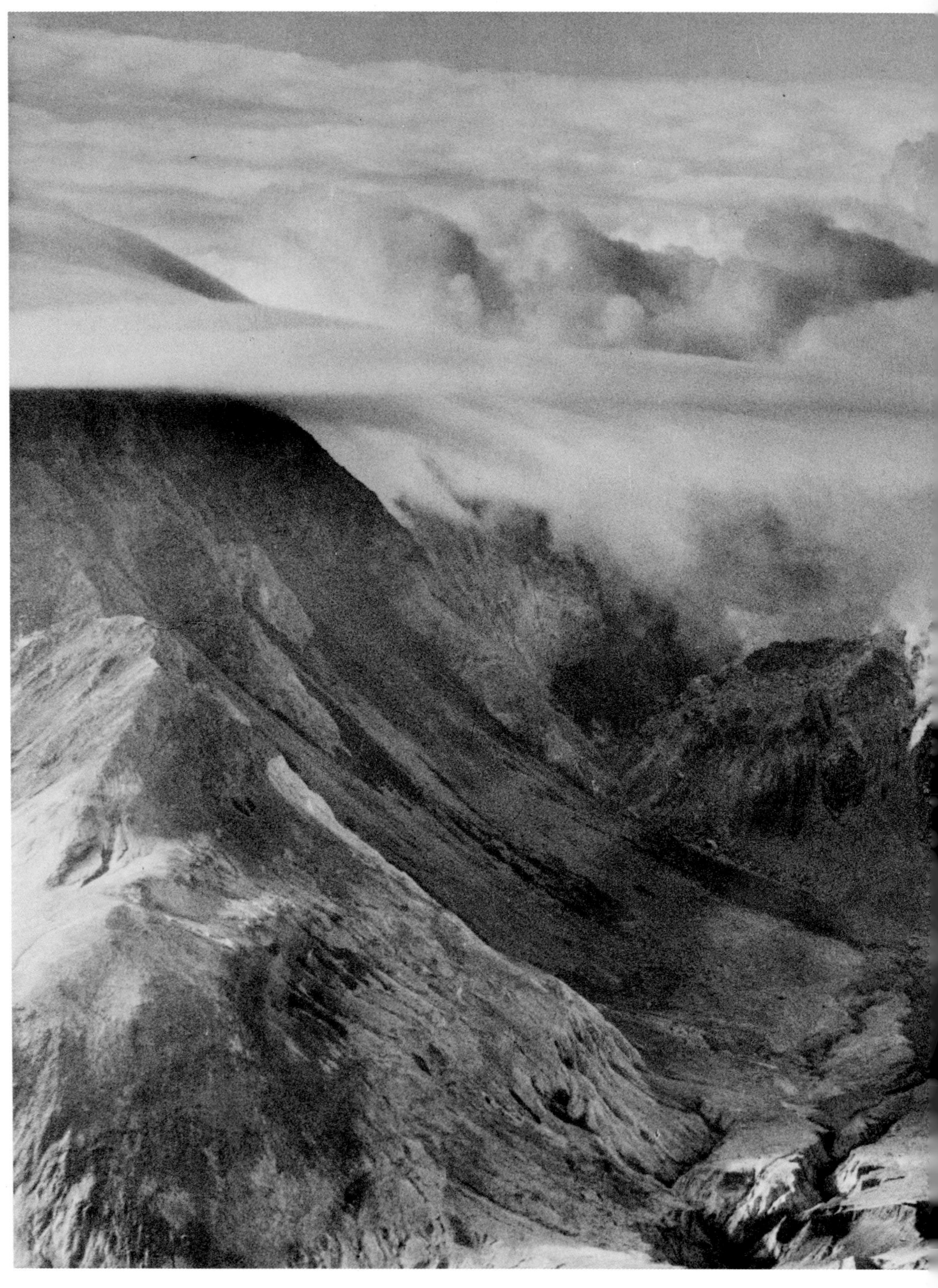

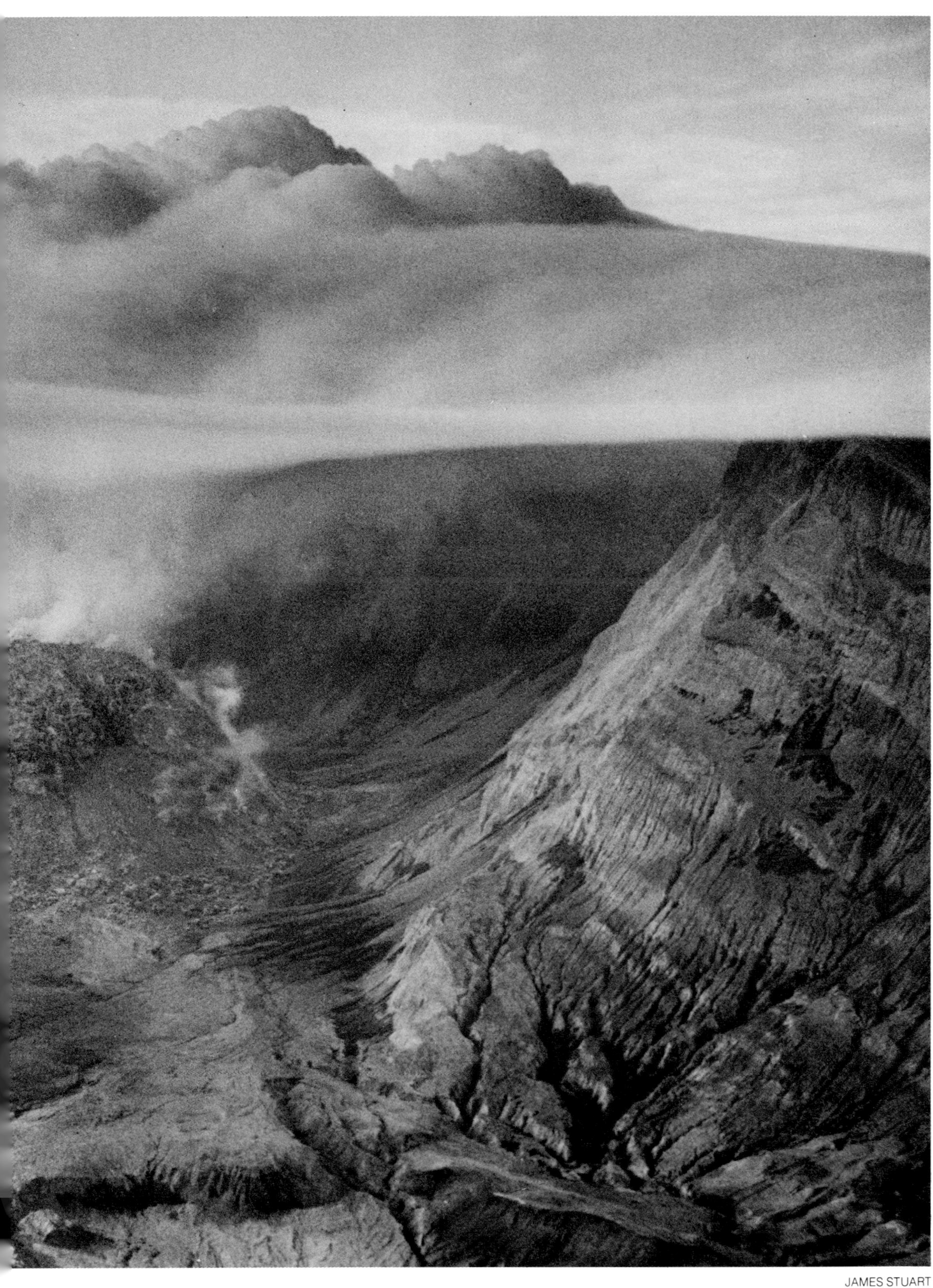

JAMES STUART

Lava dome forming on Mount St. Helens.

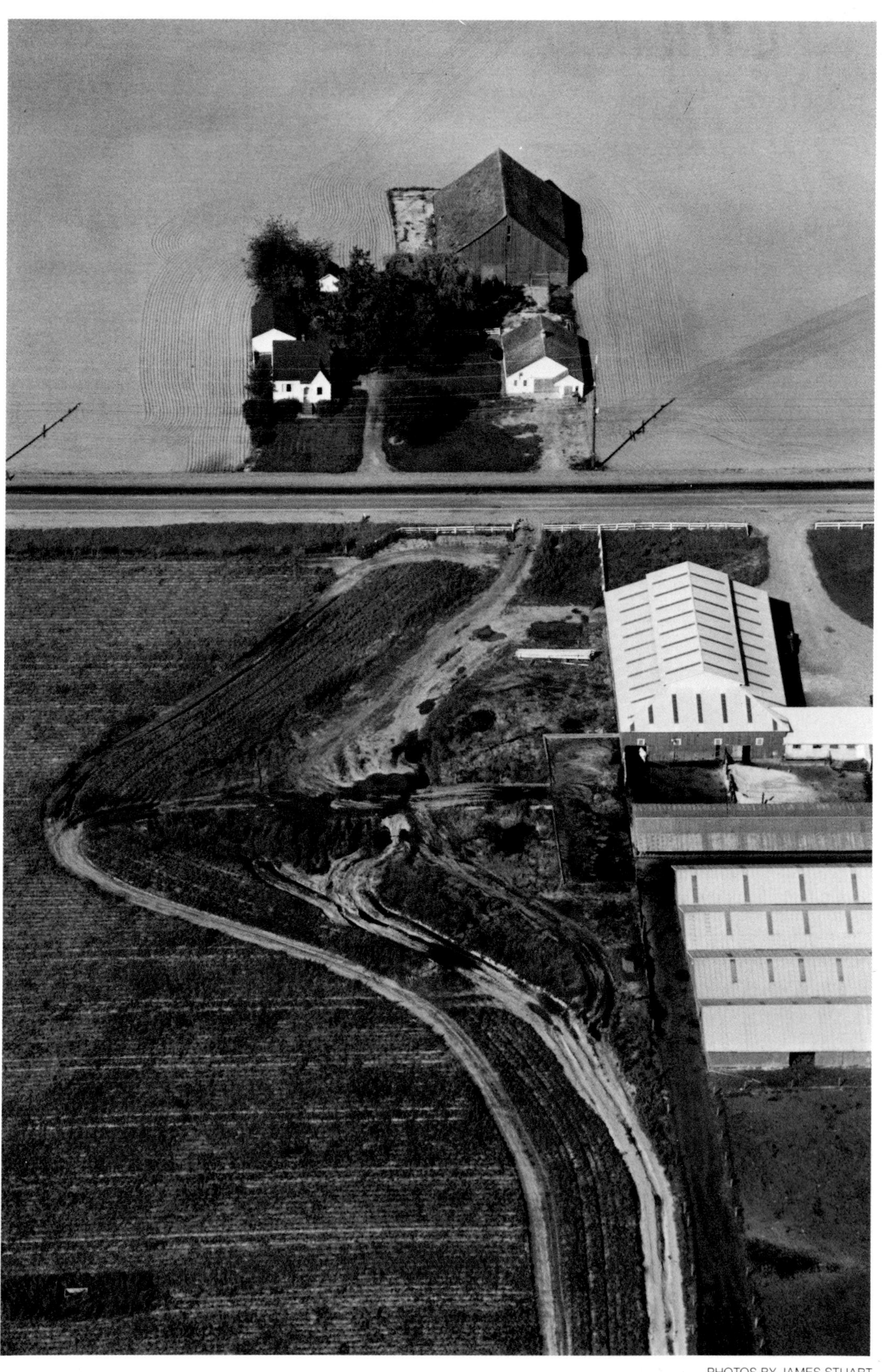

A farm near Conway in the Skagit Valley.

PHOTOS BY JAMES STUART

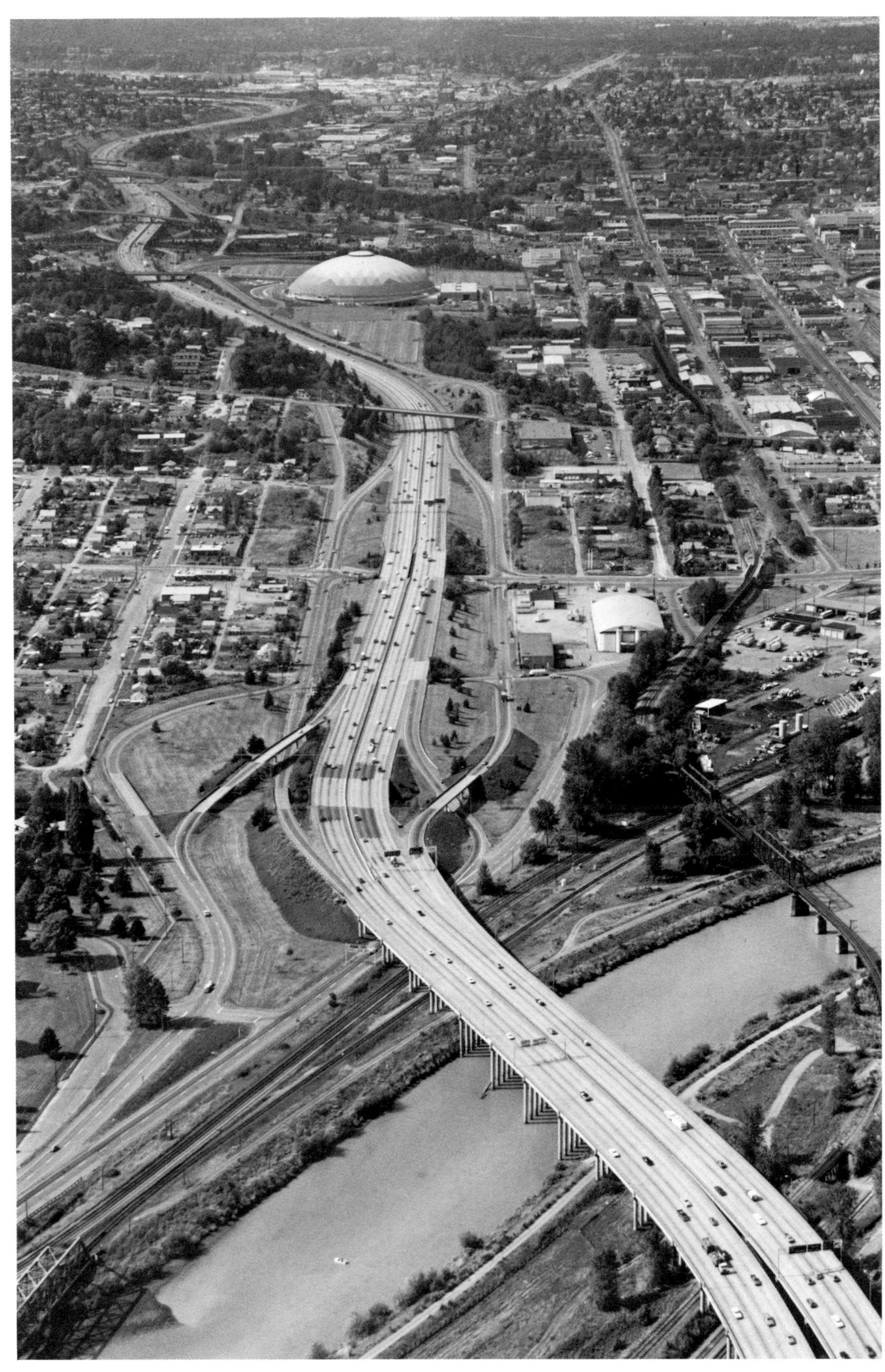

Interstate 5 crosses the Puyallup River and goes south, skirting the Tacoma Dome.

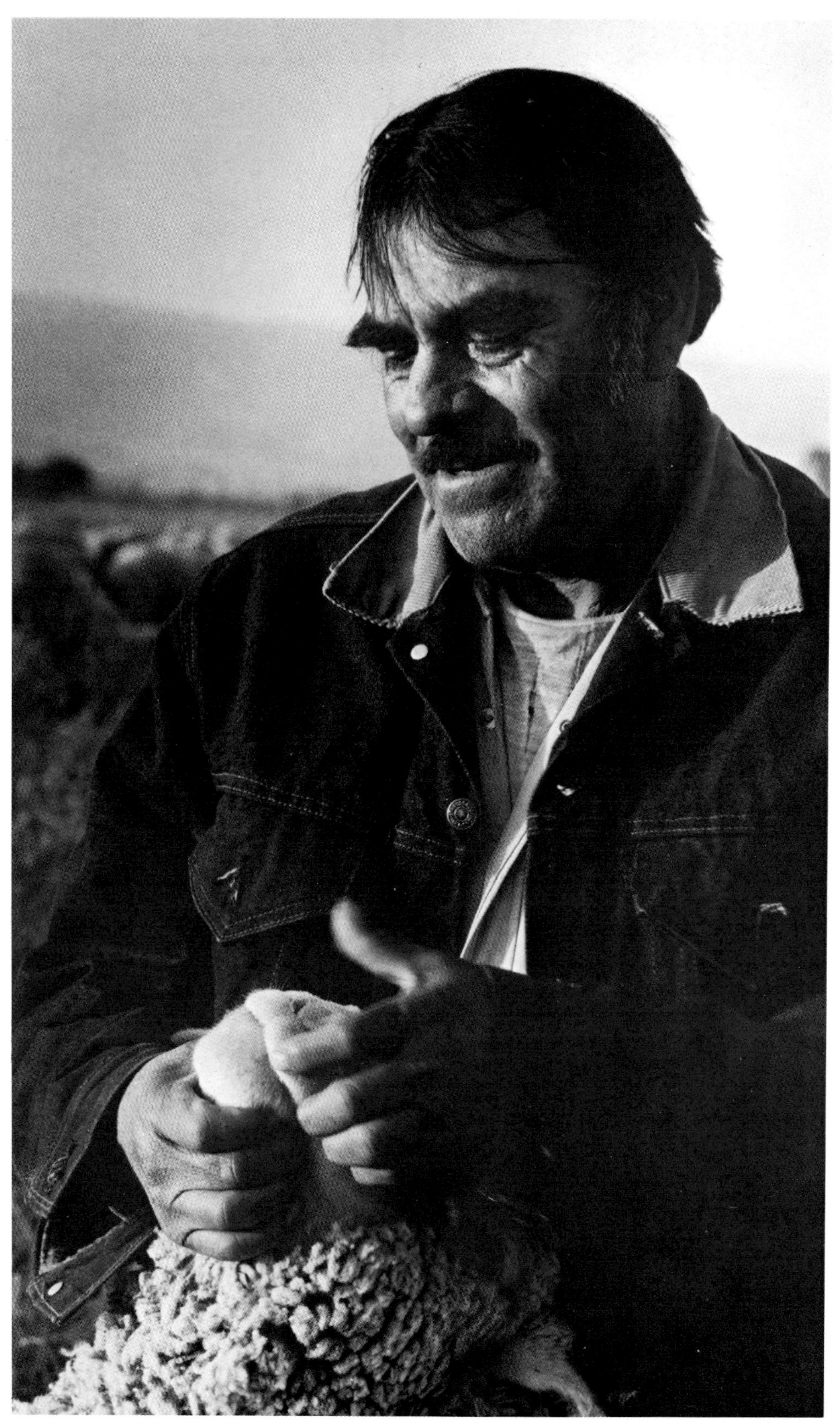

CHARLES PEARSON

Gabino Rodriguez examines sheep he has brought down to the Kittitas Valley from summer range in the high country of Wenatchee National Forest.

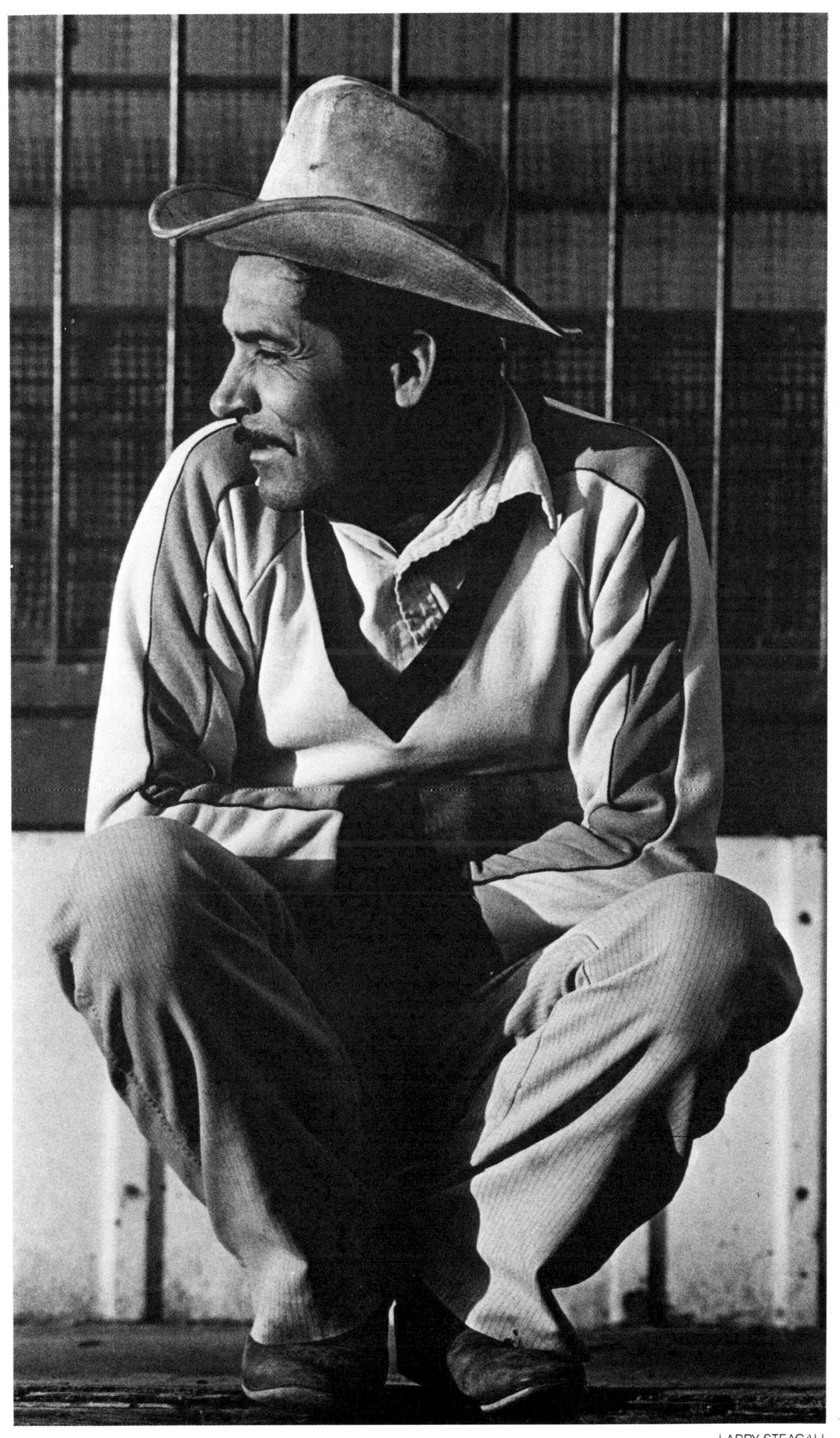

LARRY STEAGALL

A migrant farm worker in front of a hardware store in Buena, Yakima County.

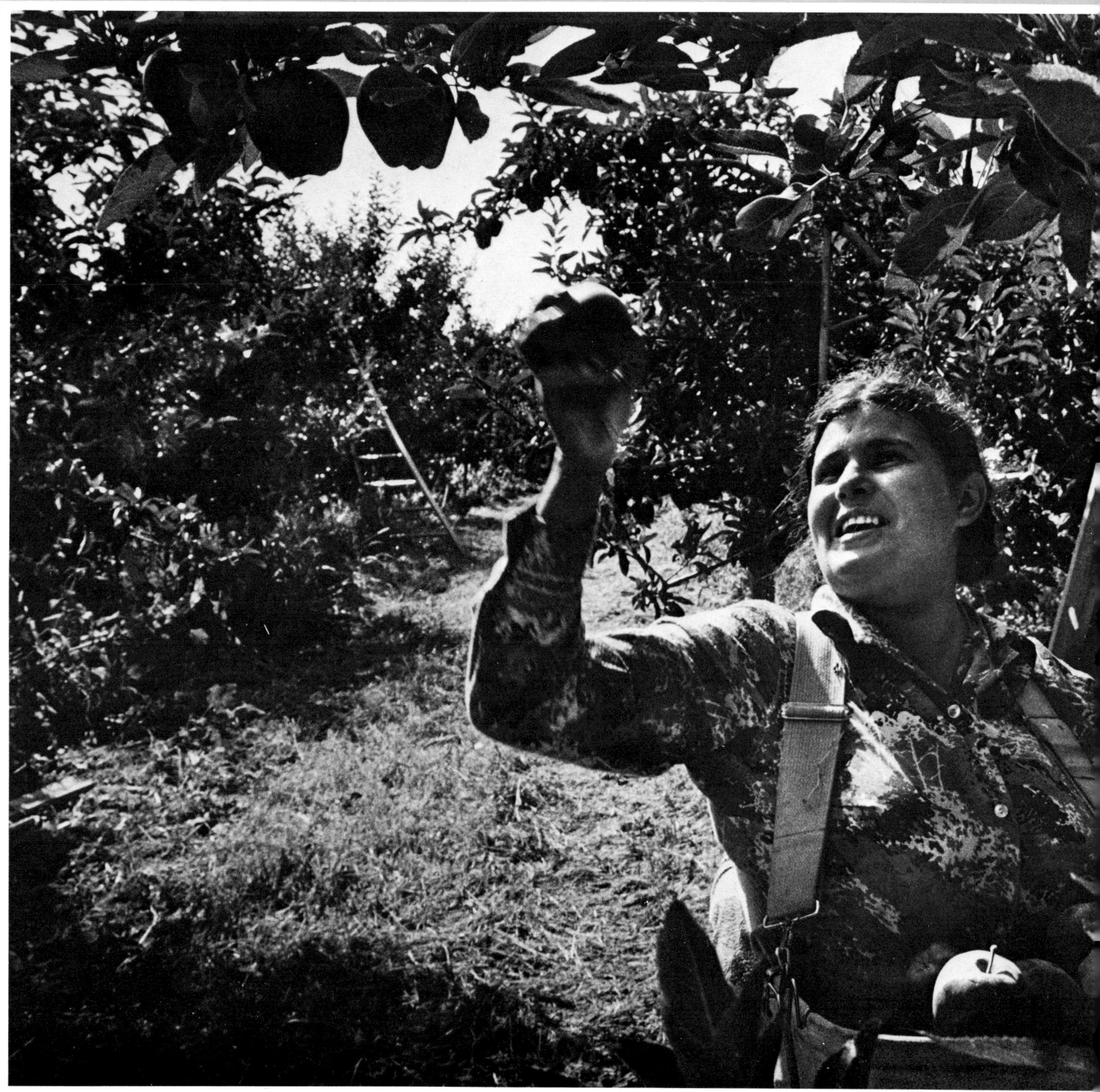

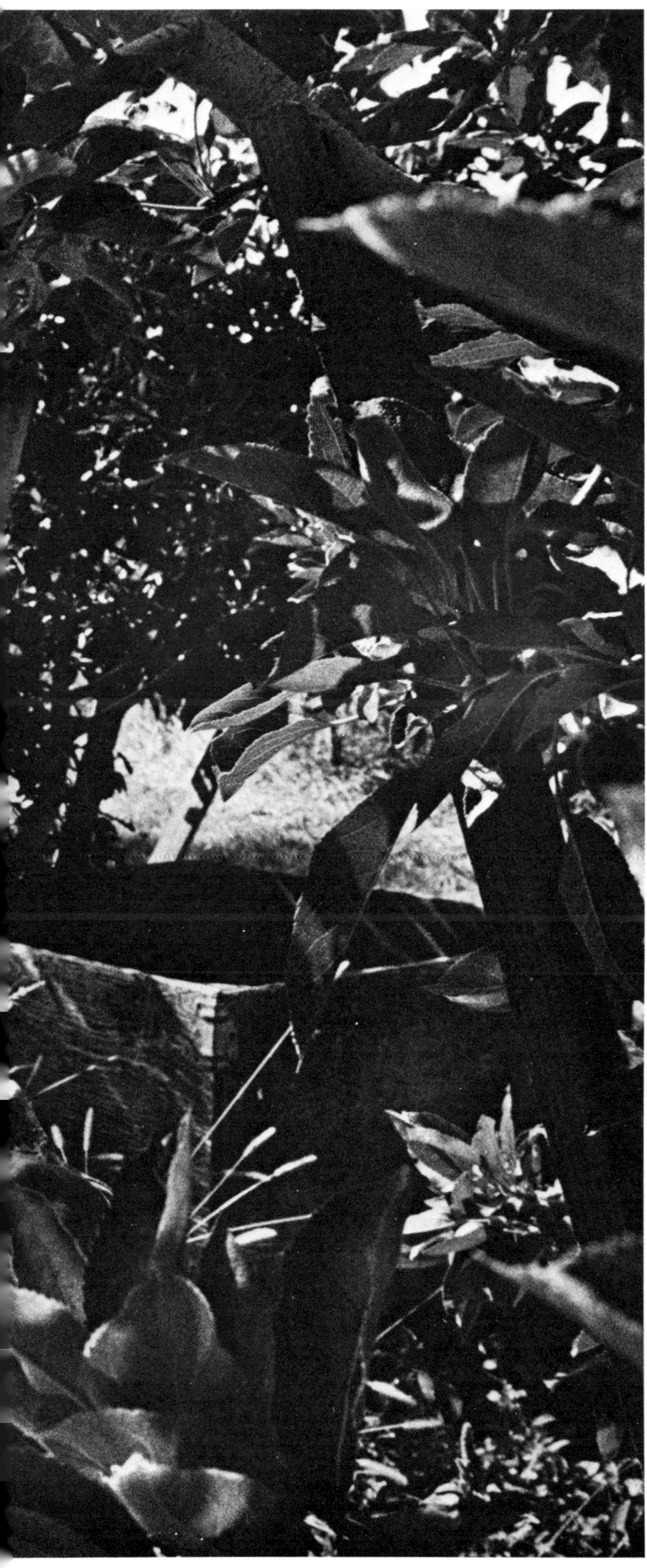

PHOTOS BY TOM TOTH

Working together, Mario and Felipa Coronado pick a box of Red Delicious apples in about 45 minutes. They earn $8 a box and pick about 14 boxes a day. At noon, they have lunch with friends and a small child at the Five Star Orchard, south of Yakima.

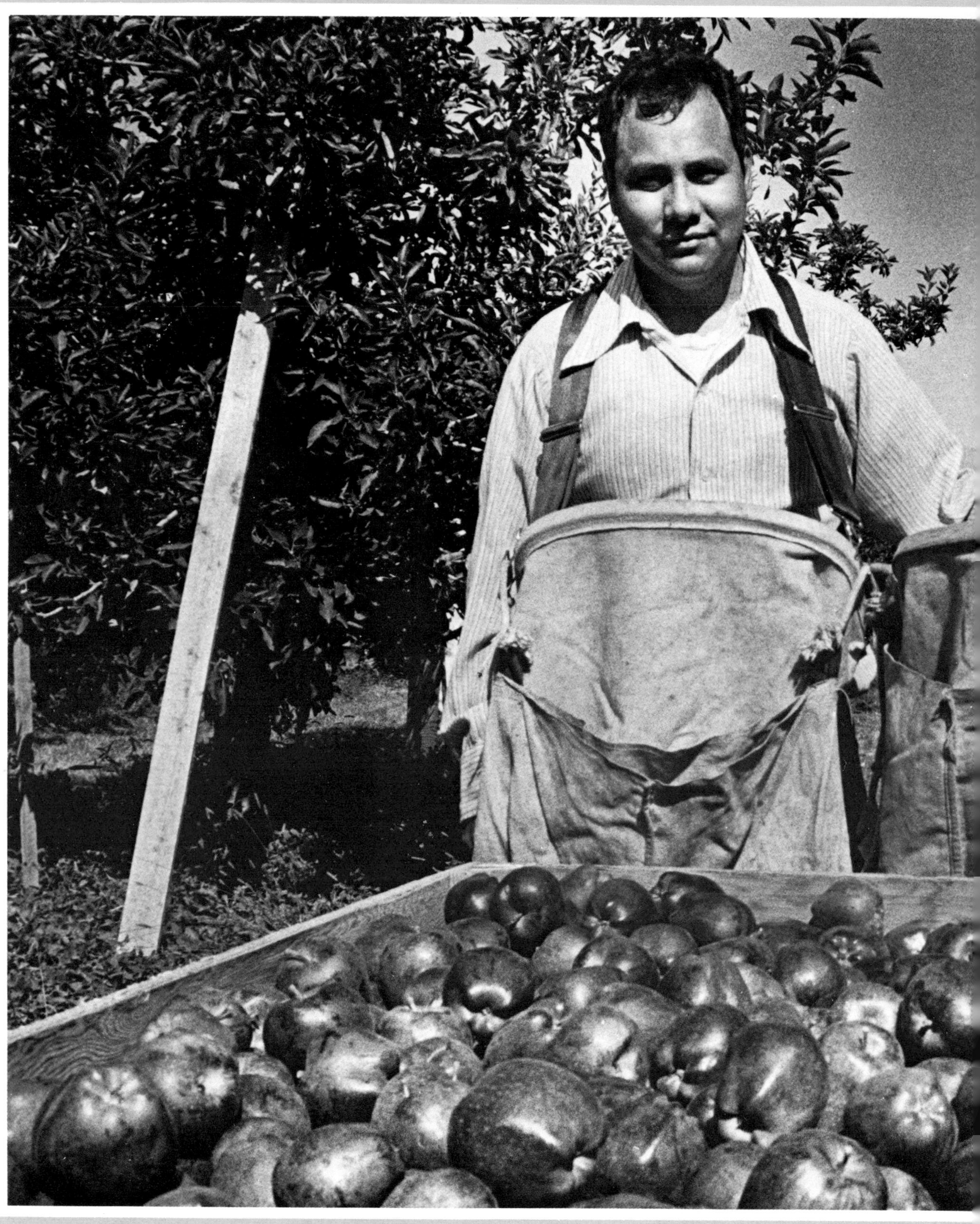

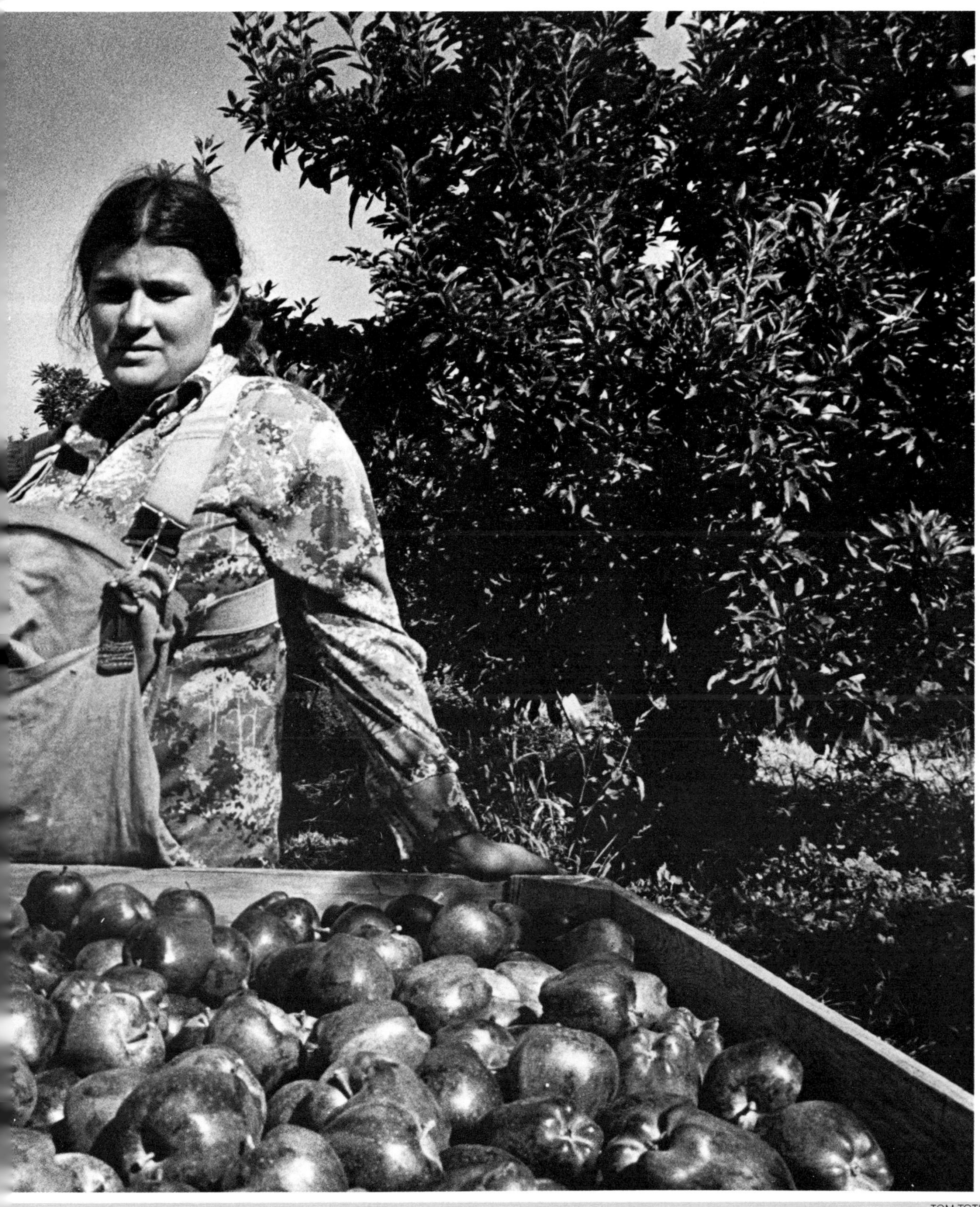

TOM TOTH

Following pages:
Marie Morris and daughter, Marisa Mancillas, 16, at a Burger King on Seattle's Rainier Avenue.
GRANT HALLER

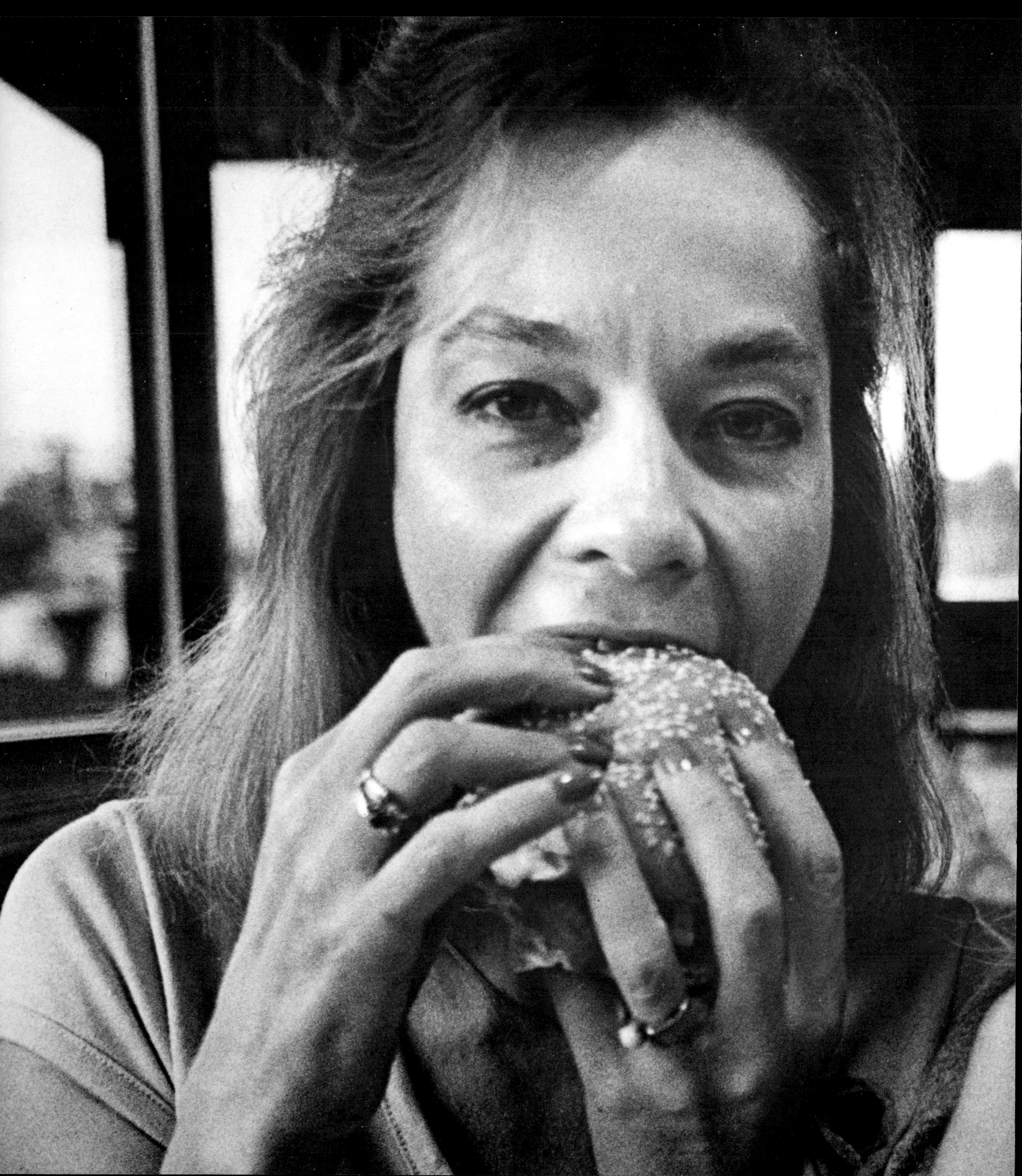

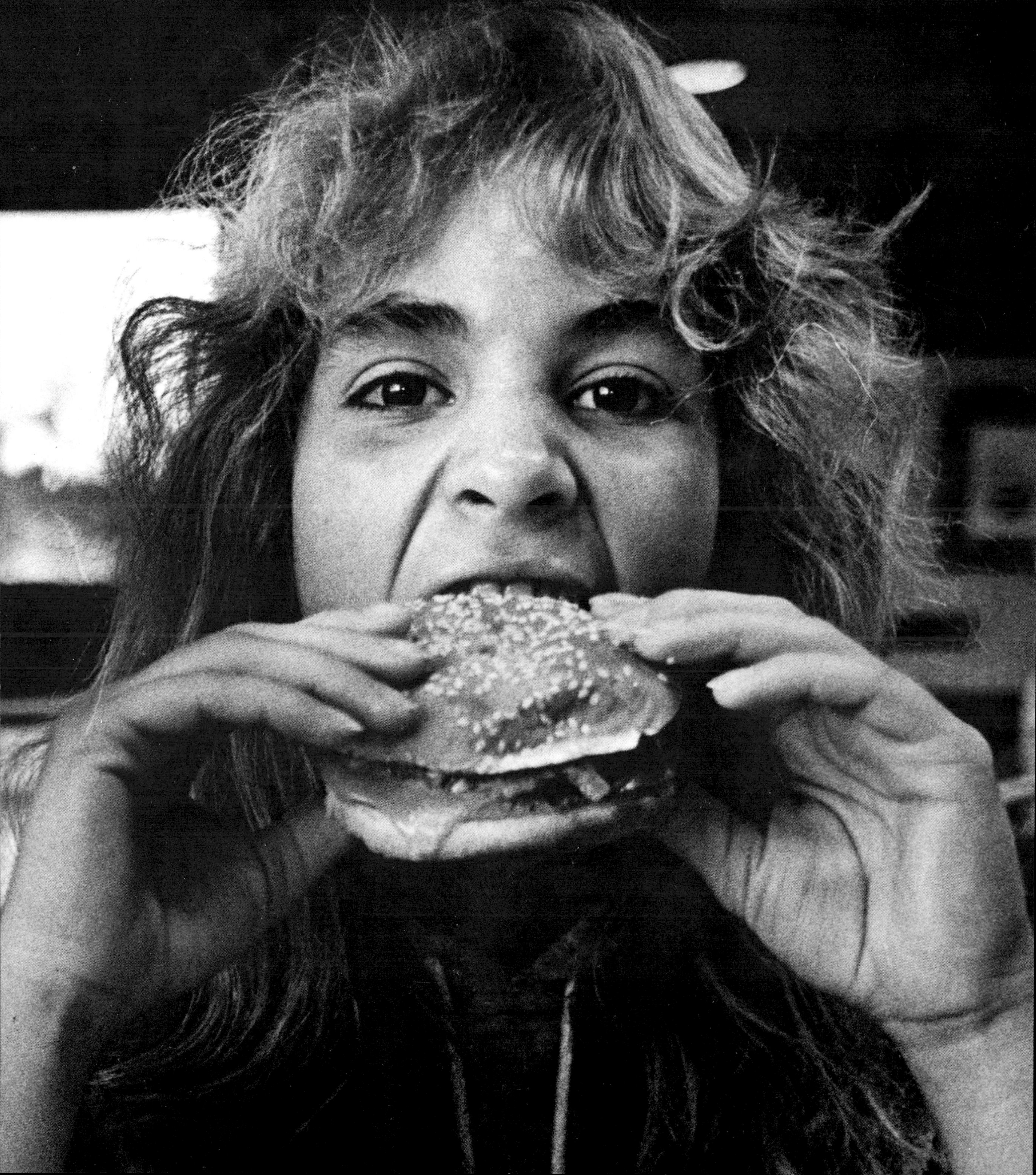

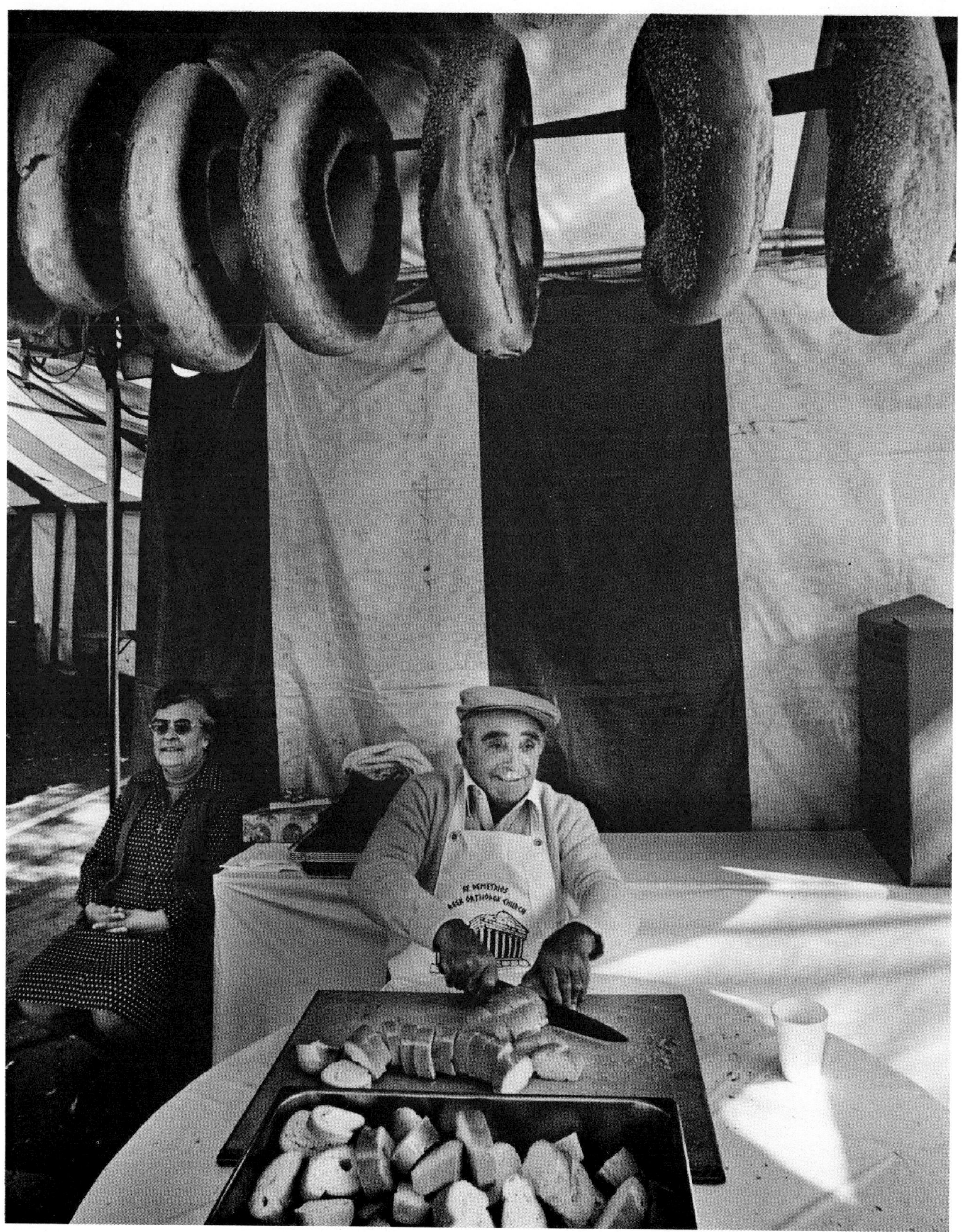

ROBERT DEGIULIO

Meletios Papanastasiou at the souvlakia stand at Seattle's St. Demetrios Greek Orthodox Church's annual Greek festival.

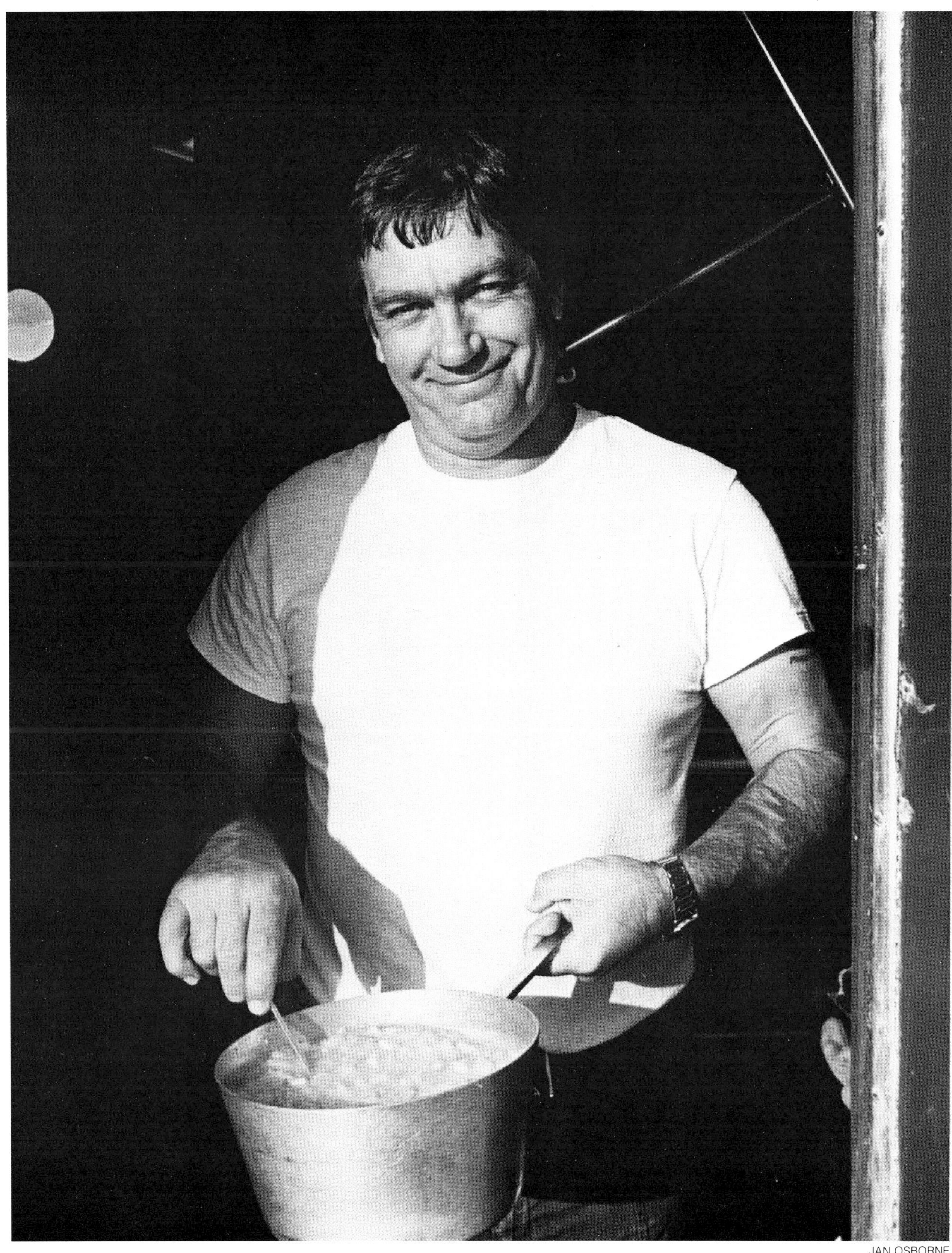
JAN OSBORNE

George Tweter, cook on the Foss tug Shelby Foss.

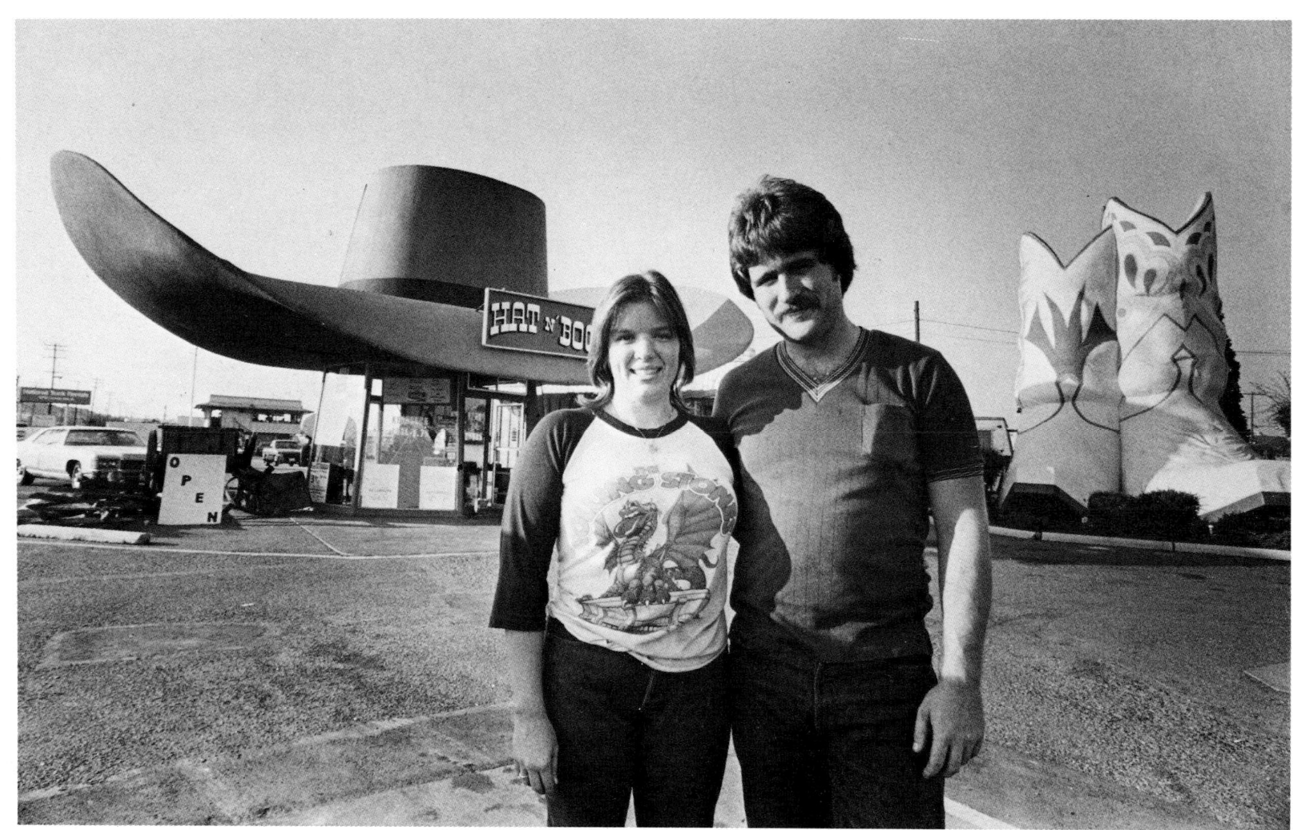

A Texas trucker and his girlfriend pause for gas at Hat N'Boots in South Seattle.

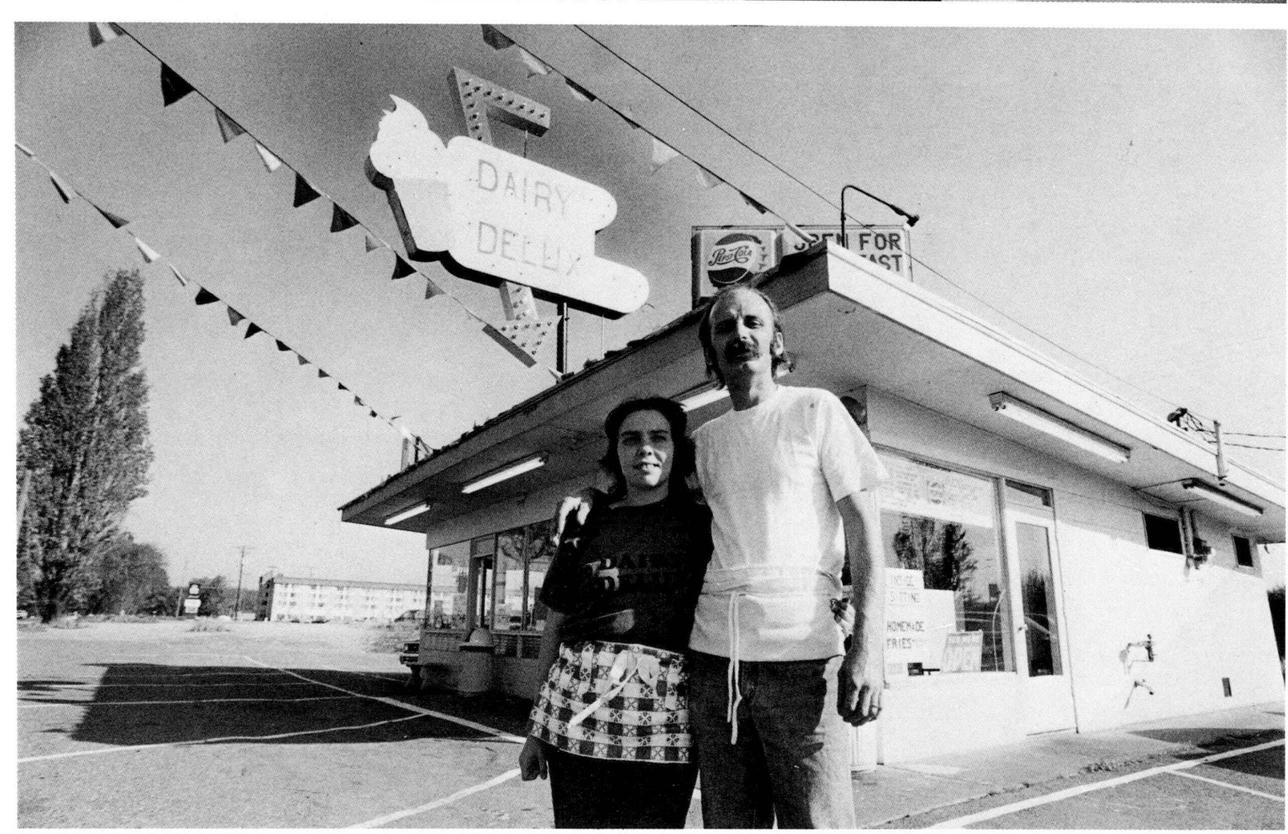

Owners of the Dairy Deluxe on Pacific Highway East in Tacoma.

PHOTOS BY JENNIFER WERNER

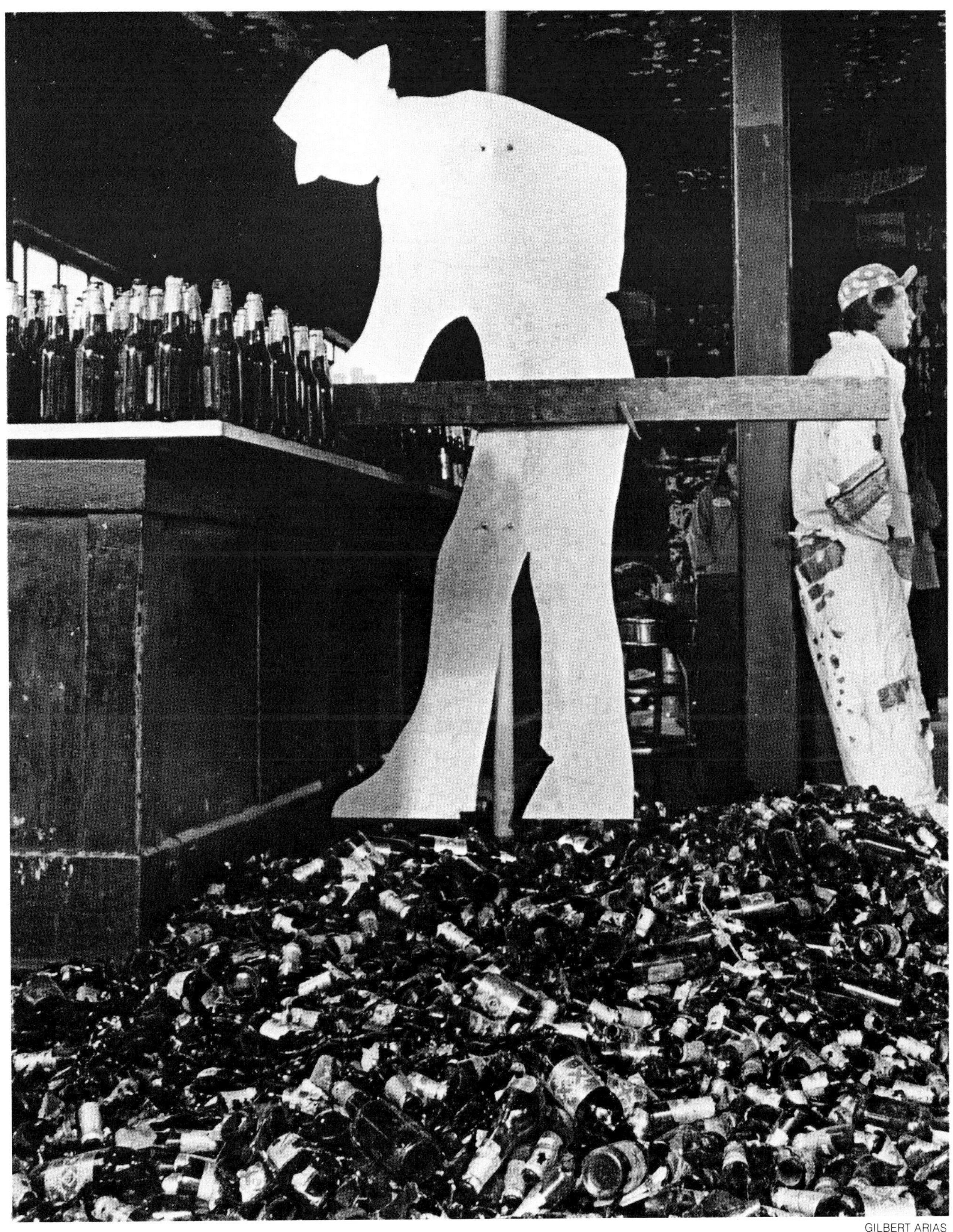

GILBERT ARIAS

Buster Simpson's bottle-smasher: The metal man is connected to another figure on the roof of the old Pine Street Tavern. When the wind blows, everything moves and bottles fly to the floor and break.

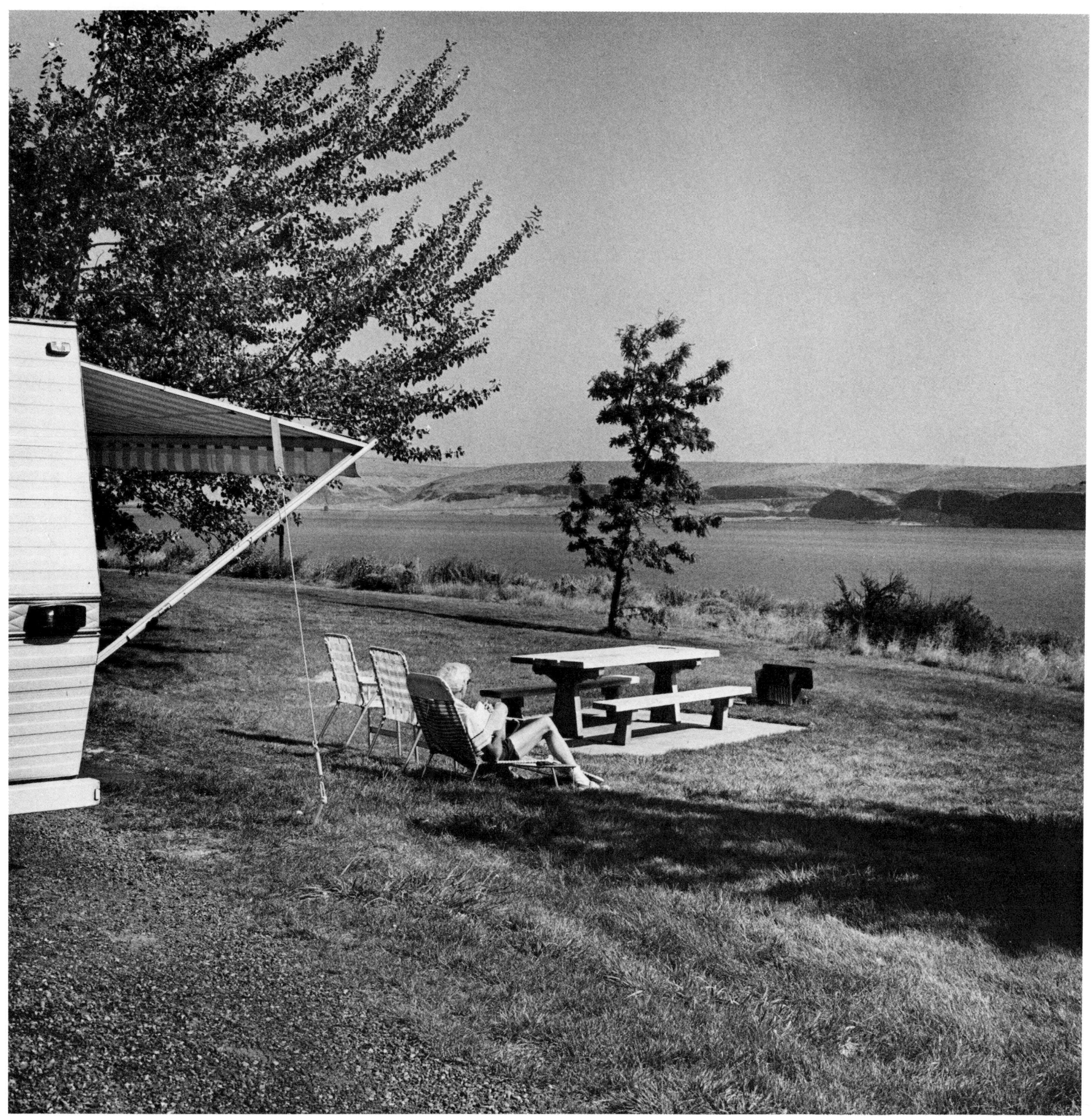

PHOTOS BY DON NORMARK

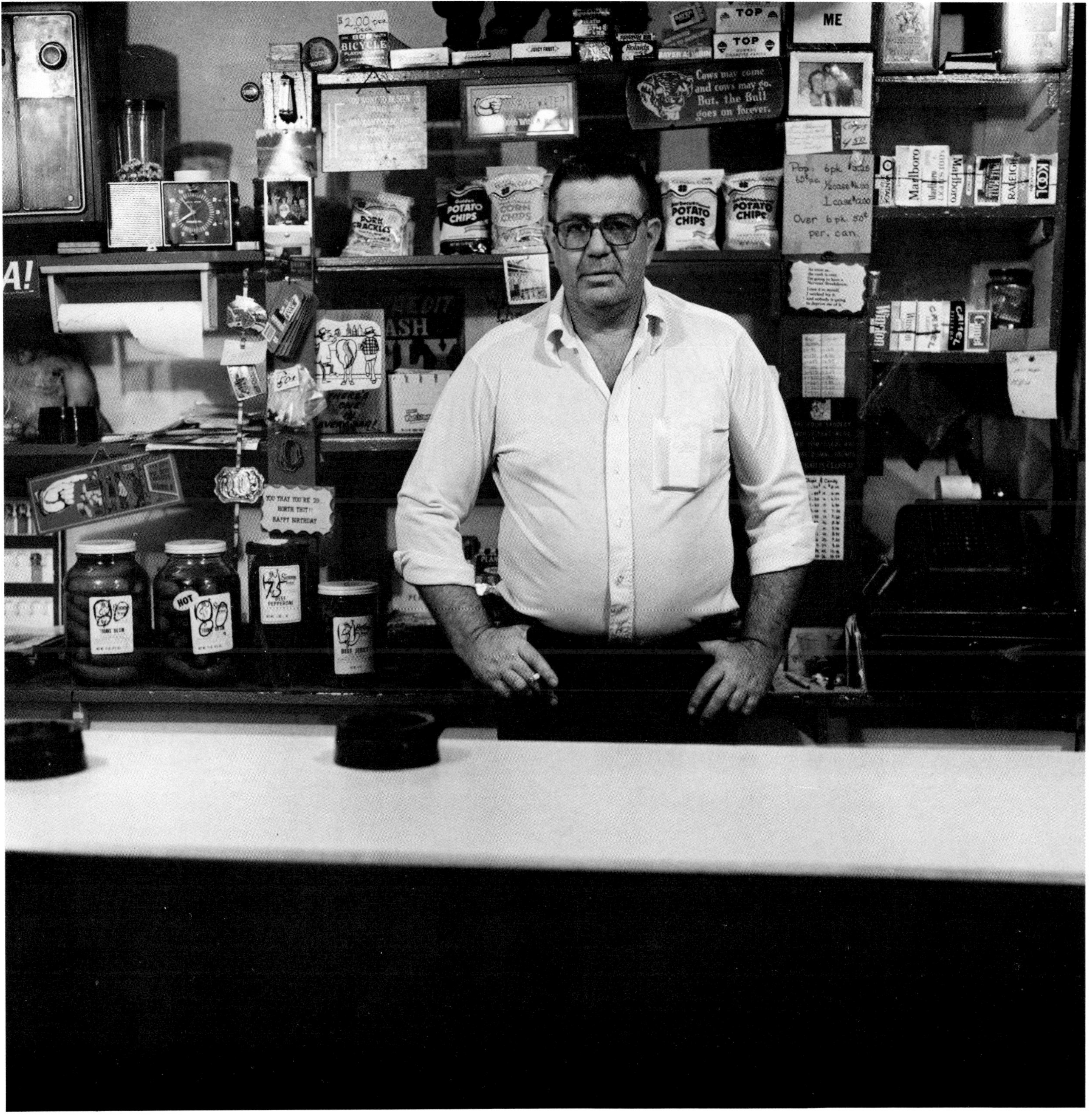

ME
TOP
BICYCLE
Cows may come
and cows may go.
But, the Bull
goes on forever.
PORK CRACKLES
POTATO CHIPS
CORN CHIPS
POTATO CHIPS
POTATO CHIPS
Over 6 pk. 50¢
per. can.
Marlboro
Marlboro
RALEIGH
KOOL
Winston
Camel
HAPPY BIRTHDAY
HOT
BEEF PEPPERONI
BEEF JERKY

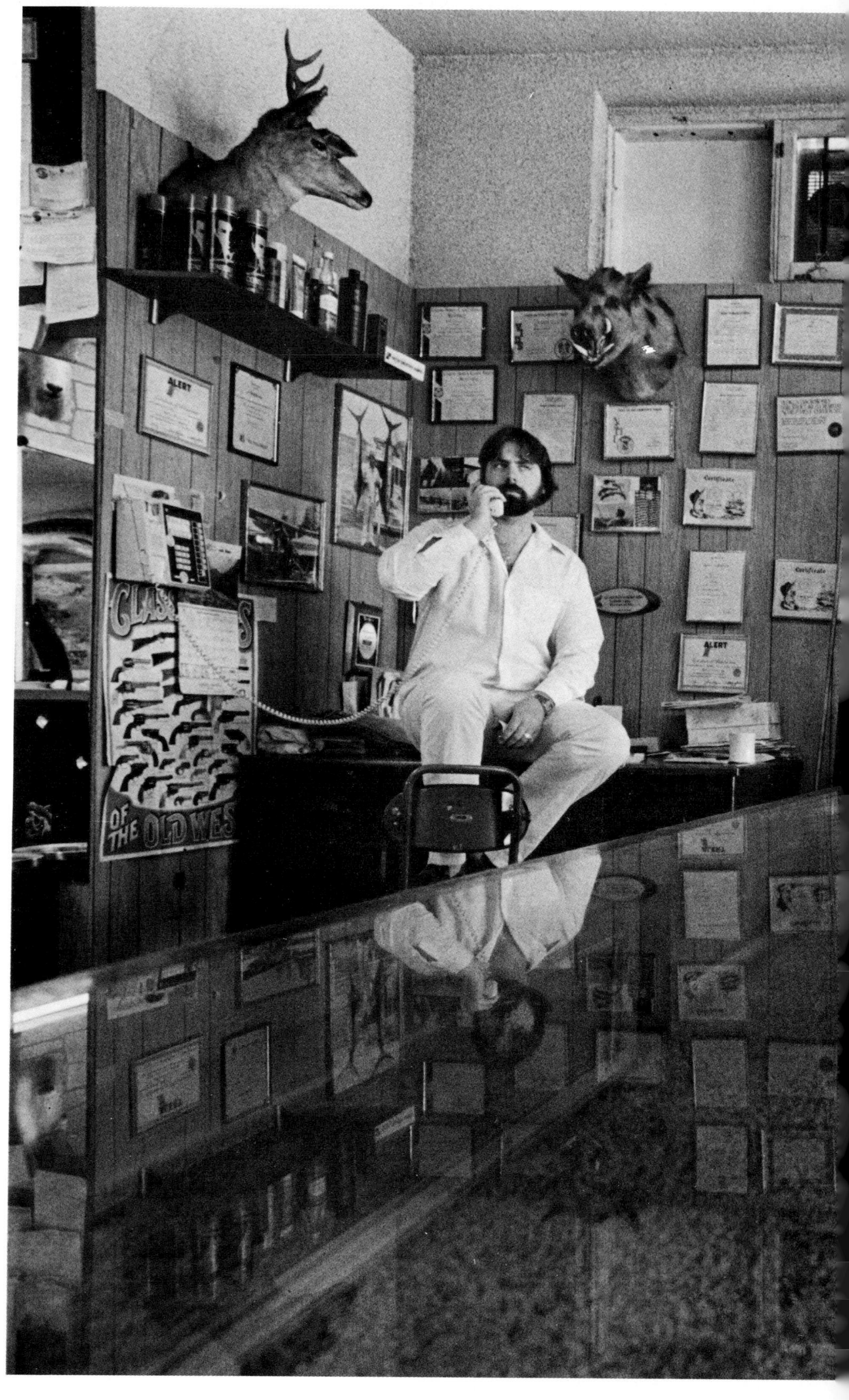

Preceding pages:
122, The Wanapum Recreation Area on the Columbia River.

123, Don Read, bartender at The Shanty in Roosevelt.

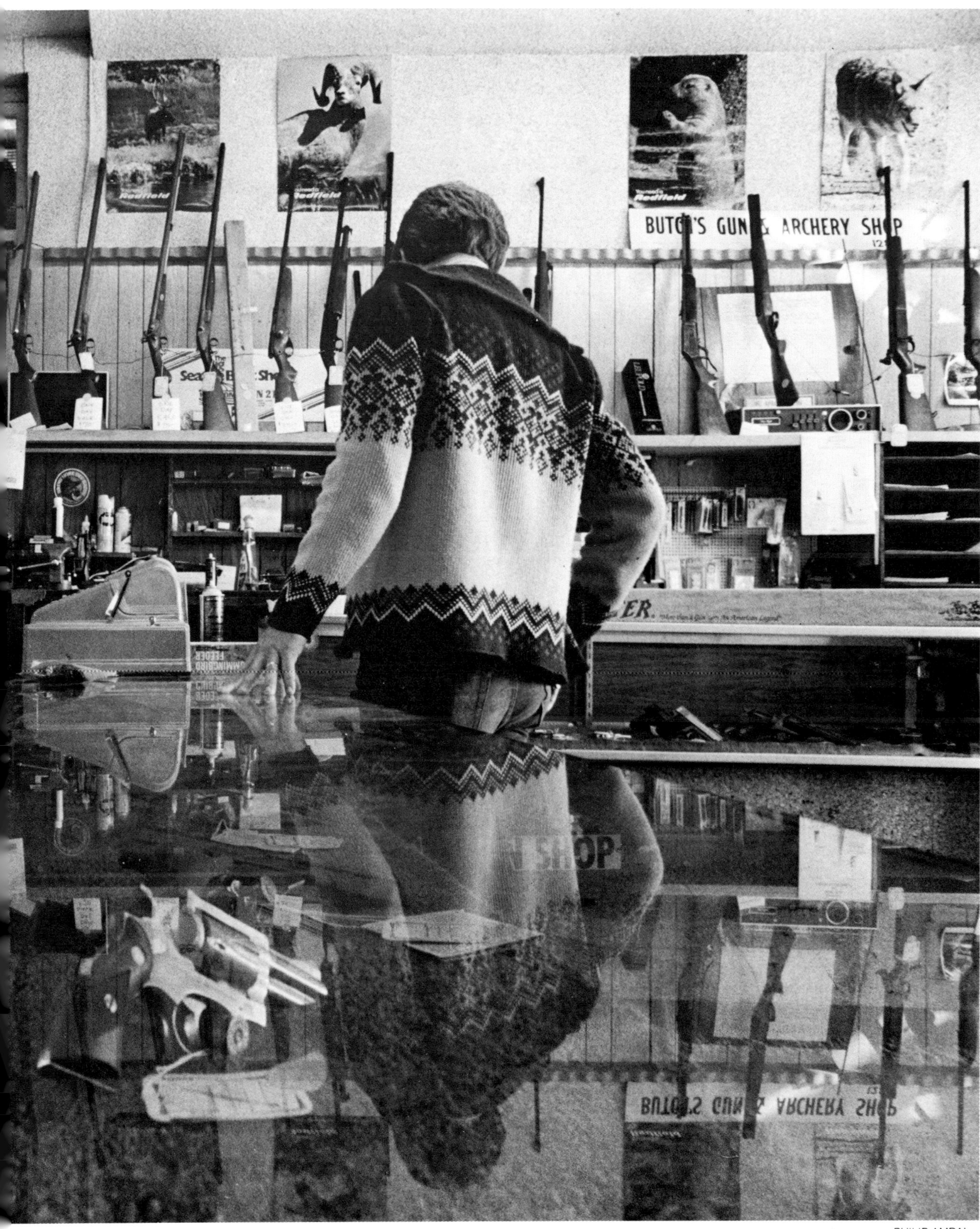

PHILIP AMDAL

Walter "Butch" Hulit's gun shop on Seattle's Aurora Avenue.

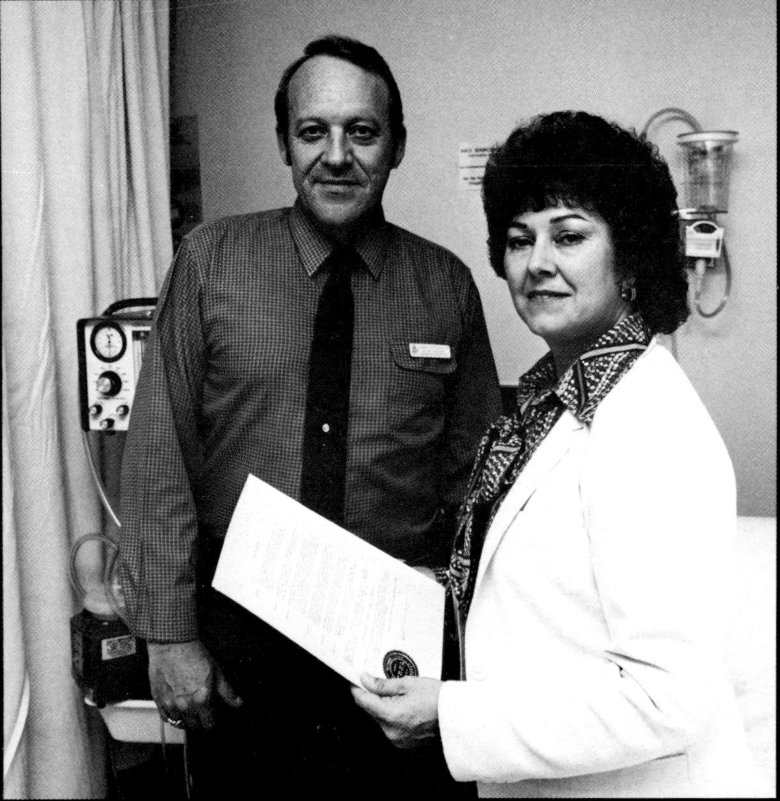

Yakima Mayor Lynn Carmichael with Darwin Steffenhagen, Sr.

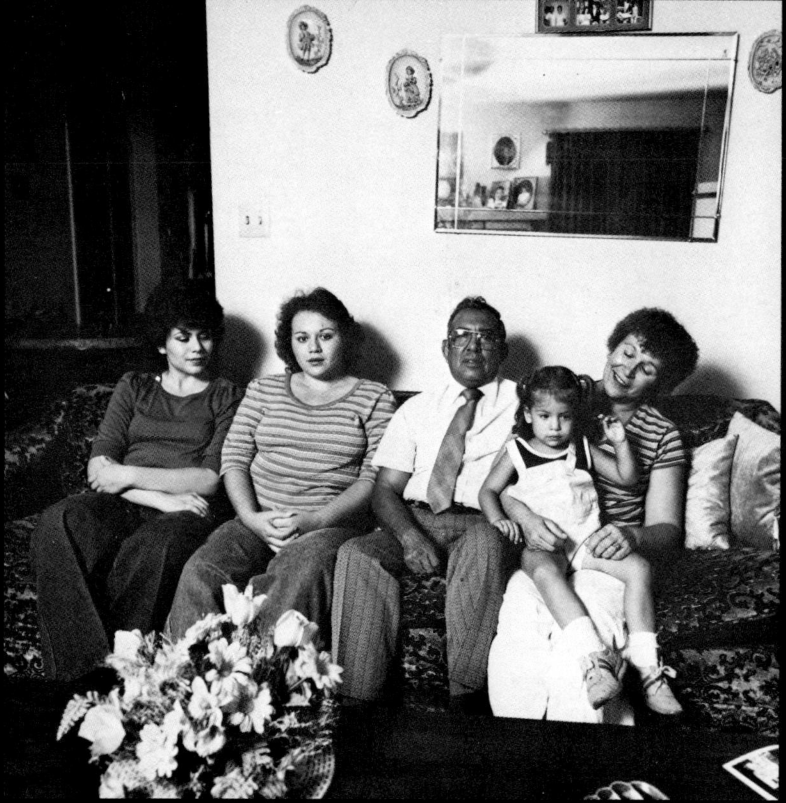

Mabton Mayor Rudy Cortez and family.

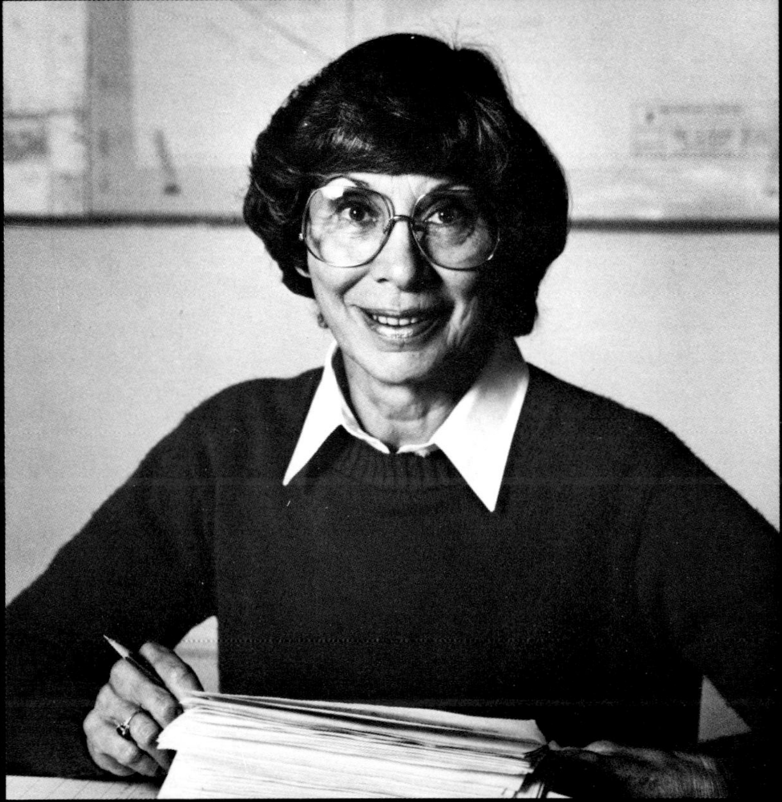

Naches Mayor Mary E. Tenney.

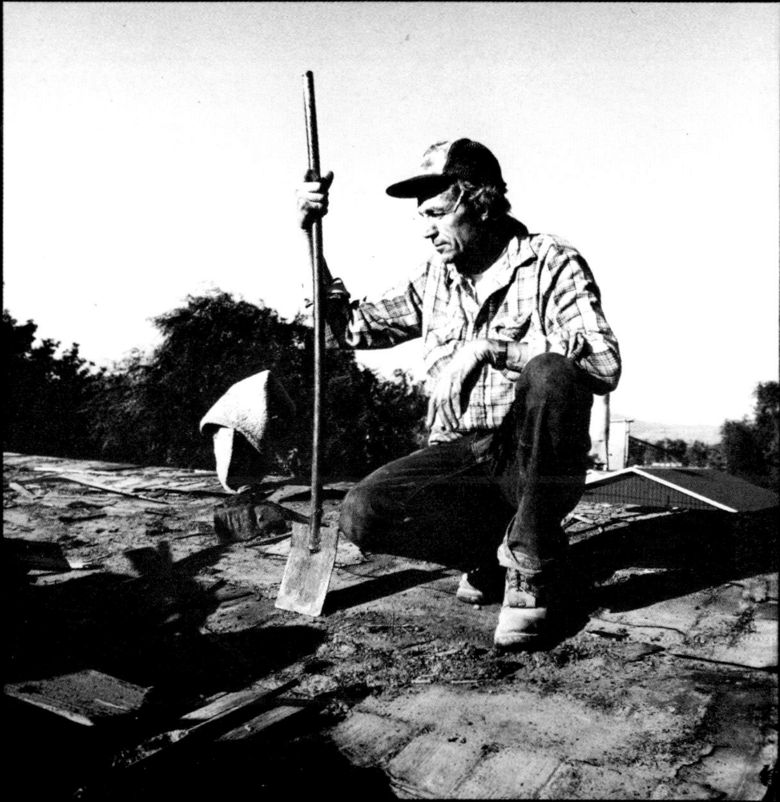

PHOTOS BY GEORGE WHITE

Kittitas Mayor Jerry Gilmour.

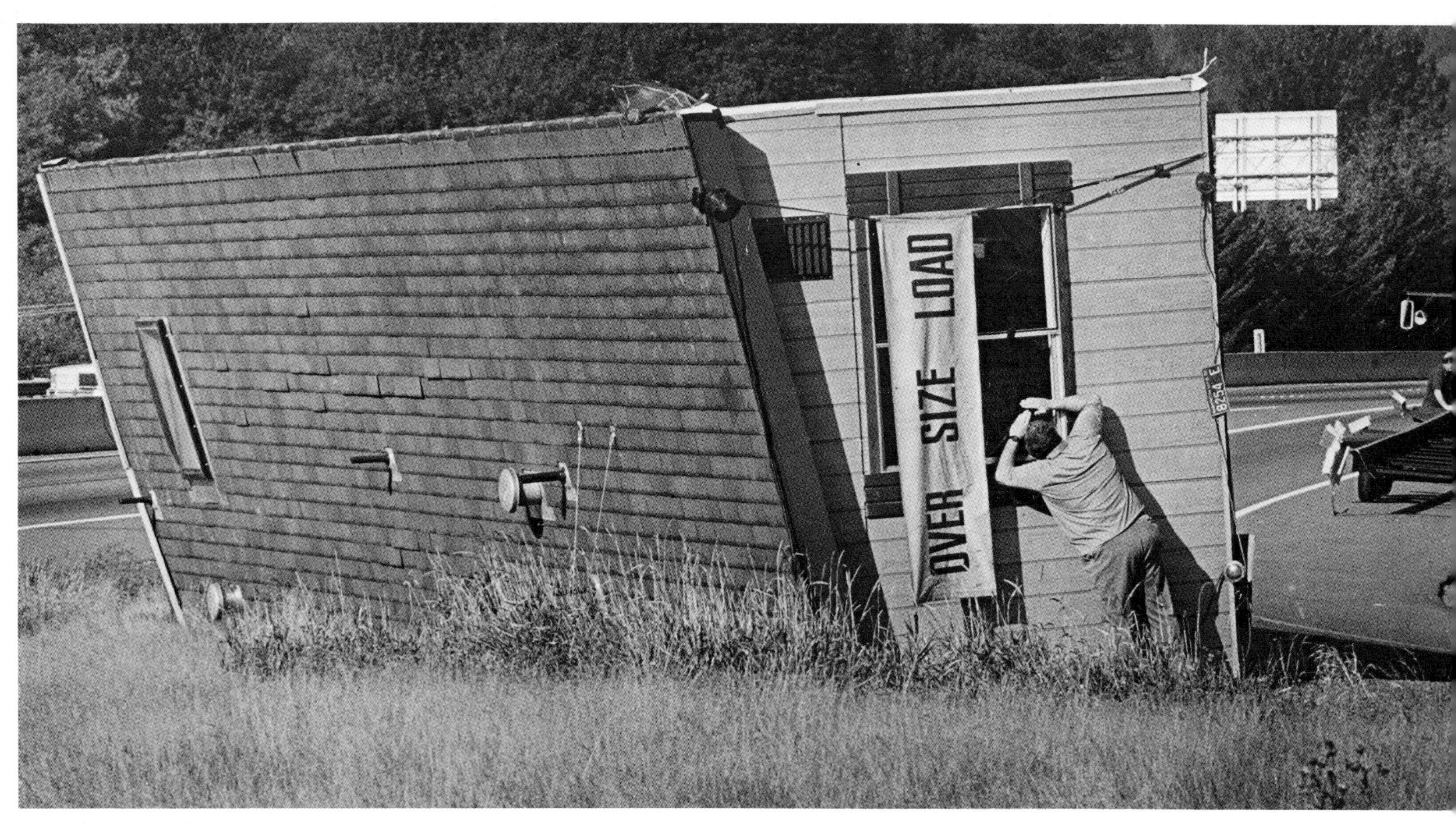

A mishap on Highway 18 in Auburn.

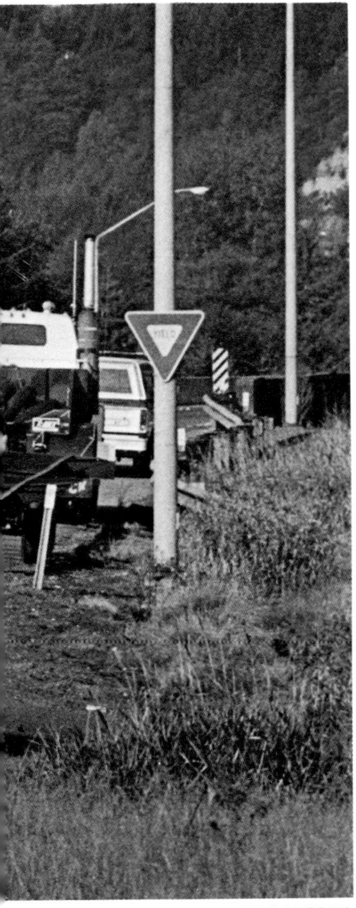

MARK MORRIS

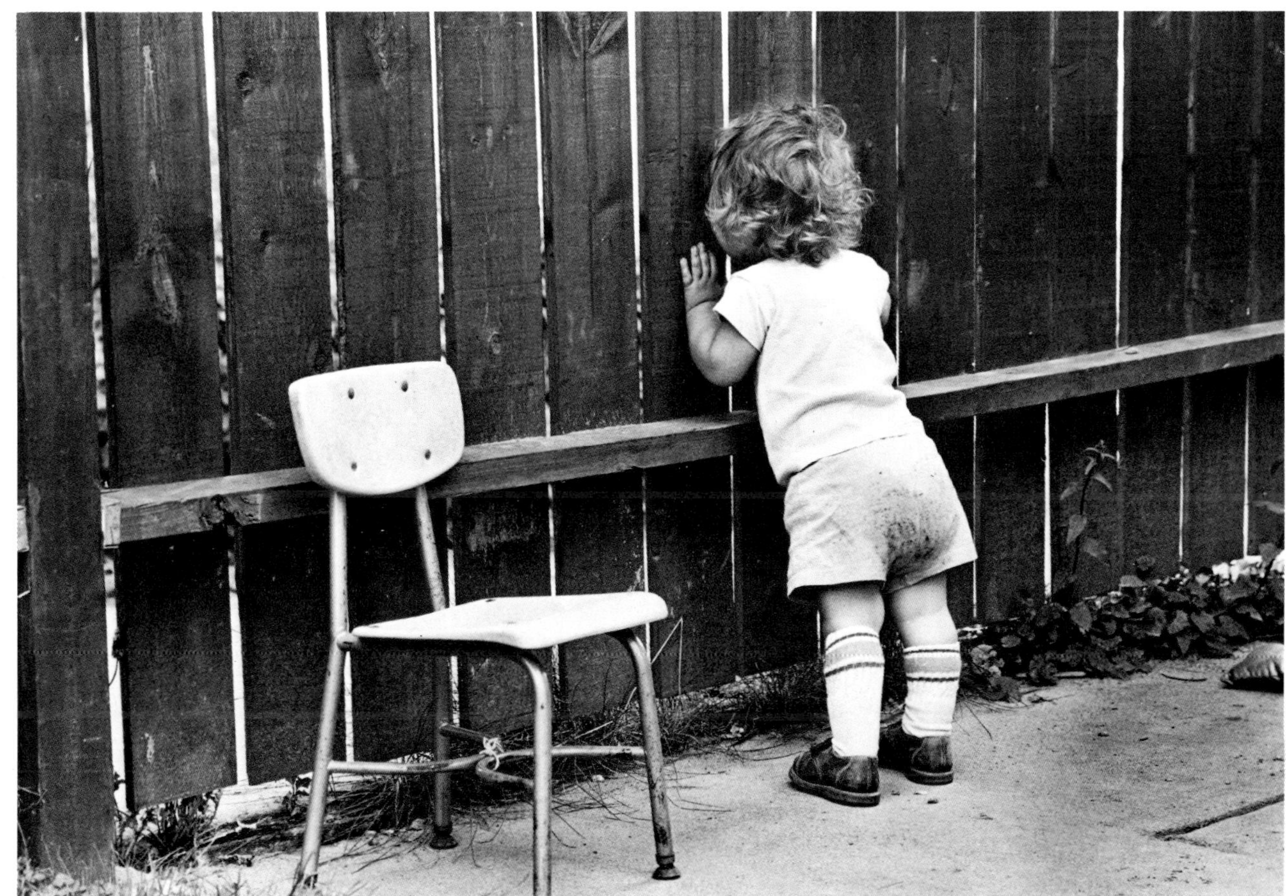

NATALIE FOBES

Looking through the fence from a day-care center on Capitol Hill, Seattle.

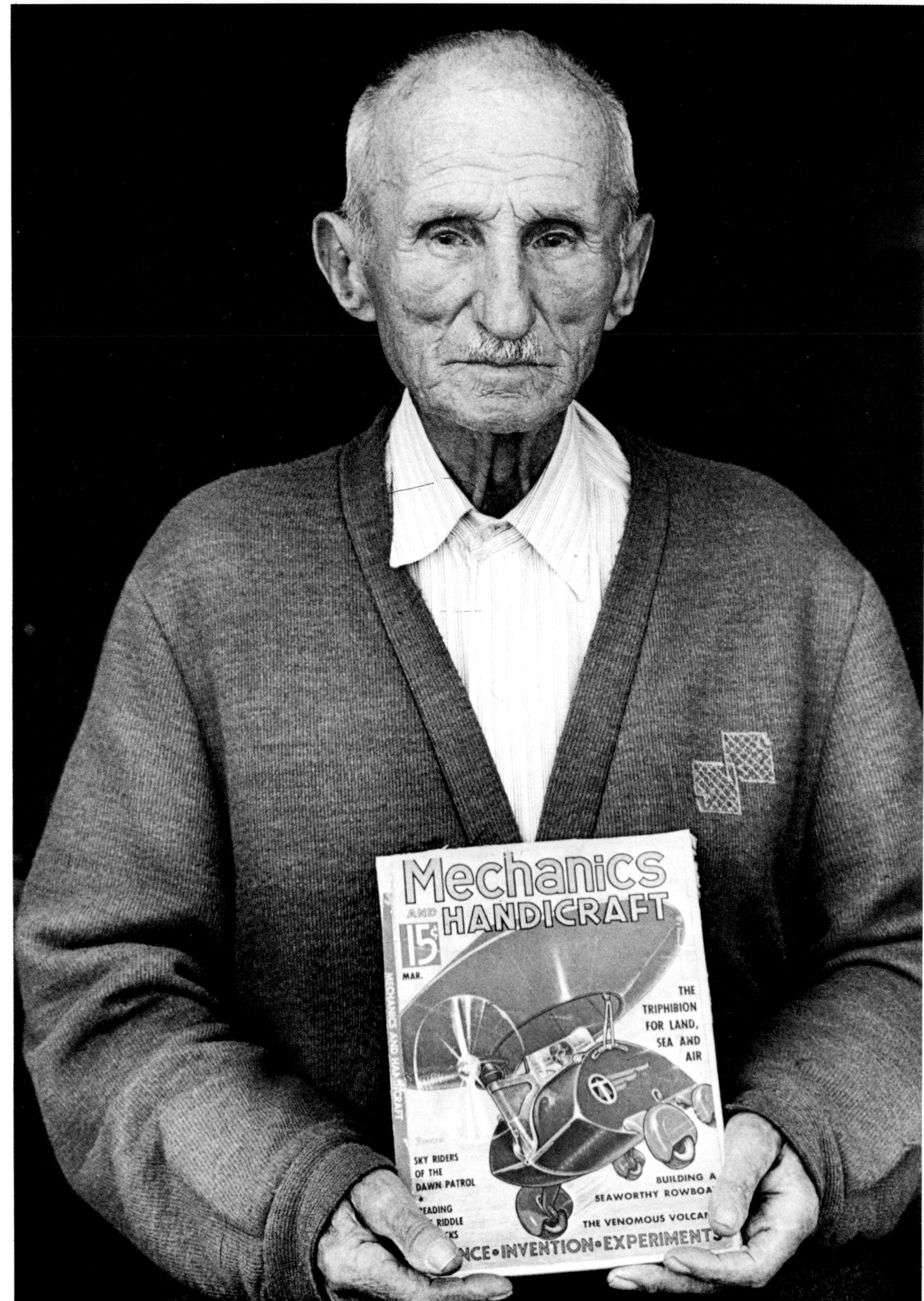

JAMES JOHNSON

Constantinos H. Vlachos, 90, holds the cover of a 1935 magazine containing a story about his triphibion, a vehicle that could travel on land or sea or in the air. Unfortunately, it exploded during a takeoff and Vlachos spent nine months in the hospital.

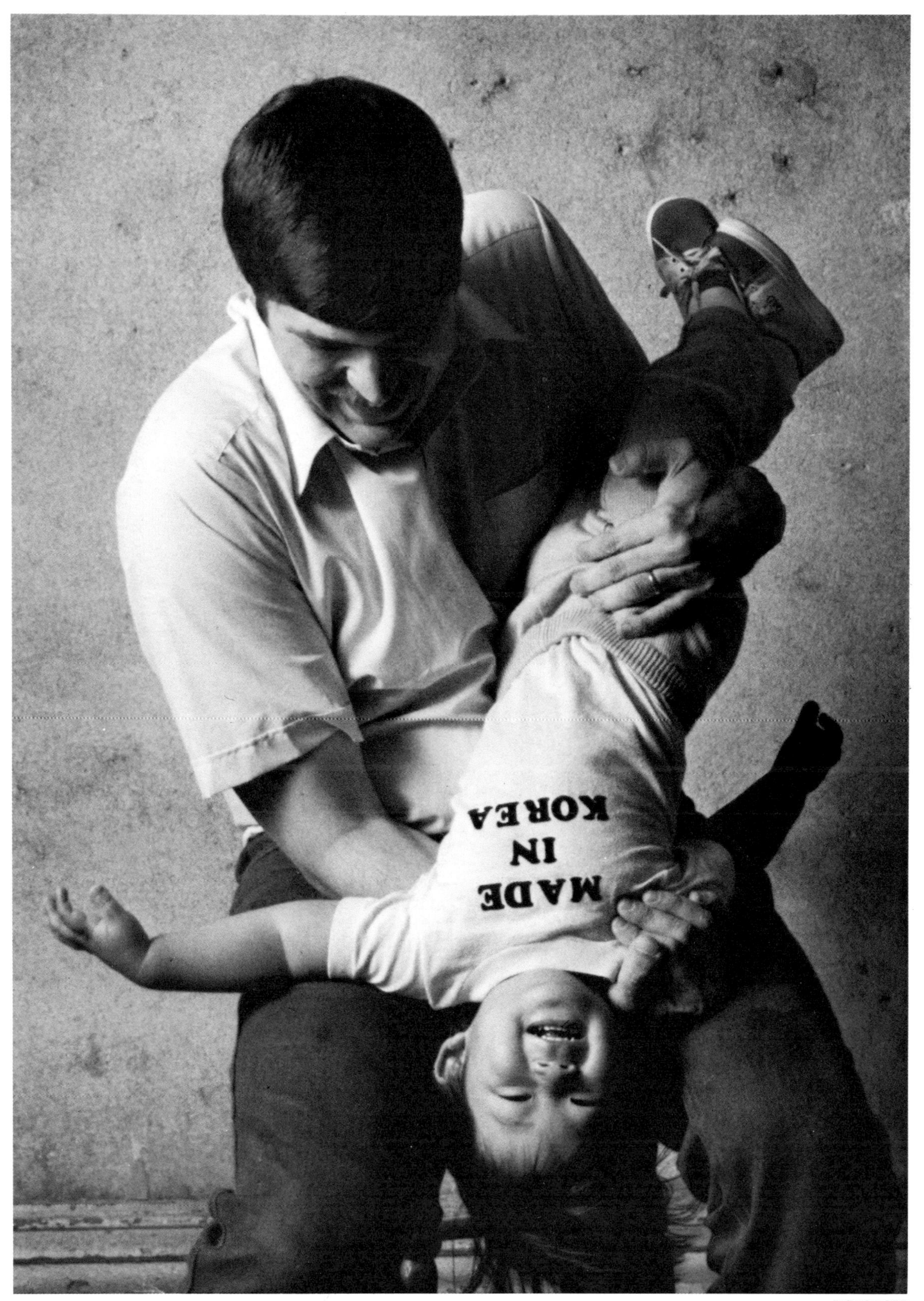

RICK SINGER

Gary Singer of Spokane plays with his newly adopted son, a 1½-year-old Korean orphan, Daniel Jonathan Singer.

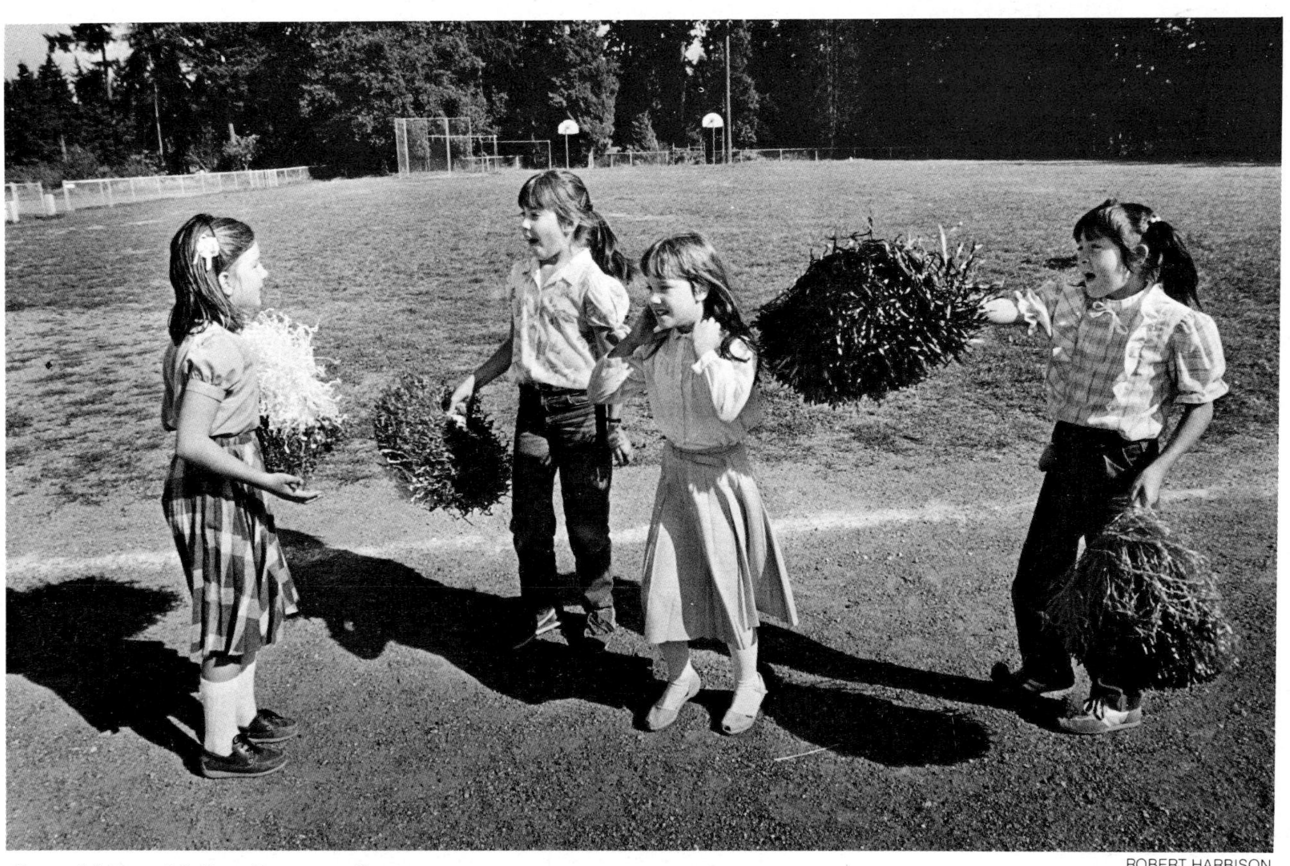

ROBERT HARBISON

Casey Nelson, Melissa Svenson, Gwen Lighty and Shelly Scharnickel practice their cheerleading at Wildwood Elementary School, Federal Way.

Annie Rose and The Thrillers at the Rainbow Tavern in Seattle's University District.

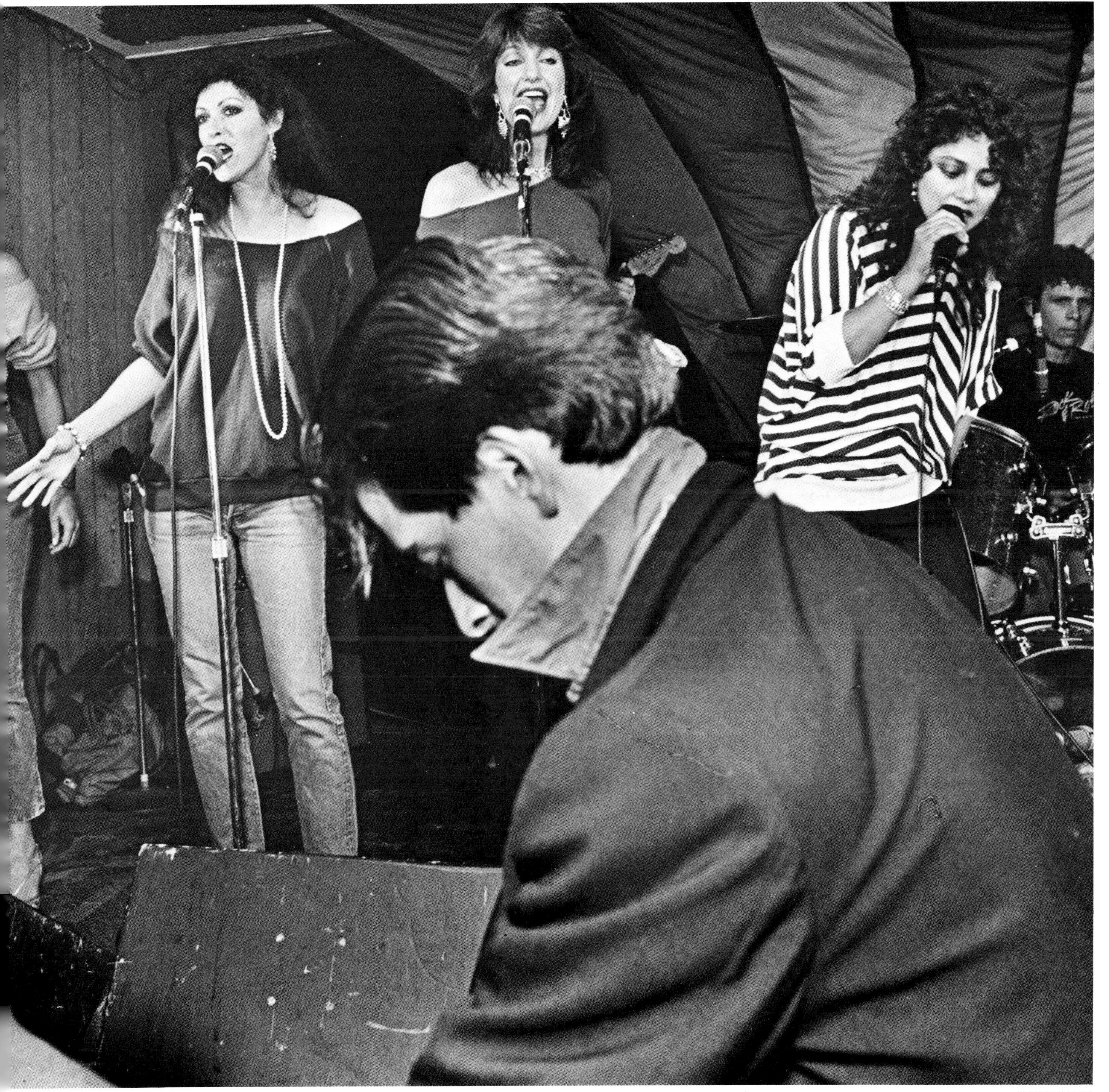

GRANT HALLER

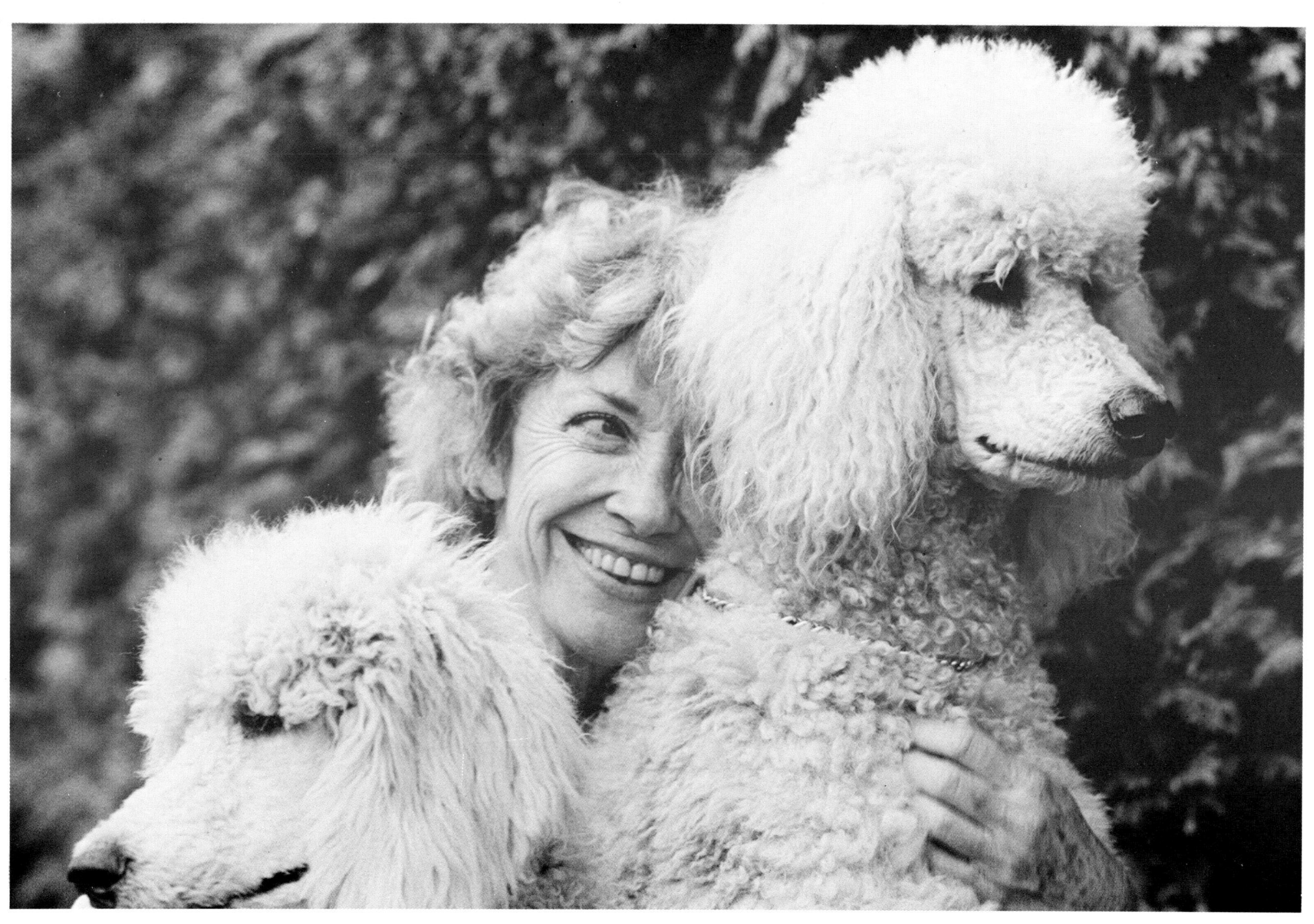

NATALIE FOBES

Woman sitting in her front yard in Seattle's University District.

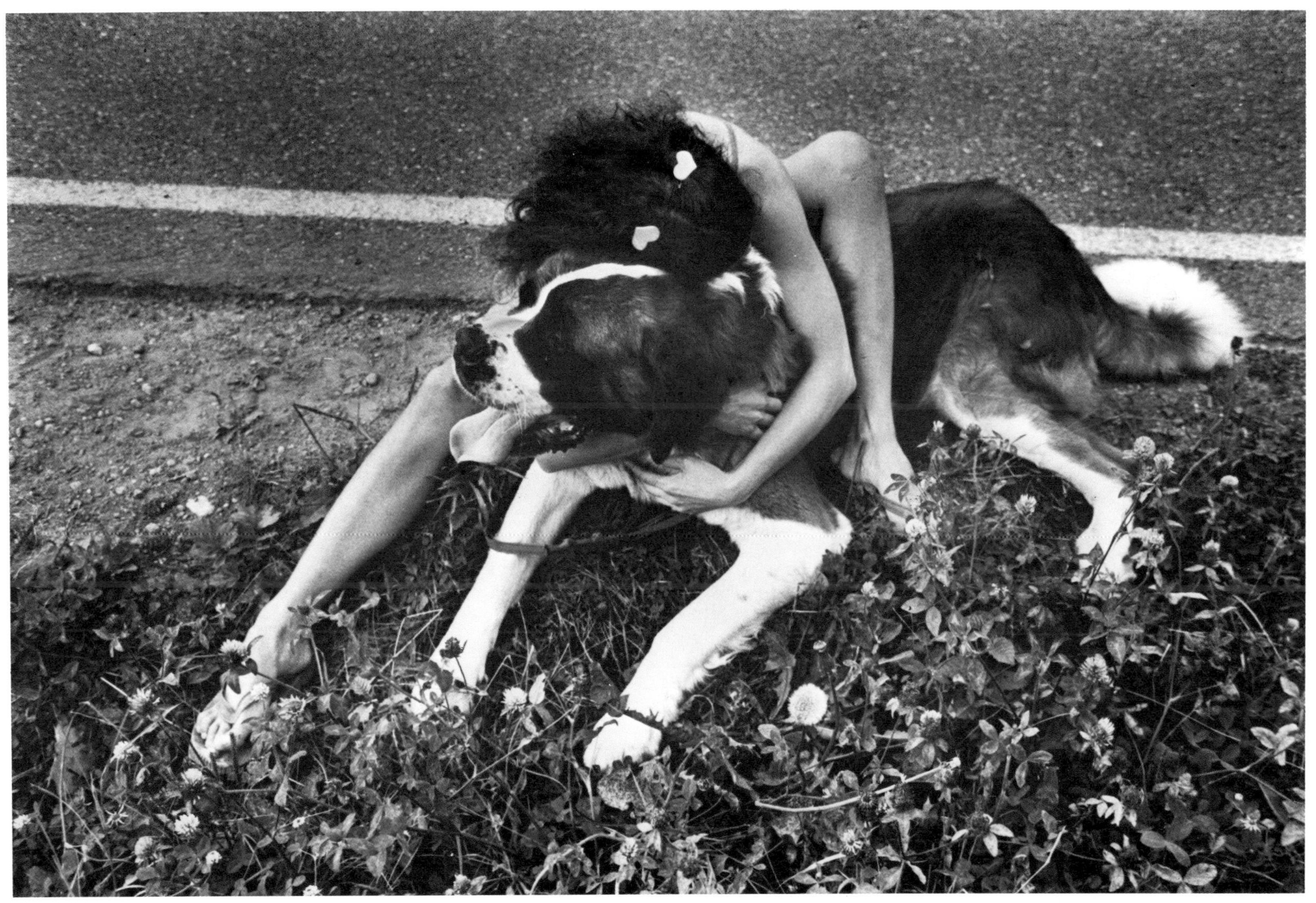

DALE BLINDHEIM

Joanna Levcon and her dog Bear.

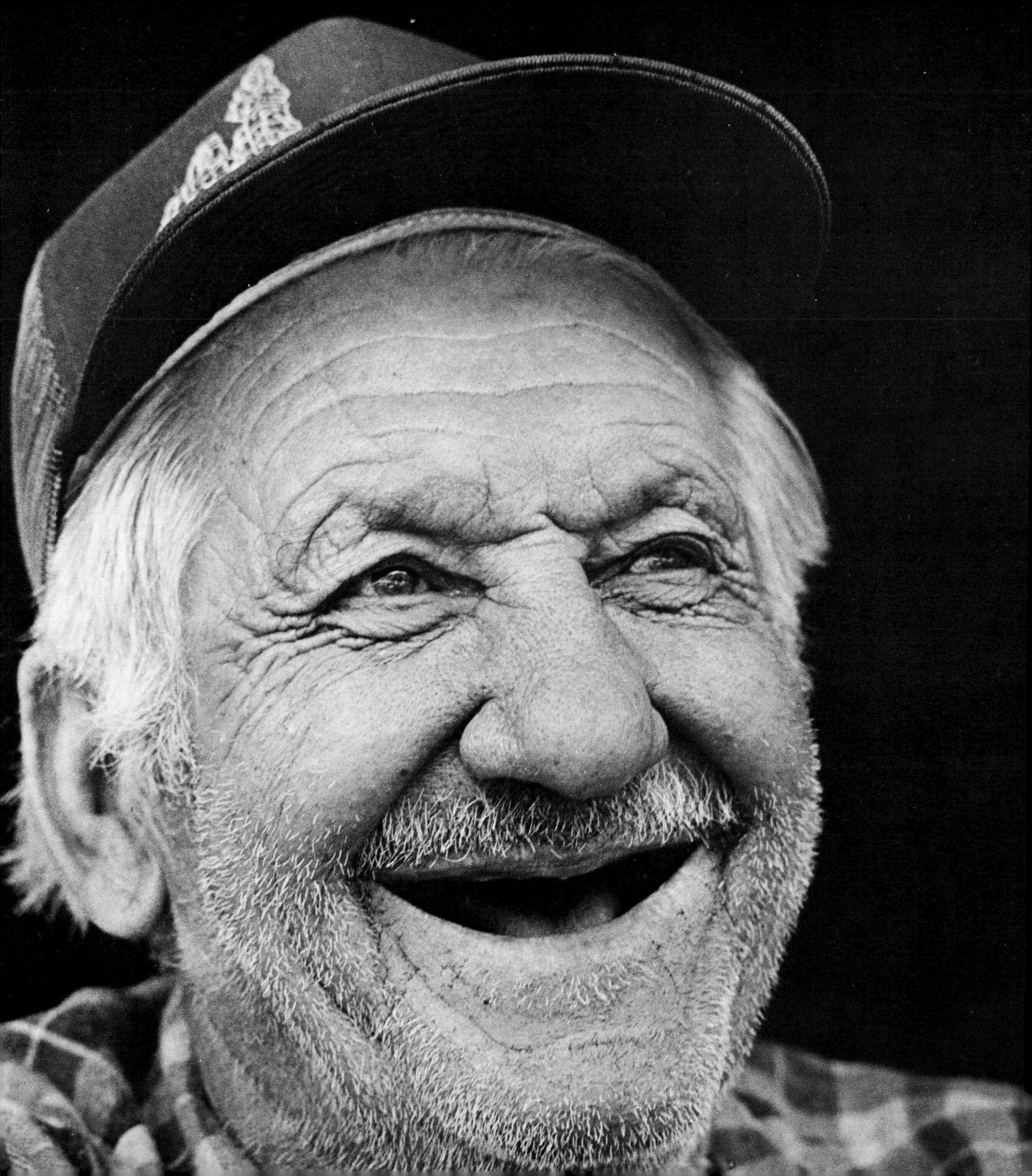

Left: *Frank Grens was known as Miner Frank when he clawed coal from the mines in eastern King County.*
MARK MORRIS

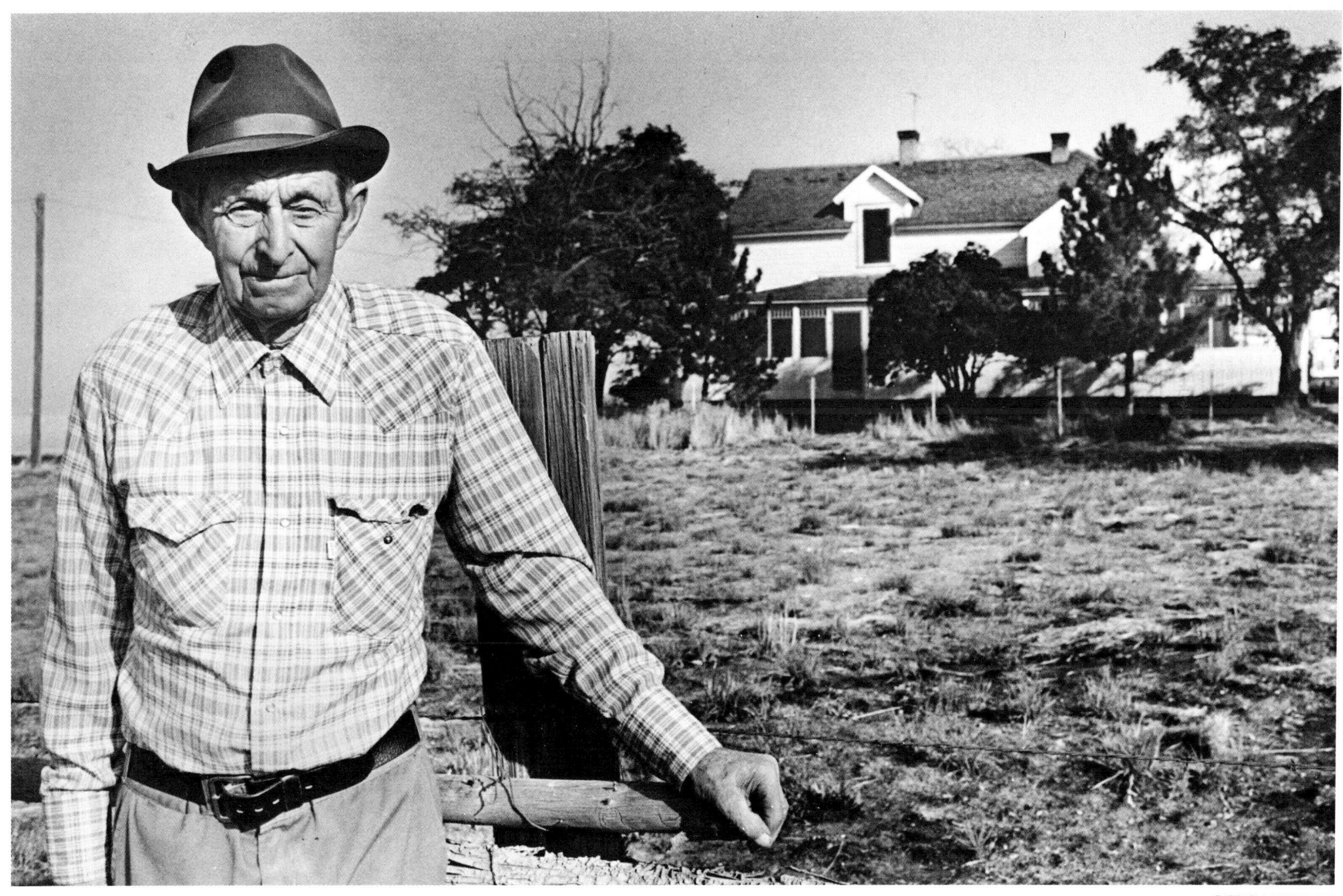

PATRICIA FRIDLUND

Elmer Anderson, 82, runs the family wheat farm started by his parents in the Rattlesnake Hills near Yakima.

Following pages:
Bill Schluter, 82, entertains his 107-year-old mother, Appie Kroll.
JIMI LOTT

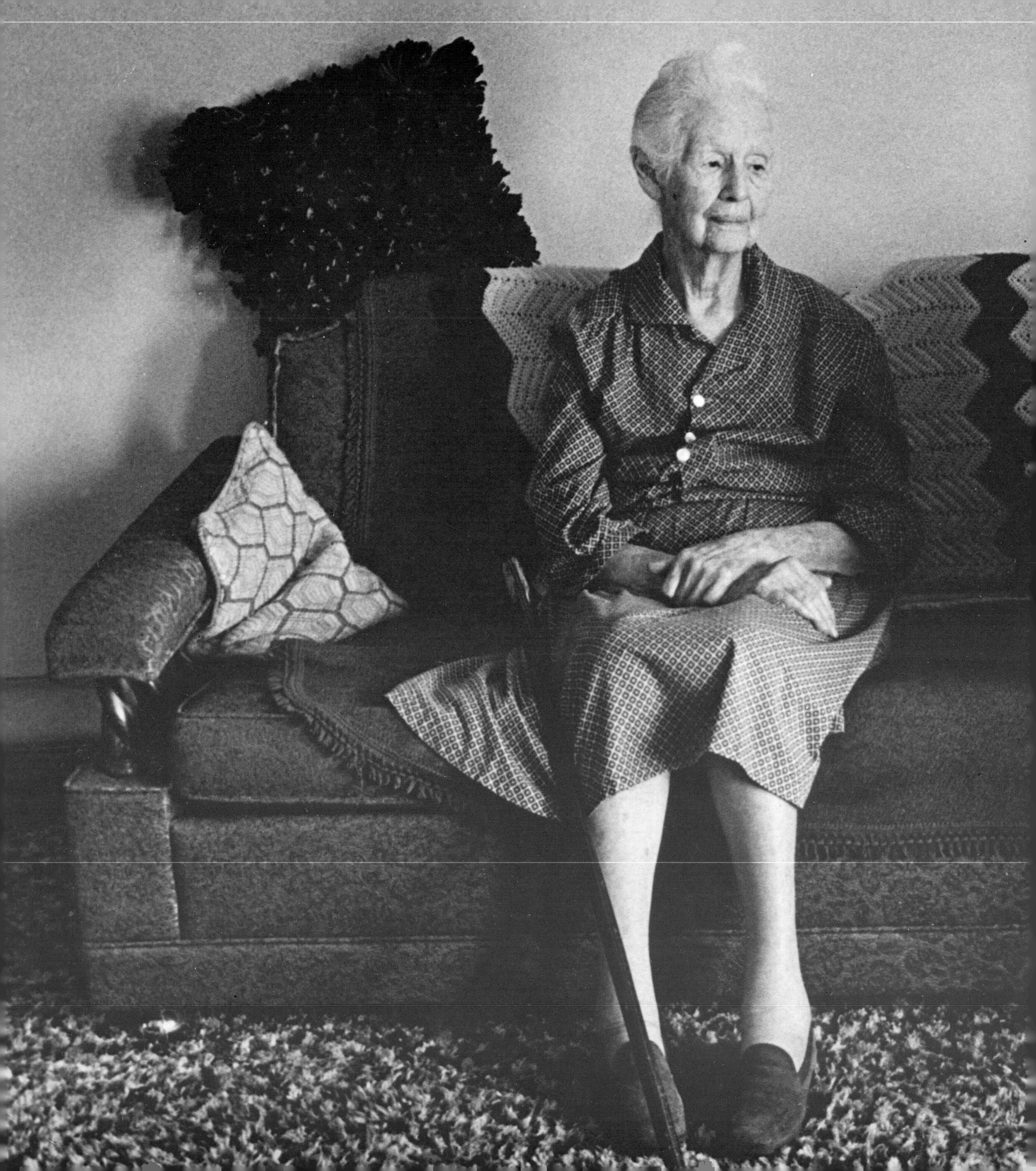

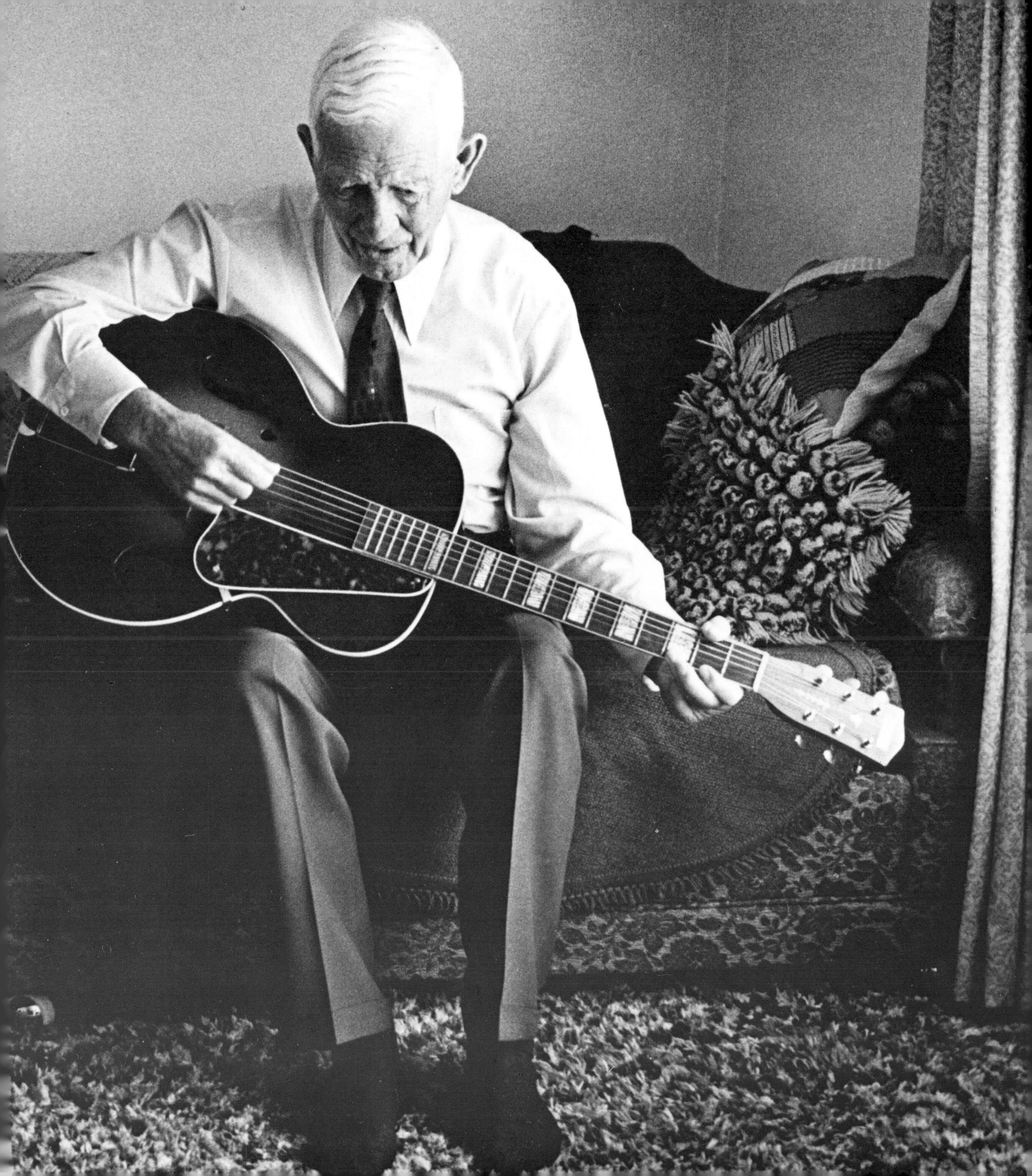

TWINS

Right: *Kim Peck and Kay Jones*

Far right: *Anita and Angela Brown*

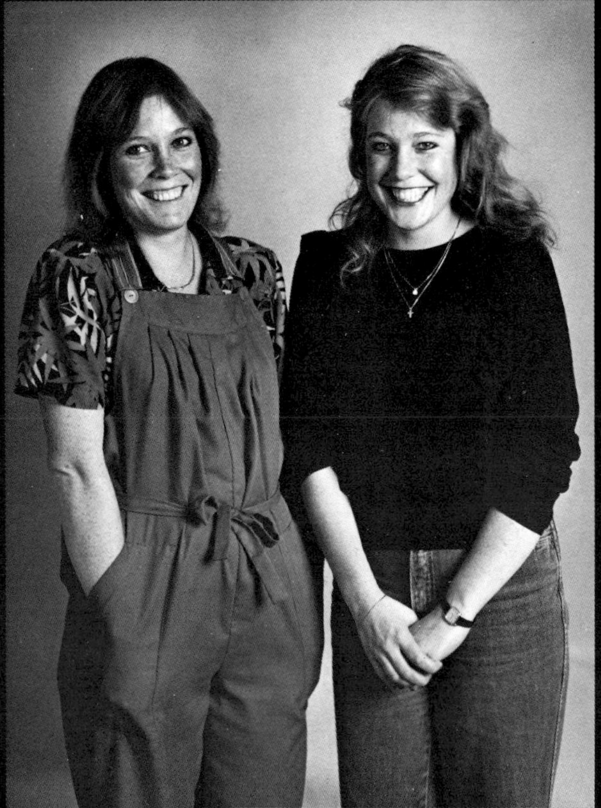

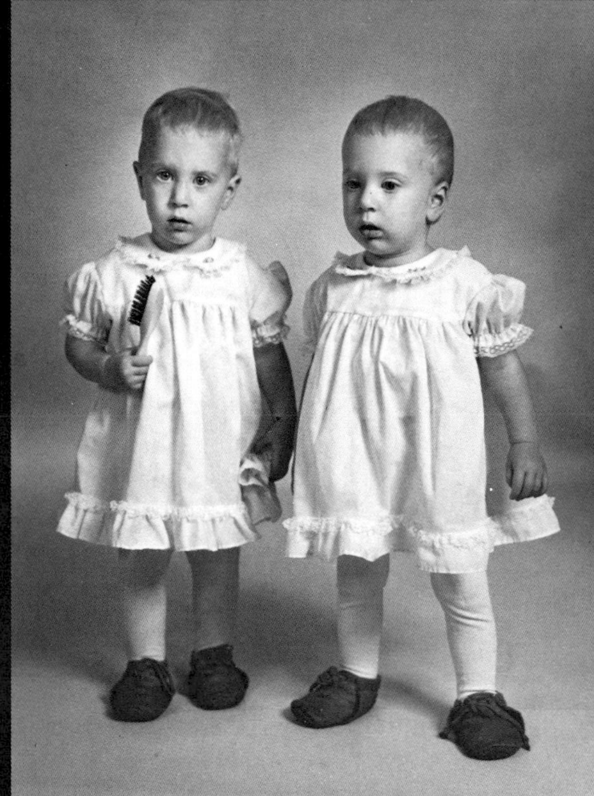

Right: *Tony and Terry Stephens*

Far right: *Marie and Naomi Lord*

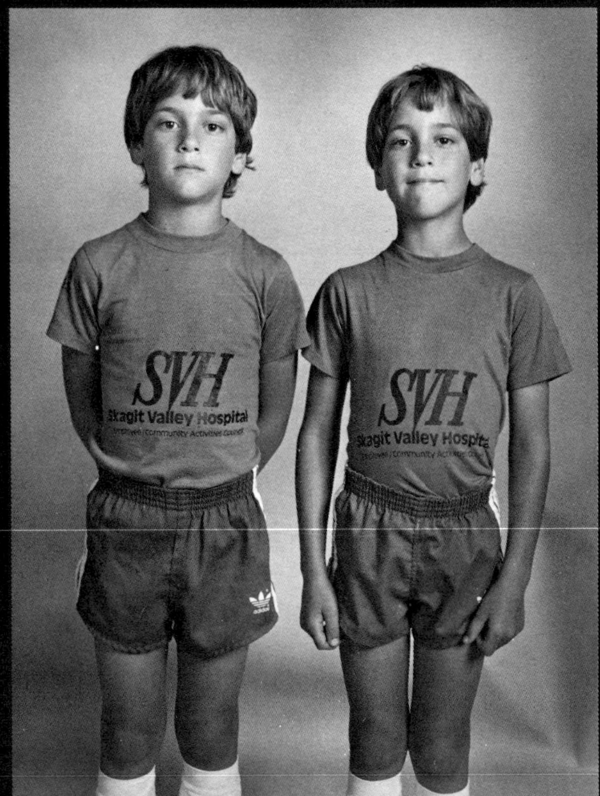

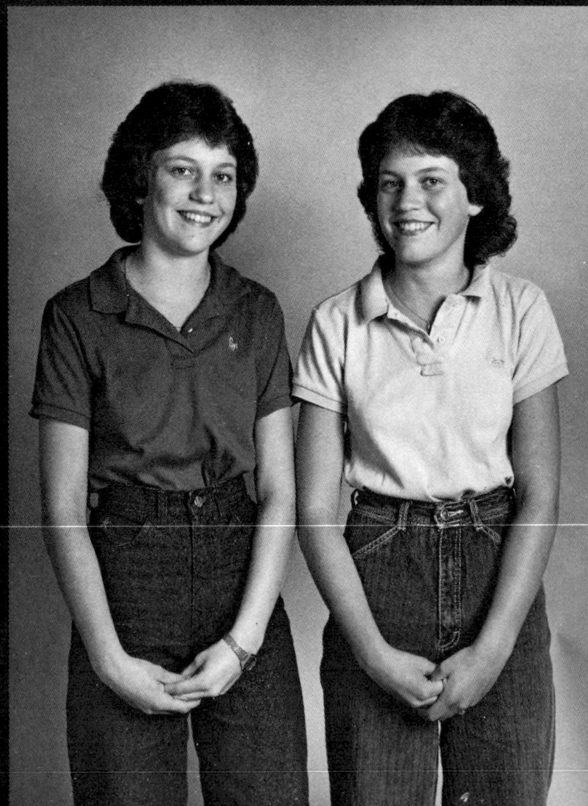

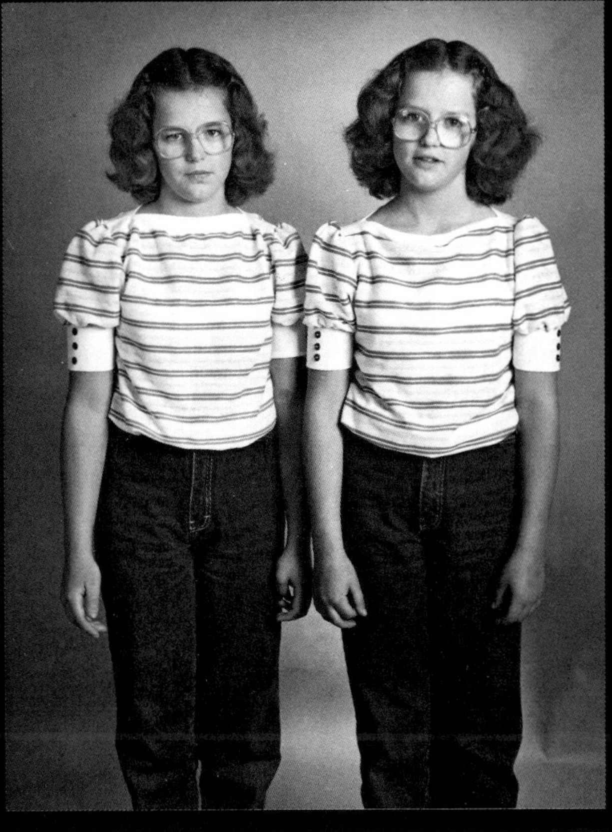

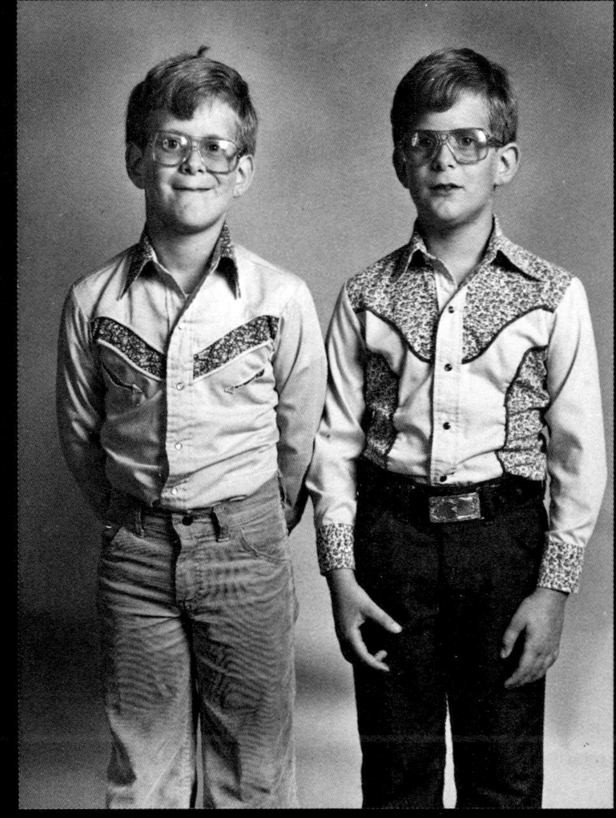

Far left: *Dawn and Melissa Ivison*

Left: *Tyson and Garry Danielson*

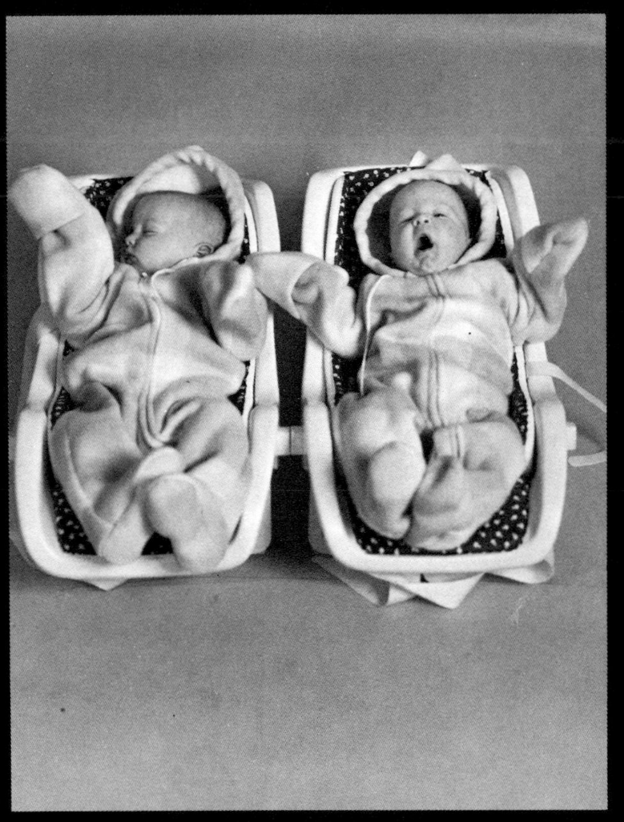

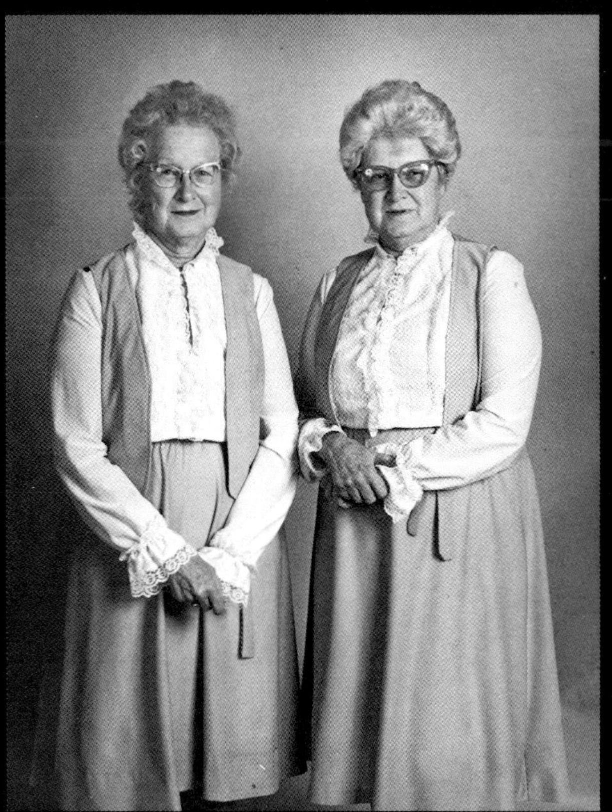

Far left: *Billy and Bobby Bauder*

Left: *Dorothy Hall and Dora Hofstad*

PHOTOS BY JON BRUNK

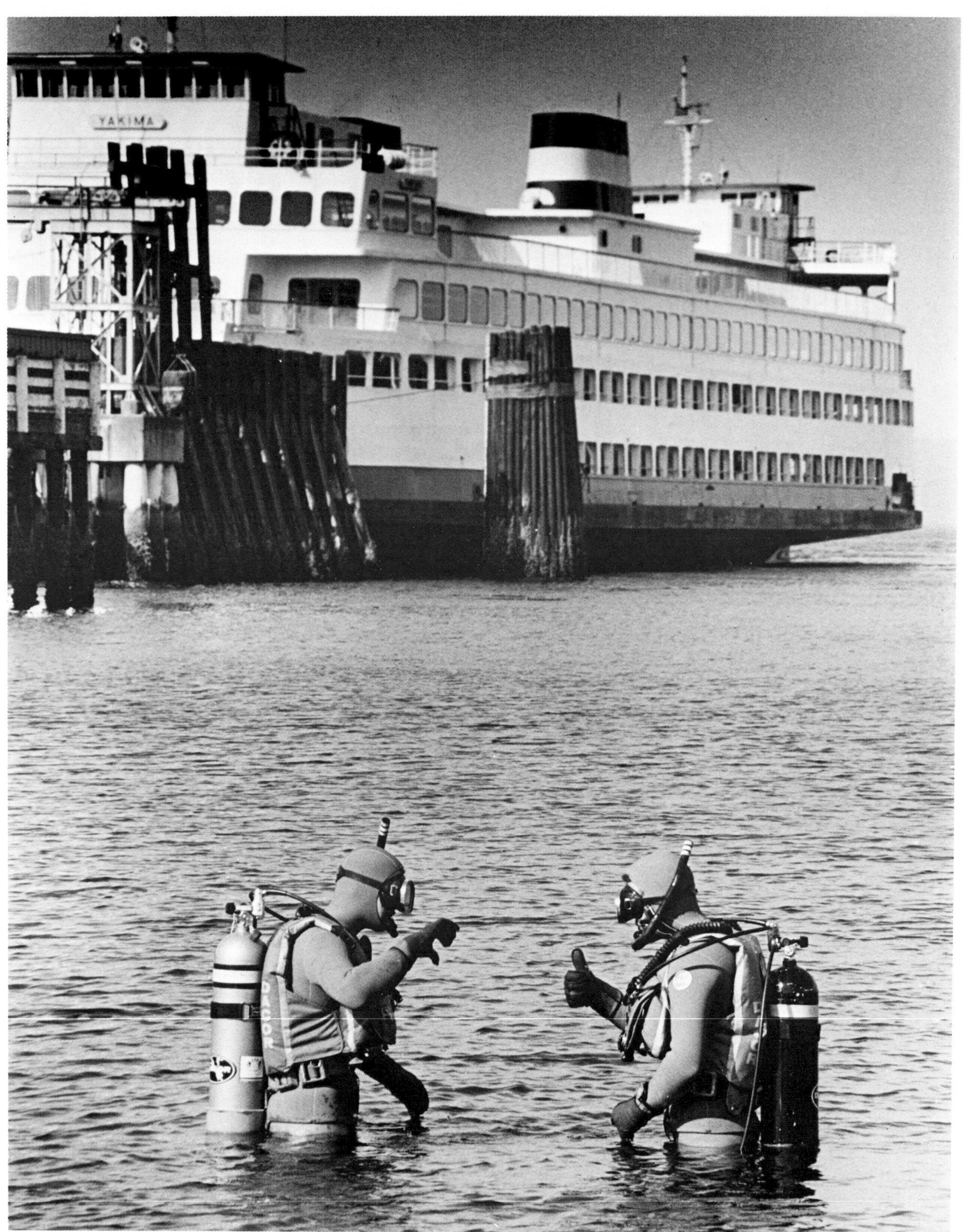

Dan Gartner and Tom Jovanovich at a marine park and sanctuary developed by the city of Edmonds near the ferryboat terminal.

R. BRUCE COLWELL, JR.

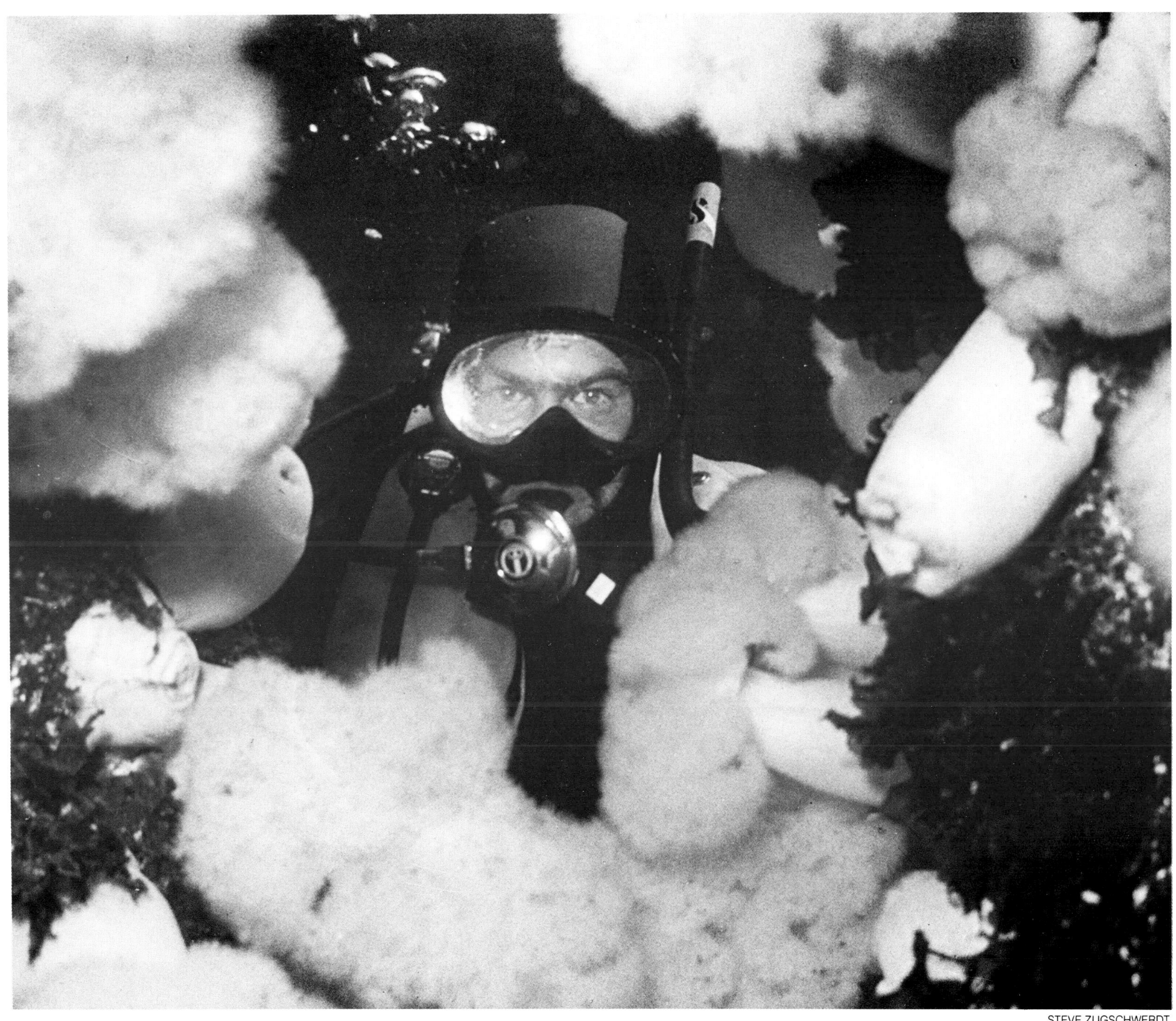

STEVE ZUGSCHWERDT

Steve Wojcik framed by a wall of anemones in Puget Sound.

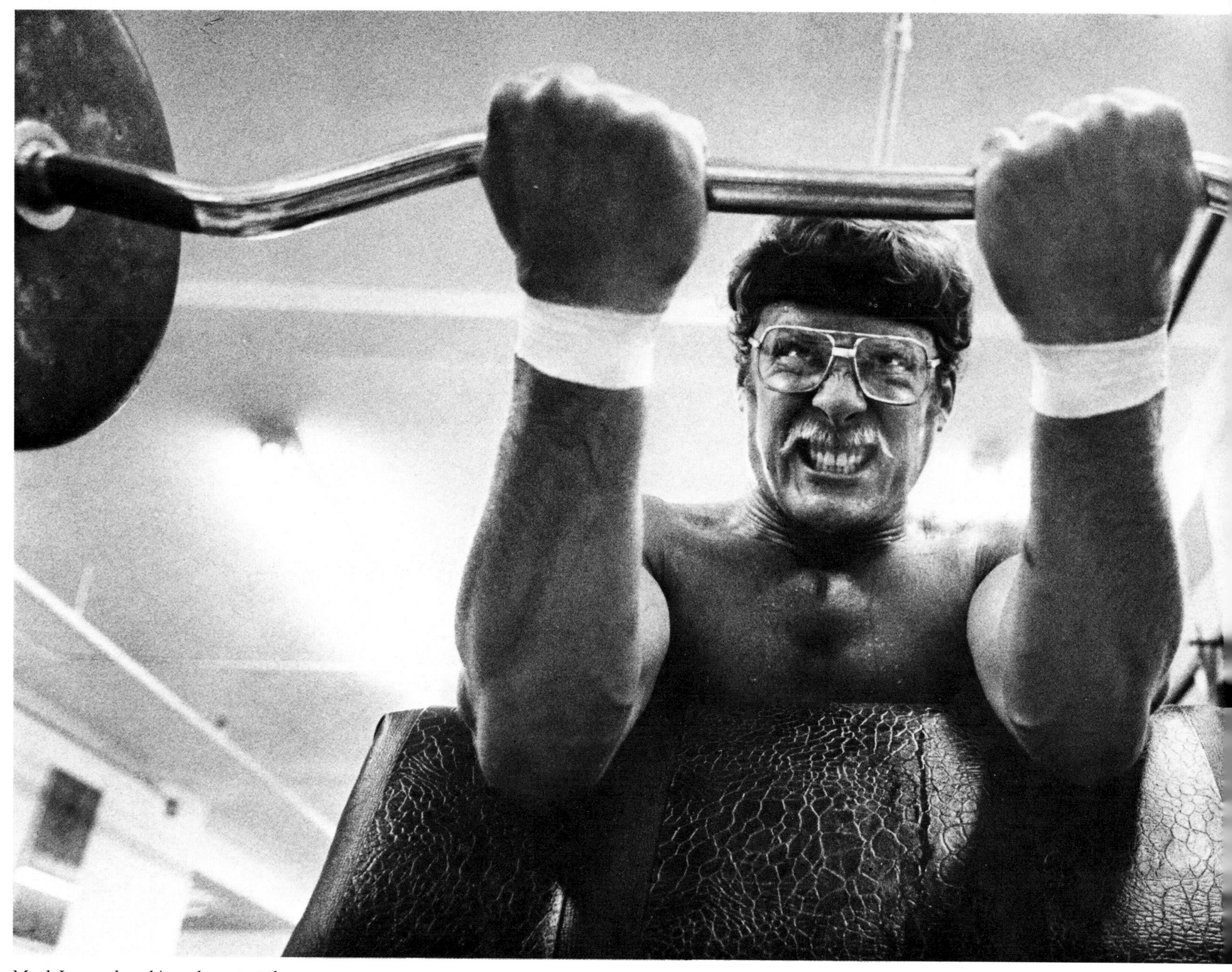

Mark Lewondowski works out at the Metropolitan Health Club in downtown Seattle.

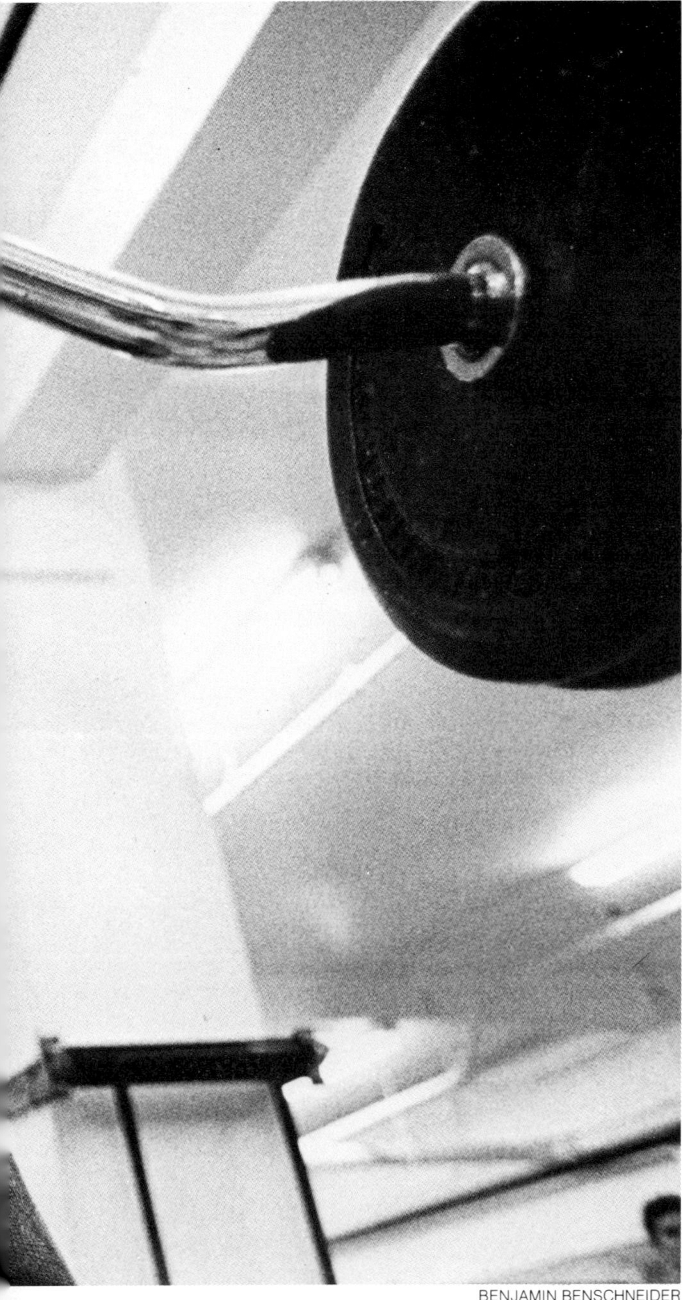

BENJAMIN BENSCHNEIDER

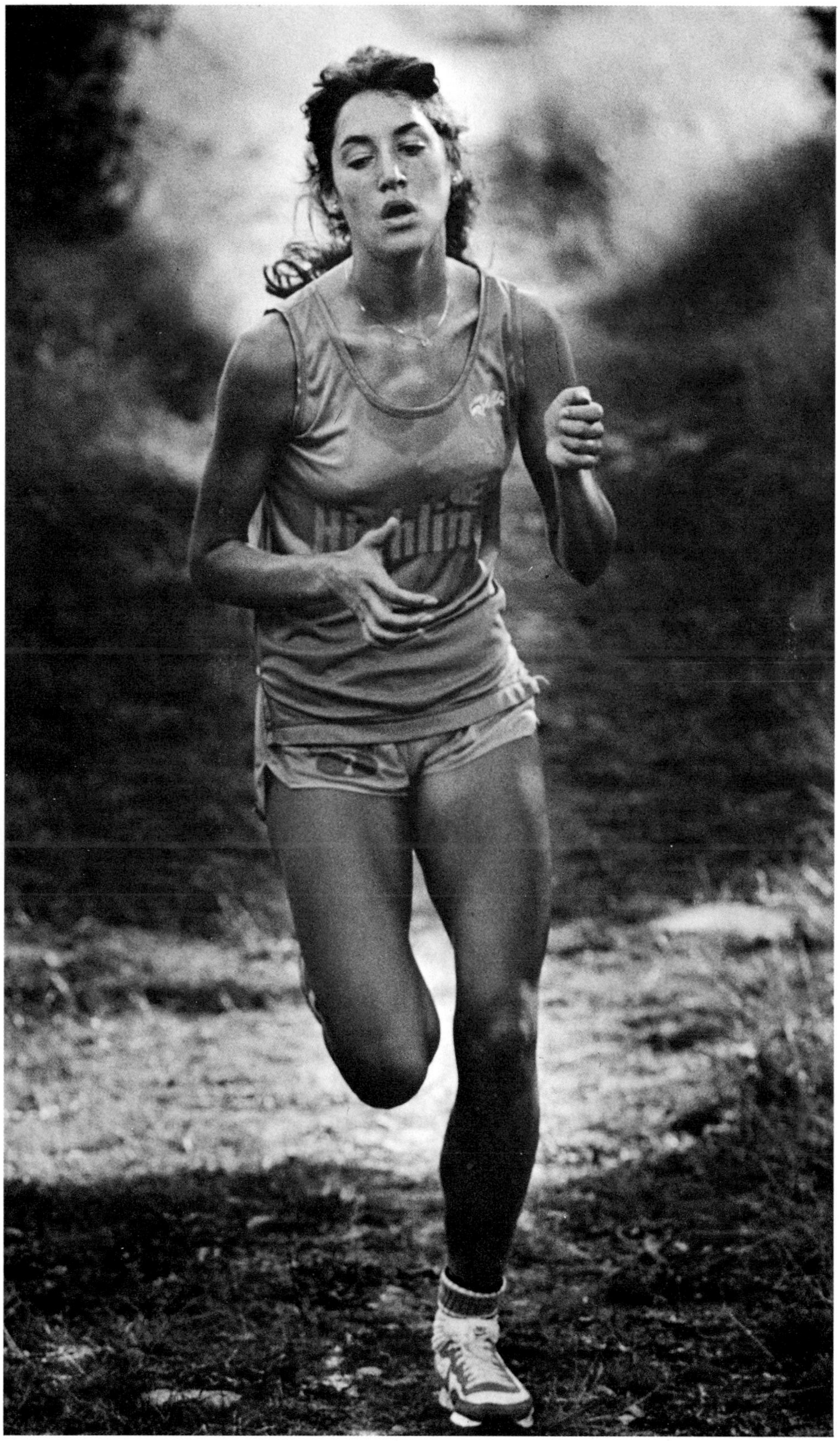

Gina Hulsman of the Highline High School cross-country team.

Following pages:

Terry Minteer of Bremerton goes to aerobics classes three times a week.

THERESA AUBIN

SCOTT TERRELL

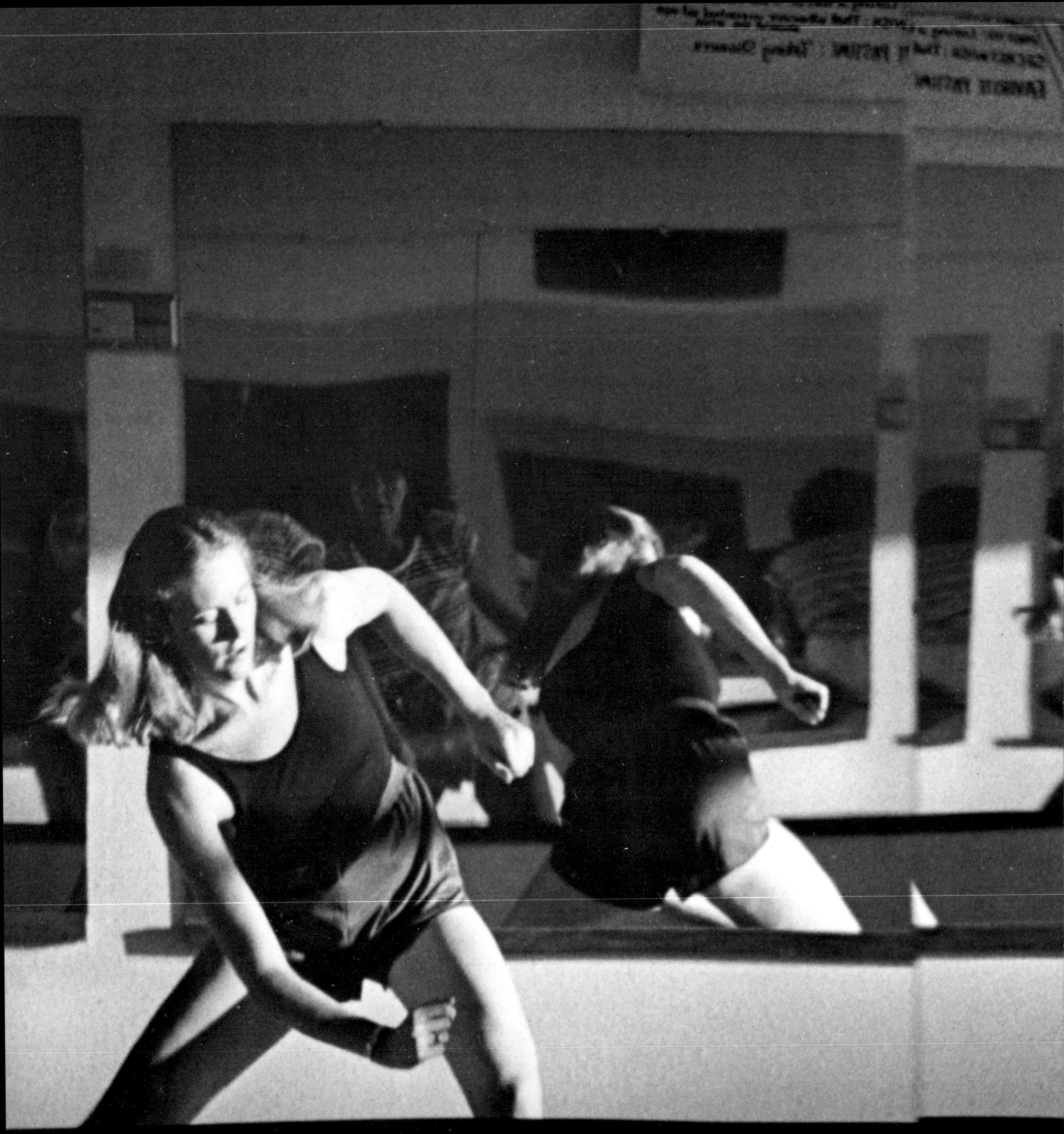

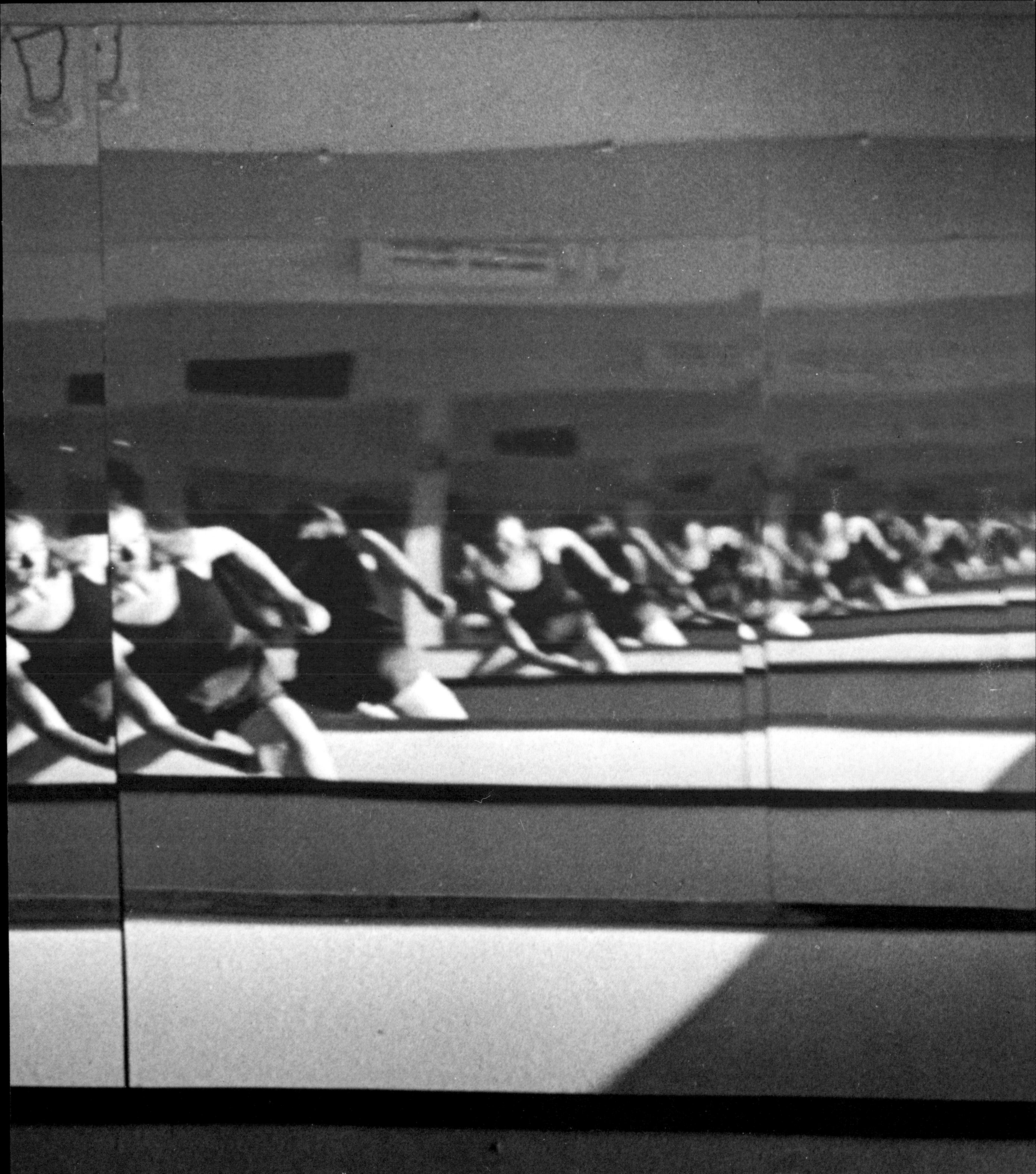

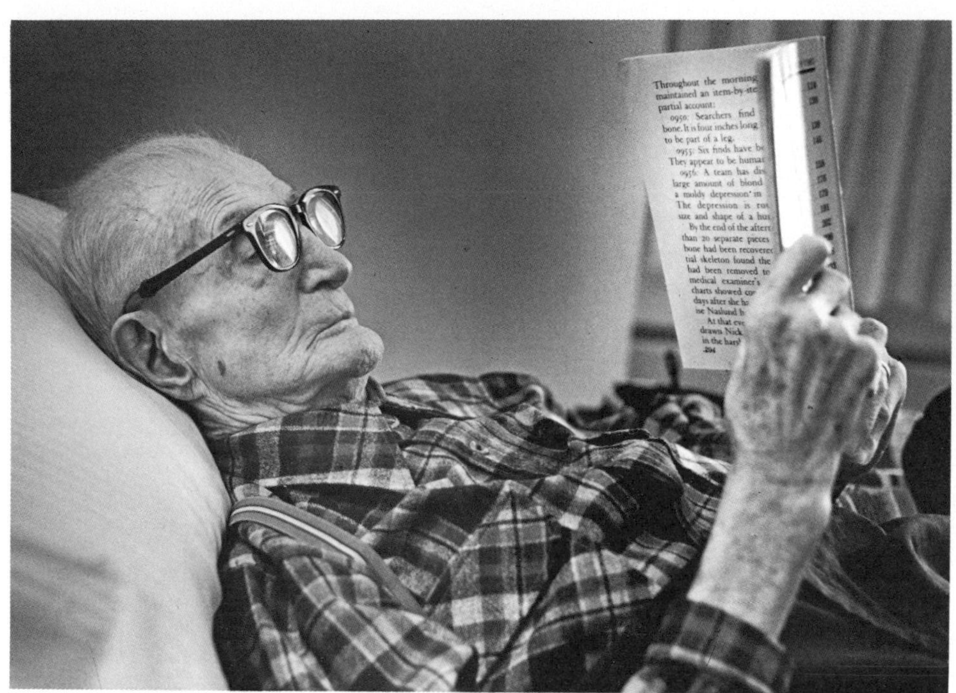

REX-ZANE RUDEE

Will Cook, 104, a veteran of the Spanish-American War, at the Restil Veterans Home.

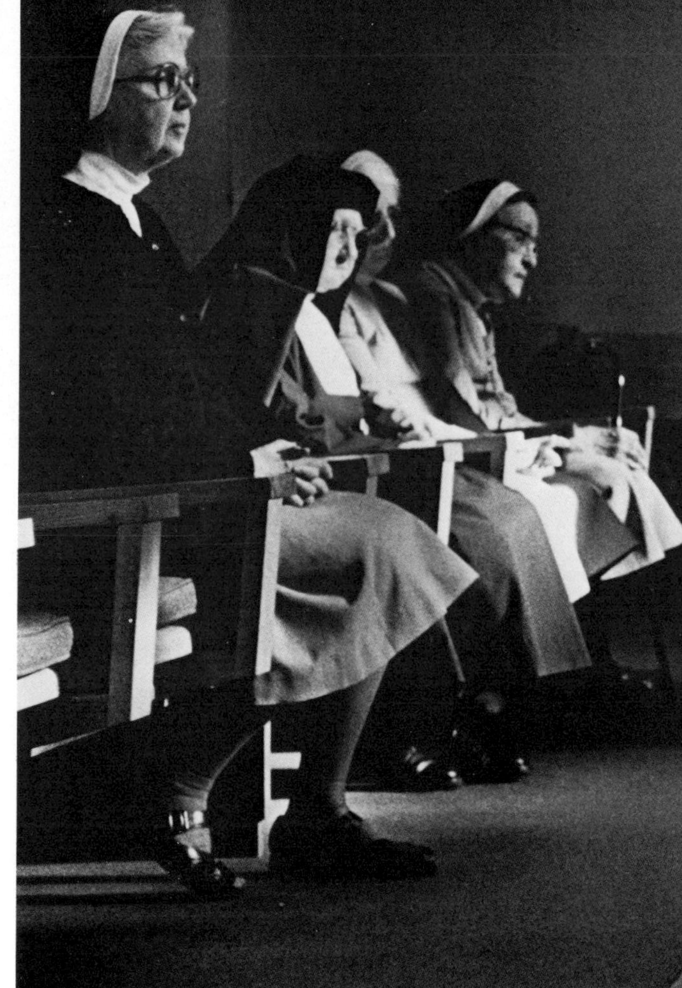

The Sisters of Visitation, Pierce County.

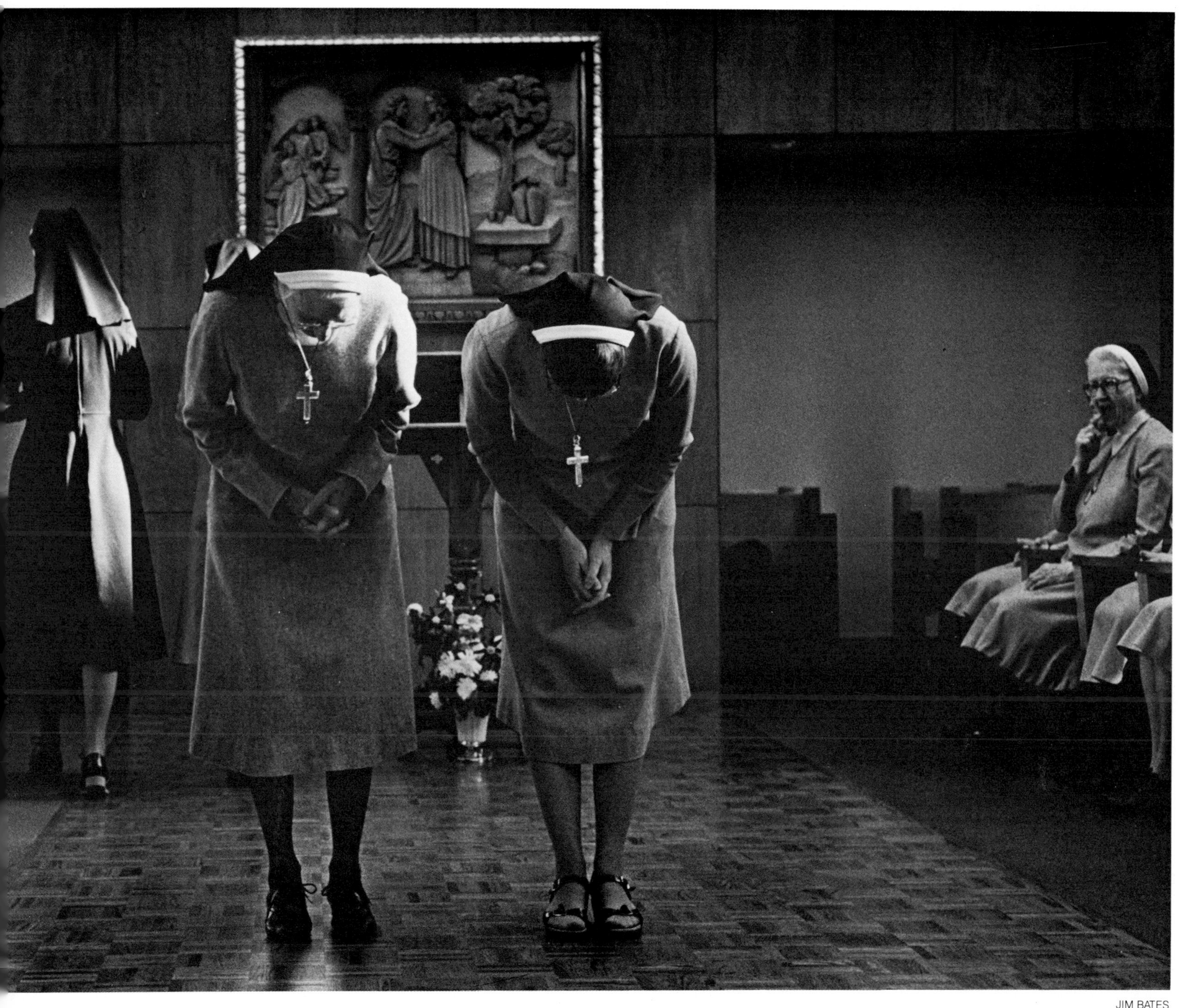

JIM BATES

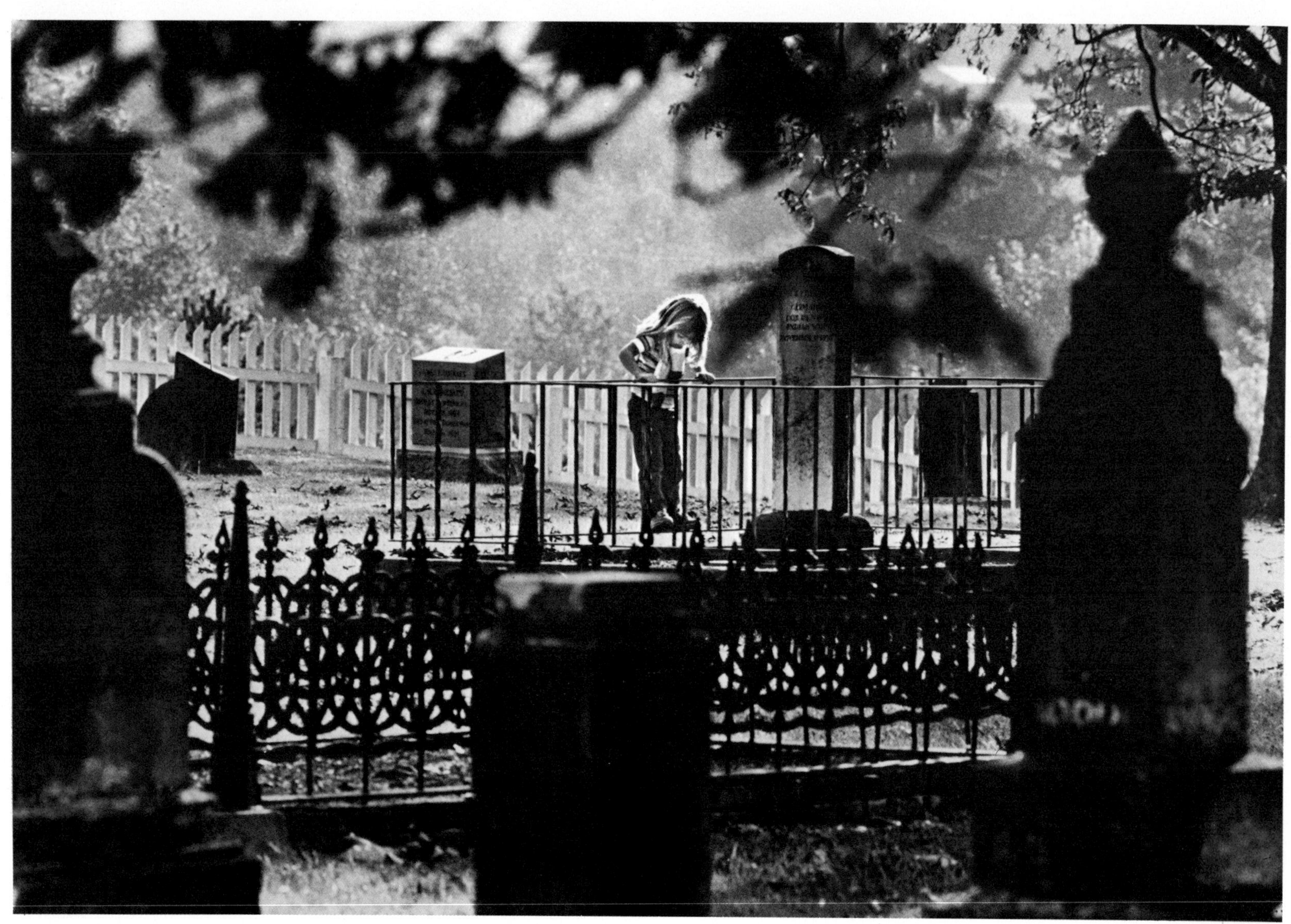

MIKE SIEGEL

Kelli Renee Breeton-Fairall, 4, of Silverdale, at the grave of the first Navy man to die in the Pacific during the "Indian Depredation of 1856." The cemetary, a national historic monument, is in Port Gamble.

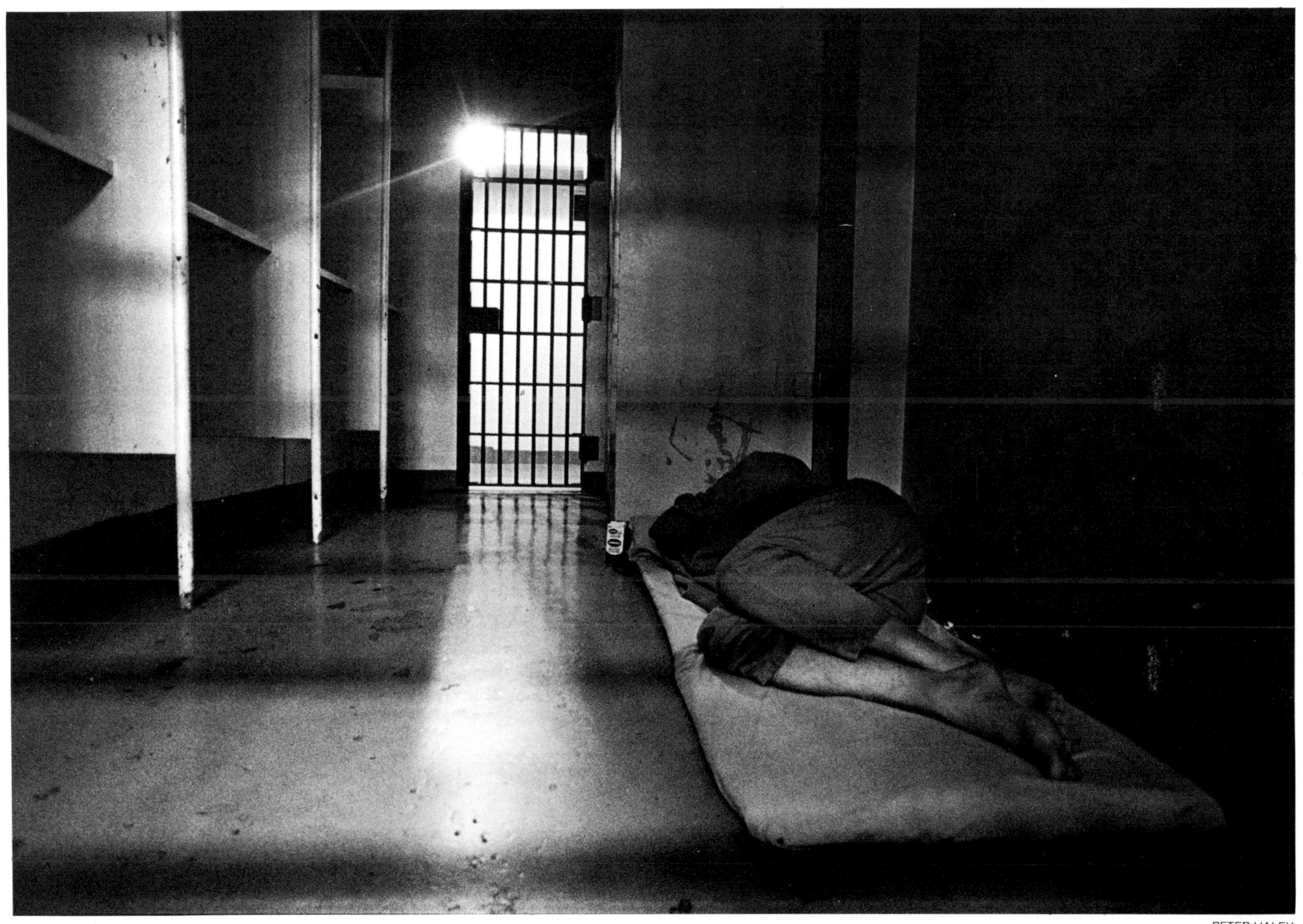

PETER HALEY

In the King County jail.

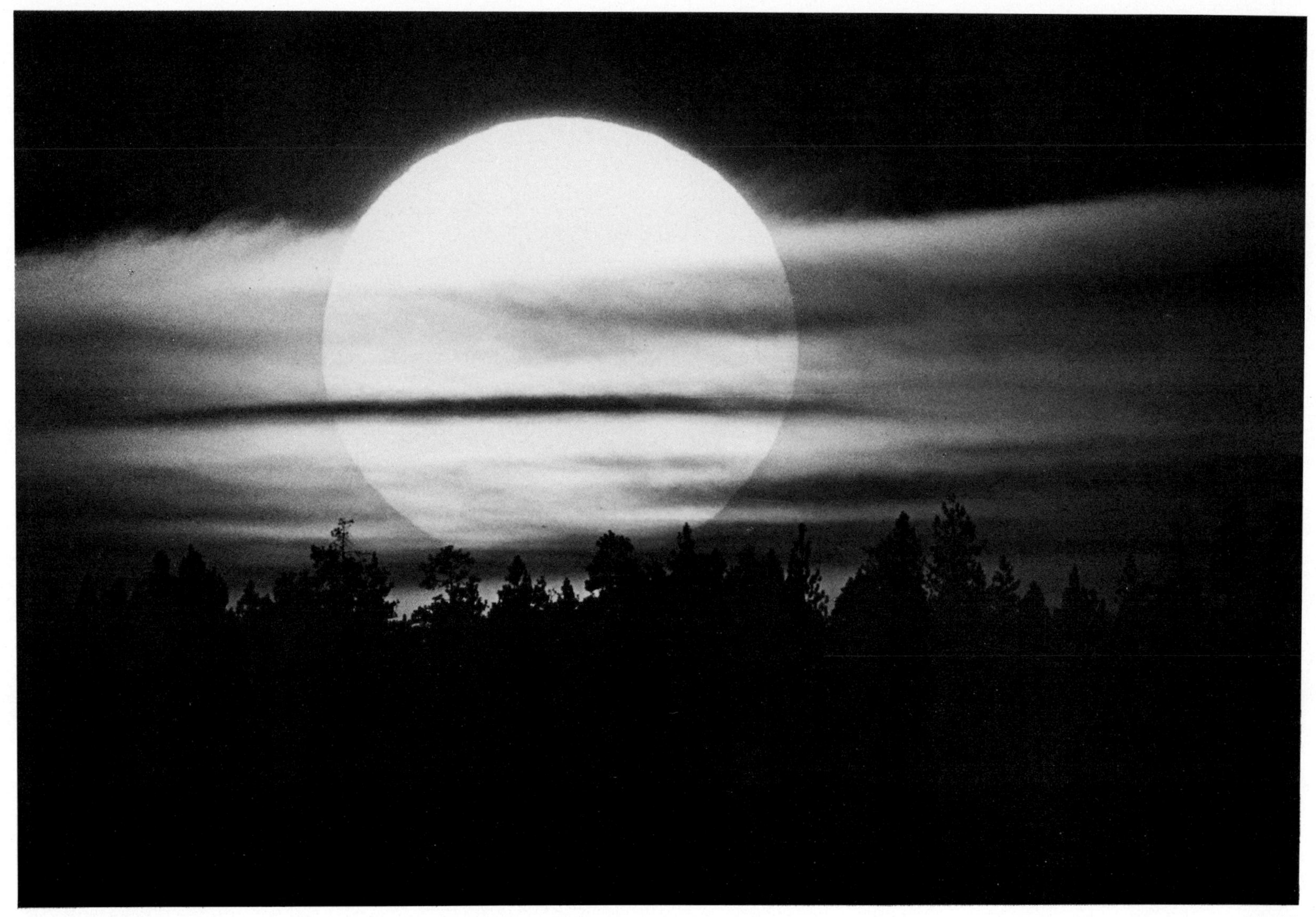

JIMI LOTT

Sunset, Spokane.

Right: *A Washington State Ferry in Elliott Bay.*

ALAN BERNER

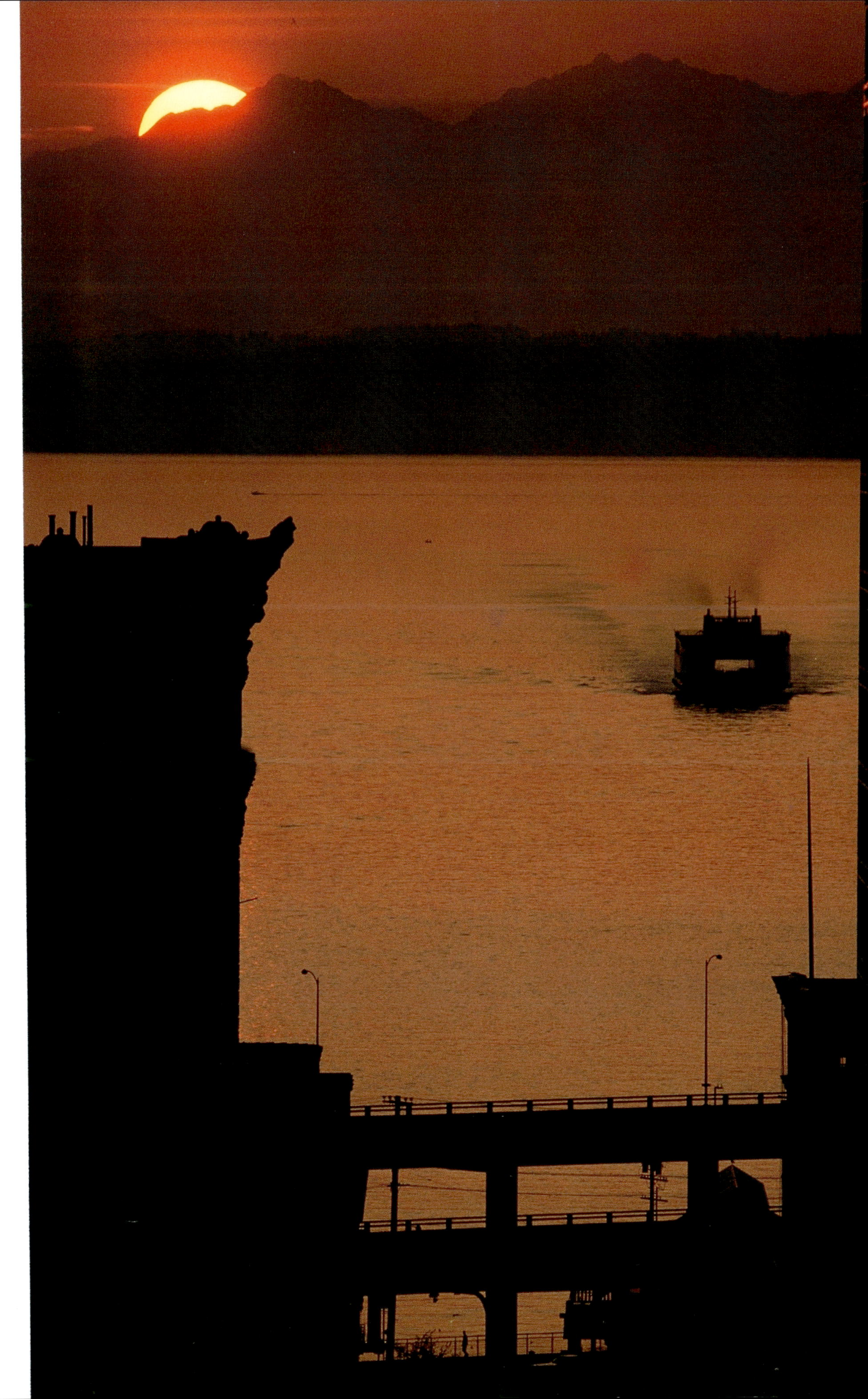

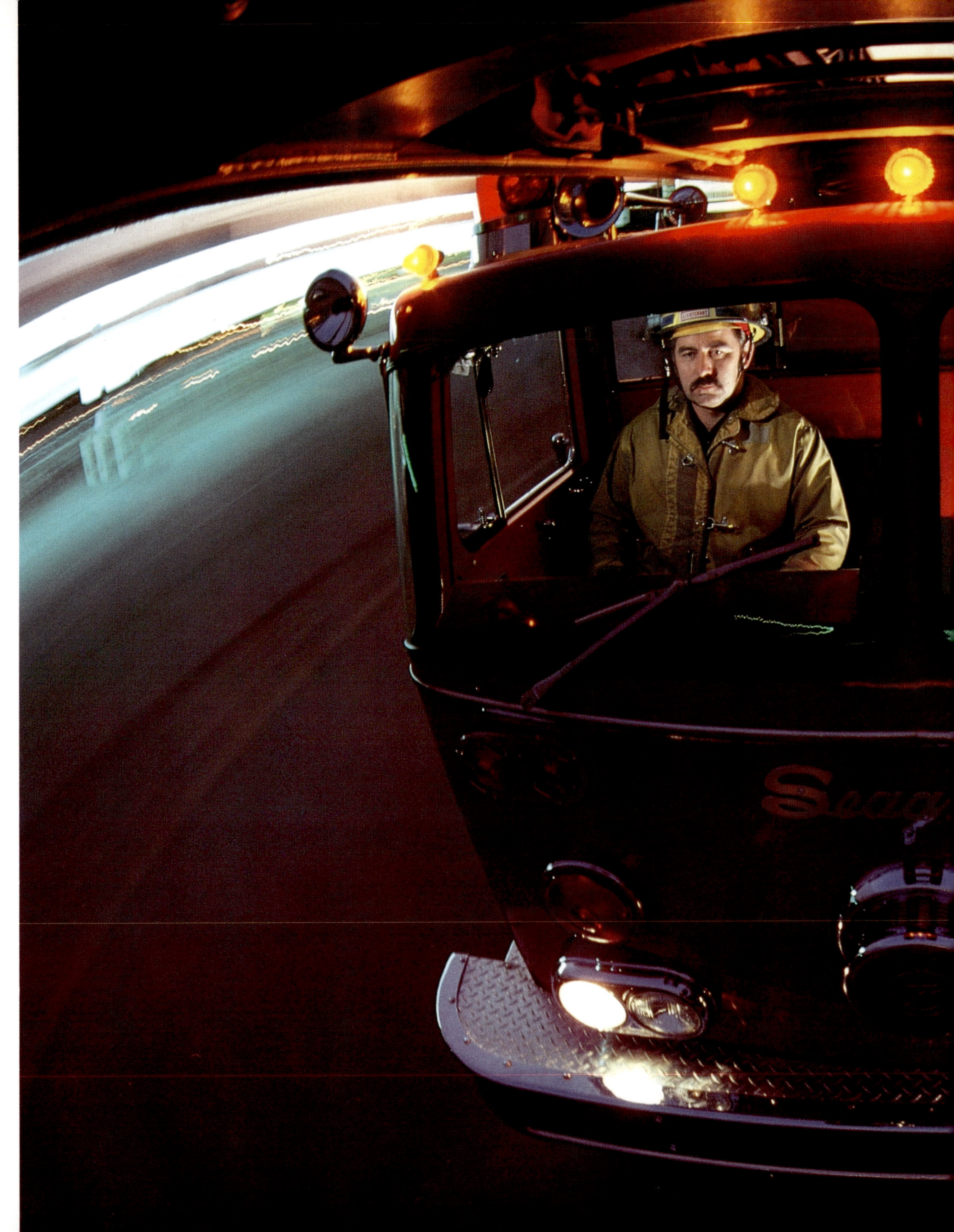

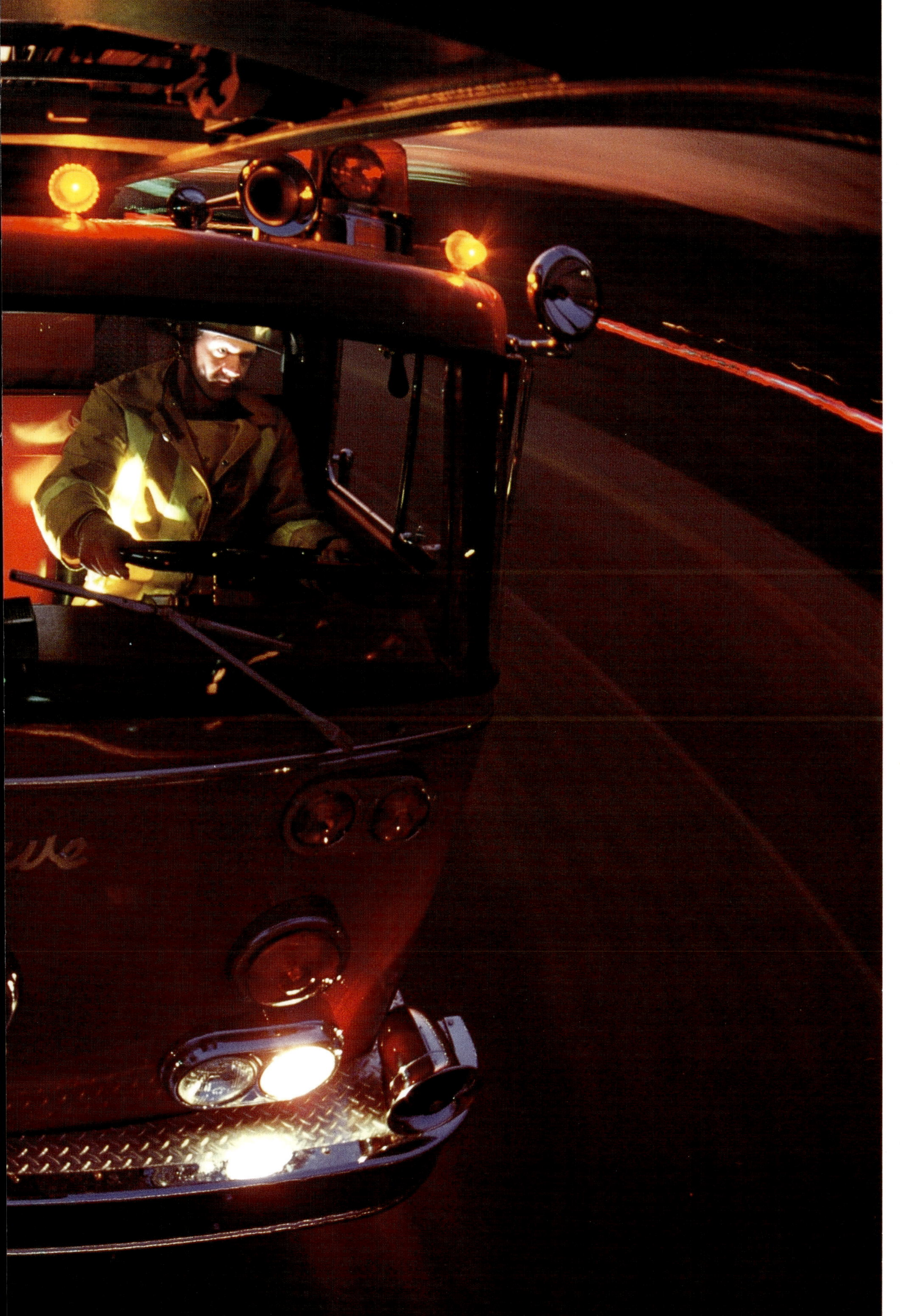

Mount Vernon fire truck.
STEPHEN SCHROEDER

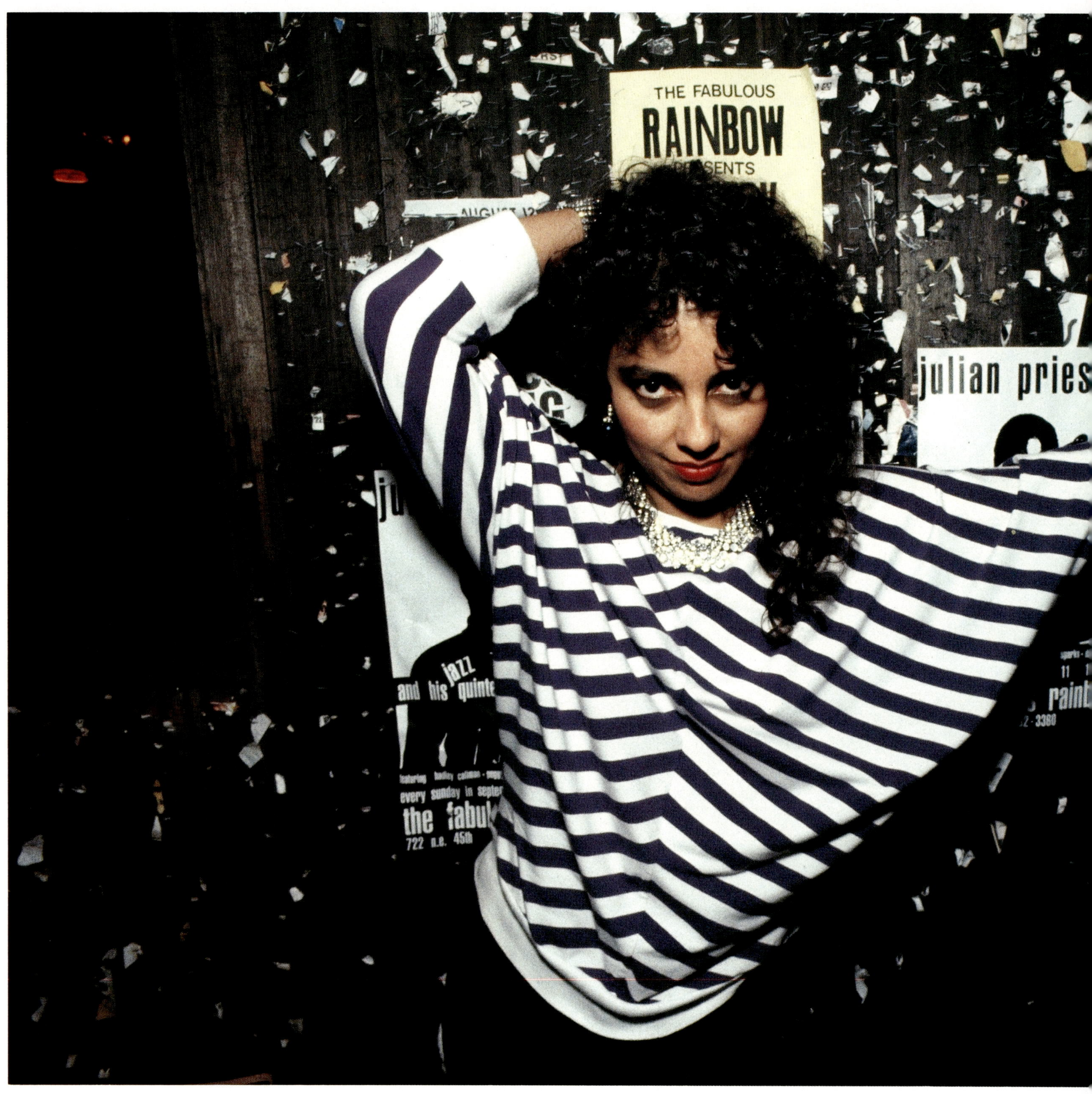
THE FABULOUS
RAINBOW
julian pries
jazz
and his quinte
every sunday in septe
the fabul
722 n.e. 45th

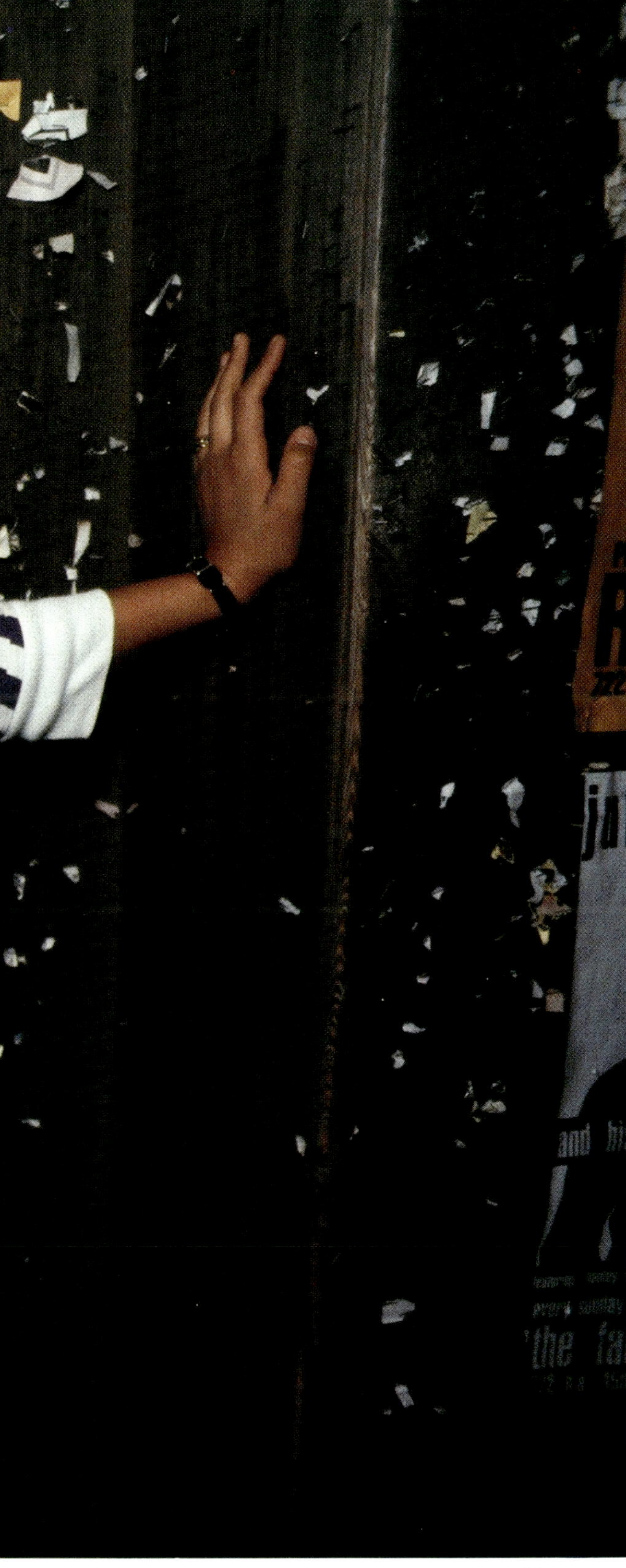

GRANT HALLER

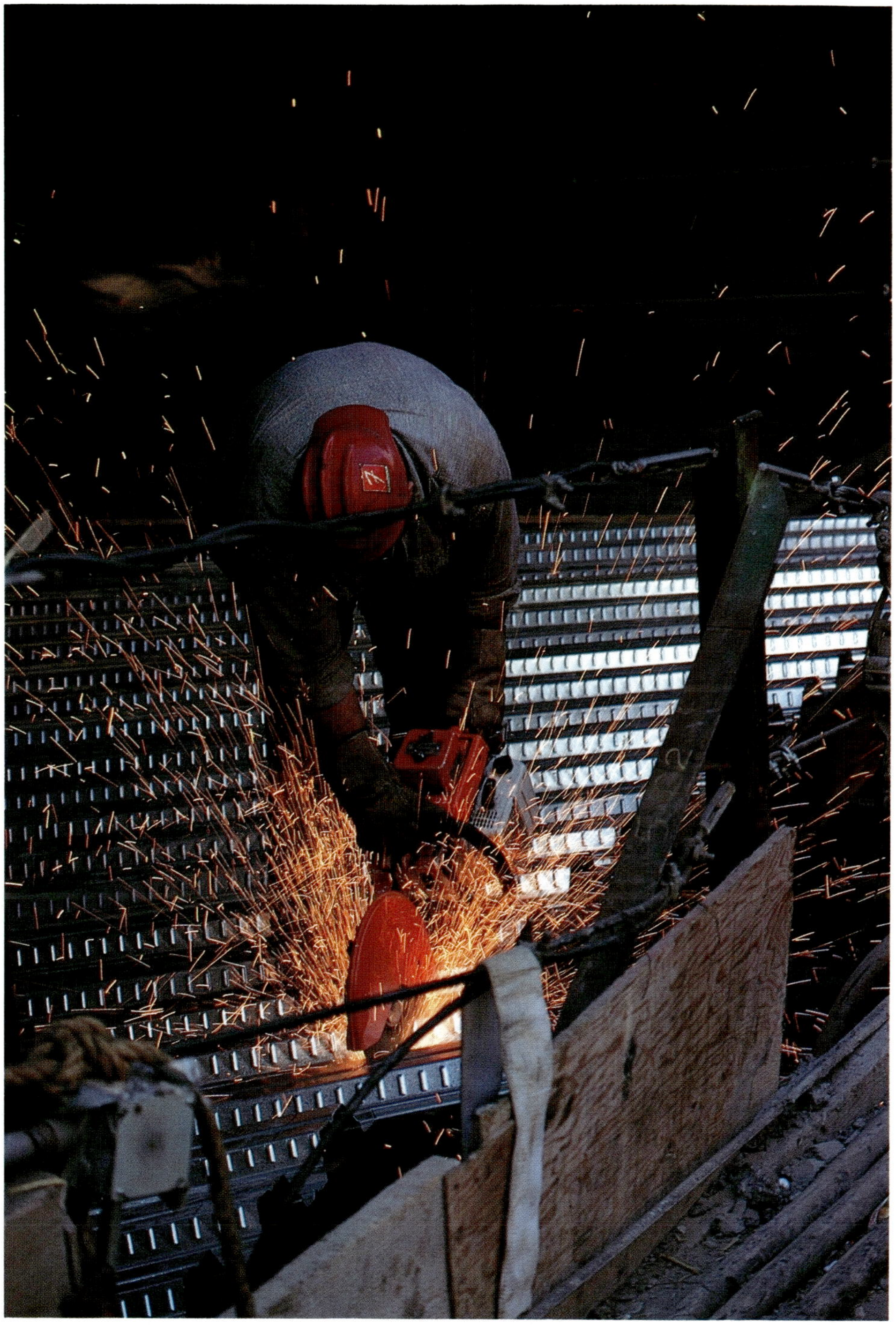

CHARLES GORDON

Left: *Annie Rose.*

Above: *Metal cutter on Columbia Center.*

Following pages: *Oil refinery at Anacortes.*

STEPHEN SCHROEDER

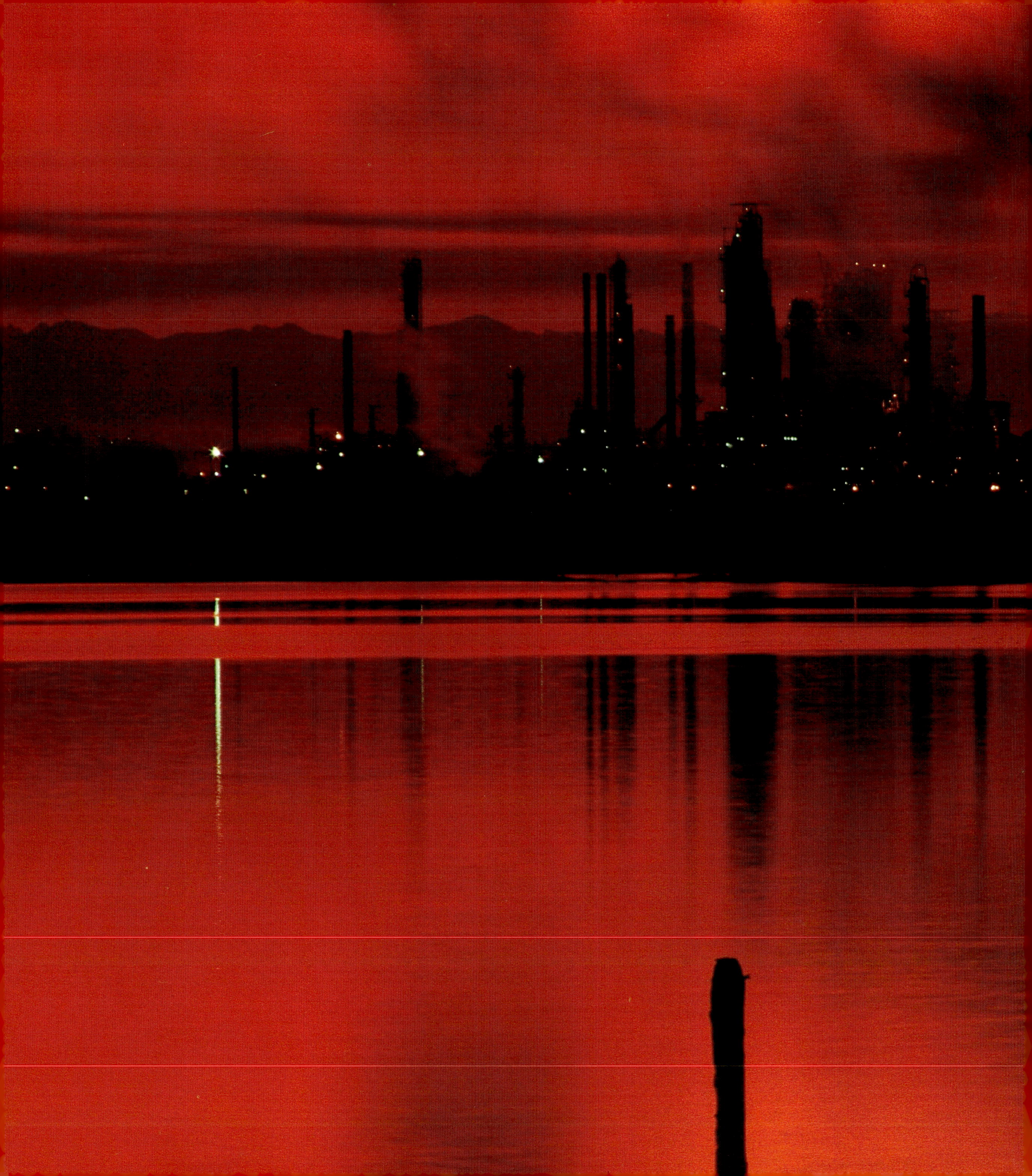

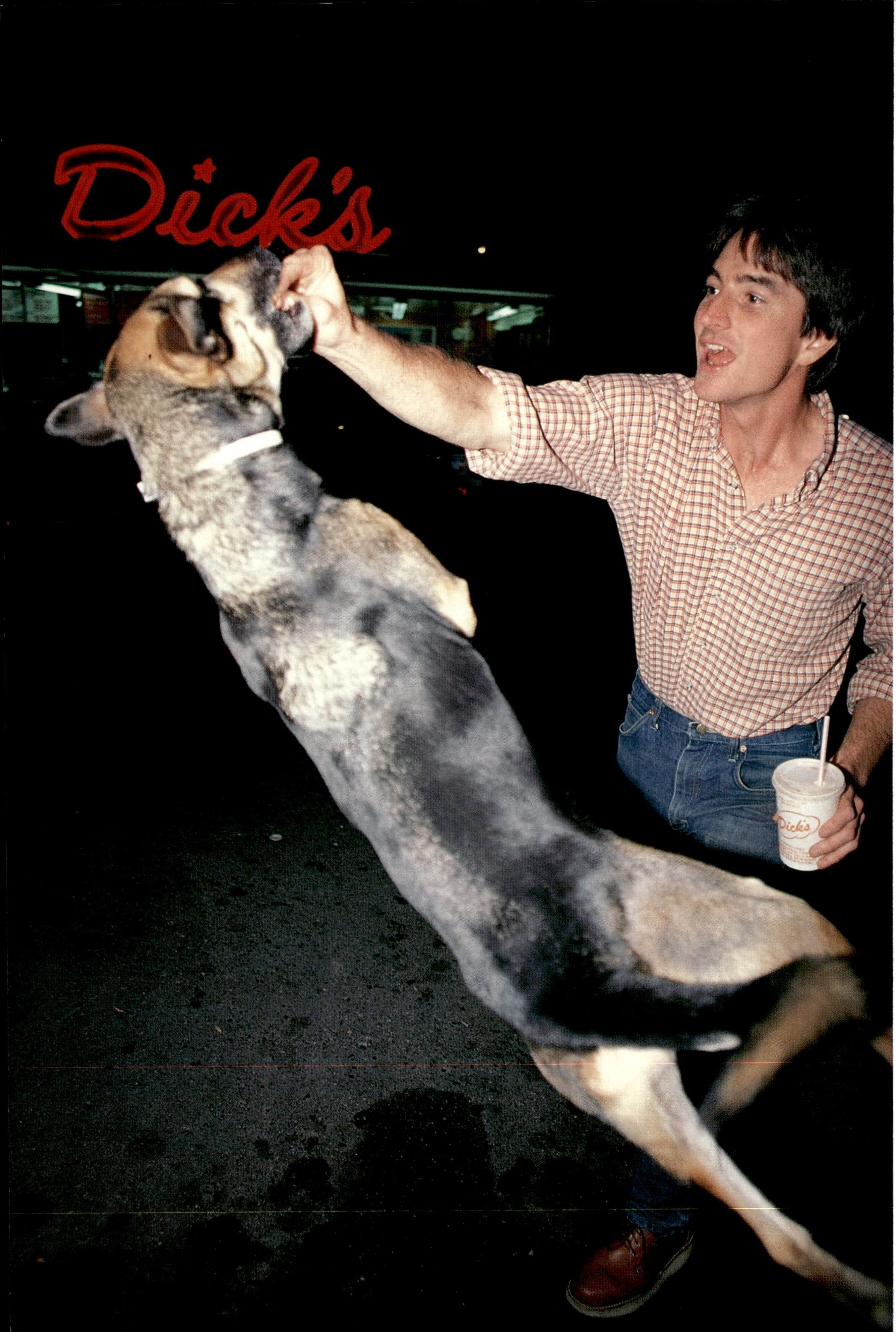

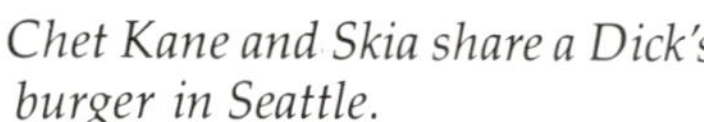

Chet Kane and Skia share a Dick's burger in Seattle.

PEGGY PEATTIE

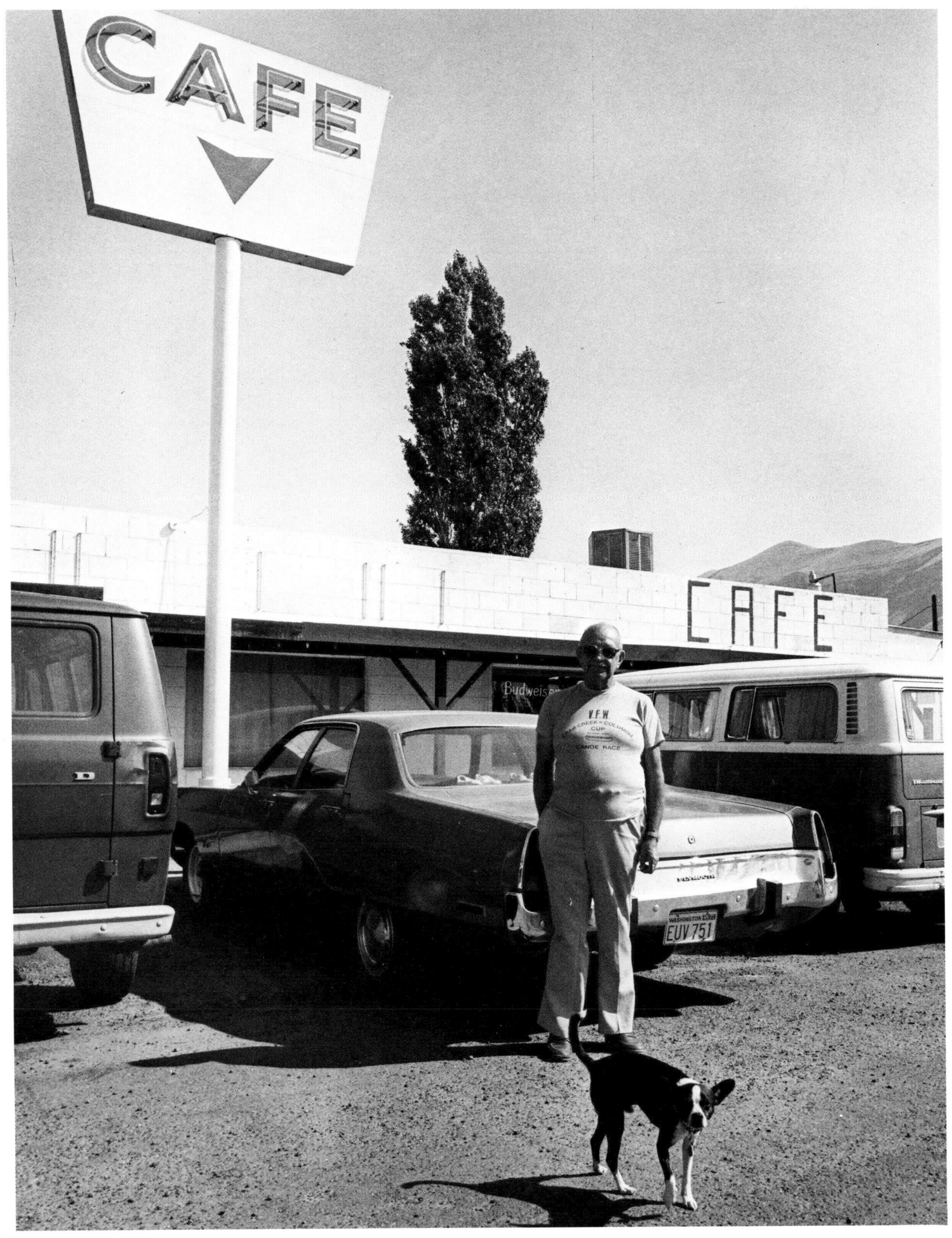

DON NORMARK

Arthur Turner, his cafe and his dog Charlie in Schwanna, Grant County.

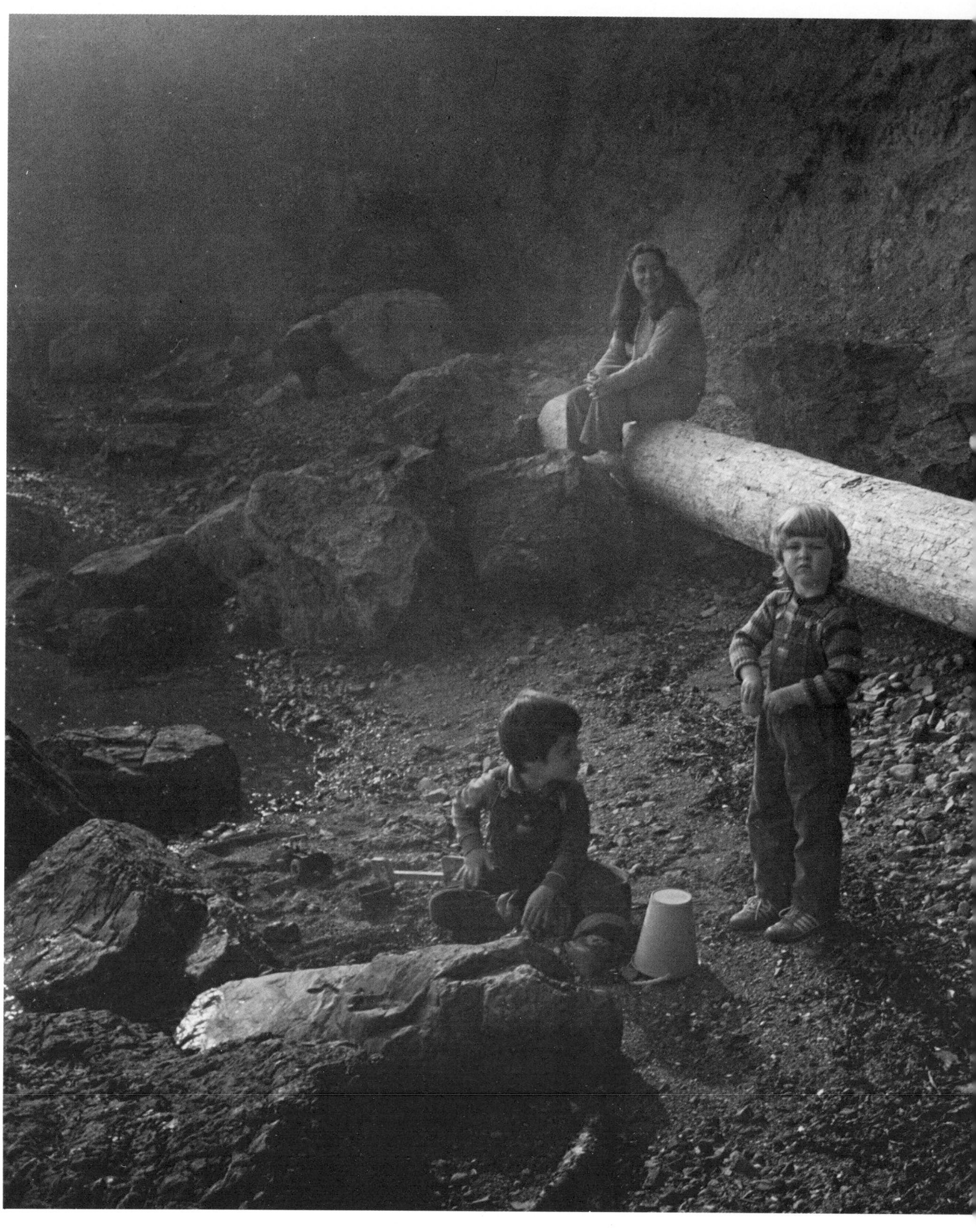

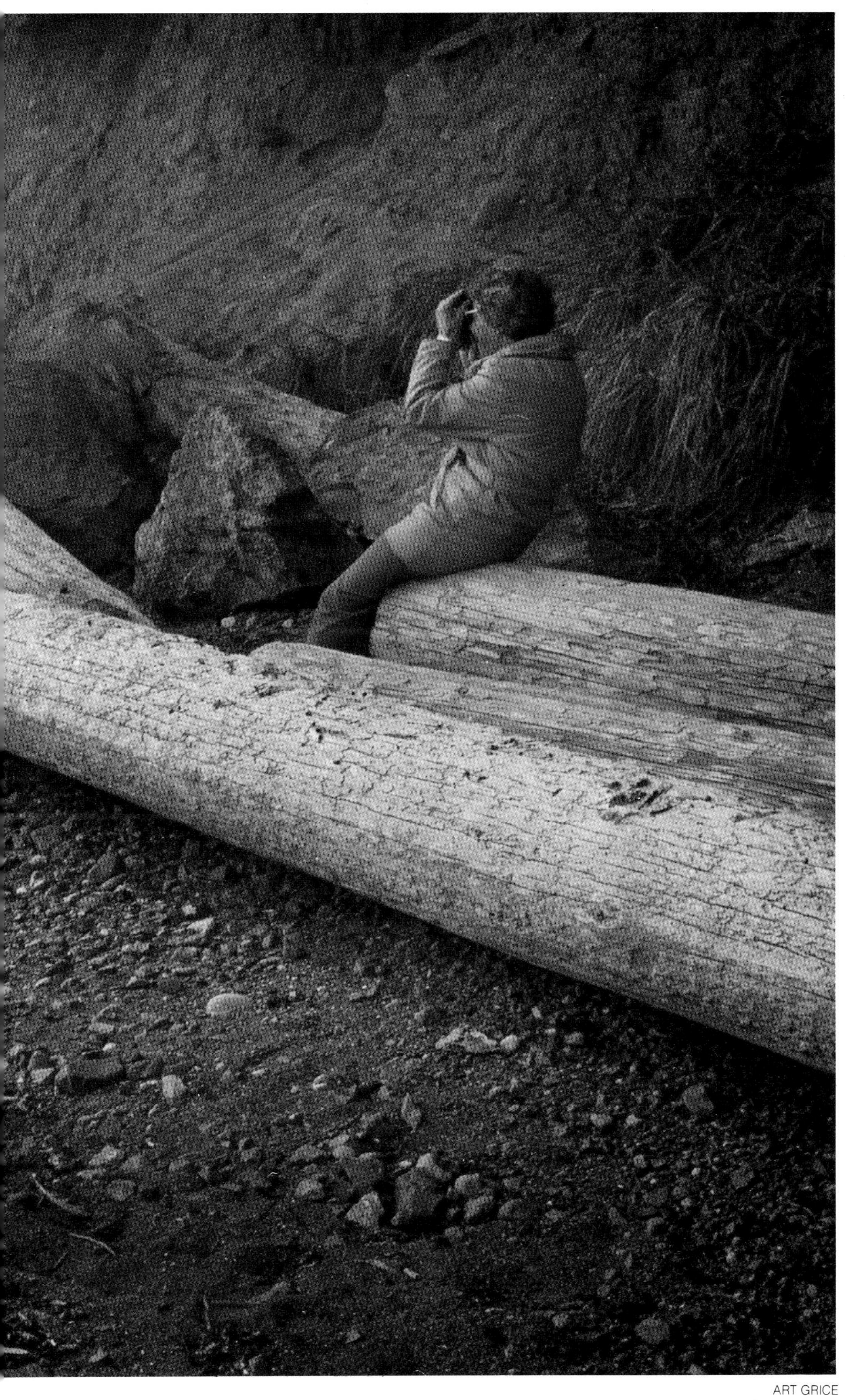

ART GRICE

The Art Grice family at Deception Pass State Park.

Robert "Bob" Cummings, 78, the dean of the state's government reporters.

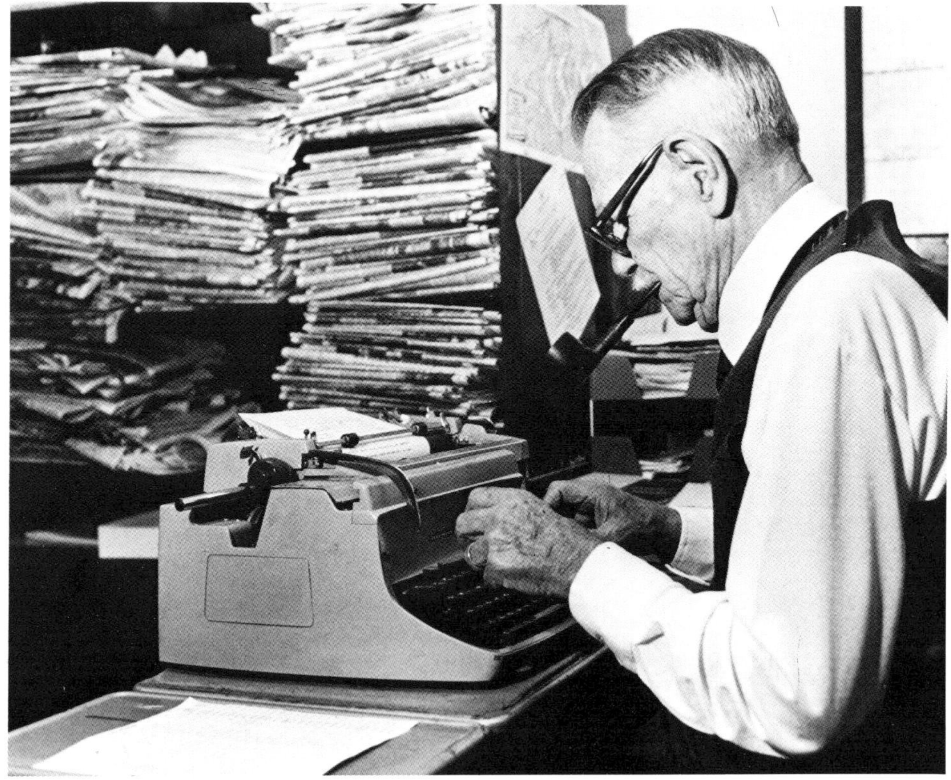

DICK BALDWIN

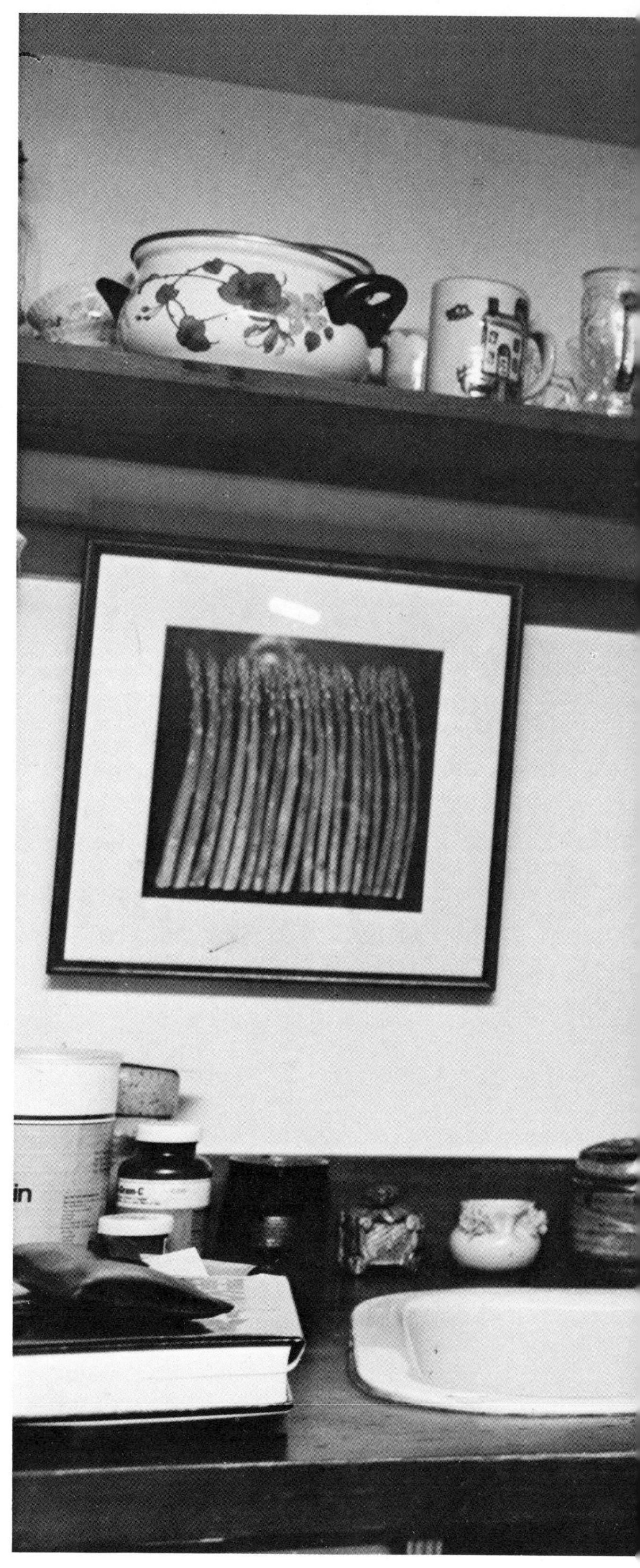

Author Tom Robbins in his kitchen at La Conner.

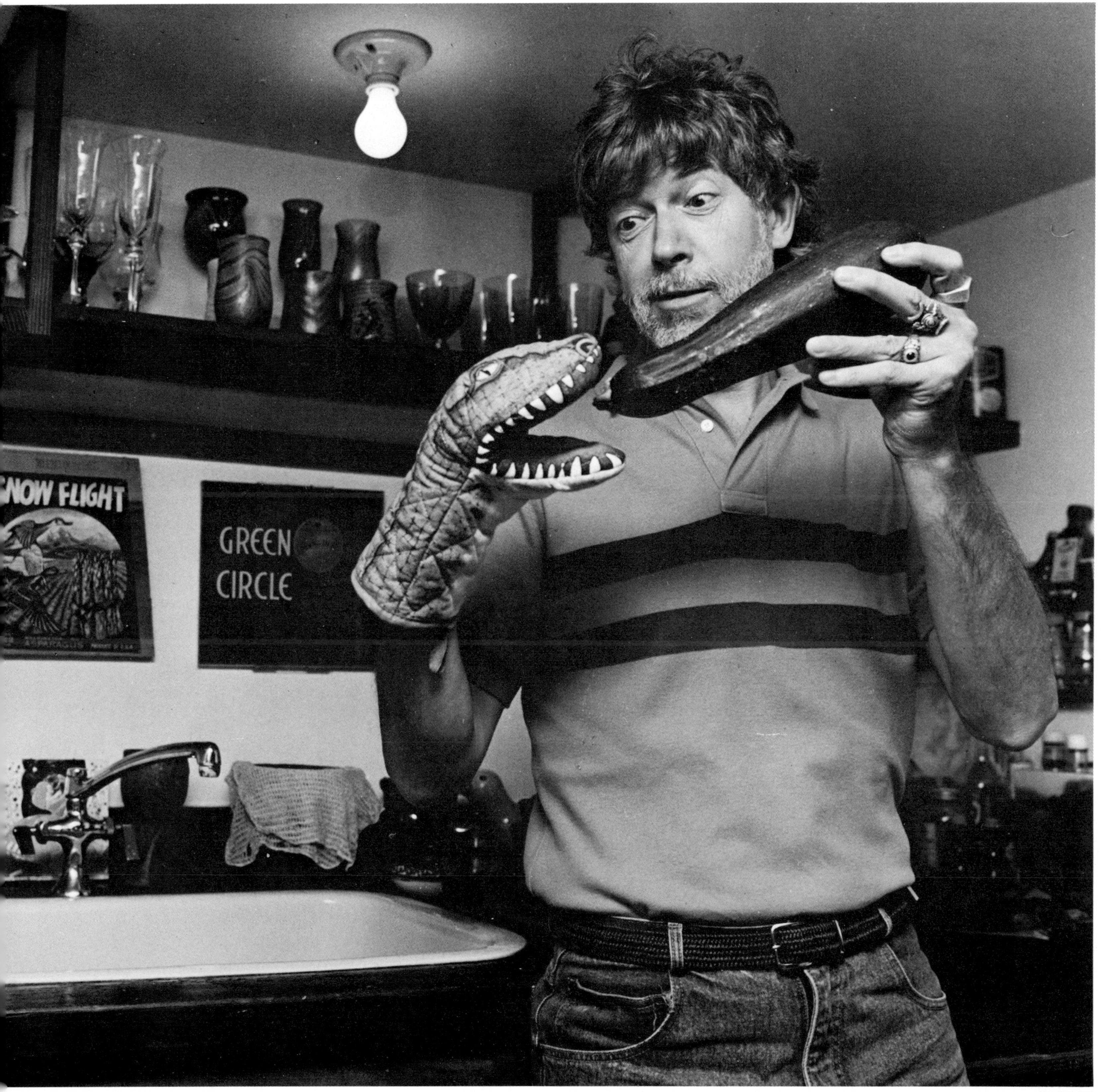

JON BRUNK

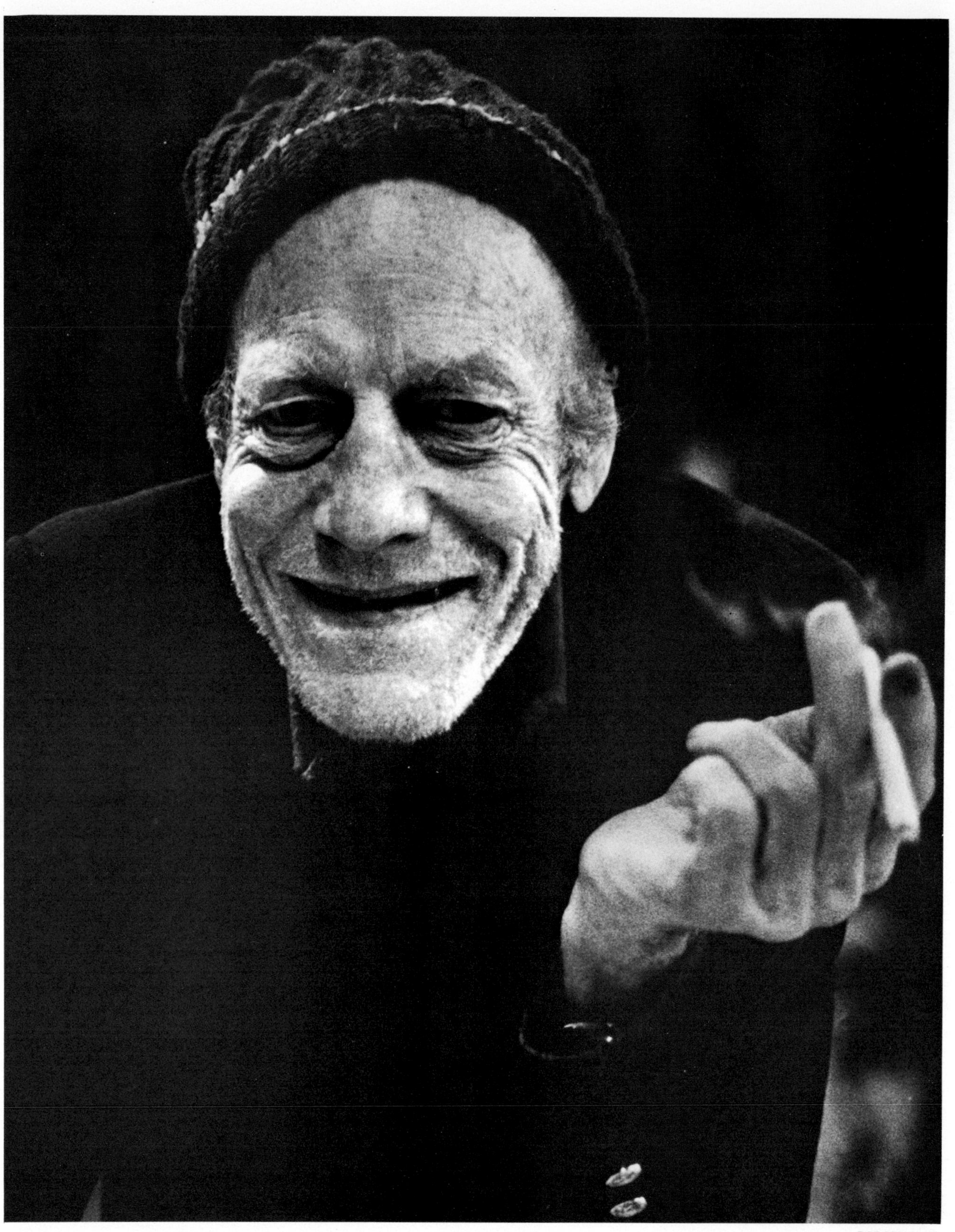

DOT STENNING

Jack Brandon, 65, at the Emergency Shelter Center in Seattle's Morrison Hotel.

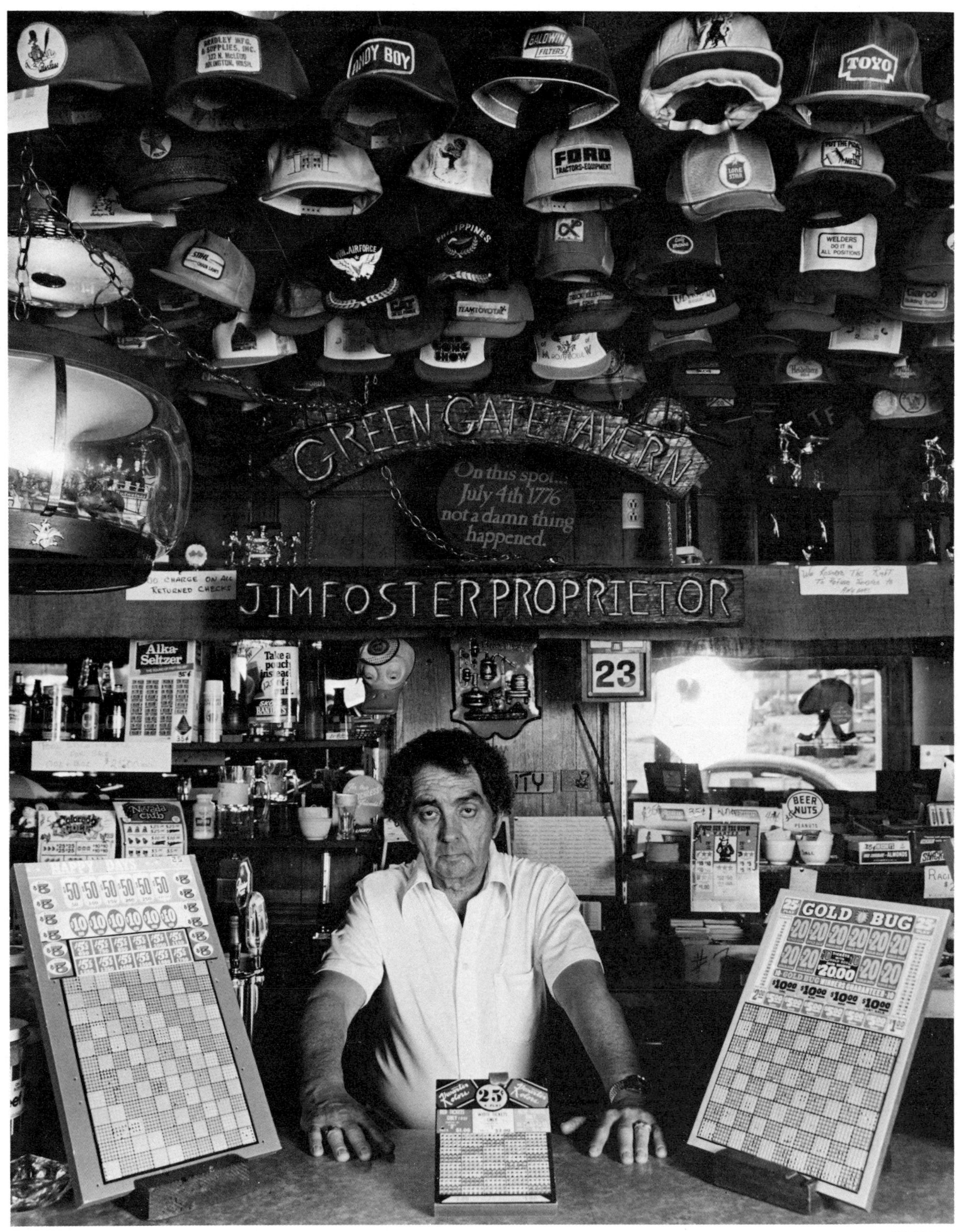

JON BRUNK

Jim Foster's Green Gate Tavern in Burlington has a collection of 1,584 baseball-style caps stapled to the ceiling.

A forest of aspen trees on the Benson Creek Road, south of Twisp.

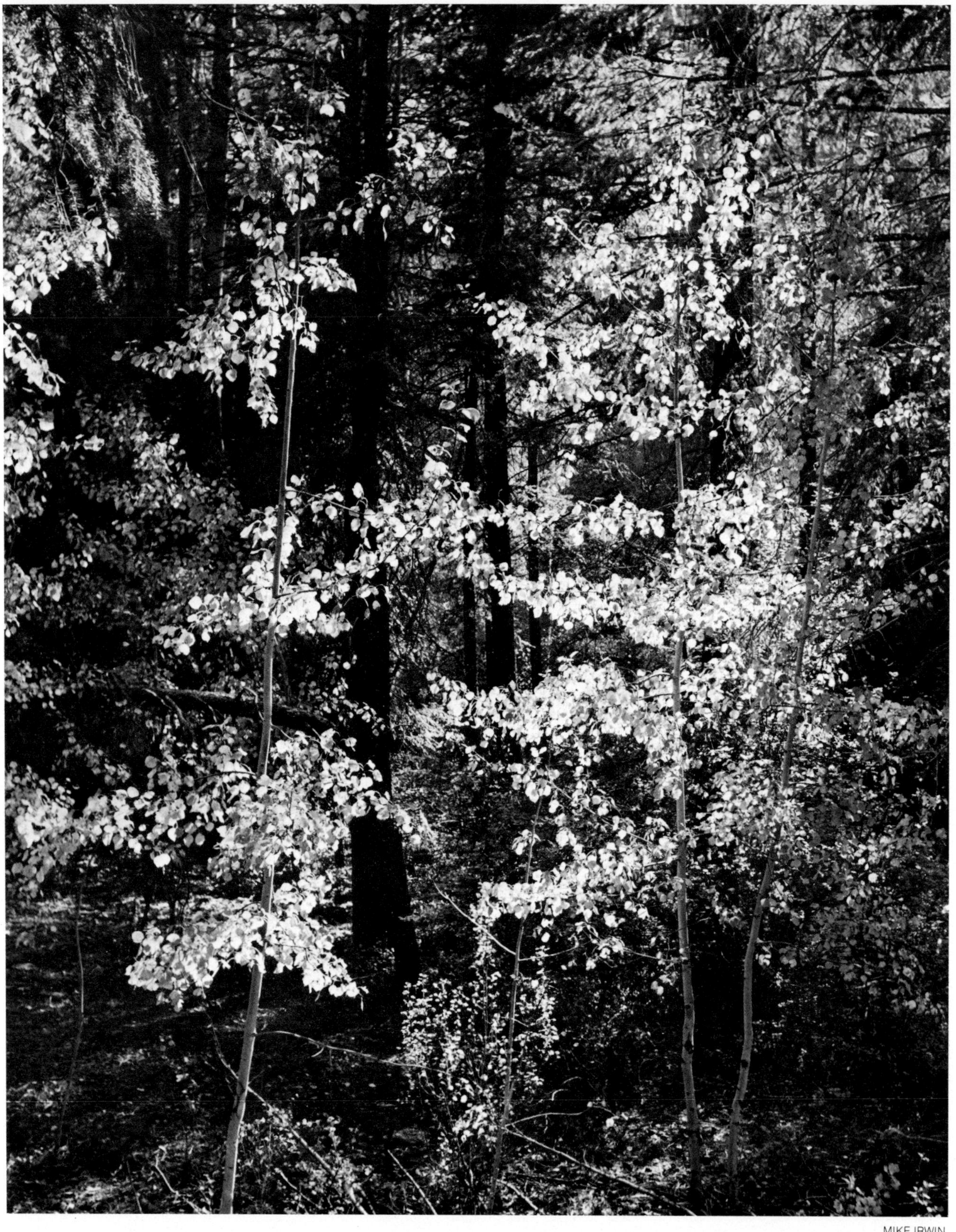

MIKE IRWIN

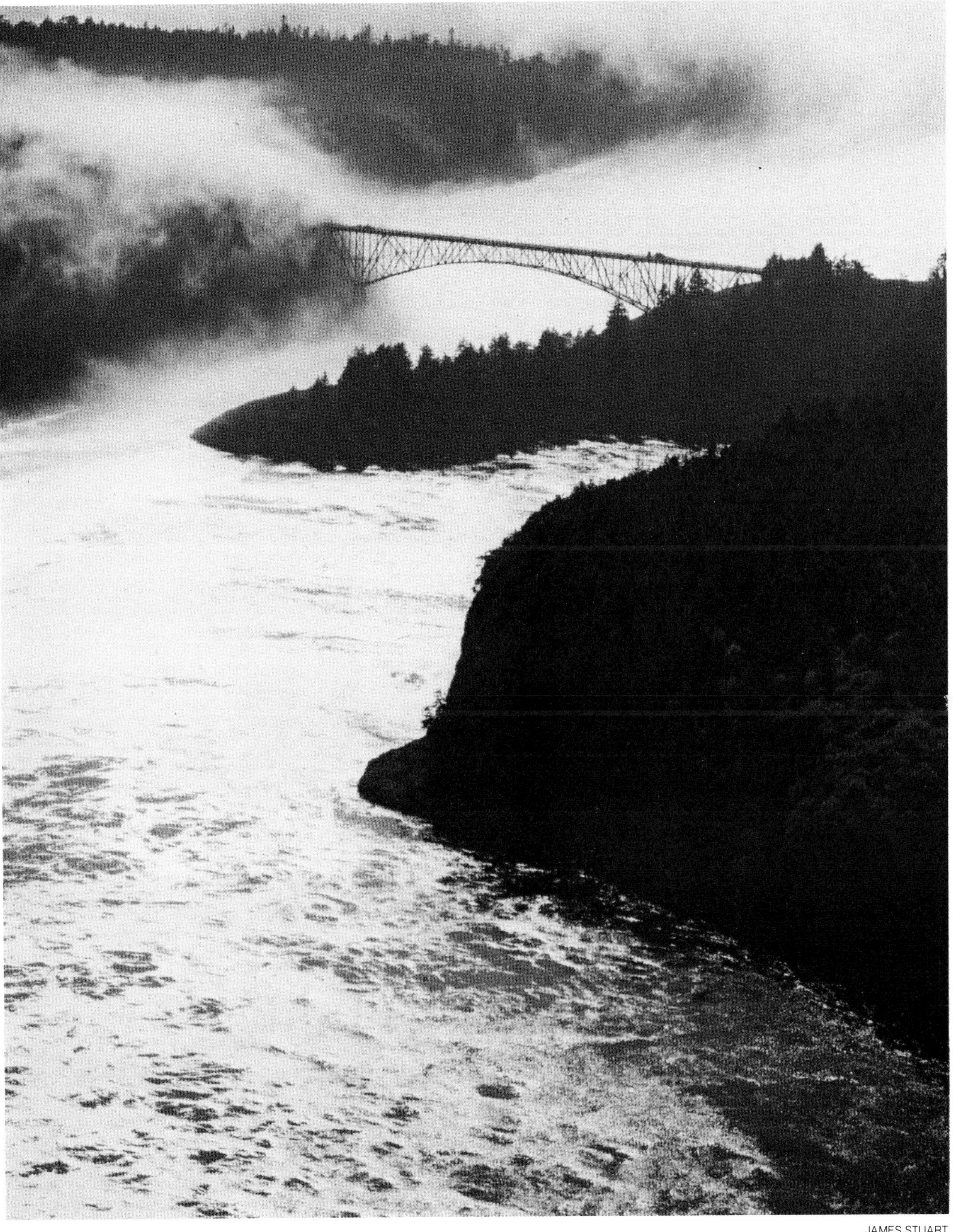

JAMES STUART

Deception Pass.

Following pages:
A bench in Seattle's Pioneer Square.

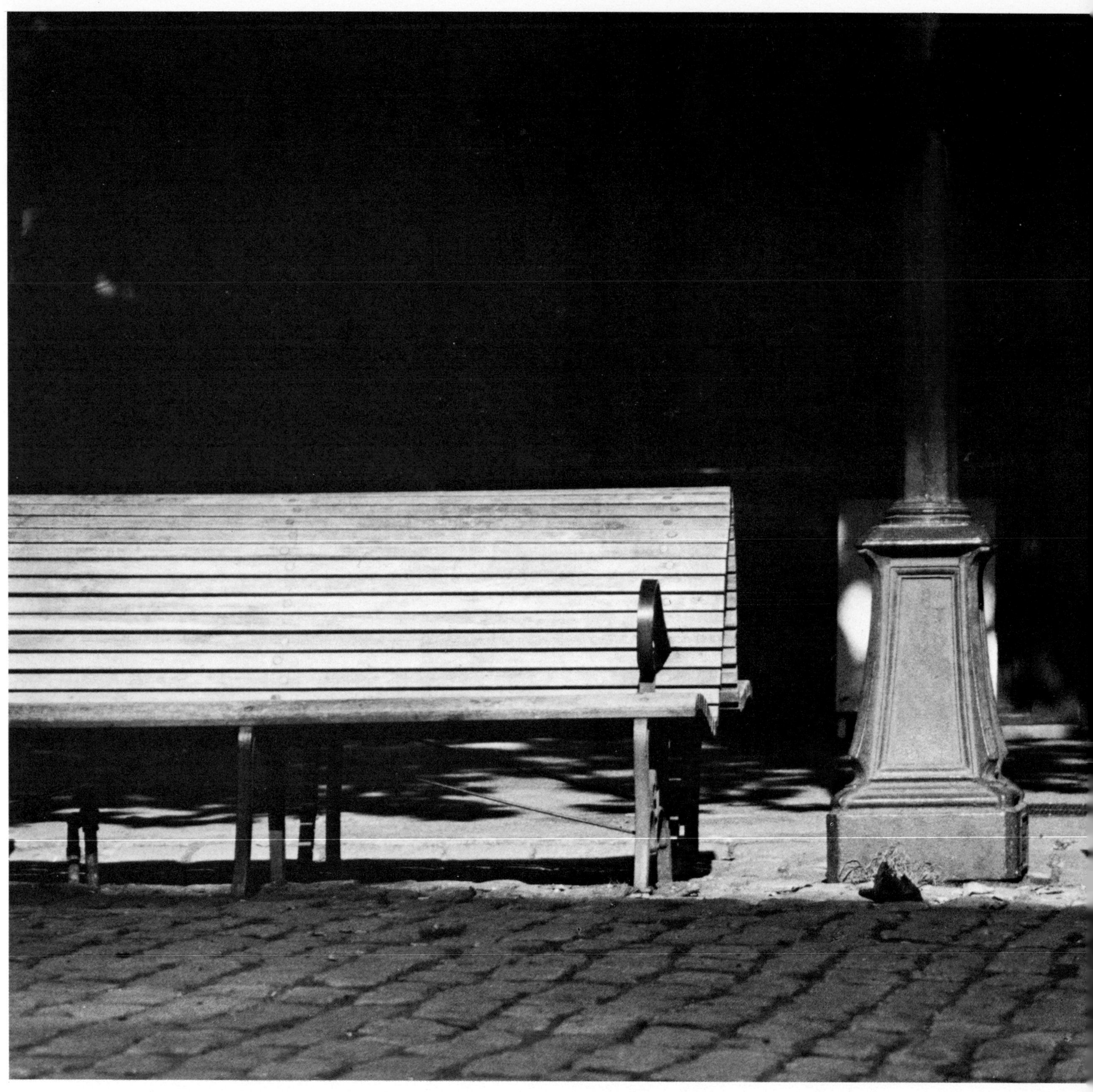

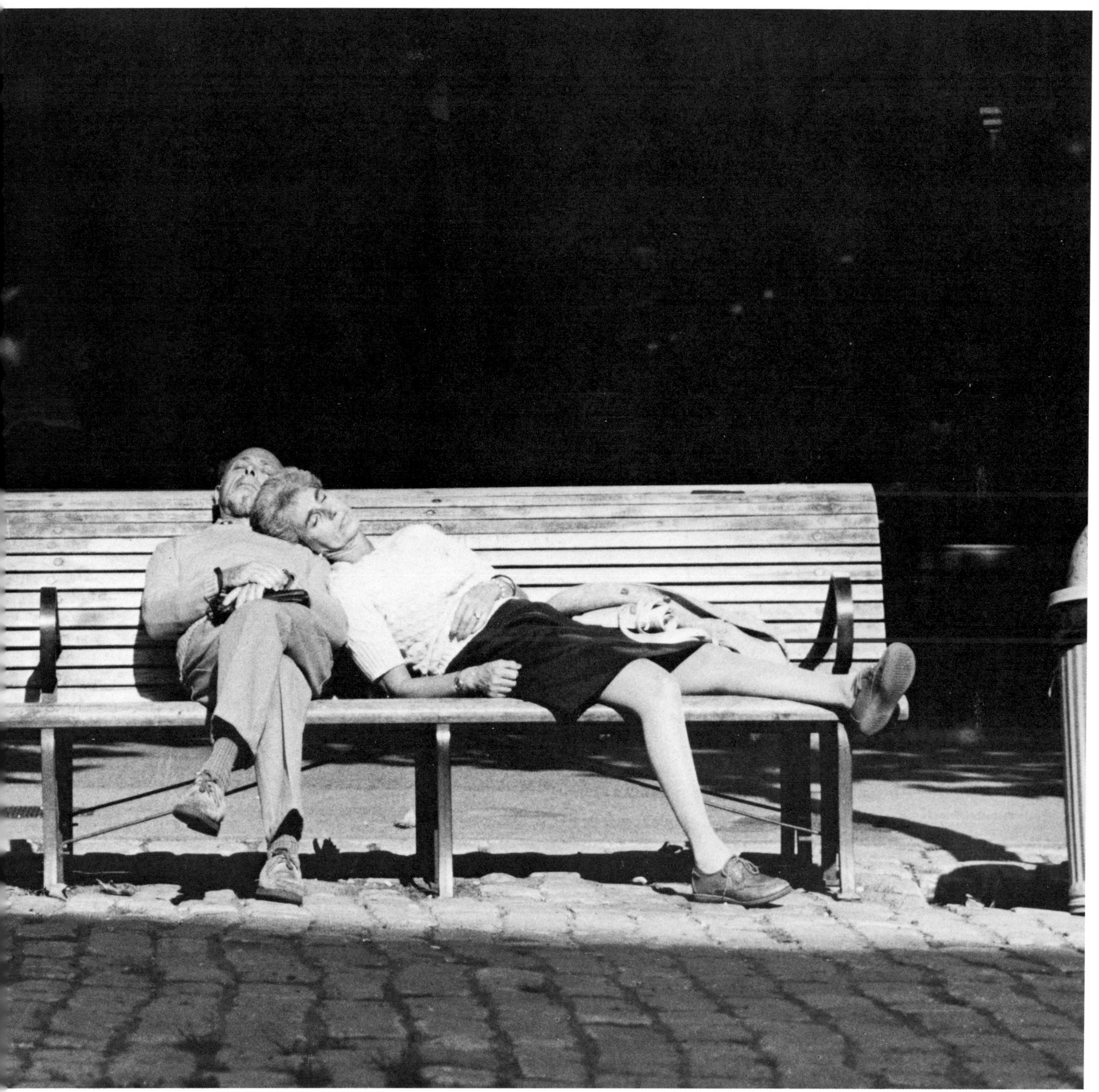

BRUCE CARROLL

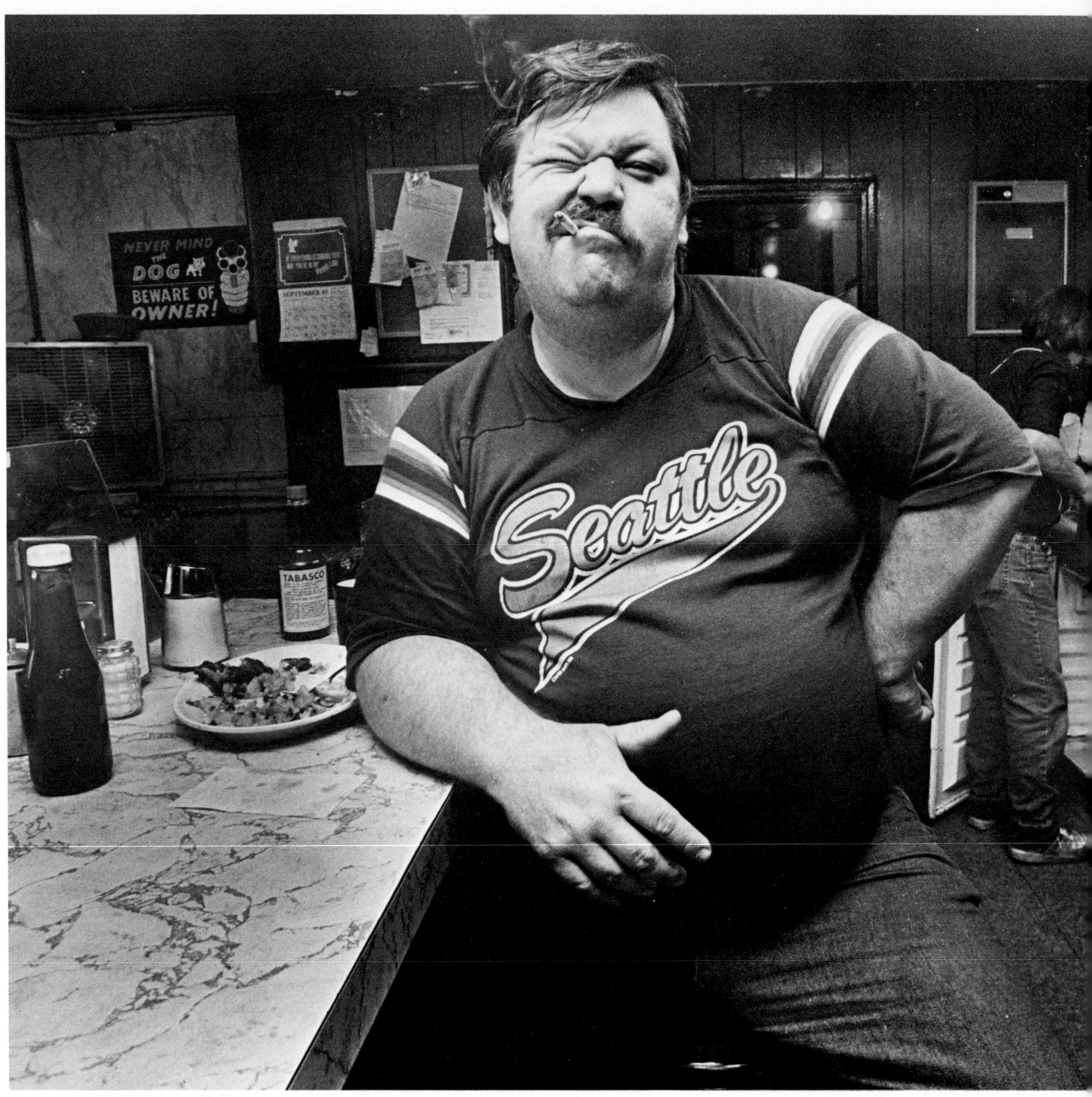
NEVER MIND
THE
DOG
BEWARE OF
OWNER!
TABASCO
Seattle

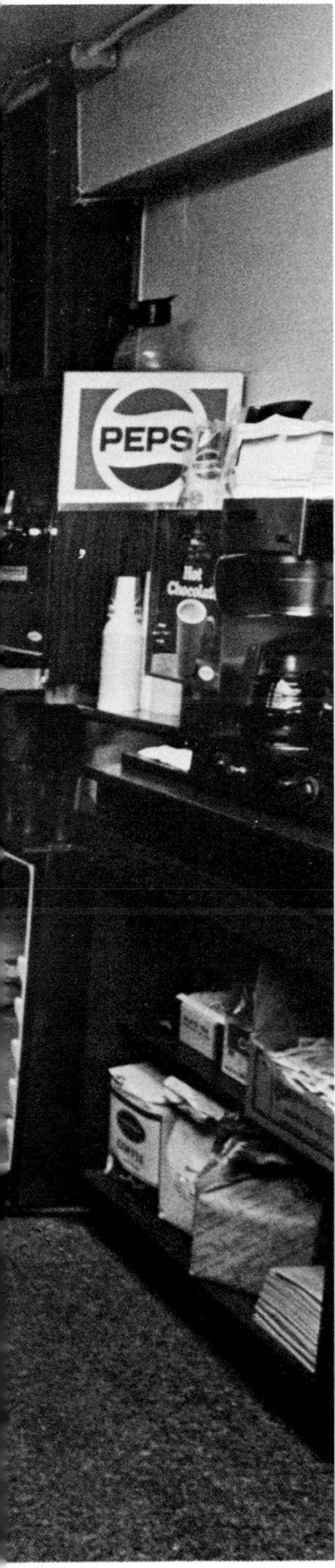

GRANT HALLER

Michael Fletcher breakfasts at Beth's Cafe on Seattle's Aurora Avenue.

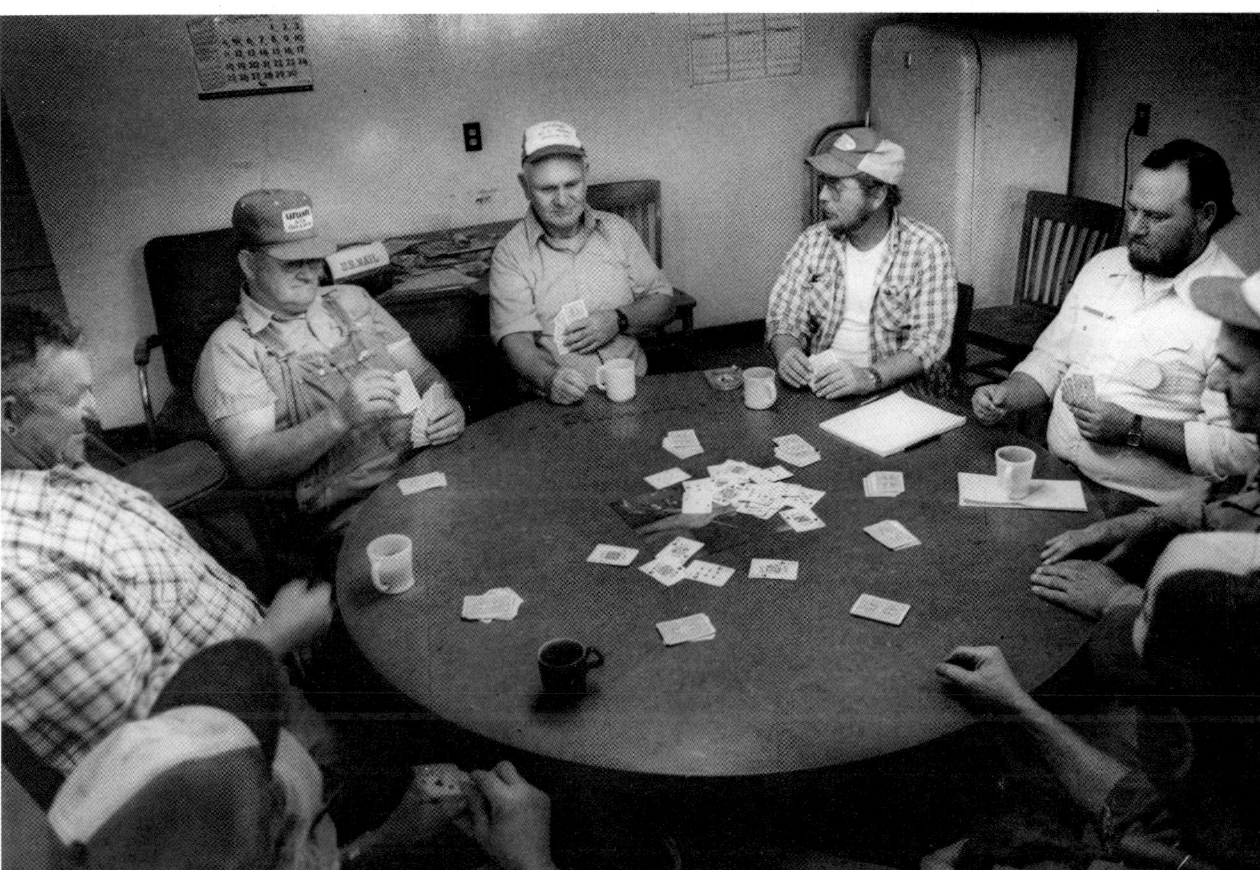

PAUL FRIDLUND

Playing double-deck pinochle at the Emergency Shelter Center in Seattle's Morrison Hotel.

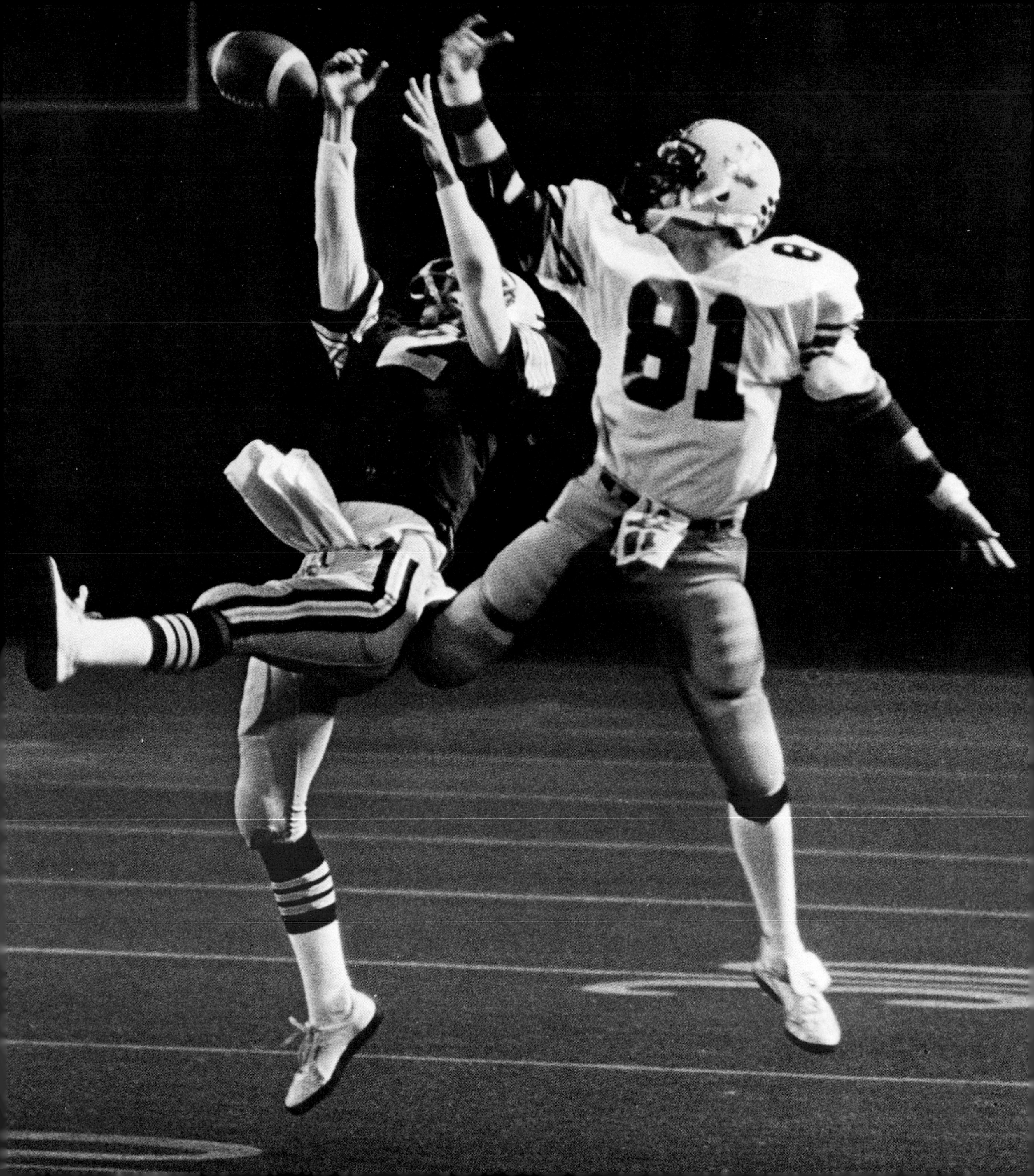

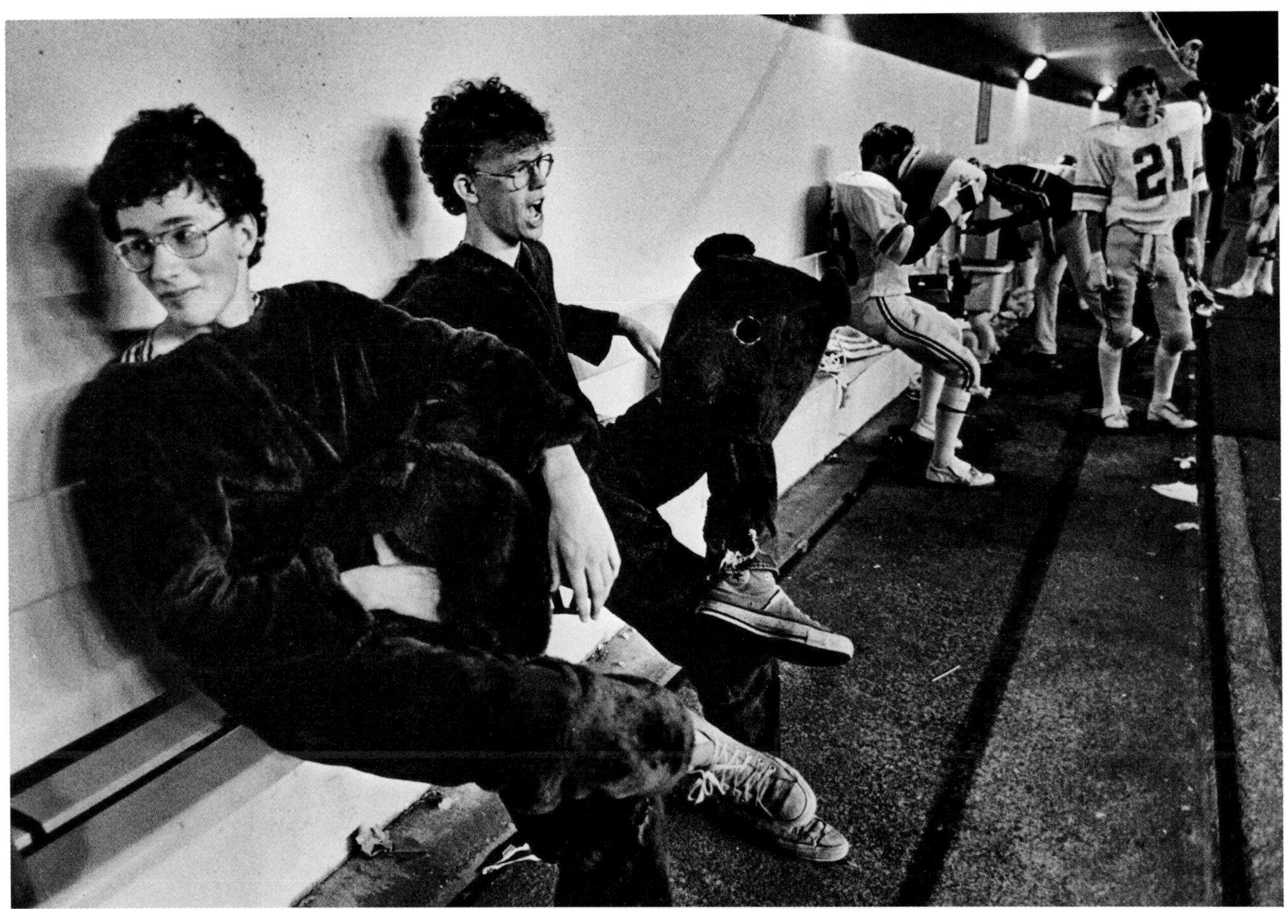

Sebastian Jones and Brady Smith don Teddy Bear costumes as Roosevelt High School mascots.

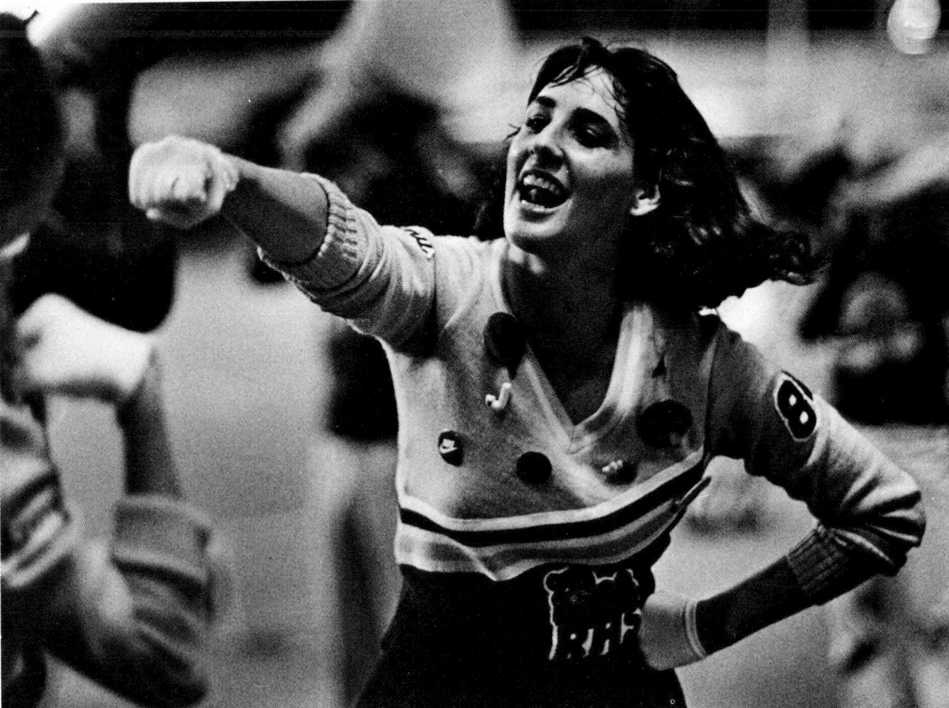

Left: *Roosevelt High School cheerleader Jennifer Sider.*

PHOTOS BY PETER HALEY

Far left: *Kentridge High School defender Louie Albrecht intercepts a pass against cross-town rival Kentwood.*

MARK MORRIS

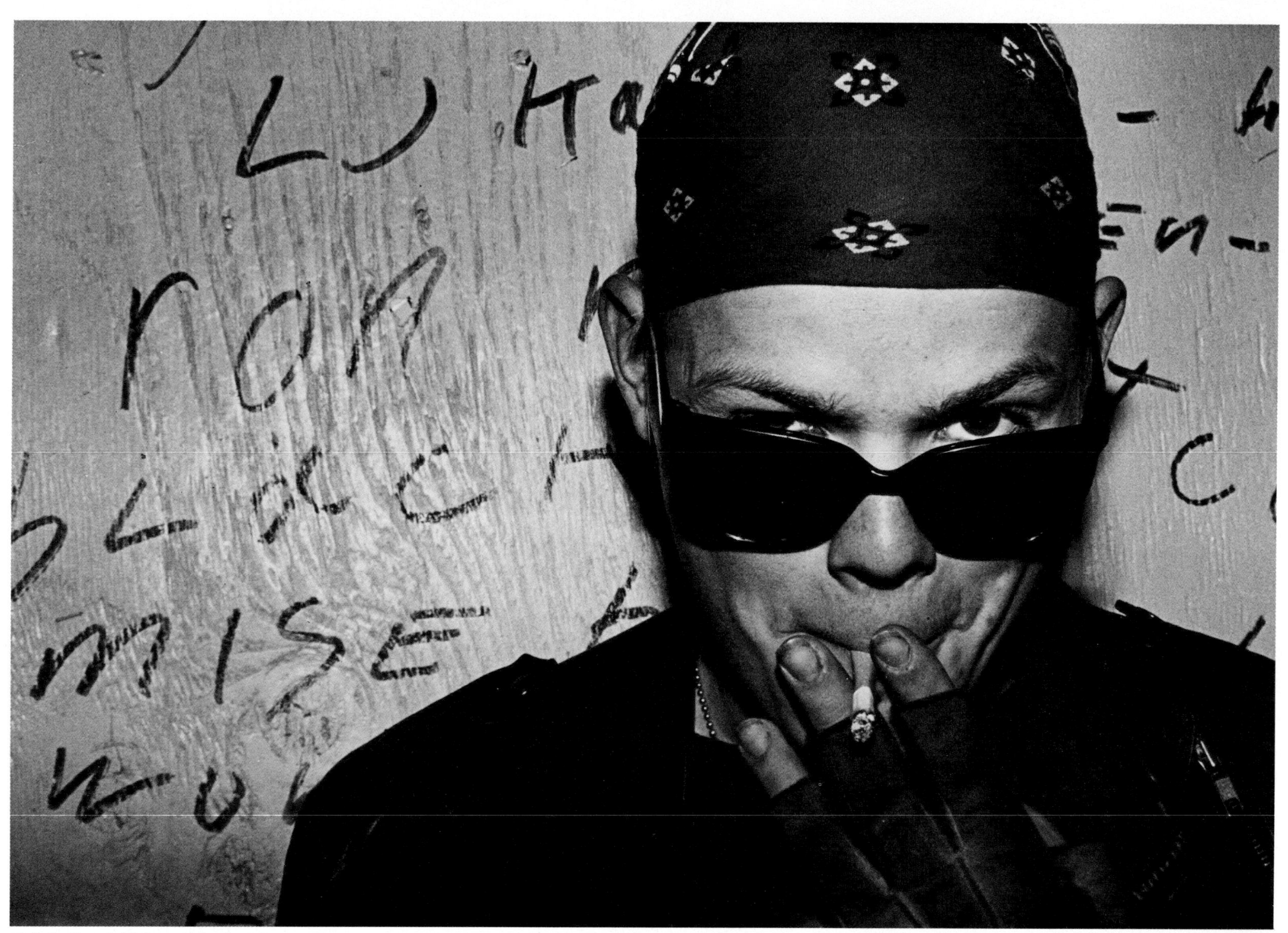

*Calvin Lee Stidel outside the Metropolis,
Seattle's largest punk rock club.*

CHRISTINA EKSTED

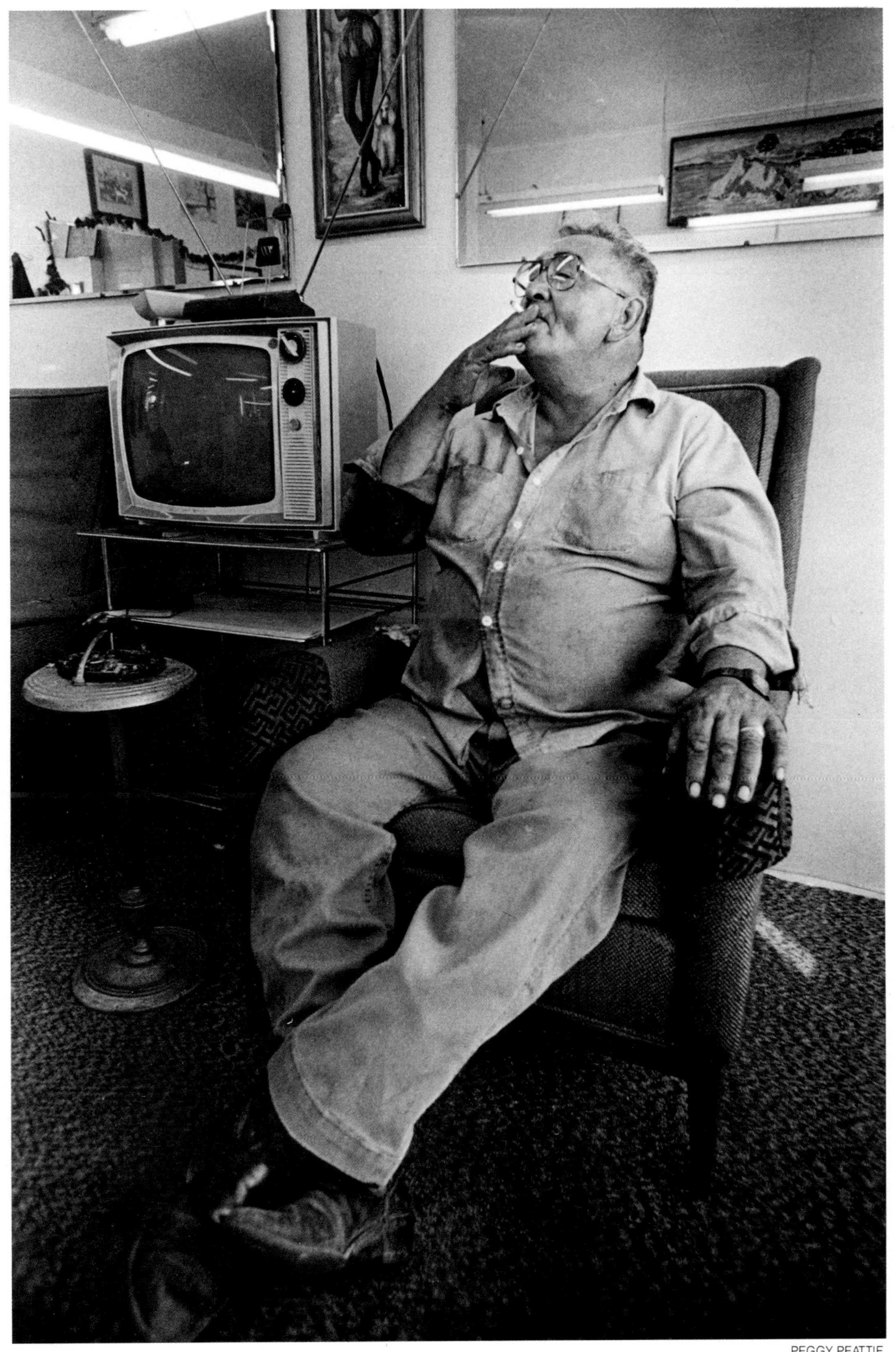

PEGGY PEATTIE

Gene, an Indian, just after having his waist-length braids cut off, for $3.50, at a cut-rate barber shop between White Center and Burien.

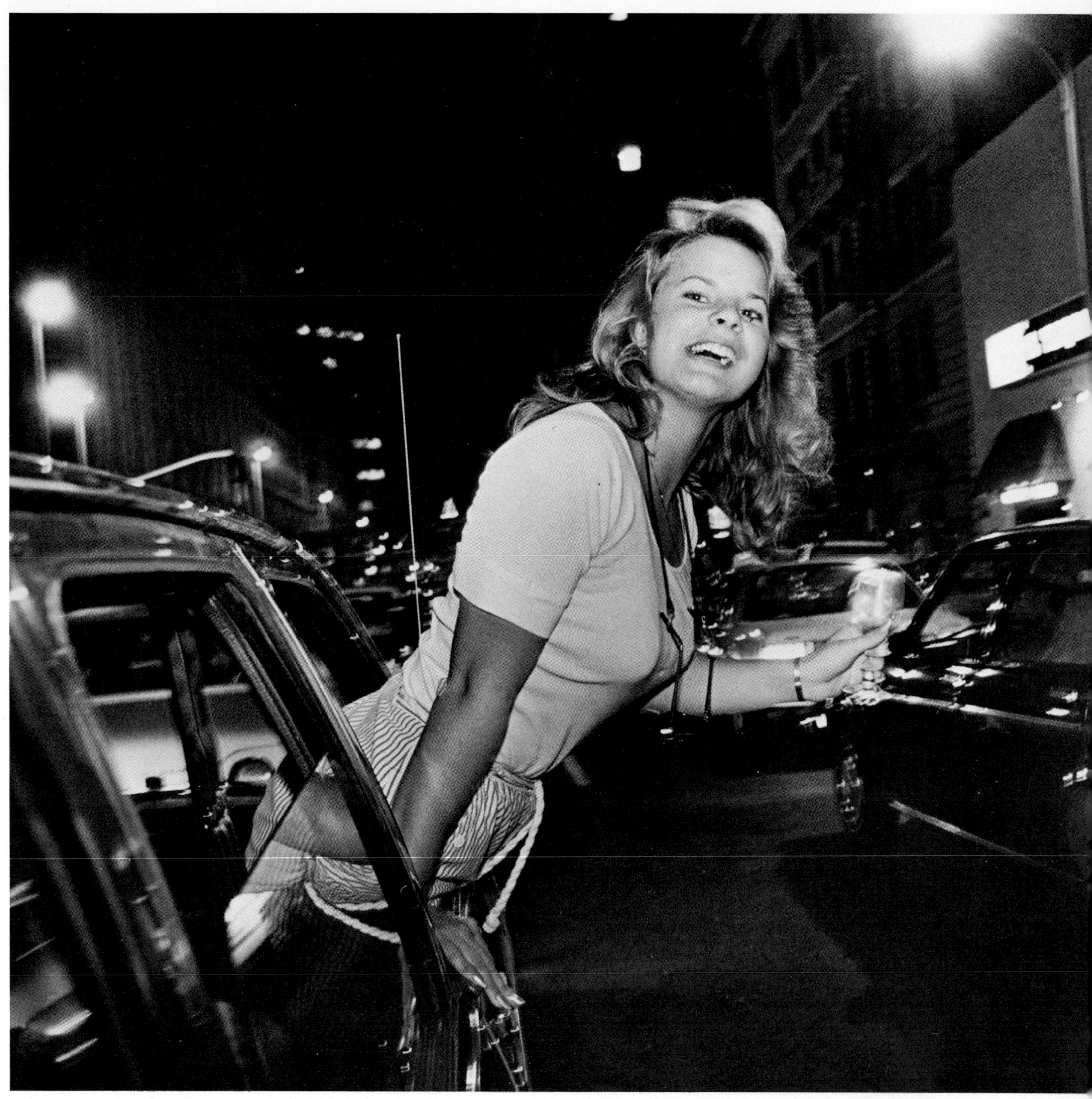

JIMI LOTT

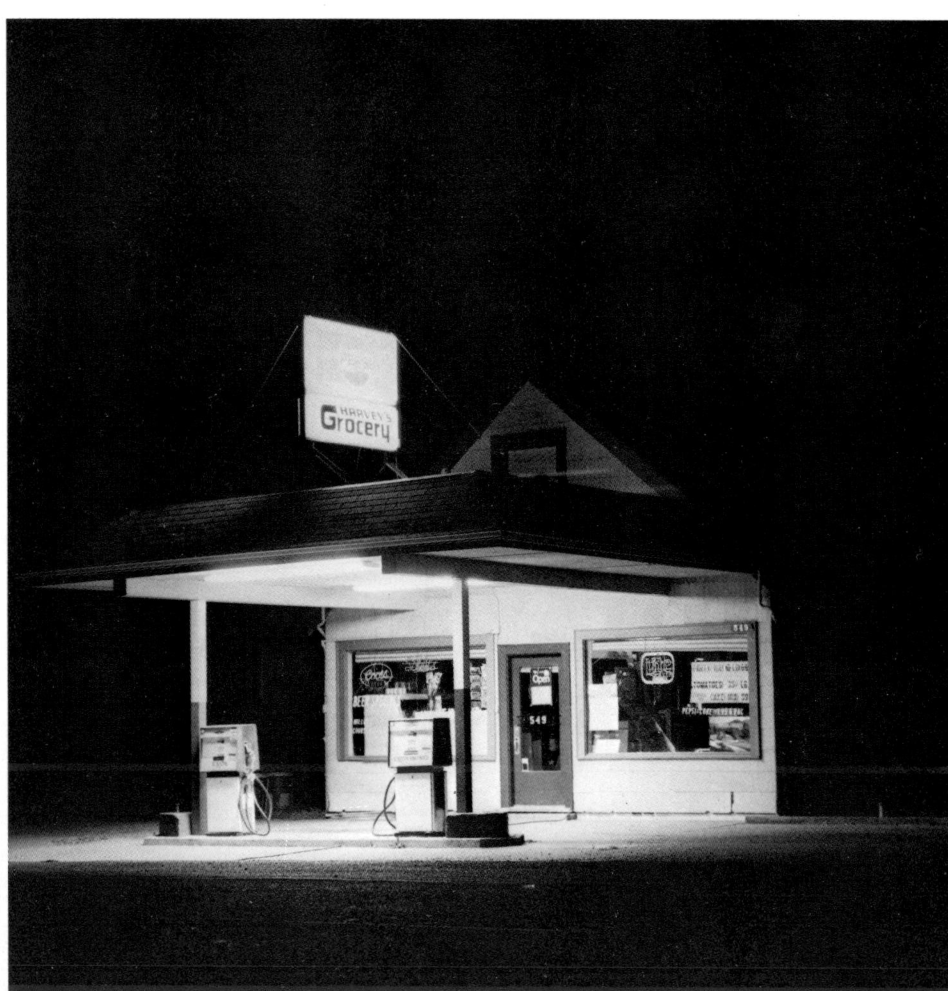

MARIA MAYER

Harvey's Grocery on Chuckanut Drive near Edison.

Friday night "cruising" on Spokane's Riverside Avenue.

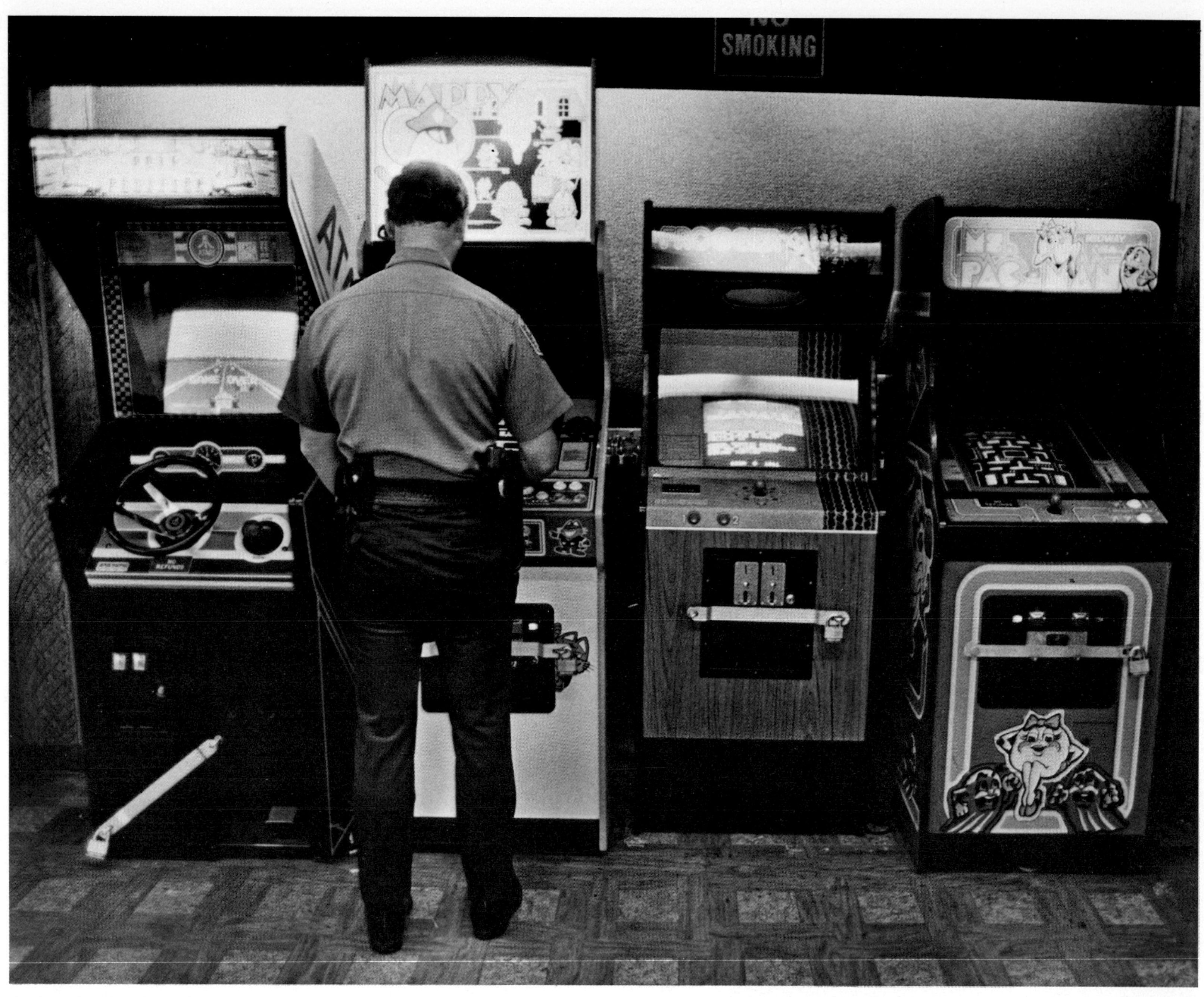

At Seattle's Greyhound bus terminal.

PETER HALEY

A late-night withdrawal.

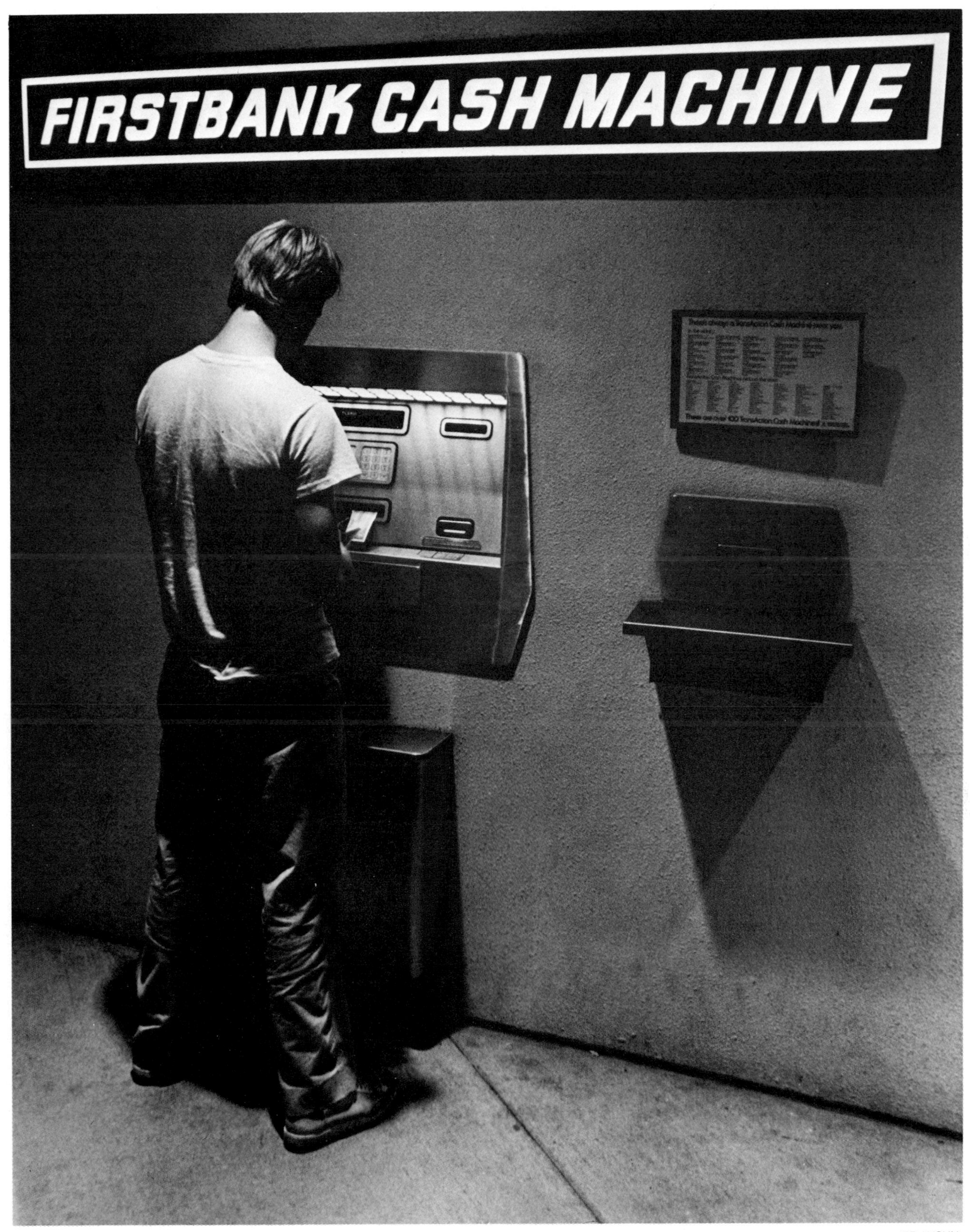

JEF JAISUN

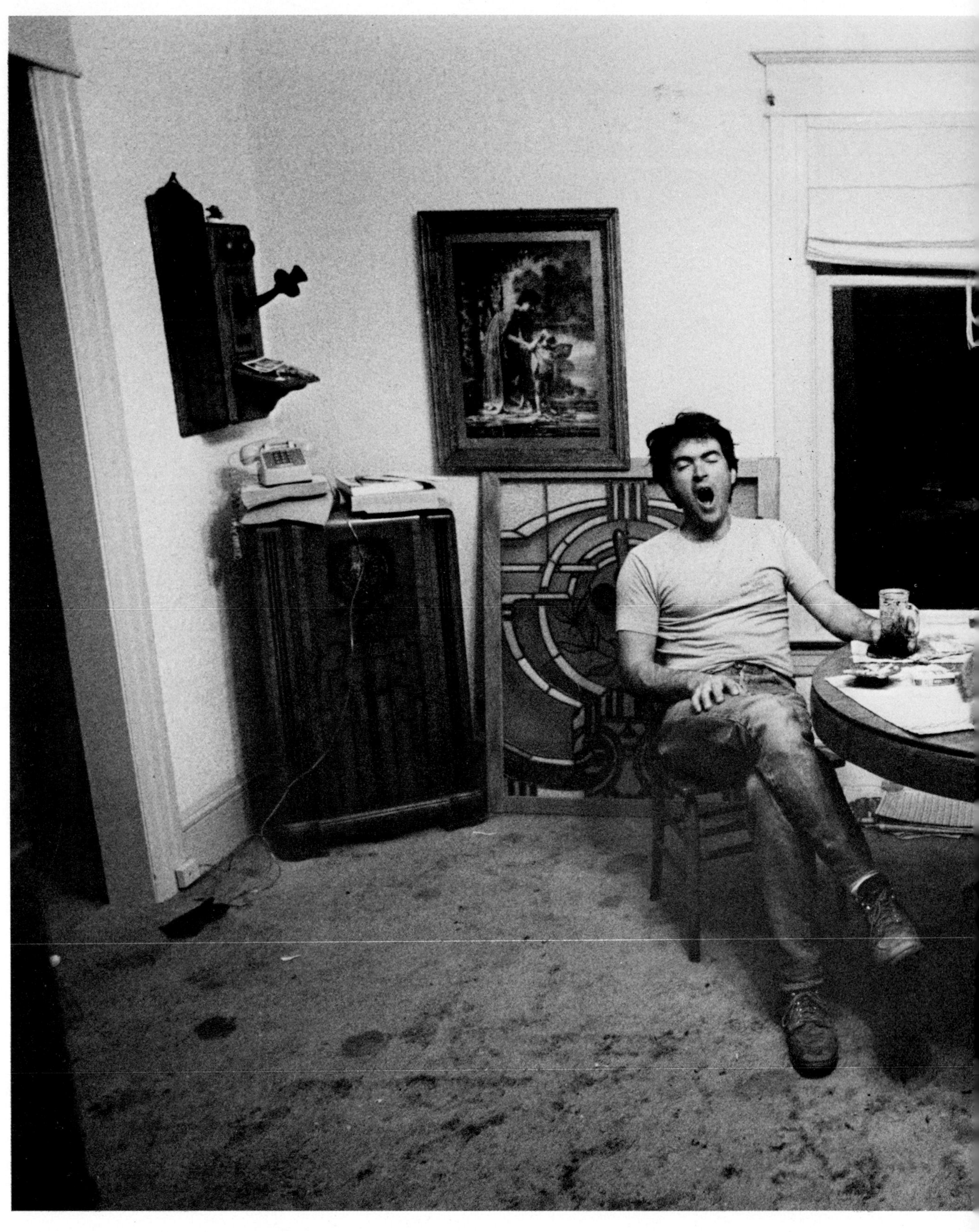

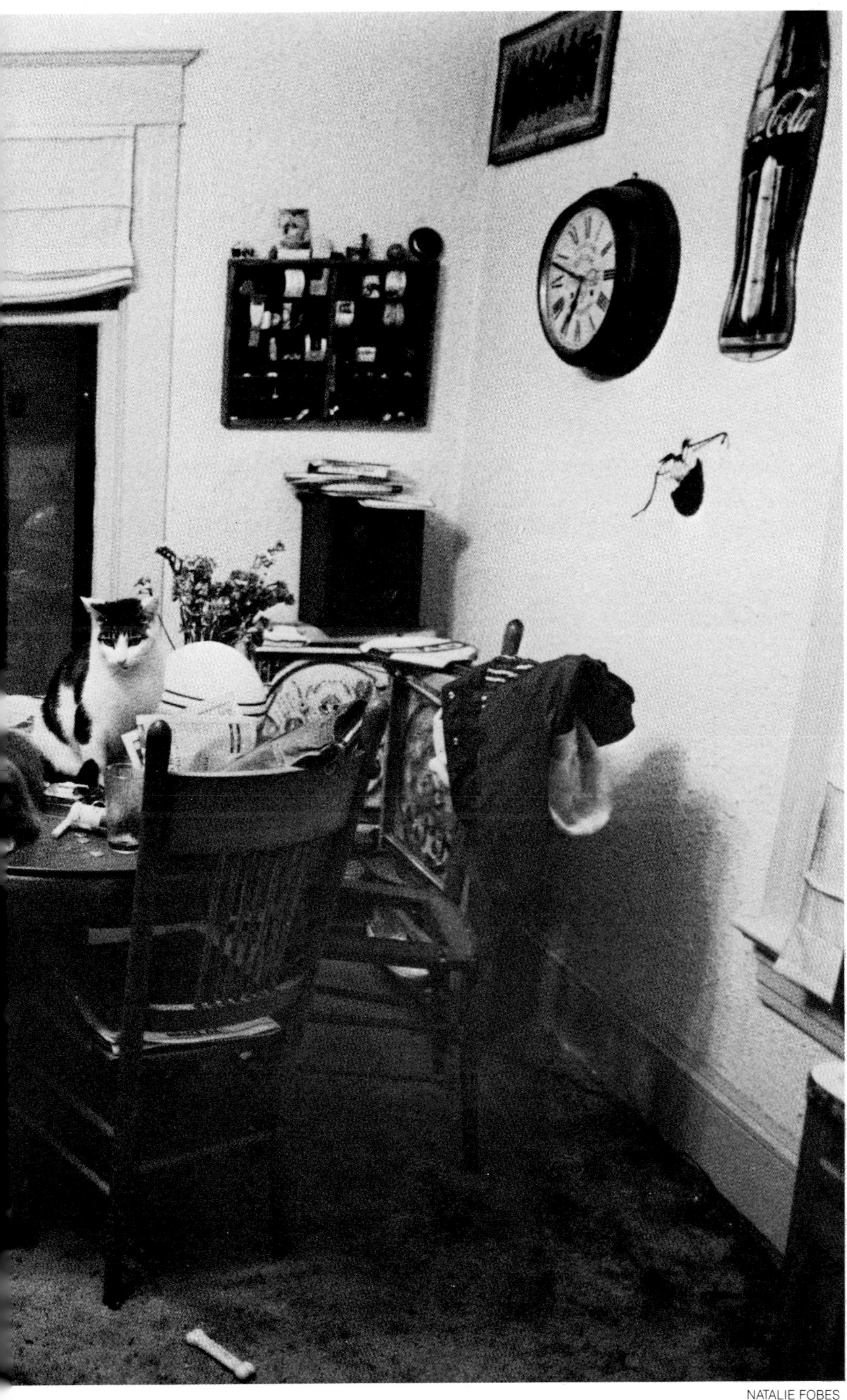

NATALIE FOBES

David Nixon after a day's work as a carpenter and cabinetmaker in Seattle.

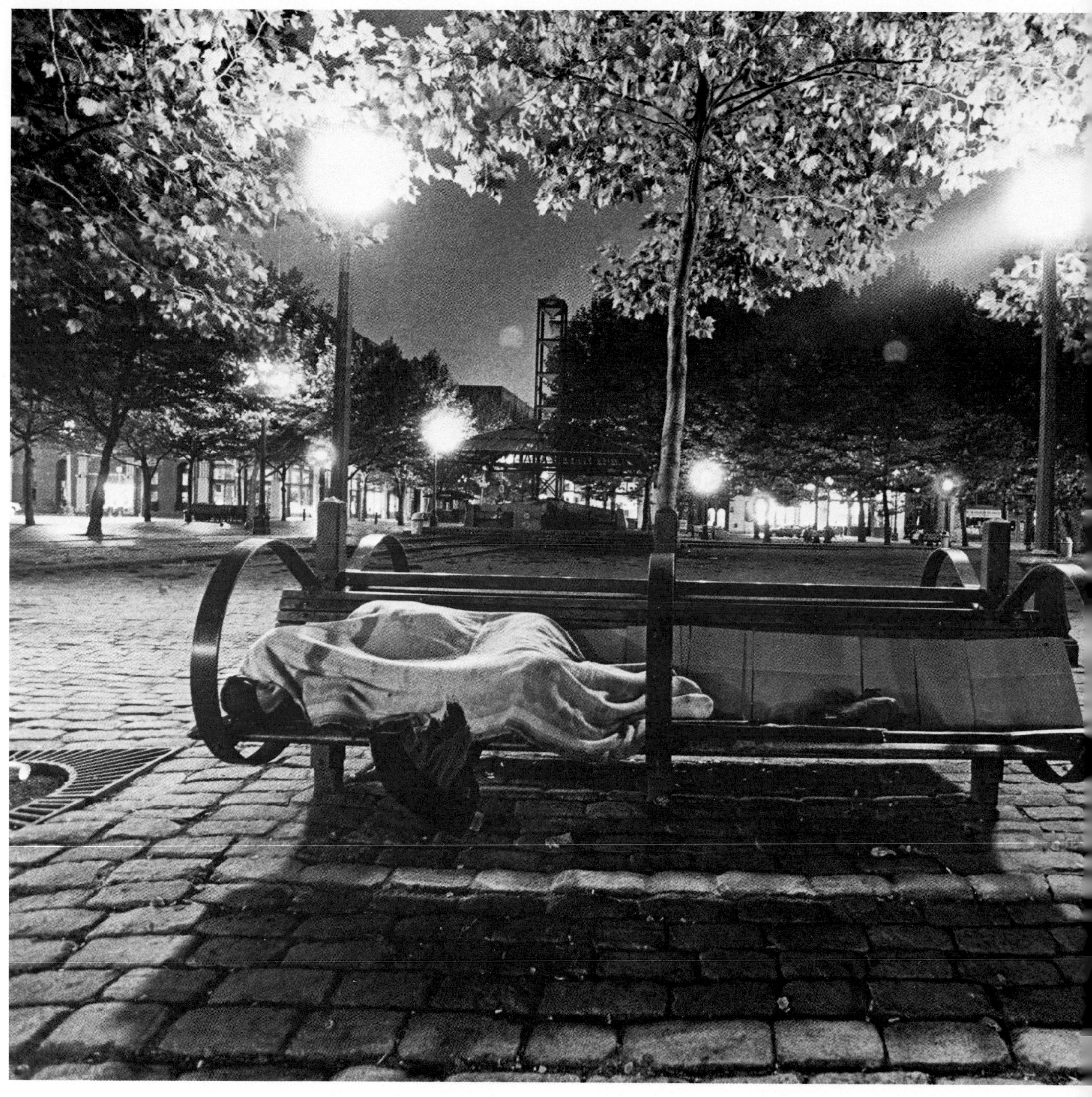

Rena Grice at her Bainbridge Island home.

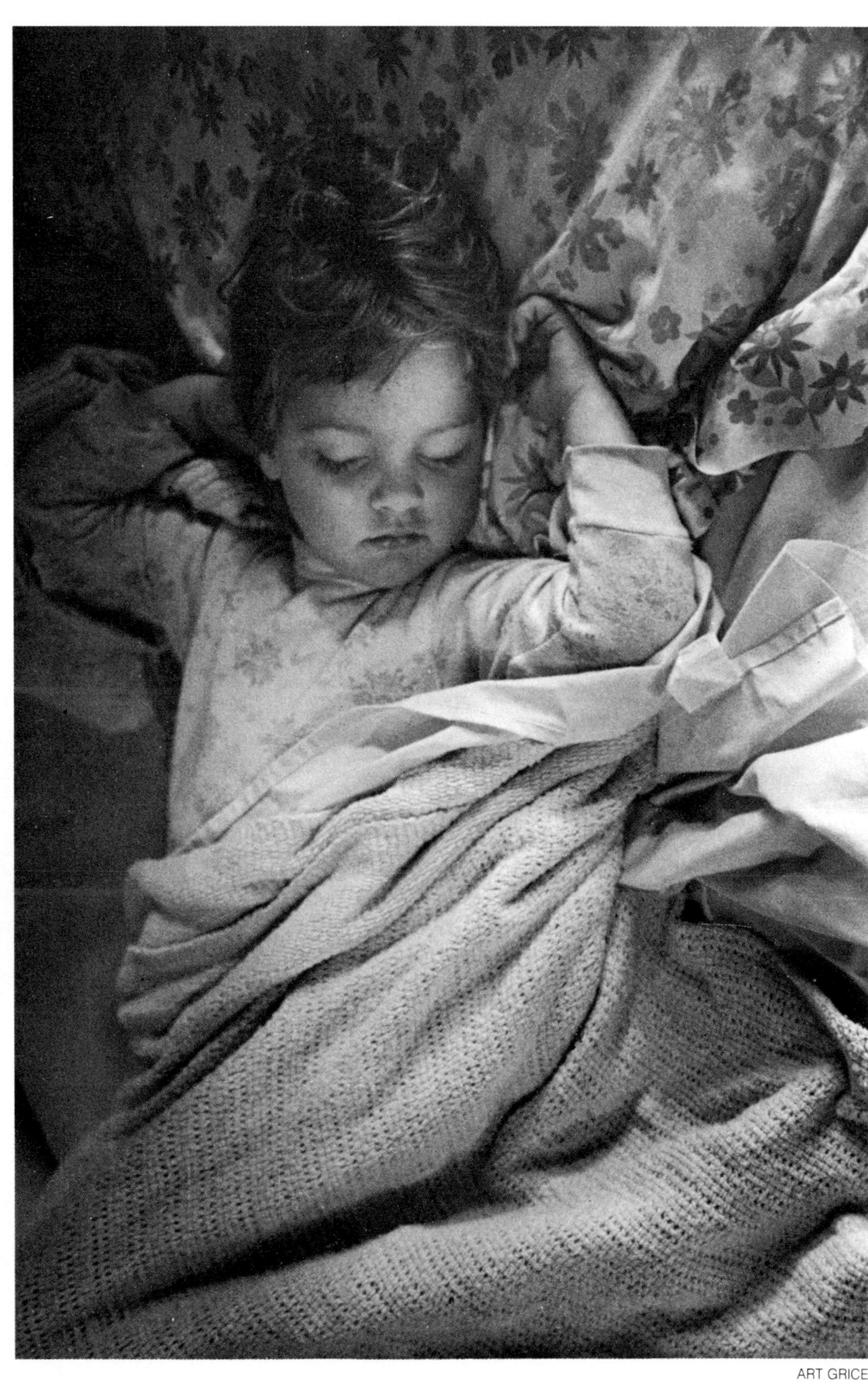

ART GRICE

Occidental Park in Seattle.

PETER HALEY

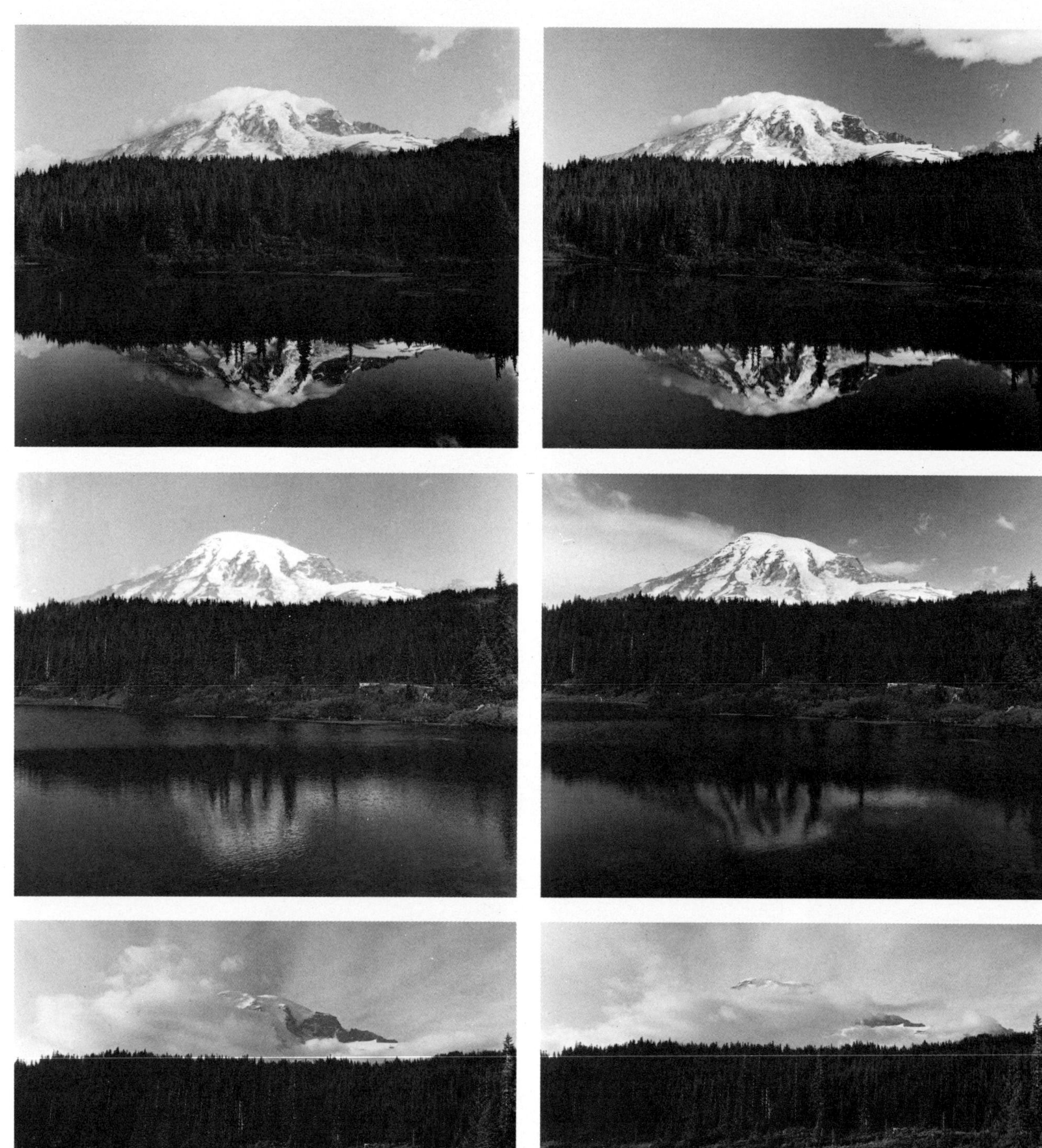

It's 14,210 feet tall, breathtakingly beautiful on a clear day, and many simply call it The Mountain. Lana Harris snapped portraits of Mount Rainier and its cloud formations every hour, on the hour, for 12 consecutive daylight hours.

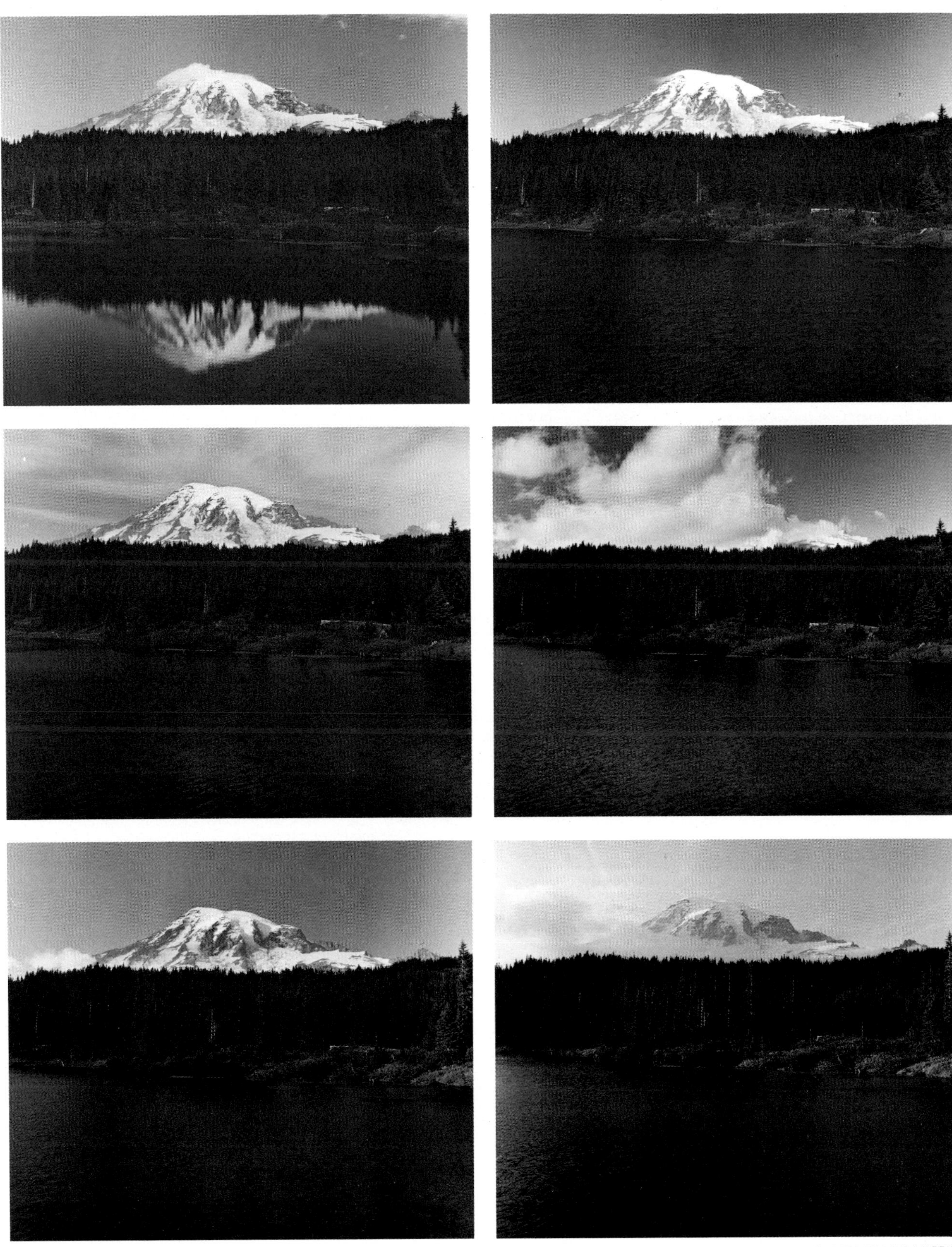

PHOTOS BY LANA HARRIS

PARTICIPANTS

NED AHRENS, *freelance*
PHILIP AMDAL, *freelance*
CHRIS ANDERSON, *Spokane Review-Chronicle*
DON ANDERSON, *Bellingham Herald*
GILBERT ARIAS, *Seattle Post-Intelligencer*
THERESA AUBIN, *Bremerton Sun*
DICK BALDWIN, *Washington State Senate*
PHIL BANKO, *freelance*
JIM BATES, *Valley Newspapers*
BENJAMIN BENSCHNEIDER, *Seattle Post-Intelligencer*
ALAN BERNER, *Seattle Times*
DAVID ALAN BJUR, *Columbia Basin Community College*
DALE BLINDHEIM, *freelance*
STEVE BLOOM, *Olympian*
RICK BOCKWINKEL, *freelance*
SHERRY BOCKWINKEL, *Seattle Post-Intelligencer*
JON BRUNK, *freelance*
AL CAMP, *Omak-Okanogan County Chronicle*
BRUCE CARROLL, *freelance*
MARK CLAESGENS, *Washington State University*
JERRY CLARK, *Longacres Race Track*
MARY-LOUISE COLWELL, *freelance*
R. BRUCE COLWELL, JR., *freelance*
ROBERT DEGIULIO, *Seattle Post-Intelligencer*
JEAN DONG, *freelance*
BOKMON DONG, *freelance*
DENNIS DORAN, *freelance*
RICHARD DOWNEY, *freelance*
KIRTHMON DOZIER, *Bellingham Herald*
GANT EICHRODT, *Washington State Senate*
CHRISTINA EKSTED, *freelance*
CAMILLE FLATEN, *Columbia Basin Community College*
NATALIE FOBES, *Seattle Times*
PAUL FRIDLUND, *Grandview Herald*
PATRICIA FRIDLUND, *Grandview Herald*
GORDON GOOS, *Columbia Basin Community College*
CHARLES GORDON, *freelance*
ART GRICE, *freelance*
EMILY GRICE, *freelance*
DIANNE HAGAMAN, *Bellevue Journal-American*
PETER HALEY, *Seattle Times*
GARY HALL, *freelance*
GRANT HALLER, *Seattle Post-Intelligencer*
DIXON HAMBY, *freelance*
ROD HANSON, *freelance*
ROBERT HARBISON, *Federal Way News*
LANA HARRIS, *freelance*
CHERYL HASELHORST, *Vancouver Columbian*
JOHN HAUGEN, *freelance*
GEFF HINDS, *Skagit Valley Herald*
JOHN HOLMBERG, *Seattle Post-Intelligencer*
DIANA HOTTELL, *Methow Valley News*
MIKE IRWIN, *Methow Valley News*
DENNIS JACOBSON, *freelance*
JEF JAISUN, *freelance*
JAMES JOHNSON, *Northshore Citizen*
MAHRIA JORDAN, *Columbia Basin Community College*
ED KANE, *freelance*
BRUCE KELLMAN, *Tacoma News Tribune*
GARY KISSELL, *Federal Way News*
MAGGIE KREIDLER, *Pullman Herald*
GREG LEHMAN, *freelance*
JIMI LOTT, *Spokane Review-Chronicle*
MIKE LUNDSTROM, *KOMO-TV*
GORDON MACDONALD, *freelance*
DAVID MANN, *The Facts*
MARIA MAYER, *freelance*
JEFF MILLER, *freelance*
DICK MILLIGAN, *Olympian*
LINDA MOORE, *freelance*
MARK MORRIS, *Valley Newspapers*
ROY MUSITELLI, *Yakima Herald Republic*
JEFFRY MYERS, *freelance*
LISA NELSON, *freelance*
DON NORMARK, *freelance*
MERRILL OLIVER, *Tri-City Herald*
BARBARA OLMSTEAD, *Grandview Herald*
JAN OSBORNE, *freelance*
J. DAVID PANTER, *Columbia Basin Community College*
JEAN PARIETTI, *Columbia Basin Daily Herald*
CHARLES PEARSON, *freelance*
PEGGY PEATTIE, *West Seattle Herald*
COLE PORTER, *Seattle Times*
KATHY QUIGG, *Aberdeen World*
JOEL ROGERS, *freelance*
REX-ZANE RUDEE, *Port Orchard Independent*
M. CRAIG SANDERS, *freelance*
PHIL SCHOFIELD, *Spokane Review-Chronicle*
STEPHEN SCHROEDER, *Skagit Valley Herald*
RICK SCHWEINHART, *Northshore Citizen*
DON SEABROOK, *Wenatchee World*
BLAKE SELL, *UPI Newspictures*
MIKE SIEGEL, *Bremerton Sun*
RICK SINGER, *freelance*
DOUG SLY, *Columbia Basin Daily Herald*
KURT SMITH, *Seattle Post-Intelligencer*
LINDA SMITH, *freelance*
BOB SPIWAK, *Methow Valley News*
BILL STALEY, *freelance*
LARRY STEAGALL, *Yakima Herald Republic*
DOT STENNING, *freelance*
MELISSA STEVENSON, *Washington Christian News*
JAMES STUART, *freelance*
SCOTT TERRELL, *Highline Times*
TIM THOMPSON, *freelance*
TOM THOMPSON, *Port Angeles Daily News*
CARY TOLMAN, *Seattle Post-Intelligencer*
LYN TOPINKA, *U.S. Geological Survey*
TOM TOTH, *Yakima Herald Republic*
VIRGINIA TREADWAY, *Columbia Basin Community College*
CRAIG TROIANELLO, *Yakima Herald Republic*
MILES TURNBULL, *Leavenworth Echo*
ED VIDINGHOFF, *freelance*
MARTIN WAIDELICH, *Bellingham Herald*
PHIL WEBBER, *Seattle Post-Intelligencer*
JENNIFER WERNER, *Seattle Post-Intelligencer*
ROGER WERTH, *Longview Daily News*
GEORGE WHITE, *freelance*
KURT WILSON, *Longview Daily News*
JOAN WITHERELL, *Columbia Basin Community College*
BOB WODNIK, *Columbia Basin Daily Herald*
STEVE ZUGSCHWERDT, *Bremerton Sun*

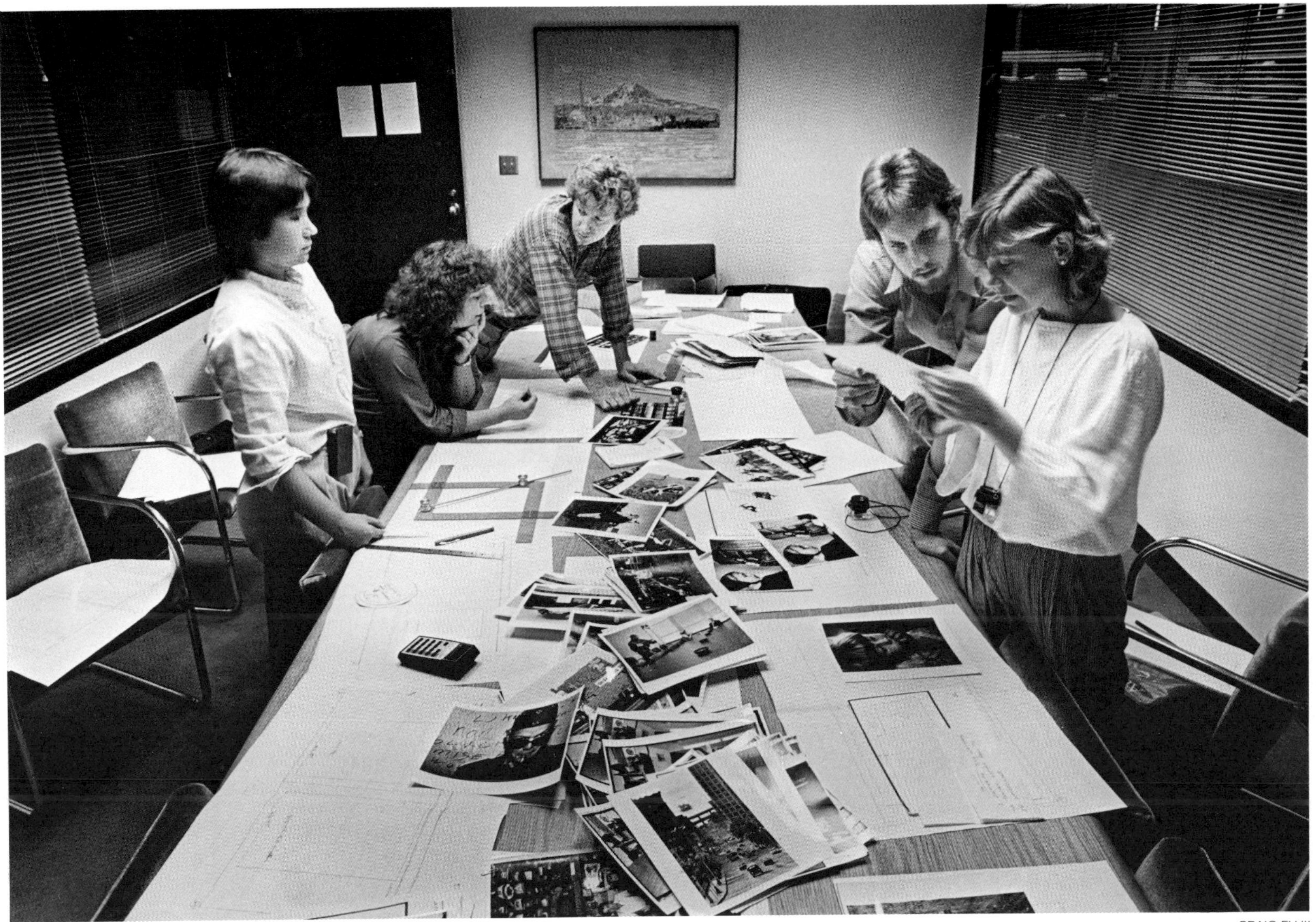

CRAIG FUJII

Editors work on page layouts for One Day in Washington. *From left to right: Geri Migielicz, Theresa Aubin, Fred Nelson, Mark Morris, Jennifer Werner.*

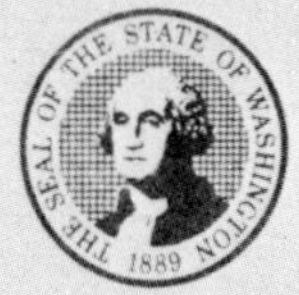

State of Washington

PROCLAMATION

WHEREAS, "Washington Daybook" is a photo documentary project being sponsored by the National Press Photographers Association, Region II; and

WHEREAS, the project is being administered by local, unpaid volunteers from within the profession of photojournalism; and

WHEREAS, the intention of the project is to visually define Washington as it enters the mid-eighties; and

WHEREAS, all prints submitted for the "Washington Daybook" will constitute the "Dayshoot Collection"; and

WHEREAS, the project is scheduled to be exhibited at Seattle's Museum of History and Industry in June of 1984; and

WHEREAS, because the resulting "Dayshoot Collection" will comprise a valuable and unique visual record of contemporary history, the collection will become a part of the permanent archives of the Museum of History and Industry;

NOW, THEREFORE, I, John Spellman, Governor of the state of Washington, do hereby proclaim September 23, 1983, as

PHOTOJOURNALISM DAY

in Washington State.

Signed, this 21st day of September, 1983.

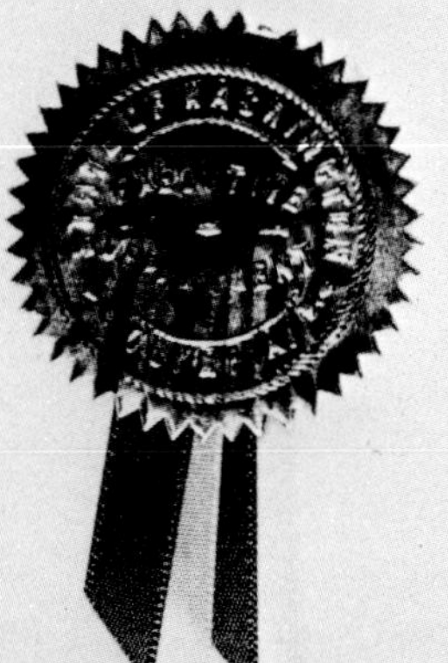

John Spellman

Governor John Spellman

CREDITS

Project Director
Jennifer Werner

Co-Director
Theresa Aubin

"Dayshoot" Organizing Committee
Jennifer Werner
Theresa Aubin
Grant Haller
Jim Bates
Larry Steagall
Jimi Lott
Sherry Bockwinkel

Photo Editors
William Kuykendall
Steve Small
Ron Ramey
Jennifer Werner
Theresa Aubin
Mark Morris

Designers
Theresa Aubin
Mark Morris
Jennifer Werner
Fred Nelson
Geri Migielicz

Caption Writers
Don Duncan
Lansing Jones

Photo Printers
Gilbert Arias
Mike Bainter
Jim Bates

Contributors to Project
Eastman Kodak Co.
Ilford
Ivey-Seright
The Seattle Times
The Seattle Post-Intelligencer
The Bremerton Sun
Valley Newspapers
The Museum of History and Industry

Pilots for Aerial Photos
John O'Ryan, Seattle Post-Intelligencer
Chuck Sicotte, KIRO-TV

Video Project
Bill Strothman, KOMO-TV
Bill Fenster, KING-TV
Steve Ramaley, KOMO-TV

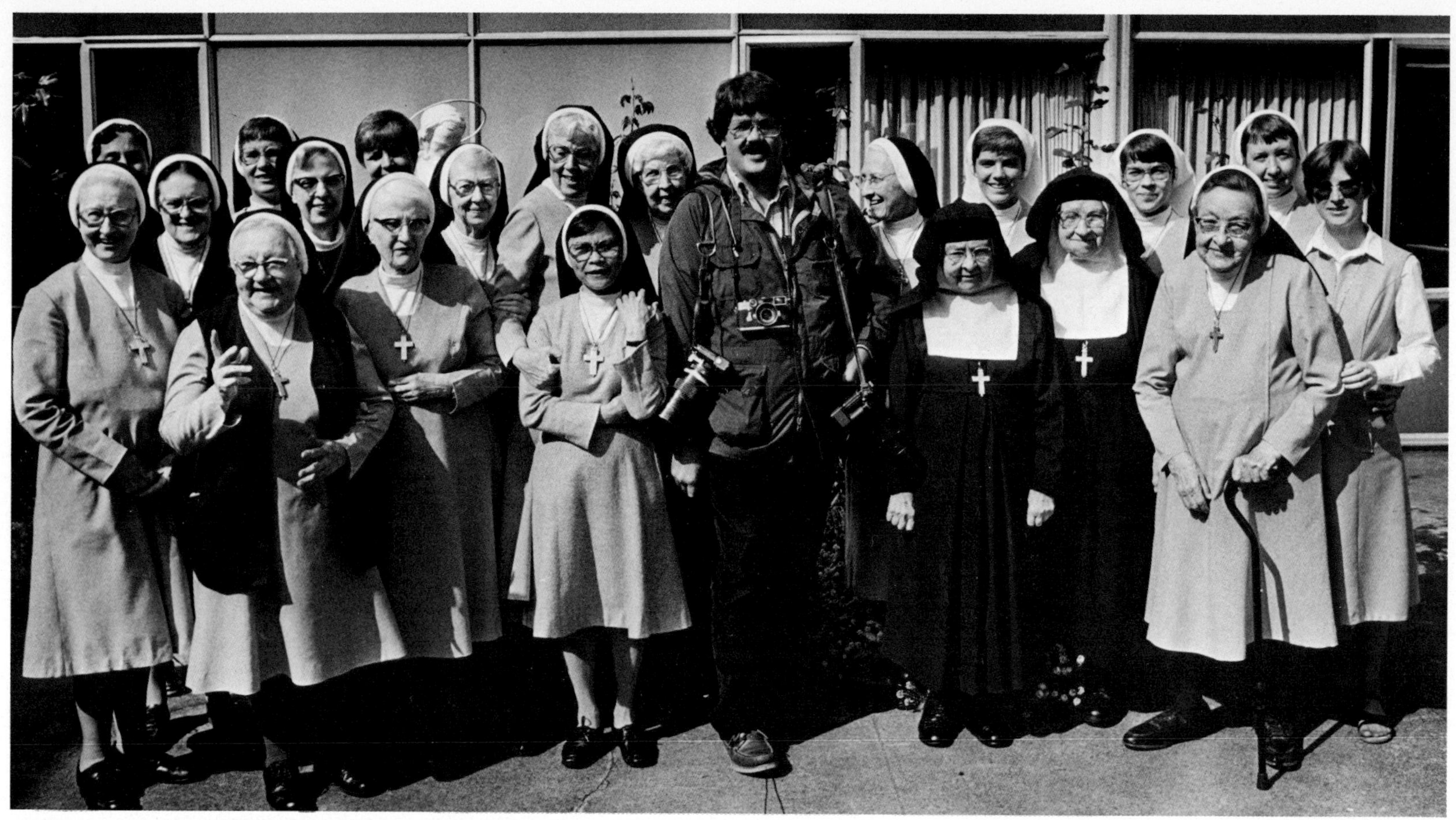

JIM BATES

Photographer Jim Bates with the Sisters of Visitation.